ACTS OF UNION

Contents

Illustrations appear between pages 144 and 145.

Contributors

Thomas Bartlett is Professor of Modern Irish History at University College, Dublin.

Claire Connolly lectures at the School of English, Communication and Philosophy, Cardiff University.

Jane Elizabeth Dougherty lectures in the English Department at Bentley College, Boston.

Patrick Geoghegan is a historian with the *Dictionary of Irish Biography*, Royal Irish Academy.

James Kelly is Head of the History Department at St Patrick's College, Dublin.

Dáire Keogh lectures in the History Department at St Patrick's College, Dublin.

James Livesey lectures in the History Department, Trinity College, Dublin.

Daniel Mansergh is a doctoral candidate in the School of History, Cambridge University.

Allan Macinnes is Burnett-Fletcher chair of history, University of Aberdeen.

Willa Murphy lectures in the Religious Studies Department at St Patrick's College, Dublin.

Gillian O'Brien is the Irish and British Government Scholar at Liverpool University.

Ruán O'Donnell lectures in the Department of Government and Society at the University of Limerick.

Nicholas Robinson is a lawyer, cartoonist and co-founder of the Irish Architectural Archive.

Kevin Whelan is Michael Smurfit Director of the Keough-University of Notre Dame Centre, Dublin.

Abbreviations

Aspinall, *George III*	A. Aspinall (ed.), *The later correspondence of George III 1784-1812* (5 vols, London, 1962-70)
Auckland corr.	*The journal and correspondence of William, Lord Auckland* (ed.) Bishop of Bath and Wells (4 vols , London, 1861-2)
Barrington, *Rise and fall*	J. Barrington, *The rise and fall of the Irish nation* (Dublin, 1853)
Barrington, *Historic memoirs*	J. Barrington, *Historic memoirs of Ireland* (2 vols, London, 1833)
Bartlett, *Fall and rise*	T. Bartlett, *The fall and rise of the Irish nation: the Catholic question 1690-1830* (Dublin, 1992)
Beresford corr.	*The correspondence of Rt Hon. John Beresford*, ed. W. Beresford (2 vols, London, 1854)
BL	British Library
BNL	*Belfast News Letter*
Bolton, *Union*	G. Bolton, *The passing of the Irish Act of Union* (Oxford, 1966)
Burke corr.	*The correspondence of Edmund Burke*, ed. T.W. Copeland (10 vols, Cambridge, 1958-78)
Castlereagh corr.	*Memoirs and correspondence of Viscount Castlereagh*, ed. Marquess of Londonderry (4 vols, London, 1848-9)
Charlemont	*The manuscripts and correspondence of James, first earl of Charlemont* (HMC, 2 vols, London, 1891-4)
CKS	Centre for Kentish Studies, Maidstone
Cornwallis corr.	*Correspondence of Charles, first marquess of Cornwallis*, ed. C. Ross (3 vols, London, 1859)
CUL	Cambridge University Library

Dickson *et al.*, *United Irishmen*	D. Dickson, D. Keogh & K. Whelan (eds), *The United Irishmen: republicanism, radicalism and rebellion* (Dublin, 1993)
Drennan-McTier letters	*The Drennan-McTier letters 1776–1819*, ed. J. Agnew (IMC, 3 vols, Dublin, 1998–9)
ECI	*Eighteenth-Century Ireland*
EHR	*English Historical Review*
Fortescue	*The manuscripts of J.B. Fortescue, preserved at Dropmore* (HMC, 10 vols, London, 1892–1927)
Geoghegan, *Union*	P.M. Geoghegan, *The Irish Act of Union* (Dublin, 1999)
IHS	*Irish Historical Studies*
Kelly, 'Origins'	J. Kelly, 'The origins of the Irish Act of Union; an examination of unionist opinion in Britain and Ireland 1650–1800', *Irish Historical Studies*, xxv (1987), pp 236–63
Lecky, *Ire.*	W.E.H. Lecky, *History of Ireland in the eighteenth century* (5 vols, London, 1892)
McDowell, *Ireland*	R.B. McDowell, *Ireland in the age of imperialism and revolution 1760–1801* (Oxford, 1979)
NA	National Archives of Ireland
NLI	National Library of Ireland
PRO HO	Public Record Office of England, Home Office Papers
PRONI	Public Record Office of Northern Ireland
SHR	*Scottish Historical Review*
TCD	Library of Trinity College Dublin

Preface

Acts of Union had its origins in two conferences held to commemorate the bicentenary of the legislative union of Ireland and Great Britain. The Byrne-Perry Summer School was held in Gorey, County Wexford; the second conference, hosted by the Keough-University of Notre Dame Centre in assocation with the Research Institute of Irish and Scottish Studies (RIISS) of the University of Aberdeen, met in Newman House, Dublin. To these proceedings, essays specifically commissioned for this volume have been added.

The editors wish to thank the individual contributors for their efficiency and courtesy. In addition, they would like to thank generous sponsors who made both the seminars and the publication of this volume possible: Seamus Brennan TD, chair of the Commemoration Committee of the Government of Ireland, and Martin Naughton; the Byrne-Perry Committee (Fr Walter Forde, Matthew Duggan, John Woodbyrne, John McEvoy, Kevin Swords, Rev. Charles Mullen, Ronnie McCormick, Terry McCabe, Michael Leacy, Peter Donnolly, Eileen O'Loughlin, Michelle Sinnott, Michael Warren, John Cullen, Fiachra Ó Lionnáin, Bernard Browne, Sean Mythen, Colin Webb and Senator Avril Doyle); Martin Mansergh, Alice Kearney, Seamus Deane and Jane Ohlmeyer. A special thanks to Katie Keogh, who reduced an amazing diversity of disks into an elegant unity, and who provided invaluable editorial assistance. Finally, we would like to thank Michael Adams and his staff at Four Courts Press for their unstinting backing of this project.

The other within: Ireland, Britain and the Act of Union ·

Kevin Whelan

Looked at in long-term perspective, the Act of Union of 1800 marked both the end and the beginning of an historical sequence. Looking back from an imperial perspective, it marked the logical conclusion of a process of consolidation of the British state, which had begun with the incorporation of Wales in 1534 and continued with the Scottish Act of Union of 1707. Looking forward from an Irish nationalist perspective, it inaugurated over a century of illegitimate rule, terminated by the establishment of the Free State in 1922, which in turn set in motion two further historical sequences, one rapid – the break up of the British empire, one protracted – the break up of Britain.

THE IRISH ACT OF UNION

In 1794, Edmund Burke had argued that a union would only be justified 'in some nearly desperate crisis of the whole empire.'[1] William Pitt, bruised by the failure of his commercial propositions of 1785-86, had turned his back on Irish issues throughout the turbulent 1790s. However, immediately news of the rebellion reached London, Pitt instantly saw the opportunity to implement his frustrated union plans. To Pitt, the Irish parliament should be a client parliament, there to do England's bidding; any increase in its competency or power was a corresponding diminution of the imperial sway. The 1782 settlement was a disaster for Britain, a fundamental loss of authority and of assumed Irish subordination, prised reluctantly from them at a moment of imperial vulnerability.[2] Since 1782,

---

1 E. Burke to Earl Fitzwilliam [c.26 Sept. 1794], in *Burke corr.*, viii, p. 21.   2 J. Kelly, *Prelude to union. Anglo-Irish politics in the 1780s* (Cork, 1992).

the government of Ireland had become a government of contingency, with no settled policy (except for the politically impossible union option). The English response was to rely increasingly on the undersecretary Edward Cooke and a new Irish 'cabinet', and their ability to control the Irish borough parliament. Camden noted that Ireland's 'corrupt parliament is the only means which we have left to preserve the union between the two countries'.[3]

English strategists were worried about the unworkability and volatility of the new relationship. Unable to push through their preference for a union, they sought control throughout the 1780s by cultivating a new group of political handlers, notably John Foster, John Fitzgibbon and John Beresford. Foster, Fitzgibbon and Beresford – 'The three Jacks' – were all ambitious, skilful politicians, resolutely anglophile. All were new men, recruited from outside the traditional networks of Irish power politics. They became the crucial managers of the Irish parliament in the English interest. For the radicals, these men were the epitome of Irish corruption, who cynically promoted English policy in Ireland to advance their own careers. Theobald Wolfe Tone fulminated on the failure of the 1782 settlement:

> The revolution of 1782 was a revolution which enabled Irishmen to set at a much higher price their honour, their integrity, and the interests of their country; it was a revolution, which, while at one stroke it doubled the value of every borough monger in the kingdom, left three-fourths of our countrymen slaves as it found them, and the government of Ireland in the base and wicked and contemptible hands who had spent their lives in degrading and plundering her … The power remained in the hands of our enemies, again to be exerted for our ruin, with this difference, that formerly we had our distresses, our injuries, and our insults gratis, at the hands of England; but now we pay very dearly to receive the same with aggravation, through the hands of Irishmen; – yet this we boast of, and call a revolution.[4]

The promotion of a resolutely anglophile 'cabinet' who controlled the House of Commons via patronage was the only means left for England to stiffen its wavering grip. From this English perspective, the Regency crisis of 1789 demonstrated the danger of an Irish 'government by expedients'

3 Cited in Kelly, *Prelude*, p. 89.   4 T.W. Tone, *An argument on behalf of the catholics of Ireland* (1791) in *The writings of Theobald Wolfe Tone 1763-98*, i (ed.) T.W. Moody, R.B. McDowell & C.J. Woods (Oxford, 1998), pp 112-13.

(Pitt).[5] The rebellion happened at a particularly low ebb in Pitt's career. The fiscal crash of 1797 (with its humiliating retreat from the gold standard), the palpable war weariness as the siege mentality deepened, the strains in the war cabinet of Pitt, Dundas and Grenville, dealing with an (always) irascible and (intermittently) mad king – all these placed extreme pressure on Pitt, overworked, stressed, isolated, ill. News of an Irish rebellion was one more headache, to which Pitt proposed the instant solution of union. Pitt's unionist predeliction was always there since 1782 but it had to remain dormant until the right circumstances presented itself. The rebellion was that circumstance, as Pitt quickly grasped: 'Cannot crushing the rebellion be followed by an act appointing commissioners to treat for an union?'[6] He followed this by appointing Cornwallis with a pro-union mandate:

> Lord Cornwallis will I am sure carry with him the fullest determination to employ the utmost vigour and energy in speedily crushing the rebellion, though he must certainly feel a wish … not to preclude the hopes of clemency towards those who may submit, and must ultimately and as soon as possible have in view some permanent settlement which may provide for the internal peace of the country and secure its connection with Great Britain. This object I am more and more convinced can be attained only by an union.[7]

The union itself was a vital component of imperial strategy. Cornwallis argued that its 'great object' was 'consolidating the British empire'.[8] According to Cornwallis, the captured Wolfe Tone 'when he was recognised by Sir George Hill on board the Hoche, said "Mr Pitt is mad" if he does not attempt an union and the French are mad if they do not attack Ireland before it can be effected'.[9]

Indeed, the Irish union began a process of imperial rationalisation after the demise of the first British empire. It thus cleared the deck for a new phase of expansion (in India, Canada and elsewhere), while eliminating what had become (from a British perspective) a vexing constitutional anomaly. There was also a pressing strategic imperative to prevent Ireland destabilising the war effort against France. Faced with this threat, Britain could no longer take the risk of running its colony by remote control. Pitt understood this as early as 1788:

5 J. Ehrman, *The younger Pitt*, iii (London, 1996).   6 Pitt to Camden, 28 May 1798, Camden papers, CKS.   7 Ibid., 11 June 1798.   8 Cornwallis to Ross, 1 July 1798 in *Cornwallis corr.*, ii, pp 384-5.   9 Cornwallis to Pitt, 31 Mar. 1800, Dacre Adams papers, PRO 30/58/3.

> To preserve from further dismemberment and diminution, to unite
> and connect what yet remained of our reduced and shattered empire
> of which Great Britain and Ireland were now the only considerable
> members.[10]

The rebellion demonstrated the compelling military and fiscal rationale of
an incorporating union. It would eliminate a debilitating internal security
weakness, as the war cabinet wearily tried to build a second coalition against
France. Richard Musgrave claimed that:

> Ireland in her present state may be considered as an intestine thorn
> in the side of England, as a strong outpost easily accessible to her
> enemies, who may at all times annoy her through it: instead of afford-
> ing her strength, it will be an incessant source of weakness.[11]

Union would promote recruiting for 'the British armed nation' (one-third
of it to be Irish by 1815).[12] Pitt, his cabinet and an overwhelming (4:1)
majority of the London parliament supported a measure whose British (not
Irish) benefits were seen as paramount. Viewed from London, Ireland was
simply one among many pressing issues of foreign policy. This act of
imperial consolidation would also definitively resolve the long-running
problem of 1782, which has vexed historians as much as politicians: was
Ireland dependent or independent? a colony?, a province?, a confessional
state?, a dual kingdom? As early as 1719, it had been noted 'the words province, colony, plantation, conquest and depending kingdom are ever in these
men's mouths'.[13] After 1 January 1801, these clamorous mouths were
silenced constitutionally. The union was to answer the Irish question posed
on 22 January 1799 at the opening of the Irish parliamentary session – what
would be:

> the most effectual means of maintaining and improving a connexion
> essential to their common security, and of consolidating as far as
> possible into one firm and lasting fabric the strength, the power, and
> the resources of the British empire.[14]

10 Cited in Kelly, *Prelude*, p. 138.   11 R. Musgrave, *Memoirs of the different rebellions
in Ireland.* Fourth edition (Enniscorthy, 1995), p. 851.   12 J.E. Cookson, *The British
armed nation 1793-1815* (Oxford, 1997).   13 *Some considerations upon the late attempt
to repeal the Test Act, humbly offered to the dissenters* (London, 1719), p. 17. [NLI
P284].   14 Cited in F. Plowden *An historical review of the state of Ireland*, ii, p. 826.

To achieve these aims in what Cornwallis pithily described as 'a corrupt country', the government was even willing to subvert its own laws.[15] Much to his displeasure, the old imperial hand Cornwallis had to engage in the 'dirty work'[16] of getting the Irish gentry on board, a gentry which he (in common with the rest of English elite society) despised as a crude colonial class, fond only of 'hanging, shooting, burning'.[17] From top to bottom, the Irish protestant elite named their price. Agar held out for the archbishopric of Dublin and a permanent seat in the House of Lords; there were 18 creations and 15 promotions in the peerage; 74 MPs were given jobs and offices; 11 lawyers and 10 ecclesiastics got advancement; 16 annuities were granted; parliamentary seats were purchased and over a million was paid out in borough compensation. The recently released Home Office papers 'prove beyond doubt that the government bent the law'.[18] No one in Britain cared. As commentator after commentator bewailed, the English knew little and cared less about Ireland.

The Act of Union immediately raised the issue of catholic emancipation. On a-nod-and-a-wink basis, it had been assumed by catholics that their acquiescence in union would guarantee their emancipation by a grateful and impartial imperial parliament. The 1793 Relief Act had still excluded them from key executive (lord lieutenant, chief secretary, privy council), legal (lord chancellor, judge, sheriff) and political (MP) positions. Pitt wished to introduce emancipation but was stymied by George III (suitably alarmed by extremist opponents of the measure like John Fitzgibbon); the king stated categorically in 1801 that he would 'in future consider any man who proposed further concessions to catholics as a personal enemy'.[19] Pitt resigned and with him went the union management team of Cornwallis, Castlereagh and Cooke. Jonah Barrington provided a sardonic commentary on the treatment of Irish catholics by British administrations: 'In 1798, they were hanged: in 1799, they were caressed; in 1800, they were cajoled; in 1801, they were discarded.'[20] The tantalising question is what would have happened if emancipation and the union had been carried together: would grateful catholic gentry, bishops and politicians have then actively supported the union? However, the weight of elite and popular anti-popery (with a strong xenophobic dimension), established church and parliamentary opposition (from an exclusively protestant house of commons and house of

15 Cornwallis to Ross, 21 Jan. 1799, cited in Bolton, *Union*, p. 88.   16 *Cornwallis corr.*, ii, p. 270.   17 Cornwallis to Ross, 16 Nov. 1799, *Cornwallis corr.*, iii, p. 145.   18 D. Wilkinson, 'How did they pass the union? Secret service expenditure in Ireland 1799-1804' in *History*, 82 (1997), p. 251.   19 Bartlett, *Fall and rise*, p. 264.   20 Barrington, *Historic memoirs*, ii, p. 232.

lords) and the king's inflamed hostility were sufficient to block its passage.[21] Two British governments subsequently fell on the catholic issue in 1801 and 1807.[22]

The failure to accommodate the catholics constitutionally throws the protestant nature of Britishness into sharp relief. In 1707, the distinctively presbyterian nature of Scottish society had been safeguarded. In 1800, the distinctively catholic nature of Irish society had been scorned. One pamphlet, *The case of Ireland reconsidered*, asked 'What difference is there between an Irishman and Scotchman, that the religion of the one should be treated with respect, and the other with contempt?'[23] Richard Musgrave provided a simple answer: 'popery doctrinally teaches and sanctions treason and resistance to a protestant state'.[24] Another commentator asked the question:

> Can the two repugnant religions be both established and maintained? The position of England and Scotland form no precedent; for the religions are not even different in the standards of faith, far less repugnant; the difference is in church government, order, and discipline, ranks of clergy, and other secondary points. Hence both could be established by the state, without inconsistency, and they were so established – it was part of the compact of union, and neither people would have consented to it on other conditions.[25]

REACTIONS TO THE UNION

The easy passage of the union demonstrated the irreparable breach that had opened up in the 1790s between parliament and people. Thomas Hussey (first president of Maynooth College) had (correctly) forecast to Burke at the time of the Fitzwilliam crisis that the majority of Irish people no longer trusted their government: 'The contemptible light in which they will view their own parliament will induce them to lay it in the dust.'[26] All strands of opinion were agreed on this. An Orangeman believed that Irish politicians

21 C. Haydon, *Anti-catholicism in eighteenth-century England c.1714-80. A political and social study* (Manchester, 1993).   **22** F. O'Gorman, *The long eighteenth century. British political and social history 1688-1832* (London, 1997), p. 356.   **23** [P. Lattin], *The case of Ireland reconsidered in answer to a pamphlet entitled* Arguments for and against the union considered (London, 1799), p. 16.   **24** Musgrave, *Memoirs*, p. 885. **25** J. Glassford, *Notes of three tours in Ireland in 1824 and 1826* (Bristol, 1832), pp 360-1.   **26** T. Hussey to E. Burke, 3 Mar. 1795 in *Burke corr.*, viii, p. 169.

would be better off in Westminster than staying 'at home to wrangle in the little infantine squabbles of a local legislature'.[27] Archibald Hamilton Rowan, the United Irishman, welcomed the prospect of union because 'in that measure, I see the downfall of one of the most corrupt assemblies, I believe, ever existed'.[28] The Irish whig MP, Richard Griffith, saw disadvantages in union, but these would 'be more than counterbalanced by the demolition of the most corrupt assembly that ever disgraced a nation'.[29] Redesdale, the English conservative, argued that its parliament had consigned Ireland 'into the state of corruption and misrule from which the union, as it now stands, may I think completely rescue it'.[30] The English whig, George Moore, made the same point: 'An union will really emancipate the Irish people; it will emancipate them from party government; it will emancipate them from the tyranny of passion, from the despotism of prejudice.'[31] Castlereagh considered that leading catholics would 'consider any transfer of power from their opponents as a boon',[32] or as Hussey vividly expressed it, the catholics 'would prefer a union with the Beys and Mamelukes of Egypt to that of being under the iron rod of the Mamelukes of Ireland'.[33]

In that sense, the union represented the achievement of one of the United Irishmen's aims – the destruction of the power base of the borough mongers. An immediate effect of the union was the eclipse of the leviathans of the old system (Downshire, Ely, Shannon) and the loss of authority of others (Fitzgibbon, Beresford, Cooke, Agar). Their status – 'strutting on the stilts of power and title' – depended on their Irish role and the union paved the way to their obsolescence.[34] Irish members of the UK parliament, according to one of their number, 'appear bewildered and quite at a loss how to act in this large field they had entered upon'.[35] Only Castlereagh had a successful career in the union parliament and the psychological cost can perhaps be seen in his ultimate act – cutting his own throat.

This enduring popular contempt for the legitimacy of the protestant parliament, the senior political figures, and the Dublin Castle executive was

27 [H. Giffard], *Union or not? By an Orangeman* (Dublin, 1799), p. 37. **28** W. Drummond (ed.), *The autobiography of Archibald Hamilton Rowan* (Shannon, 1972), p. 340. **29** R. Griffith to T. Pelham, 15 Jan. 1799, Pelham papers, BL Add. Ms 33,106, ff 169-72. **30** Redesdale papers, PRONI, TH 3030/7/9 **31** G. Moore, *Observations on the union, Orange associations and other subjects of domestic policy, with reflections on the late events on the continent* (Dublin, 1799), p. 45. **32** Castlereagh to Wickham, 23 Nov. 1798 in *Cornwallis corr.*, ii, p. 446. **33** T. Hussey to J. Clinch, 10 Jan. 1800, Dublin Diocesan Archives. **34** D. Taaffe, *The Shamroc*, 4 Feb. 1799. Downshire died in 1801, Fitzgibbon in 1802, Beresford in 1805. **35** Broderick Chinnery (MP, Bandon) to Lord Shannon, 20 Feb. 1801, cited in P. Jupp, 'Irish M.P.s at Westminster in the early nineteenth century' in *Historical Studies*, vii (1969), p. 73.

the primary reason why the anti-union campaign never took off. From the start, it was an unnatural alliance, with diametrically opposed leaders. For hardline protestants, Grattan was discredited by his alleged United Irish linkages and had himself led the whigs out of the parliament in 1797; for the catholics, Foster and Downshire were extreme loyalists. Such an oxy-moronic coalition lacked the popular support to sustain a long campaign.

This atmosphere did not augur well for the prospects of what Burke had called 'an union of interest and affection with Ireland'.[36] This was to be the whig mantra. Charlemont in 1782 implored England to 'bind us to you by the only chain that can connect us – the only chain we will ever consent to wear – the dear ties of mutual love and mutual freedom'.[37] The whig argument was that the union would fail if unaccompanied by catholic emancipation. Henry Grattan claimed that:

> It is not an identification of people, as it excludes catholics from the parliament and the state ... The union, then, is not an identification of the two nations ... it is merely a merger of the parliament of one nation in that of another.[38]

This remained the consistent whig line. In 1805, Charles James Fox spoke in favour of 'an union of sentiment, an union of people in affection for their government', but with the ominous addition that 'catholic emancipation alone could pave the way for this union'. He believed that emancipation should be granted for British, not for Irish reasons:

> The Protestant Ascendancy has been compared to a garrison in Ireland; it is not in our power to add to the strength of this garrison, but I would make the besiegers themselves part of the garrison.[39]

Catholic opinion was seduced into believing that the union would be accompanied by emancipation. In the new dispensation, an enlightened legislature, an impartial rather than sectarian-based administration and a cordial relationship between the islands would pave the way for a peaceful settlement of the Irish problem, in which catholics would participate fully as citizens in the United Kingdom. The failure to grant emancipation until 1829 soured catholics against the union, which represented for them not a new beginning but a copper-fastening of 'Protestant Ascendancy'.

36 E. Burke to S. Span, 23 Apr. 1778 in *Burke corr.*, iii, p. 434.   37 Charlemont to Rockingham, 17 Apr. 1782, cited in Bolton, *Union*, p. 1.   38 Cited in D. Madden, *Speeches of the Rt Hon. Henry Grattan* (Dublin, 1853), p. 255.   39 Report of speech by C. J. Fox, *Dublin Evening Post*, 22 Jan. 1805.

Cornwallis had wished to promote the emancipation option and began his lord lieutenancy by self-consciously sidelining Cooke and the old Irish cabinet, who resented him for not having 'thrown himself blindly into their hands'.[40] He believed that it would be 'a desperate measure' to adopt the protestant ascendancy line, thereby making an 'irrevocable alliance with a small party in Ireland to wage eternal war against the papists and presbyterians'.[41] He stressed the necessity of making these concessions at the time of the union, 'which, if now liberally granted, might make the Irish a loyal people, will be of little avail, when they are extorted on a future day'.[42] Cornwallis was eventually overridden on this issue, and the union settlement became an exclusively protestant one. According to Edward Cooke, Pitt's sympathy for the catholics was 'a humbug on his part;' 'after making a mock battle, he will come into power again and leave them in the lurch'.[43]

The anti-union case had centred on the projected economic and social decline of Ireland, that the union sought 'to make us hewers of wood and drawers of water, to fix the servitude of Ireland, making it a draw farm for her [England's] manufactures and commerce, a nursery for her fleets and armies'.[44] The union itself was passed during a period of near famine between 1799 and 1801 – 40,000 deaths, rampant disease, unemployment, bank failures, emigration, social unrest, and cattle houghing.[45]

Barbara Verschoyle, agent on the Fitzwilliam estate and trying to complete the development of Merrion Square, predicted in 1798 that the union 'would be the ruin of this country' and especially Dublin – 'the ground would remain unbuilt and the land about Dublin considerably fall in price'. By 1799, she was reporting that:

> now no one wishes for any thing but to get shut of what they have here – the union is the terror of every one and I am sorry to say I am sure it will be and if it is – even here in this delightful spot Merrion Square – we shall have grass where it was once pavement.

---

40 Cornwallis to Portland, 16 Sept. 1798 in *Cornwallis corr.*, ii, p. 406.   41 Cornwallis to Pitt, 17 Oct. 1798, *Cornwallis corr.*, ii, pp 418-20.   42 Cornwallis to Ross, 8 Oct. 1800, *Cornwallis corr.*, iii, p. 294.   43 E. Cooke to Castlereagh, 23 Feb. 1801, *Cornwallis corr.*, iv, p. 61.   44 Taaffe, *The Shamroc*: a Dublin newspaper described Ireland as 'a nursery for soldiers' in 1807. *Dublin Evening Post*, 22 Jan. 1807.   45 R. Wells, 'The Irish famine of 1799-1801: market culture, moral economies and social protest' in A. Randall & A. Charlesworth (ed.), *Markets, market culture and popular protest in eighteenth-century Britain and Ireland* (Liverpool, 1996), pp 163-93.

As late as 1811, tenants on the Square remained in arrears, still pleading the negative impact of the union as an excuse.[46]

When duties were finally equalised in the 1820s, following a decade of post-war difficulty, the cumulative impact was sufficient to wipe out the luxury textile industries of the Liberties, as well as precipitating a collapse in the artisanal sector, also concentrated in the old heart of the city. This was not helped by the exodus of aristocratic families and the collapse of the Dublin winter season, which also dented the luxury retail and services sector. The great gentry houses fell to institutional uses: Aldborough House (only completed in 1796) became a school in 1813; Leinster House was acquired by the Royal Dublin Society in 1814; Moira House became the Mendicity Institute in 1818. In that same year, Lady Morgan described Dublin as 'a fallen capital' whose centre was 'still, silent and void'.[47] That stillness was predicated on Liverpool's dominance. By the 1840s, over ninety per cent of Dublin's imports came from the United Kingdom – an overwhelming dominance.

THE BRITISH RESPONSE TO UNION

The union raised the stakes more for Britain than Ireland. Within the novel aegis of the Ukanian state, its problems could no longer be summarily dismissed as the result of Irish (protestant and papist) inability to rule themselves. Hitherto, the Irish parliament had effectively screened Ireland from Britain; with these ball bearings gone, a more abrasive friction came into play between Ireland and London. With Emmet's insurrection of 1803, Irish separatism now threatened the break-up of Britain. Three short years after its passage, the union itself was now the issue and this shocked the London elite. Their response was to safeguard the union through a policy of coercive integration. The Emmet insurrection demonstrated that 1798 (and the subsequent union) had not provided the sense of an ending in Ireland. Unlike 1688, the inaugurating moment of the British whig narrative (with its political exorcism of the unquiet seventeenth century), 1798 and the union provided no constitutional closure in Ireland. Instead, it

46 Cited in E. McAulay, 'Some problems in building on the Fitzwilliam estate during the agency of Barbara Verschoyle' in *Irish architectural and decorative studies*, ii (1999), p. 115. 'We'll all live in clover then' was one unionist reply to the Dublin complaint that 'you will have grass growing in College Green after the union' (*Irish Magazine*, March 1811).   47 Lady Morgan, *Florence Macarthy. An Irish tale*, 4 vols (London, 1818), i, p. 21.

merely demonstrated Irish cyclicity – 1641, 1690, 1798, 1803 ... The malignant passions just kept on resurfacing in what the *Westminster Review* defined as 'a constantly revolving cycle of anarchy, injustice and misrule'.[48] What more could be expected from what Coleridge called 'a wild and barbarous race', brutalised by the oppression of centuries?[49]

After the failure of the 1805 attempt to bring in catholic emancipation, which was quickly followed by the despatch of five million bullets to the garrison in Ireland, Thomas Moore caught the despondent mood of the catholics in his 'A pastoral ballad for John Bull':

> I have found out a gift for my Erin,
> A gift that will surely content her;
> Sweet pledge of a love so endearing!
> Five millions of bullets I've sent her.
>
> She ask'd me for Freedom and Right,
> But ill she her wants understood;
> Ball cartridges, morning and night,
> Is a dose that will do her more good...

In choosing the protestant and coercive strategies, the British government ensured that catholics would be turned from neutrality to hostility towards the union, that local rancour would be institutionalised, and that the catholic question would quickly become the Irish question. Once catholic political activism revived, it would inevitably be pitted against the sectarian adminis-tration at home and a hostile, or indifferent, imperial parliament in London. In such circumstances, catholic emancipation could only be taken, not granted, and the adversarial stance between catholic and protestant and between catholics and the British state would be hardened and perpetuated.

The union, then, did not deliver Ireland from sectarianism, but rather deepened its insidious influence, as the distinguished commentator Edward Wakefield noted a decade later:

> Protestantism became the watchword and unionists encouraged this distinguishing appellation for the purpose of separating the loyal from the disaffected. By this, an arbitrary Pale was drawn around the constitution, which excluded every Roman Catholic in the island.[50]

---

48 *Westminster Review*, April 1829, p. 349.   **49** D. Erdman (ed.), *The collected works of Samuel Taylor Coleridge*, 3 vols (London, 1978), i, p. 106. This article originally appeared in the *Morning Post*, 15 Jan. 1800.   **50** Wakefield, *Ire.*, i, p. 363.

Archbishop Troy, who had (according to no less an authority than Lord Grenville) been 'justified in entertaining great and sanguine expectations that the [union] measure would lead to the consequences anxiously desired',[51] sadly admitted in 1809 that they were now governed 'by a state & people notoriously prejudiced against our religion, & particularly hostile to Irish catholics'.[52]

Prior to the union, Irish problems could be decisively attributed to the incompetence and corruption of its national legislature. It was axiomatically assumed in Britain that the self-evident virtues of an impartial imperial legislature would painlessly extend the manifold blessings of British civilisation to Ireland. But Irish poverty and violence increased spectacularly rather than diminished after the union, posing a severe conundrum: why was Ireland not improving under the aegis of this marvellous modern empire – a civilised empire of trade and moral progress, not an ancient one of force and fear? It was unthinkable that the imperial project itself could be problematic, that its civilising mission could collapse so impotently on the shores of its nearest neighbour and oldest colony. But how then could one explain Irish 'turbulence' – 'one wide stream of discontent, dark and turbid, perpetually flowing, and deepening the longer it runs'?[53] This anxiety explains the intense English interest in Ireland: between 1810 and 1833, the parliamentary system generated a paper panopticon on Ireland with 114 commissions and 60 select committees sitting on Irish issues.[54]

In the nineteenth century, the aggressive British imperial mission again crystallised identity formation, bringing prolonged awareness of an alien, recalcitrant empire. From this often anxious contact with a highly visible other, self-definition clarified. Extending this argument into an Irish context, catholicism became that highly insistent other (all the more visible because internalised in the state itself) against which British protestant identity was defined. Irish catholics joined the French as the alien *doppelganger* of British identity. They were the brutish barbarians against whom British civility was measured. Under the pressure of politics, an emerging racial theory was deployed against the Irish. This dangerous, bestial Paddy appears in the 1790s – at precisely the same moment when the ludic, antic and politically harmless stage Irishman disappears from the British stage.

51 Lord Grenville, speech of 10 May 1805 in *Cobbett's parliamentary debates 1803-1812*, 22 vols (London, 1804-1812), iv, pp 659-60.   52 Troy to J. Carroll, 29 Mar. 1809, cited in H. Fenning, 'Troy to Carroll: letters from Dublin to Baltimore 1794-1815' in *Collect. Hib.*, xxxix-xl (1997-8), pp 176-209.   53 *I.L.N.*, 28 Mar. 1846, p. 201.   54 N. Mansergh, *The Irish question 1840-1921* (London, 1965), p. 49. See also G. Hooper, 'Stranger in Ireland: the problematics of the post-union travelogue' in *Mosaic*, xxviii

In the 1790s and subsequently, Ireland assumed the French stereotypes – papist, republican, anti-monarchical – in both elite and popular British perceptions. Under the union, it became the other within, whose poverty, violence and surly separatism became a curiously comforting antithesis to British virtue, prosperity and stability. The first half of the nineteenth century witnessed the reorganisation on a narrowly racial basis of the older European version of national character, inspired by the enlightened model of Montesquieu, with its sophisticated and relatively sympathetic understanding of the inter-relationship among geography, history and culture.[55] The new science claimed that each country had a unique and unchanging racial destiny, genetically imprinting its national character. Ireland was obviously celtic, a lower racial order, which accounted for the country's inferiority to anglo-saxon England. Celts were naturally lazy, feckless, violent and communitarian, lacking the sober integrity, sturdy individualism and self-reliance of the saxon. Combined with popery, these racial flaws determined Ireland's endemic poverty and violence. As the German Knut Clement argued in 1845, these defects also explained why Ireland should be subject to a political union:

> If ever the Irish should succeed in extricating themselves from the English clench, it is hardly likely that they will ever cast off their old Paddy habits and develop a completely new kind of person, for the Celt, the Slav and the Jew are unchangeable in their ancient ways.[56]

The racial and sectarian perspectives squared this Irish circle: Irish problems were not socio-economic or political in character, but genetically and confessionally rooted. Irish crime and poverty were endemic, irrational and 'natural', and were therefore impervious to moral or political persuasion, amenable only to force and fear. In 1814, Sir Robert Peel pronounced that the Irish had a 'natural predilection for outrage and a lawless life which I believe nothing can control'.[57] In a paradoxical doubling, Irish poverty and disorder (whose obliteration was the initial justification) now became the justification for the union.

Obviously, not every English commentator adopted these perspectives. In 1808, Sydney Smith assailed the prevalent view of the Irish as irredeemably turbulent:

(no. 1), (1995), pp 25-47. **55** S. Deane, 'Montesquieu and Burke' in G. Gargett & G. Sheridan (ed.), *Ireland and the French Enlightenment 1700-1800* (London, 1999), pp 47-66. **56** Cited in E. Bourke, *Das Irelund bild der Deutschen* (Tubingen, 1991); see also E. Bourke, 'German travel writers in Ireland 1828-50' in *History Ireland*, v (1997), pp 21-5. **57** R. Foster, *Modern Ireland 1600-1972* (London, 1988), p. 294.

Before you refer the turbulence of the Irish to incurable defects in
their character, tell me if you have treated them as friends and equals?
… Nothing of all this. What then? Why you have confiscated the
territorial surface of the country twice over; you have massacred and
exported her inhabitants; you have deprived four fifth of them of
every civil privilege; you have at every period made her commerce
and manufactures slavishly subordinate to your own; and yet the
hatred which the Irish bear to you is the result of an original turbulence of character, and of a primitive, obdurate wildness, utterly
incapable of civilisation.[58]

THE FRENCH REVOLUTION AND BRITISH IDENTITY

The union also opened up a debate on the relationship between nationalism
and imperialism, between the local and the universal. From the British
perspective, the advantages overwhelmingly lay with the imperial side of the
argument and here they could draw on both the arguments of the Scottish
Enlightenment (Adam Smith and Adam Ferguson had been vigorous
advocates of union since the 1780s) and on the increasingly prestigious arguments of Edmund Burke.

Burke inflected the Scottish Enlightenment model of civilisation in his
celebrated reflections on the consequences of the French Revolution.[59]
Burke asserted that there is a uniform and universal human nature, as
profound as it is unchanging. Civility (in the Scottish Enlightenment sense)
could be calibrated against this universal set of values. Burke's innovation
was to argue that the French Revolution had failed to meet this standard of
civility, because it had fundamentally altered human nature itself in its
brutal pursuit of an unattainable and abstract human perfectibility. Revolutionary jacobinism also backlit the essential features of that universal human
nature which it had so rudely assaulted – the domestic values of feeling,
fidelity, loyalty, and a profound at-homeness. Burke then argued that the
new France had betrayed the old values while the placid, dull, almost bovine
English had not. The placidity of their national character, grooved in
immemorial routine, firmly rooted them in their traditions, unlike the
volatile, frivolous French. This allowed Burke to make the larger claim:
because Great Britain opposed the French Revolution and its novel

58 Cited in S. Deane, *A short history of Irish literature* (London, 1986), p. 60.   **59** S.
Deane, 'Factions and fictions: Burke, colonialism and revolution' in *Bullán*, iv (no.
2), (2000), pp 5-26.

ruthlessness, it became the defender of human nature as it once was, and as it should always be. The very particularism of British nationalism paradoxically underpins its claim to be undeniably linked to universal human nature.

This curious British reworking of the Scottish Enlightenment and the French Revolution had massive Irish repercussions. The identification of civility as the apex of human development and its instantiation in Great Britain meant that other forms of identity, like the Gaelic, were deemed incapable of aspiring to the universal. Similarly, the British imperium in Ireland had to be seen as a defender of universal human values indelibly identified with the British way of life and British nationalism. Any one who repudiated these values *ipso facto* betrayed themselves as inhuman barbarians, delinquents who lacked feeling and who acted against the deepest instincts of human nature.

Burke and, later, Coleridge are then able to theorise the relationship between Englishness and civilisation, and the British state which preserved and guaranteed them as a system of universal values. The Irish can then only be celts in a saxon world, like greeks in a roman one, whose function is to be absorbed – either coercively (through punitive means) or genially (the Gladstonian project). The Gael occupied the space of the past, as the celts became the memory of the saxon. Wordsworth observed the Highland Scots, after a century of union with England and the attendant 'conquests of civility:'

> The pibroch's note, discountenanced or mute;
> The Roman kilt, degraded to a toy
> Of quaint apparel for a half-spoilt boy;
> The target mouldering like ungathered fruit;
> The smoking steam-boat eager in pursuit,
> As eagerly pursued; the umbrella spread
> To weather-fend the Celtic herdsman's head –
> All speak of manners withering to the root …[60]

The sheltering British reign kept out the ruinous celtic rain, as a distinctive culture withered at the roots, a metaphor soon to leap to shocking life – and death – as the blight assailed the potato-based culture of Gaelic Ireland.

These tropes were to resound off Irish unionist platforms for generations to come. Here is a typical example from Belfast in 1898:

60 W. Wordsworth, *Yarrow revisited and other poems* (London, 1835), poem vii.

The union between Great Britain and Ireland must occupy a higher platform, as it is destined to achieve nobler issues, the progress and prosperity of a united people, whose name, prestige, and power among the nations are acknowledged; whose flag is honoured, whose trade is blest, and whose Queen and Empress was so recently honoured by the representatives of the nationalities of the world. The flag of England is fanned by the breezes of every clime; her commerce grasps the entire earth; the oceans separating continents are only her great highways; the 'marriage ring' which binds them together in commercial activity, so that it may well be quoted, 'The sea is England's glory, the bounding wave her throne.' Let us not forget that august and princely tribute paid to our good Queen Victoria by the several nationalities of the world on the occasion of her Jubilee, the varied languages represented, the different nations and peoples all gathered to her hearth like children of a common family, not conquered by force of arms, but captivated by goodness, reform, and progress. Had you witnessed that scene in London, you would have seen the natives of Hindostan, the savage tribes of North America, the Negroes of West Africa, the Maories of New Zealand, Chinese, and Zulus, Kaffirs and tenants of the Oceanic Islands, vying with one another in honouring our own Victoria, side by side with the kings and princes of Europe, India, Japan, and Siam, all joining with the many colonial representatives in bearing witness to England's goodness, to England's greatness, and to England's model monarch. The only blot on the escutcheon of that memorable day was the apathy of the so-called Nationalists of Ireland. They apparently sulked, and could neither associate with savage nor civilised.[61]

The concept of Britishness therefore cloaked a strategic essentialism, masquerading as an universal civilisation, as opposed to the allegedly narrow nationalism of Ireland. This British civilisation, at once national and imperial, masked, moralised and mitigated its colonial thrust. Even in it most liberal forms, it endorsed imperialism by consigning cultural difference to erasure. Colonised cultures could only exist in a provisional form, destined to be cancelled by exposure to the superior civilisation. The adult-child metaphor was deployed to suggest that such cultures were sunk in an eternal colonial childhood, which required the parent imperialism for tutelage and

61 Cited in K. Whelan, 'The politics of memory' in M. Cullen (ed.), *1798. 200 years of resonance* (Dublin, 1998), p. 158.

discipline, as the child-culture underwent the necessary reform and reconstruction which raised it into the mature imperial world, and made it worthy of the gift of British liberties. This was the mainstay of English liberal thinking, derived from contact with Scotland, Ireland and India.[62] James Mill, writing in the *Edinburgh Review* in 1810, advanced the Indian arguments, which Peel was to champion in Ireland:

> Is a legislative assembly to be convoked in India? Certainly not. The stage of civilisation, and the moral and political situation in which the people of India are placed, render the establishment of legislative assemblies impracticable... A simple form of arbitrary government, tempered by European honour and European intelligence, is the only form which is now fit for Hindostan.[63]

There is a neat encapsulation in his son John Stuart Mill's *Utilitarianism*:

> Nobody can suppose that it is not more beneficial to a Breton, or a Basque [to be assimilated into advanced French forms of civilisation] than to sulk on his own rocks, the half savage relic of past times, revolving in his own little mental orbit, without participation or interest in the general movement of the world. The same remark applies to the Welshman or Scottish Highlander as members of the British nation.[64]

The forceful expansion of French and English imperialism therefore offered an expansion not a contraction of liberty.

CONCLUSION

Once catholics were spurned by the nascent United Kingdom state, the only available option was to manage Ireland on the old protestant lines, thus institutionalising and perpetuating the sectarian state, and in so doing, decisively turning Irish catholics from a wary neutrality to vehement hostility towards the union. It was then incorporated into their capacious

62 U. Singh Mehta, *Liberalism and empire. A study in nineteenth-century British liberal thought* (Chicago, 2001). 63 *Edinburgh Review*, xvi (1810), p. 155, cited in K. O'Brien, *Narratives of enlightenment. Cosmopolitan history from Voltaire to Gibbon* (Cambridge, 1997), p. 237. 64 J.S. Mill, *Utilitarianism* (Oxford, 1998), p. 86. See also J.S. Mill, *Essays on England, Ireland and the empire*, ed. J. Robson (Toronto, 1982).

and constantly ramifying narrative of betrayal, evicting them from their
warm constitutional fireplace back out into the penal cold. It also acquired
a starker anti-British dimension. In the absence of an Irish parliament, the
issue of parliamentary reform evaporated. The 'catholic question' became
the sole Irish question. Hitherto, the Irish parliament had screened Ireland
from Britain: after the union, catholic Ireland and protestant Britain chafed
together in a more abrasive relationship. In these circumstances, emancipation could only be grasped not granted, grudgingly conceded by a reluctant
state, which in itself concentrated the most visible anti-catholicism. The
liberal Peter Burrowes posed the issue: 'Is it possible that the catholics of
Ireland can be permanently alienated and the two countries permanently
united?'[65]

Burrowes' unanswered question exposed the empty heart of the union.
So much energy had been expended on the short term issue of getting the
measure passed that there was little effort to develop either a clear
conceptual framework or pragmatic blueprint for making the union work in
the long term. It was casually assumed that, as in the Scottish case, Westminster alchemy would magically metamorphose the unruly Irish into pliant
citizens. There was no attempt to streamline or standardise Irish administrative procedures: the Irish administration was allowed to trundle along on its
old sectarian grooves. No effort was made to run the island by British
standards, and Ireland was thereby delivered over to 'Irish animosities,
prejudices and conceptions' – precisely from which pro-union spokesmen
had claimed it would relieve Ireland. Dublin Castle settled back into its
comfortable sectarian mould, aided by the idea that (though theoretically
part of a British state) Ireland was actually a foreign country, which should
be run on the lines of a colony.[66] On the verge of the union passing,
Cornwallis gloomily observed that the rulers of the new state must:

> feel ourselves under the melancholy necessity of considering the
> majority of the Irish people as our enemies, and employ a large
> portion of the force, which ought to act against a foreign invader, to
> keep our own countrymen in subjection.[67]

Ireland remained only ambiguously British. In 1803, an insurance company
offering substitutes to English volunteer corps unable to fill their com-
plements inquired whether they would accept 'foreigners or Irishmen'.[68] It

65 P. Burrowes to L. Parsons, 23 Oct. 1800, in PRONI, T 3489/D/2/11. 66 S.
Deane, *Strange country. Modernity and nationhood in Irish writing since 1790* (Oxford,
1997). 67 Cornwallis to Portland, 2 Sept. 1800, in *Melville*, p. 55.

is a neat vignette of Ireland's awkward fit with the British project – not fully internalised, like the Scots and Welsh, but not fully foreigners, like the Hessians or Swiss.

Robert Peel (known derisively to catholics as 'Orange Peel') would eventually assert that 'an honest despotic government is by far the fittest government for Ireland. Ireland is not to be governed as England is: the character and the spirit of the government are completely different.'[69] Peel endorsed Protestant Ascendancy and used the state as an instrument of it. He also found it expedient to co-operate with the raw sectarianism of the Orange Order – 'a most difficult task when anti-catholicism and loyalty are so much united ... to appease the one without discouraging the other'.[70] In 1813, Peel concluded that 'the government could scarcely wish to see the lower classes in northern Ireland united'. He wished instead that they should always be disunited: 'The great art is to keep them so and yet at peace, or rather not at war with each other.'[71] In these ways, the United Kingdom state embarked on 'an experiment of a forced union', turning Burkean principles entirely on their head.[72]

The refusal of catholic emancipation was ultimately the failure of the Act of Union. Unlike Scotland after 1707, Ireland failed to bed itself down into the constitutional marriage.[73] The religious failure was matched by the economic and civil failure – the worsening of the Irish economic and demographic situation, the graphic violence of the Irish countryside. The Famine represented the moral, political and fiscal bankruptcy of the union settlement for Irish catholics.

By contrast, Irish protestants moved closer to Britain under the union settlement. Lord Redesdale, a key player in post-union Ireland, had argued for the maintenance of a protestant state in Ireland:

> Neither can I agree with some who think it immaterial to England whether the principal people here are catholics or protestants, or whether the whole nation was catholic. For, though the maxim, divide and govern, has been often reprobated, it is nevertheless true

68 L. Colley, *The significance of the frontier in British history* (Austin, 1995), p. 11.   69 R. Peel to Gregory 15 Mar. 1816, BL Add. Mss 40, 290, f. 150.   70 Cited in S. Connolly, 'Union government 1812–23' in *N.H.I.*, v, p. 66.   71 BL Add. Mss. 40, 286. Cited in R. Shipkey, *Robert Peel's Irish policy 1812–1846* (New York, 1987), p. 126.   72 Glassford, *Notes*, p. 362. It is an egregious error to argue, as Paul Bew has tried to do, that the union operated on Burkean principles. P. Bew, 'Where is Burke's vision of the union?', *T.L.S.*, 16 Mar. 2001, pp 6–7.   73 T. Devine, *The Scottish nation 1700–2000* (London, 1999).

that the division facilitates the governing of the country. It may be problematical whether the connection would be more secure if all the people here were protestants: but it seems evident that it would not be secure if they were catholics, for notions of aboriginal possession, which are very strong, as well as religion, would be and are always working in the minds of the catholics against the connection.[74]

The dispassionate, impartial, imperial legislature that Irish catholics had hoped for was a chimera and Dublin Castle embraced an Orange policy. In choosing orangeism, Britishness and the empire, while copperfastening the position of Irish protestants within it as a privileged minority, conservative protestantism effectively ceded the concept of the Irish nation to the catholics. The long-run split was to divide Irish politics into two confessionally defined monoliths, nationalism and unionism. The pernicious long run political outcome was partition. As Edward Said puts it: 'Imperial powers begin by divide and rule; they end by divide and quit.'[75]

Looked at in the long term, the union marked a decisive shift in the balance of power between Ireland and Great Britain. In 1800, when the union passed, the ratio of population was 2:1 (ten million to five million). When the union began to break up 120 years later, the ratio was 10:1 (forty million to four million). The union was indubitably an English measure, and it is instructive that the word 'colonialism' first appears in 1886 in an English text on Ireland, when the imperial theorist Albert Dicey, in resisting Home Rule arguments, observed that 'English colonialism works well enough' in Ireland.[76]

Britain's self-interest was such that it was unable to countenance an independent Ireland and its imagined community was also so narrowly envisioned as to be incapable of absorbing catholics as citizens. That imaginative and political failure of Britishness was to be at the heart of the Anglo-Irish problem in the 1790s: its effects can be seen ever more clearly as the concept of Britishness decomposed in the 1990s. The arc of empire and the arc of Britishness were directly synchronous. With empire gone, with protestantism fading in the face of a secularising and multi-cultural society, and with its old continental adversaries now its partners in the EU, Britishness no longer has a coherent principle. Recent developments in Scotland and Wales indicate the new realities, while in a sense reverting to

74 Redesdale papers, PRONI, T 3030/7/9   75 E. Said, 'Palestine and partition,' lecture delivered to the inaugural Notre Dame Irish Seminar, Dublin, July 1999.   76 A. Dicey, *England's case against Home Rule* (London, 1886), p. 273.

pre-imperial and pre-union politics. These developments have also striking implications for Northern Ireland, where they are slowly surfacing in the political arena. Within decades, we may use the term post-British like we now do the term post-Soviet. In the words of Hugo Young, 'Britain is a brief artefact, not a continuous entity.'[77]

This discussion makes clear that what is sometimes conceived of as Britain's Irish problem is more properly seen as Ireland's British problem. Recent developments in east-west relationships show the first serious efforts to acknowledge the fundamental problem at the core of the concept of Britishness. These changes also involve a rethinking of Ireland's relationship with England, Scotland and Wales: the Britain against which we so insistently defined ourself no longer exists, no more than the command culture of the first half century of the Irish state. Those who continue to cling barnacle-like to the sunken hulks of the old certainties, nationalist and unionist, are like the Beckett character with an amputated leg – all that remains is the unappeasable urge to scratch an unbearable itch where the amputated limb should be.

ACKNOWLEDGMENTS

I would like to thank Sara Gunderson and Seamus Deane for their generous assistance.

77 H. Young, review of N. Davies, *The Isles: a history* in *London Review of Books*, 6 Jan. 2000, p. 18.

2

The making of the union

Patrick Geoghegan

The Irish Act of Union was made out of the embers of the 1798 rebellion. It was remade in 1799 after its initial failure in the Irish House of Commons. It was unmade in 1801, when the collapse of the British government ensured that catholic emancipation would not accompany it. Nevertheless, although the 1798 rebellion is a good starting point for any study of the Act of Union, a convincing case can also be made for union being a long-term ambition of successive British governments.[1] However, the crisis generated by the rebellion forced a reluctant Prime Minister William Pitt and his ministers into making an immediate decision on the question. On 28 May, his thirty-ninth birthday, Pitt heard news of the insurrection in Ireland, and immediately wrote to the Irish lord lieutenant, Earl Camden, asking if it was possible to follow the termination of rebellion with an act appointing commissioners to treat for a legislative union.[2] But if 28 May 1798 is the correct date for when a union was fully decided, it remains important to chart the development of the idea in Pitt's thinking.

There is a dangerous tendency amongst historians, including Pitt's best biographer, to assume that the prime minister had deliberately avoided Irish affairs in the lead-up to 1798.[3] This perception is prevalent, but it is also wrong. Throughout the 1790s the threat posed by Ireland to an empire at war was always a consideration in Pitt's imperial thinking. Security was his overriding imperative, and he was determined to put the welfare of the empire above any local or regional concerns. The commercial propositions of 1784-5 had been Pitt's grand attempt to link Ireland and Britain economically so that they would be, to all intents and purposes, united.[4]

---

1 See Geoghegan, *Union*, chapter one. 2 Pitt to Camden, 28 May 1798, PRONI, T2627/4/221. 3 J. Ehrman, *The younger Pitt*, iii (London, 1996). Thomas Pakenham, indeed, even went so far as to attribute the rebellion to Pitt's failure to have any policy whatsoever for Ireland: *The year of liberty* (London, 1969), p. 13.

Their failure had made Ireland 'that unlucky subject' for him, and had forced him to investigate other ways of creating an unity of interest and purpose between the two countries. Inexorably, his thoughts turned to legislative union as the only way of resolving the ambiguities in the Anglo-Irish relationship that had been created by the 'Constitution of 1782'. However, from a British perspective, war with France in the 1790s made any tampering with the constitutional framework in Ireland at best unwise and at worst suicidal. And the demands of war increasingly required the loyalty of the Irish catholics, both as a source of manpower in the conflict, and because their dissatisfaction threatened exposure of the weakness at the heart of the relationship between the islands.[5]

In politics Pitt was a conservative, often applying a pragmatic Burkean approach to politics in a way that was frequently beyond the ability of Burke himself. As prime minister, therefore, he was never likely to press for a union as long as Britain was at war. Nevertheless, by 1797 union had become (as it was later to be called by Richard Brinsley Sheridan) his 'favourite project', and one that he was determined to introduce as soon as an opportunity arose. The Irish-born earl of Mornington, Richard Wellesley, elder brother of the future duke of Wellington, was a close friend of Pitt and had a number of discussions with him early in 1797 about the advantages of a legislative union.[6] Pitt subsequently dispatched one of his closest advisors, Lord Carrington, to Ireland in the summer of the same year to investigate the possible support in the country for the measure. Carrington discussed the project with Camden, who became increasingly concerned about the likelihood of it being attempted, and his own inability to see it through.[7] This reluctance, as much as the rising itself, resulted in his replacement as lord lieutenant in June 1798.

The Carrington mission is highly significant, and proves that Pitt was thinking seriously about Ireland at a time when he publicly appeared to have given up all interest in the country. It also explains why the idea of union was pounced upon as soon as the outbreak of the rebellion was reported, and how easily it was adopted as policy, circumventing the usually cumbersome decision-making process. George III immediately applauded the scheme, urging the manipulation of public opinion in Ireland, so as to use 'the present moment of terror' to persuade the protestants to support the union. Cornwallis, veteran of imperial conflicts in America and India, was immediately enlisted to take command in Ireland as lord lieutenant and

4 Kelly, 'Origins'. 5 See Geoghegan, *Union*, for a wider examination of these issues; Bartlett, *Fall and rise*, pp 152-5. 6 Wellesley to Grenville, 21 Oct. 1801, *Fortescue*, vii, p. 63.

commander-in-chief. The appointment of Cornwallis has correctly been identified as an indication that the government was, at a minimum, keeping an open mind on the catholic question. But the case is overstated when it is suggested that the whole union project was predicated in a desire to bring about catholic emancipation.[8] Although Pitt was aware that union offered the best (and probably the only) mechanism for allowing such relief, it was never his most important consideration. In the months ahead he was quite prepared to ditch the catholics when they became a liability; security not emancipation was always his prime consideration.

II

When discussing the making of the union, it is necessary to differentiate between the failed attempt in 1799 and the successful one the following year. The union that succeeded in 1800 was substantially different, in form and content, from the one envisaged the previous year. It is not, therefore, misleading to talk about 'two' unions and it is necessary to appreciate the significant differences between them both. The 1799 union was largely decided in the summer and autumn of 1798. Pitt and Lord Grenville, his first cousin and foreign secretary, produced a substantial paper on the subject in June that included catholic emancipation within its terms.[9] In August, Edward Cooke, the Castle under-secretary for the civil department, sent over another detailed paper which added to the ministers' views on the subject.[10] A major weakness of the scheme, however, was that the government was never clear about how the terms of union would be decided. This uncertainty created confusion in the lead-up to January 1799, as Dublin Castle was frequently unsure about the task in hand. Pitt's immediate inclination was to follow the precedent of the Scottish union of 1707.[11] Commissioners could be appointed in both countries to negotiate the terms of the measure, and revealingly this was the exact question Pitt asked of Camden on 28 May. Pitt was never likely to allow control over the union details to devolve away from Whitehall, and thus spent much of his time discussing with leading figures what those very terms would be. In the autumn of 1798 he invited the earl of Clare, Irish lord chancellor and

7 The mission is mentioned in Camden to Pitt, 10 Oct. 1797, CUL, Add. MS 6958, f. 2245. The letter was mistakenly dated 1799, which is impossible from internal evidence. A.P.W. Malcomson has initialled a correction to the manuscript in the Cambridge University Library collection of Pitt papers, dating it 1797. 8 Bartlett, *Fall and rise*, p. 246. 9 CUL, Add. MS 6958, f. 3700. 10 Referred to in Pitt to Auckland, 14 Aug. 1798, PRONI, T3229/2/35. 11 Ibid.

therefore the leading Irish legal expert, over to England to discuss the union, in a crucial set of meetings. Clare was astonished to find that the ministers were 'as full of their popish projects as ever', and that they were committed to bringing in emancipation.[12] Threatening to lead opposition to an union, if such a policy was to accompany it, the ministers' determination wilted and they conceded the point. The catholic component of the union had been sabotaged by Clare's intransigence, and the discussions ended, unsatisfactorily, 'with much drunkenness at Bellamy's.'[13]

The decision to keep the catholic question separate from the union was to be a major factor in its failure in 1799. A month after Clare's visit, John Foster, speaker of the Irish House of Commons, also visited London to discuss the subject. Foster was a key figure in the commons, perhaps the most important, and his support was critical. While it was not clear that he would ever accept the merits of a union, his admiration for Pitt was complete, and made any negotiations with the prime minister much more conducive to an agreement. The visit was completely mishandled, the character of the visitor was misjudged, and the mood of the talks was compromised by blatant rudeness.[14] Foster may have had great respect for Pitt, but the prime minister had none for the speaker. Indeed Foster's broad Irish accent soon became a source of much amusement. William Wilberforce, one of the prime minister's closest friends, mocked him as 'Mr Spaker', and Pitt failed to show any consideration for his visitor's feelings. This may have stemmed from the incompetent Camden's faulty advice. In cabinet once more, Camden (a regular, if unremarkable advisor on Irish affairs) dismissed Foster's importance and integrity, predicting that the promise of a good peerage would be enough to secure his support. The resolute speaker was not so accommodating, and his mood was not helped by the complete breakdown of his relationship with Dublin Castle. Cornwallis correctly identified Foster as one of the chief culprits in the exacerbation of tensions in the 1790s; after his arrival in June, he isolated him from all political decisions. Discarded in Ireland, Foster had now also been snubbed in London. In an appalling display of presumption, Pitt left the speaker waiting days before seeing him, and then, characteristically, left the meeting thinking that he had secured Foster's support for the union.[15]

Arriving back in Dublin in January 1799, Foster immediately began organising opposition to the union. He refused to meet with Viscount

12 Clare to Castlereagh, 16 Oct. 1798, *Castlereagh corr.*, i, p. 393. 13 Clare to Auckland, 28 Oct. 1798, PRONI, T3287/7/22; Canning to Windham, 23 Oct. 1798, BL, Add. MS 37844, f. 274. 14 Malcomson, *Foster*, p. 78. 15 See Geoghegan, *Union*, chapter two.

Castlereagh, the chief secretary, in a snub that reflected his own recent experiences. As a hard-line supporter of Protestant Ascendancy, Foster was always likely to have opposed the union, but he later attributed the strength of his opposition to his cold treatment at the hands of the administration. A further blow to the union cause was the decision of the catholics to remain aloof from the measure. Without the offer of relief, they were unwilling to take sides, although Archbishop John Thomas Troy of Dublin and the catholic bishops remained largely sympathetic to government designs. In late January it appeared that the catholics would be offered emancipation by the protestant anti-unionists in return for their public opposition to the measure. This unlikely alliance would probably have prevented any future attempts to secure a union. In the event no such deal was made; the strength of the prejudices of Foster and his like on the subject made any agreement impossible.

The most significant factor in the failure of the 1799 union was the refusal of the government to accept the principle of borough compensation. While it was generally accepted that seats were a form of personal property, the ministers were aware that compensating borough proprietors for their abolition would raise unwelcome allegations of corruption against them. There was also an even greater consideration – money. The one and a quarter million pounds that it was estimated would be needed for proprietors was too much to contemplate. Whatever about the ethical implications of compensation, the government was determined to pass the union as cheaply as possible, and their frugality was a significant factor in the rejection of the measure in the commons.

The Irish parliament met on 22 January, with an unusually large attendance for the traditional king's address. Although union was not explicitly mentioned in the speech, it was implied, and the opposition attacked the principle from the outset. Lord Tyrone, son of the marquess of Waterford and a government supporter, attempted a traditional vote of thanks but was interrupted by George Ponsonby, one of the leading opposition MPs, who questioned the legality of Castlereagh's parliamentary seat. Ponsonby argued that the chief secretary had vacated it upon accepting that office the previous autumn. Two hours of debate on this point followed, which was only resolved after the attorney general intervened and explained that Castlereagh had not needed to seek re-election.[16]

Both sides had been expecting a battle over the union, but only the opposition was ready for one. Government numbers, which had looked solid

16 *A report of the debate ... 22 and 23 January 1799* (Dublin, 1799).

going into the chamber, haemorrhaged as the debate intensified. The speeches continued after midnight, and went on into the afternoon of 23 January. Unionist morale was shaky to non-existent, while the opposition was buoyed by their successful humiliation of their adversaries. Opposition speeches were loudly cheered, while the government benches remained half-empty with 'members affecting carelessness and inattention.'[17] As waves of abuse descended upon ministers, the twenty-nine year old chief secretary, Viscount Castlereagh, became the principal target for taunts. Arrogant, aloof and lacking in charisma, even Cornwallis found him 'so cold that nothing can touch him'; Castlereagh was also hampered by his deficiencies as a speaker.[18] William Plunket, the fiery opposition member for Charlemont borough, showed no mercy and taunted Castlereagh for being an 'unspotted veteran', an 'unassuming stripling' and ' a green and sapless twig'.[19] This last barb was a cruel reference to Castlereagh and his wife's apparent inability to have children. Castlereagh was so taken aback at this vicious onslaught that he appeared to shrink visibly from the encounter. That said, the chief secretary was at his best when under pressure, and responded well to the attacks. Even Jonah Barrington, who was not prone to praising unionists, admitted that his speeches 'far exceeded the powers he was supposed to possess'.[20] One seasoned observer, John Beresford, the first commissioner for the revenue and a government apologist, was disgusted by the behaviour of the members: 'direct treason spoken, resistance to the law declared, encouraged and recommended. I never heard such vulgarity and barbarism.'[21]

Lady Bessborough, the sister of a cabinet minister, blamed the failure of the measure on the Castle; 'not that I believe that corruption and bribery were wanting: there was as much as you could wish for.'[22] Barrington provides some clear examples upon this score. Early in the day, one unassuming

---

17 Carysfort to Grenville, 23 Jan. 1799, *Fortescue*, iv, p. 450. **18** Martha McTier to William Drennan, 3 Sept. 1794 in *Drennan-McTier letters*, ii, p. 95; Charles Greville's profile quoted in H.M. Hyde, *The strange death of Lord Castlereagh* (London, 1959), p. 7. **19** *A report of the debate ... 22 and 23 January 1799*, p. 48; J. C. Hoey (ed.), *Speeches at the bar and in the senate by the Rt Hon. William Conyngham* (Dublin, 1873), pp 45-6. In the printed report of the debate, the comment is a 'green and limber twig', but Hoey quotes the 'sapless' version and Hyde states that this was generally regarded to be the correct one (*Castlereagh*, p. 298, fn. 1). Emily, Castlereagh's wife, watched all of this from the gallery. The pair remained childless to Castlereagh's death. **20** Barrington, *Historic memoirs*, ii, p. 309. **21** Beresford to Auckland, 24 Jan. 1799, *Beresford corr.*, ii, p. 194. **22** Castalia Countess Granville (ed.), *Private correspondence of Lord Granville Leveson-Gower 1781-1821*, 2 vols. (London, 1916), i, p. 239.

country member, Frederick Trench, expressed his opposition to the union, but by the end of the debate had publicly recanted his error. Barrington's version of Trench's seduction is one of the writer's finest descriptive passages. It begins with Cooke and Castlereagh murmuring, and looking earnestly at Trench, unsure about whether his vote was critical. After some quick calculations, 'they whispered – again looked most affectionately at Mr Trench, who seemed unconscious that he was the subject of their consideration. But there was no time to lose – the question was approaching – all shame was left behind,' and so Cooke left his seat, went over to Trench, and with 'a significant and certain glance' indicated that the Castle had agreed to his conditions. The terms decided, Cooke returned to his seat, and 'with a parting smile completely told the house that Mr Trench was that moment satisfied'.[23] In 1800 Trench was raised to the peerage as Lord Ashtown.

When the twenty-one hour debate finally concluded, the battered government found that they could only pass the king's address by 107 votes to 105. Worse, Ponsonby's amendment protecting the Irish constitution was defeated by a single vote. As a policy the union was dead, and Castlereagh was forced to admit to the commons that it would not be proceeded with again until the mood of the country and the parliament had changed.

III

The 1800 union was to be substantially different, in tone and content, from the one that had been so aggressively rejected. Within ten months the three 'C's' had been adopted to guarantee victory: compensation, catholic emancipation, and corruption. Pitt immediately dropped the idea of appointing commissioners, and decided instead to press the union through as a bill in both parliaments, with the act to come into effect on 1 January 1801. The government's shyness when it came to money was now abandoned with abandon. Borough compensation was accepted as a point of principle, as well as practicability, removing a major obstacle in the way of securing the landowners' support. Patronage was also employed with even more liberality than before, as Dublin Castle went out of its way to avoid an embarrassing repetition of the scenes in the house of commons in January 1799. Although humbled, the ministry remained as ruthless as ever.

The catholic question now became a decisive issue. In the autumn of 1799, Castlereagh visited London and informed the ministers that the union would fail unless the catholics were willing to acquiesce in its passing. Determined to see the measure succeed, the cabinet came to a crucial

23 Barrington, *Rise and fall*, p. 405.

decision in November to make catholic emancipation a corollary of the union.[24] It was the most serious shift in the entire union policy, and one that ensured that there was little popular resistance in the country to the measure. Ultimately, it also ensured the failure of the project, as the catholic question tore Pitt's ministry apart in the autumn of 1800.

Perhaps the most significant aspect of the 1800 union was the role of corruption in its passage. Barrington led the critique of the union on the grounds of the illegality with which it was achieved, but for many years these claims were dismissed as polemical products of his hyperactive imagination. An unique figure, Barrington was a man of many parts. A deadly duellist and an incorruptible politician, he was also a highly inaccurate diarist, and an eminently corruptible judge. Barrington is now best remembered for his trenchant attack on government corruption in his *Rise and fall of the Irish nation*. Ironically, he spent his own final days in France, having fled the country to avoid prosecution for embezzlement. In his work, Barrington included the 'red' and 'black' lists of those that voted during the union debates, and added personal details of how the members fared subsequently. Those on the 'red' list (opponents of the measure) usually ended up badly; Barrington reserved special venom for those on the 'black' list, gleefully citing their subsequent promotions, peerages, and pensions. A particular hero for Barrington was his one-time debating adversary John 'Bully' Egan, a successful barrister and MP, so called for his large-size and boisterous manner.[25] During the union debates, however, Egan was threatened with dismissal from his office of chairman of Kilmainham unless he supported the union. As it was his principal source of income, the decision weighed heavily with him as he sat in the commons waiting to state his opinion to the house. Finally he rose to speak, and throwing aside his personal interests, exclaimed 'Ireland! Ireland for ever! And damn Kilmainham!'[26]

The charge of 'general corruption' was levelled against the government throughout the union debates, and it was often extended to include the traffic in patronage, as well as borough compensation. Historians have been keen to distinguish these elements, and separate things that were generally accepted as part of the political system at the time, from hard cash, which

24 Castlereagh to Pitt, 1 Jan. 1801, CUL, Add. MS 6958, f. 2827. 25 On one famous occasion, Barrington had humiliated Egan by continuously laughing during a speech, in which the word 'obdurate' featured prominently. Egan was finally forced to stop, and he angrily asked Barrington if he was laughing because he was mispronouncing the word: Barrington replied that he was in fact laughing because Egan had managed to pronounce the word correctly. Barrington, *Personal sketches*, i, pp 215-6. 26 The story is quoted by Barrington, who noted with some regret that Egan died in poverty in 1810, although not with enough sympathy to alter some of his crueller descriptions of the man.

was never moral practice. Because of the paucity of evidence to substantiate the claims of Barrington, Henry Grattan and the opposition that large sums of money changed hands during the union debates, these have usually been dismissed as anti-union propaganda. The discovery of 'lost' secret service papers in the Public Record Office in Kew in 1996, however, provides the missing evidence. [27] In themselves the documents are unimpressive, but they prove that £30,850 of secret service money was diverted to Ireland for use in the government's campaign, contravening Burke's Civil List Act (1782) and the Irish Civil List Act (1793). Secret service funds were to be used solely for detecting or preventing treasonable conspiracies, within limits set by parliament, and all monies had to be carefully accounted for. In the context of the union, such restrictions were illegally circumvented by Cooke and Castlereagh with the full knowledge of George III, Pitt, and the Home Office.[28] The purpose of the money was to establish a covert slush fund which could be used to deal with whatever emergency arose. Part was spent on the propaganda war, paying for pamphlets, and possibly even buying and destroying opposition ones. It was also a convenient way of keeping MPs happy until an official place or sinecure that would give them an annual pension could be found for them. As a last resort, the money could also be used for direct bribes, although the price of a vote had increased by January 1800, was still increasing, and was not likely to be diminished.

The neo-corruption interpretation of how the union passed has largely concentrated on the misuse of these secret service funds.[29] This money, however, does not represent the entire budget of the illegal slush fund that was set up to facilitate government business. A further £18,000 was diverted from the Irish civil list in the autumn of 1800, and channelled secretly into the union campaign.[30] Although the union had passed in the commons by this stage, it was now time to settle debts, and the Castle became increasingly concerned about whether they could meet all their commitments. Indeed the appropriation of the £18,000 from the saving made on the civil list in 1800 almost lead to the exposure of the entire illegal dealings in 1801. As late as the autumn of 1801, the Castle needed even more money, to pay for printers' bills, borough seats that had been purchased, and other debts. Therefore a request was made to the Alien Office, or as it was referred to at the time in treasury documents 'His Majesty's Secret Service', seeking an additional £14,800. This figure should also be included in any calculation

27 These have been catalogued by David Wilkinson of the History of Parliament. 28 See Geoghegan, *Union*, chapter four.   29 D. Wilkinson, 'How did they pass the Union?' in *History*, 82 (1997), pp 223-51.   30 Pitt to Addington, 26 June 1801 in Aspinall, *George III*, iii, p. 565.

about the extent to which illegal funds were used to assist the union, and shows that the amount of money at the Castle's disposal was greater than has perhaps been realised.[31] In total then, the entire slush fund at the Castle's disposal between 1799 and 1801 amounts to £63,650, and this is only the figure that can be verified from documentary sources; it may have been much higher. Even after the passing of the union in June 1800, the Castle still needed to raise extra funds to honour the commitments it had made in the previous year. It reveals just how important the sums were in maintaining unionist support, and more importantly just how desperately the Castle relied on the fund.

When the Irish parliament met at the beginning of 1800, the government was in a considerably stronger position than it had been the previous year. The secret service money sustained morale whenever it was threatened, and the opposition was divided over possible tactics. Castlereagh called the funds 'the means by which so much depends' and warned the Home Office not to shirk from continuing their covert activities.[32] £10,000 was sent to the chief secretary in January, with a promise that 'the fund was good security for a still further sum'.[33] Barrington provides some examples of how the money was employed. On every day that parliament sat, the Castle held a lavish dinner for about thirty irresolute members. The dinner was held in the committee rooms, so that in the event of a snap division, they could be rushed as voting fodder to the chamber. One happy consequence was that 'wit and puns' accompanied the passing of the bottle. Edward Cooke supervised the proceedings, and according to Barrington, 'with significant nods, and smirking innuendoes, began to circulate his official rewards to the company ... [until] every man became in a prosperous state of official pregnancy'.[34]

IV

The 1799 union had been drowned out by the heckles and taunts of the opposition. In 1800 the government benches were loudest, and Barrington admitted that they showed much more spirit than the opposition, having left their dinners 'fully resolved to eat, drink, speak and fight for Lord Castlereagh'. Recognising the weakness of their position, the opposition attacks centred on the corruption of the government. On one significant occasion, Castlereagh turned these allegations to his advantage in a

31 John King to Cooke, 10 Oct. 1801, BL, Add. MS 60338, f. 80. 32 Castlereagh to John King, 2 Jan. 1800, *Cornwallis corr.*, ii, p. 156; PRO HO 100/93, f. 2. 33 *Cornwallis corr.*, iii, p. 156 34 Barrington, *Historic memoirs*, ii, p. 336.

particularly stunning piece of oratory. Loftily insisting that 'there are bribes I am not prepared to offer', he constructed an ingenious defence of the unionist case: 'if bribery and public advantage are synonymous, I must readily admit that it is a measure of the most comprehensive bribery that was ever produced'.[35] The overall effect of Castlereagh's arguments, however, was somewhat diminished by his insistence early on in the debate that 'everyone knows the ignorance of the lower classes in this kingdom'. The opposition's best speakers were quick to pounce on the illegal practices of the administration. George Ponsonby warned the country that 'your peerage is to be disgraced, your commons purchased'. Or as Henry Grattan put it with a characteristic blend of melodrama and hyperbole, it was a question of 'whether your children shall go to your graves saying a venal, a military court, attacked the liberties of the Irish ... Such is an epitaph that the king cannot give his slaves.'[36]

Unfortunately for the anti-unionists, the venality of many members of the house was never in doubt. The union passed inexorably through the commons in 1800, and had its final reading in June. Throughout the year the opposition had been consistently out-fought, out-thought, and out-spent by the government. Unable to nurture a popular resistance to the measure out of parliament, the anti-unionist case crumbled in the commons, and there was never any significant doubt about the final result. The people had little affection for the protestant parliament and some expected that emancipation would accompany the union. Others had lost their confidence after the failure of 1798 and were unwilling to make any kind of stand. In late 1800, however, the catholic question returned as a destabilising issue for the government – and in January 1801 the cabinet collapsed, Pitt resigned as prime minister, and any hopes of accompanying the union with emancipation were dashed. George III was determined to defend his coronation oath; when the English lord chancellor, Lord Loughborough, and others, informed him that emancipation was on its way, his anger could not be contained. All the previous tensions between king and prime minister surfaced in an explosive clash that reduced Pitt to an unprecedented emotional state, and robbed George III, temporarily, of his sanity. Unwilling to allow his conception of the role of prime minister and his own power to be challenged, Pitt resigned, allowing the hard-line anti-catholics to win the day. Robbed of its corollary, the union was only grudgingly, and never enthusiastically, accepted in Ireland. The apparent exclusion of the catholics

35 *A report of the debate in the house of commons of Ireland on 5th and 6th February 1800* (Dublin, 1800), p. 37. 36 *Report ... 5th and 6th February 1800*, p. 65.

from the terms of the union ensured that a permanent weakness lay at its core. It is this problem that lies at the heart of any discussion of the unmaking of the union.

Meanwhile a swift cover-up was instituted in Britain and Ireland to prevent any details about the slush fund and the secret service monies from being revealed. The ministers had not, however, included in their calculations the mental illness of George III, which had unfortunate consequences for their schemes. When he recovered, in March 1801, he found that he was missing £18,000, the savings from the Irish Civil List Act that had been diverted into the Castle's slush fund, and immediately suspected the home secretary, Portland, of having embezzled it. For a time it appeared that the corruption at the heart of the union dealings would be exposed by the unlikely figure of the king. In the ensuing panic, even the normally unflappable Castlereagh had a nervous breakdown when it appeared that his own role would be unmasked.[37] With so much to lose, Pitt intervened and had discreet and confidential conversations with the king, finally convincing him that he had fully approved the transactions. A fictitious set of accounts were agreed, and the reputation of the union was preserved. As the threat of exposure faded, it was left to writers like Barrington to maintain the charges in print, with admittedly more than a little embellishment at times. Nevertheless his works remain important accounts of the union, how it was made, and how it was passed. In particular, his details about members who changed sides are both revealing and amusing, for example, the account of William Handcock, a brash MP for Athlone who wrote and sang songs against the union in 1799 and wrote and sang songs for it in 1800.[38] Perhaps surprisingly, Barrington does not shy away from mentioning his own complicity in some unorthodox behaviour. For example, he admits that at one point he acted as an agent for the government in persuading an anti-unionist MP to vacate his seat, probably in return for a financial reward for both men. Nor does he show any embarrassment in mentioning that he applied for the post of solicitor-general in the autumn of 1799. Had he been given the position, it is unthinkable that he would have been able to oppose the union. Thus the great exponent of union corruption, possibly unwittingly, reveals that even his own loyalty was negotiable, and that perhaps every writer has his price.[39]

---

37 See Geoghegan, *Union*, chapter eight for a more detailed account. 38 Barrington, *Rise and fall*, p. 491. 39 I would like to thank Mary Fay, Michael Brown and Rory Whelan for their generous help with various aspects of this paper.

3

The Act of Union: its origins and background

James Kelly

One of the more intriguing questions posed by the Irish Act of Union is how it came about that a scheme rejected by British political opinion when requested by the Irish parliament on three occasions between 1703 and 1709 and repudiated by Irish political opinion for most of the eighteenth century was accepted with comparatively little drama in 1800. This question is all the more compelling since the union was implemented a mere eighteen years after Irish protestants had exacted the right to make law for the kingdom of Ireland free of the restrictions imposed by Poynings' Law (1494) and the Declaratory Act (1720) and articulated a confident economic and political vision for the future. The traditional answer, elaborated by generations of nationalist historians and politicians, was that this manifested British hostility towards Ireland. The Young Ireland activist, William O'Neill Daunt, presented this viewpoint with exceptional clarity in his *Catechism of the history of Ireland* in 1844:

> The motive of the government was 'an intolerance of Irish pros-
> perity'. They hated Ireland with intense fierceness, from ancient
> national prejudice. Pitt also had his own peculiar quarrel with the
> Irish parliament, from its opposition to his views on the regency
> question in 1789; and the growth of Ireland in happiness, in
> greatness, in prosperity, in domestic harmony, and consequent
> strength, was altogether insupportable to our jealous English foes ...[1]

Predicated upon such partisan analyses and the problematic perception that the eighteenth-century Irish parliament had become 'an ever-increasing

1 [W. O'Neill Daunt], *Catechism of the history of Ireland: ancient and modern* (Dublin, 1844), p. 133.

object of national interest and national pride', nationalist historians explained the ratification of the Act of Union as the inevitable outcome of 'a naked, unsparing, unscrupulous, and unblushing corruption of individuals'.[2] Egregious examples were readily proffered,[3] and this interpretation became so entrenched that history textbooks in the Irish state maintained aphoristically that the union was carried by 'bribery and corruption'.[4] Furthermore, it was insisted that this was contrary to the will of what Hayden and Moonan denominated the 'Irish nation', and O'Neill Daunt termed 'the people' who, he maintained, had demonstrated their true feelings by ascribing to 'petitions against the union to the number of 707,000' when 'all the signatures the government could obtain in favour of the measure amounted to no more than about 3,000.'[5]

This interpretation of the origins and ratification of the Act of Union, whose intellectual ancestry can be traced to Jonah Barrington's sensationalist account of the episode, was in the historiographical ascendant in Ireland for over a century.[6] Indeed, it was not seriously challenged until 1966 when Geoffrey Bolton, in the first scholarly study of the passing of the Act of Union, maintained that the patronage resorted to by the authorities to facilitate its passage was not out of character with its quotidian application. Bolton sustained this contention by applying the methodology made famous by Sir Lewis Namier and his disciples in their accounts of the structure of politics in eighteenth-century England and by measuring union patronage against that distributed by Earl Harcourt in 1776.[7] This prompted a generation of historians to discard the long dominant 'bribery and corruption' paradigm and to present the union as just another, albeit seminal, event in the history of the eighteenth-century Irish parliament.[8] Because it liberated scholars from the reflexive nationalist predisposition to perceive the union as emblematic of the 'corruption' that was deemed endemic to the politics of protestant ascendancy, Bolton's work represented a hermeneutic

2 A.M. Sullivan, *Story of Ireland* (Dublin, 1894), p.526.   3 J.G. Swift MacNeill, *How the Union was carried* (London, 1887), pp 93-152.   4 These are the precise words used in, for example, M. Hayden & G. Moonan, *A short history of the Irish people* (Dublin, n.d.), p. 424; H. McGaffin, *Ireland in the eighteenth century* (Belfast, n.d.), p. 8. The same words are used, but not so juxtaposed, in the account of the passage of the union provided by Sullivan, *Story of Ireland*, pp 526-7 and in R. B. O'Brien (ed.), *Two centuries of Irish history* (London, 1907), p. 196   5 Hayden & Moonan, *A short history*, p. 448; [O'Neill Daunt], *Catechism*, p. 133; W. Dennehy, *The story of the Union told by its plotters* (Dublin, 1891), p.1.   6 Sullivan, *Story of Ireland*, pp 522-33, exemplifies the reliance on Barrington.   7 Bolton, *Union*, p. 4.   8 McDowell, *Ireland*; R. Foster, *Modern Ireland 1600-1972* (London, 1988); G. Ó Tuathaigh, *Ireland before the famine 1798-1848* (Dublin, 1972), p. 32; D. Macartney, *The dawning of democracy* (Dublin, 1987), p. 12.

advance of signal importance. However, his argument that the patronage resorted to in 1799-1800 was normal was misleading. Harcourt's efforts in 1776 were *sui generis* and probably exceptional: there are grounds for concluding that the patronage advanced and promised in 1799-1800 was likewise.[9] This is reinforced by recent discoveries of the illegal allocation of money from the English secret service fund and the extent of the patronage debts generated in 1799-1800.[10] There is, at the same time, no reverting to the long-established predilection to portray the union as a manifestation of English 'jealousy' or to interpret its implementation solely in 'conspiratorial terms.'[11]

Of the modern interpretations of the origins and ratification of the Act of Union, the argument that the Irish parliament had fallen so low in the esteem of the politicised population that few cared about its abolition is manifestly unsatisfactory. The Irish parliament as constituted was not a popular assembly, but it was not unresponsive to public opinion on the matter of an union as it demonstrated in 1785 when a large number of MPs resisted a proposal to create a 'commercial union' and in January 1799 when a majority rejected the union at the first time of asking.[12] One cannot at the same time assess the Commons' decision in January 1799 simply as a reflection of popular opposition; Irish MPs were quite prepared to ignore public opinion when it conflicted with their self interest, as the hostile responses to calls for parliamentary reform in the 1780s and 1790s attest; even popular voices like Henry Flood and Henry Grattan professed their unwillingness to be always guided in their political actions by what the public demanded.[13] Furthermore, the argument that the Irish parliament had so lost its way since 1782 that MPs were content to follow the lead provided by a 'junta' of ideological reactionaries who favoured political

9 No proper analysis of Harcourt's patronage efforts has been undertaken. They are described most fully in J. Hunt, *The Irish parliament 1775* (London, 1907), introduction. For some suggestion that Harcourt entered into patronage arrangements beyond the normal, see J. Kelly, *Henry Flood. Patriots and politics in eighteenth-century Ireland* (Dublin, 1998), pp 214-15. More generally see A. Malcomson. 'The parliamentary traffic of this country' in T. Bartlett & D. Hayton (eds), *Penal era and golden age* (Belfast, 1979), pp 137-61.   10 D. Wilkinson, 'How did they pass the union: secret service expenditure', *History*, 82 (1997), pp 223-51; Geoghegan, *Union*, pp 85-7; M. MacDonagh (ed.), *The viceroy's post bag* (London, 1904) provides the most detailed perspective on the post-union patronage.   11 O'Neill Daunt, *Catechism*, pp 132-4.   12 J. Kelly, 'Popular politics in Ireland and the Act of Union' in *Transactions of the Royal Historical Society*, 4th series, X (2000), pp 259-87.   13 J. Kelly, 'Parliamentary reform in Irish politics 1760-1790' in Dickson *et al.* (eds), *United Irishmen*, pp 74-87; McDowell, *Ireland*, pp 435-6; Kelly, *Flood*, p. 444; J. Kelly, *Henry Grattan* (Dundalk, 1993), p. 48.

integration with Britain is belied by the facts.[14] The Irish parliament passed
more law in the 1790s than it did in any previous decade; while the average
per session was lower than that registered in the 1780s, three of the five most
legislatively productive sessions in the eighteenth century were those held
in 1798, 1799 and 1800.[15] The refusal to allow catholic participation and the
anti-popery of so many of its members clearly disenchanted catholics with
the legislature, but the impact of this on the passing of the Act of Union is
disputed.[16] Leading catholics were well-disposed to the idea of a union since
they had concluded that the repeal of the penal laws owed more to
ministerial intervention than to the generosity of the Irish parliament and
they were hopeful that further concessions would be forthcoming in an
inclusive imperial assembly. This proved most useful to the Irish administration as it sought to elicit public declarations of support in 1800, but it is
difficult to sustain Bartlett's argument that the stance taken by catholics was
decisive in ensuring its ratification.

Clearly then, a more nuanced explanation of why a legislative union was
resorted to and why it was accepted is needed. Throughout the eighteenth
century, a legislative union was identified by a fluctuating number of
influential voices in Britain and Ireland as an alternative to the devolutionary
policy that gave the Irish protestant elite a substantive input into the
government of the kingdom via the Irish parliament. In this context, an
exploration of the changing trajectory of attitudes to a union in Britain as
well as Ireland during the seventeenth and eighteenth centuries is crucial.
Without it, the union can be perceived as a knee-jerk response to the 1798
rebellion and its ratification interpreted in terms not dissimilar to those
resorted to by nationalist historians in previous generations.[17] The Irish Act
of Union should be seen as a logical extension of the integrationist policy
pursued by England that commenced with the Anglo-Welsh union in 1541
and continued with the Anglo-Scottish union in 1707. Furthermore, since
England was the dominant force in Anglo-Irish relations, an Anglo-Irish
union was only likely when its leaders deemed it appropriate to press for
such an initiative, and that moment was not reached until the late 1790s.

14 This term favoured by Burke has surfaced in contemporary literature: see K.
Whelan, *The tree of liberty* (Cork, 1996), p. 76.   **15** Based upon *The statutes at large
passed in the parliaments held in Ireland 1613–1800* (20 vols, Dublin, 1789–1800).   **16**
Bartlett, *Fall and rise*, chapter 12 for the elaboration of the view that catholics had an
important impact upon the ratification of the Act of Union.   **17** Geoghegan's
admirable account of the Act of Union is not immune to this interpretation; note his
arresting opening sentences: 'The union was an act of arrogance. It was arrogantly
conceived, and executed with the ruthless efficiency that characterised much of
government activity in the period.' (Geoghegan, *Union*, p.1).

There was, as this suggests, greater resistance in England to the idea of a union with Ireland than with the other political entities in the archipelago. This is not to say that a union was not considered seriously before 1798. It was addressed on a number of occasions from the mid-seventeenth century, but only in the mid-eighteenth century did key elements of English opinion come to perceive a union with Ireland as potentially advantageous. Even then, prevailing attitudes crystallised slowly, but the realisation that a union was the only feasible option – between the *status quo* and to allow Ireland further autonomy – strengthened its appeal. Opinion in Ireland had further to travel at this point if a union was to become a reality; following London's refusal to implement a legislative union at the beginning of the eighteenth century, Irish political and public sentiment became overwhelmingly anti-union. It remained thus (a number of well-placed voices excepted) until the early 1790s when the realisation that London was no longer prepared to maintain an exclusive protestant political system prompted a rapid rethink. The subsequent emergence of a Francophile republican movement also exerted a weighty influence as the apprehension of revolution heightened the allure of integration to the political establishments in both kingdoms.

As its advocates swelled in number and influence in Britain and Ireland in the 1790s, the likelihood of an Anglo-Irish act of union increased but it did not ensure it would come to pass. It took the strategic, fiscal and practical implications of war with France and rebellion in Ireland to determine ministers to bring it about so that Ireland should remain securely within Britain's sphere of interest. Based upon the ready support forthcoming for the measure in 1799, this decision was endorsed by a majority of British opinion. Attitudes in Ireland were distinctly less decisive. Support for a union grew rapidly in the 1790s; it was almost accepted in January 1799 when it was first presented to the Irish parliament though the political management of the issue by the Irish executive left much to be desired.[18] A year later, the outcome was unambiguous; determined that the measure should become law, the administration successfully bolstered the ranks of Irish unionism, and carried the measure with comparatively little difficulty. Irish political and public opinion had moved far on this question since 1780 when its supporters were afraid even to mention the idea lest it 'excite a rebellion'. It also emphasises that the sizeable unionist constituency in the kingdom by the late 1790s was important in ensuring its implementation.[19]

18 The best account of this is provided in Geoghegan, *Union*, chapter 3. 19 Macartney to North, 8 Jan. 1780 in T. Bartlett (ed.), *Macartney in Ireland 1769-72*

I

One infrequently alluded to episode when the issue of an Anglo-Irish union is being considered is that there was an important seventeenth-century precedent; a union was actively contemplated in the 1650s.[20] Indeed, following the Rump Parliament's decision in March 1653 that Ireland should send thirty representatives to Westminster, a varying number of Irish members were nominated to sit in successive British parliaments in 1654, 1656 and 1659. In the latter year also, a bill for the union of Ireland and England was prepared.[21] This bill never became law, and the experience at Westminster was sufficiently disheartening to ensure that there was no groundswell of support for a repeat of the experiment or for a formal legislative union following the restoration of the Stuart monarchy in 1660. Ireland was allowed to make its own laws within the parameters defined by Poynings' Law in the parliament convened between 1661 and 1666; though there were sporadic expressions of support for the idea of a union subsequently, it did not elicit any sustained political notice. The 'considerable persons' in Ireland who promoted a union in 1668 believed it would neutralise the mercantilist restrictions that curbed their freedom to trade. Its appeal in England was founded on the conviction that it would strengthen English control of Ireland and, through the union of 'all his majesty's territories', ensure a healthy increase in economic activity.[22] These were to remain important considerations in both kingdoms, but so long as the political situation remained stable there was little prospect of a serious demand for a union emerging in either kingdom.

The deposition of James II and the elevation of William of Orange to the throne in 1688-89 created an environment more amenable to this constitutional option. Surprisingly, it was less the experience of war and rebellion that prompted declarations of support for political integration than the belief that time and self-government would open a chasm between the English in Ireland and their fellow subjects in England. The warmest

(Belfast, 1978), p. 325.   20 It figured in some of the background papers compiled to aid in the preparation for a union (NLI, Union correspondence, Ms 887).   21 Kelly, 'Origins', pp 237-8; T. Barnard, 'Planters and policies in Cromwellian Ireland', *Past and Present* (1973), pp 60-65; idem, *Cromwellian Ireland: English government and reform in Ireland 1649-60* (Oxford, 1975), pp 16, 28-9, 34; idem, 'The Protestant interest, 1641-1660' in J. Ohlmeyer (ed.), *Ireland: from independence to occupation 1641-1660* (Cambridge, 1995), p. 237.   22 Kelly, 'Origins', pp 238-40; J. Kelly, 'Public and political opinion in Ireland and the idea of an Anglo-Irish union 1650-1800' in D. Boyce & R. Eccleshall (eds), *Political thought in eighteenth-century Ireland* (London, forthcoming).

advocates of a union were recent settlers who apprehended that the English in Ireland would 'forget *England*, and ... bandy and side with the Irish' if they were allowed their own parliament.[23] Thus, the accountant general James Bonnell counselled against convening an Irish parliament on the grounds that it would result in 'this kingdom setting up for itself and having a different interest from England'.[24] Such advice was not heeded. Although the Irish parliament that assembled in 1692 proved highly assertive, it was not until the late 1690s that a distinct and manifestly Irish unionist strand can be identified. It was prompted primarily by the disappointment felt by Irish protestants that the Westminster parliament refused them the same constitutional and commercial privileges as Englishmen which they, as the 'English in Ireland,' believed were theirs by right.[25] William King, bishop of Derry, was among the earliest to maintain that a union would be mutually advantageous, claiming in 1697 that it would enable both kingdoms to 'flourish effectively'.[26] The Westminster ban on the export of wool from Ireland in 1698 strengthened the conviction that a union must be advantageous and elicited the famous declaration from William Molyneux (who did not believe the English political establishment was in any frame of mind to grant Ireland access to the rights and privileges it enjoyed) that a union was 'an happiness we can hardly hope for'.[27] Others, equally distressed by what they regarded as English mean spiritedness, were less enthusiastic but, like King, they could 'not see but it may be better for us than as it is at present'.[28] Henry Maxwell, MP for Bangor, opined that it would be 'highly beneficial to England as well as to Ireland by enlarging the foundation of its power, wealth and trade, and by strengthening the inward frame of its constitution'.[29] Continuing economic difficulties and the negotiations for the Anglo–Scottish union which opened in 1702 reinforced unionist sentiment in Ireland, and prompted both houses of the Irish parliament to approve addresses to the throne rehearsing their grievances and requesting

23 *Considerations concerning Ireland in relation to England and particularly in respect of an Union* ([Dublin], [1691]), pp 2-4.   24 [Bonnell] to Harley, 3 Nov. 1691 in *Portland*, iii, pp 479-81.   25 J. Leerssen, *Mere Irish and fíor Ghael: studies in the idea of Irish nationality* (Amsterdam, 1986), pp 340-5.   26 King to Southwell, 19 July 1697, cited in T. Moody & W. Vaughan (eds), *A new history of Ireland, iv: Ireland 1692-1800* (Oxford, 1986), p. 7.   27 W. Molyneux, *The case of Ireland's being bound by acts of parliament in England stated* (London, 1698); J.G. Simms, *William Molyneux of Dublin* (Dublin, 1982), pp 102-18.   28 King to Annesley, 12 Feb. 1702, TCD, King Papers, Ms 750/2/3, ff 106-07.   29 [H. Maxwell], *An essay towards an union of Ireland with England, most humbly offer'd to the consideration of the Queen's most excellent majesty, and both houses of parliament* (London, 1703), pp 3-6.

'a full enjoyment of our constitution, or ... a more firm and strict union with ... England' in 1703.[30] Further addresses from the same quarters urging 'a yet more comprehensive union' followed the Anglo–Scottish union in 1707.[31] These received some endorsement in England from those who saw a union as strategically and materially beneficial in the ongoing military struggle with France. Others concluded that 'the islands of Great Britain and Ireland seem intended by nature and providence for one state and civil government, our *Terra Firma* dividing us from the rest of Europe', but most could see no compelling reason – commercial, constitutional or political – to expand the concept of a British union to include Ireland.[32]

The union with Scotland and the rejection of the three overtures to the crown made by the Irish parliament between 1703 and 1709 for a similar arrangement with Ireland was a blow to the self-esteem of Irish Protestants. Jonathan Swift well captured the feelings of rejection in his allegory of 'the injured lady' (Ireland) who had been taken advantage of and ruined by a suitor (England) only to be forsaken for another (Scotland).[33] In truth, Irish protestants did not have strong grounds for feeling aggrieved since they perceived a legislative union as a means to an end rather than an end in itself. Their primary object was to secure the same commercial and constitutional rights as Englishmen; when this was not forthcoming, they reverted easily to their more familiar strategy of asserting their rights, as subjects possessed of a separate kingdom.[34] Support for the idea of a legislative union did not entirely disappear, however. In 1720, when the Westminster parliament affirmed through the Declaratory Act that it had the power to make law for Ireland and its House of Lords was the final court of appeal in Irish law cases, William Nicolson, Church of Ireland bishop of Derry, confidently pronounced that Irish protestants would welcome 'such an incorporation into the United Kingdom of Great Britain as hath been allowed the Scots' should it be offered.[35] Nicolson's opinion was never put to the test and Irish

---

30 *Journal of the House of Commons of the Kingdom of Ireland*, 19 vols (Dublin, 1796-1800), ii, pp 341-2; J. Smyth, 'Like amphibious animals': Irish Protestants, ancient Britons 1691-1707', *Historical Journal*, xxxvi (1993), p. 795.   31 More fully discussed in Kelly, 'Origins', pp 243-4; Kelly, 'Popular politics'; Smith, 'Like amphibious animals', p. 795.   32 *The queen an empress and her three kingdoms one empire, or brief remarks upon the present: and a prospect of the future state of England, Scotland and Ireland in a happy union for the consideration of parliament* [Dublin, 1706].   33 H. Davis, *The prose writings of Jonathan Swift*, ix (Oxford, 1968), pp 3-9.   34 See I. Victory, 'The making of the Declaratory Act' in G. O'Brien (ed.), *Parliament, politics and people* (Dublin, 1989), pp 9-29; F. James, *Ireland in the empire 1690-1770* (Cambridge, Mass., 1973), pp 103-9.   35 Nicolson to Wake, 30 Apr. 1721, Gilbert Library, Wake papers, Ms 27, f.283.

public and political opinion came increasingly to reject union. The impact
of economic, political and legal difficulties convinced many during the 1710s
and 1720s that it was in the kingdom of Ireland's better interest to retain its
own parliament and to devise domestic solutions to domestic problems
rather than to seek the answer in legislative integration with Britain.[36]

II

Though a current of opinion well disposed to the idea of a union persisted
throughout the mid-eighteenth century, the prevailing mood of Irish opinion
became increasingly antipathetic.[37] There was little sympathy for the idea in
Britain either during the 1730s and 1740s though, significantly, such public
reference as the issue generated there was favourable. However, rumours like
that reported in 1742 that 'a scheme [was] on foot for a union of England and
Ireland, much as in the same manner as that w[i]th Scotland' were invariably
wide of the mark.[38] The allure of a union with Ireland to British opinion
makers in the mid-eighteenth century derived primarily from doubts about
their capacity to sustain their current international involvements, and from
the conviction that a union with Ireland would convey synergistic benefits.
Influenced by such considerations, the Irish peer, Lord Hillsborough, a
member of the House of Commons at Westminster and 'a regular government spokesman', maintained in 1751 that Britain would benefit from
increased absenteeism and investment from Ireland in the happy event of an
Anglo–Irish union.[39] He also identified significant demographic, commercial
and economic advantages for Ireland.

Whereas thirty years earlier, his arguments might have been warmly
received in Ireland, the reaction in the early 1750s was overwhelmingly
critical. Hillsborough was disparaged by one hostile respondent as a 'brain-
less, short-sighted babbler'; an Anglo–Irish union was dismissed as a 'pre-
posterous, unnatural scheme' that would generate 'black and dreadful scenes

---

36 As note 34; J. Kelly, 'Jonathan Swift and the Irish economy in the 1720s', *ECI*, vi
(1991), pp 7-38; C. Kidd, 'North Britishness and the nature of eighteenth-century
British patriotism', *Historical Journal*, xxxix (1996), p. 380.   37 Most notably among
those described by Caroline Robbins as 'commonwealthmen' (*The eighteenth-century
commonwealthmen* (Cambridge, Mass, 1958).   38 Ellice to Price, 14 Dec. 1742,
National Library of Wales, Puleston papers, Ms 3577, f. 47.   39 [Lord Hills-
borough], *A proposal for uniting the kingdoms of Great Britain and Ireland* (London,
1751); R. Sedgwick, (ed.), *The history of parliament: the House of Commons 1715-54*,
2 vols (London, 1970), ii, 140-1.

of desolation, calamity and distress'.[40] Others were more measured in their remarks, but the attitude to an Anglo-Irish union and to Hillsborough's argument was unambiguous; a union was not now in Ireland's interest.[41] Such sentiments reflecting the prevailing outlook in Ireland where the family metaphor used by commentators to define the Anglo-Irish relationship was that of sisters. By contrast, British commentators employed a parent and child analogy where Ireland was assigned the dependent role. Nicholas Archdall, MP for County Fermanagh, expressed Irish thinking on the subject of a union most cogently when he observed in his impressive response to Lord Hillsborough that it was quite improper that he should treat Ireland as if it was merely 'a branch or colony of another kingdom' by suggesting that it should embrace his 'destructive plan of a union,' because Ireland was 'govern'd by its own laws made in a full parliament' and possessed of a 'constitution' settled by the 'REVOLUTION of *eighty eight*'.[42]

Archdall's lucid articulation of the patriot case (entrusting the Irish parliament with the responsibility of law-making in Ireland) was diminished in the mid-1750s by the undignified power struggle associated with the money bill dispute. One consequence was an increase in the number of Irish voices prepared to endorse union as a 'means of conciliating ... minds'.[43] A more powerful and, in the long term, more consequential set of arguments emerged in England. At one level, they were also prompted by uneasiness at the implications of the money bill dispute. For some, like Lord Chief Justice Dudley Ryder, who interpreted what was happening as evidence of Ireland 'foolishly and seditiously ... every day aiming at independency', a union offered the promise of secure long-term control.[44] The maintenance of English authority in Ireland also concerned economic thinkers like Malachy Postlethwayt, Mathew Decker and Josiah Tucker who responded to continuing concern about Britain's capacity to sustain its formidable international ambitions by arguing that a union would be economically and strategically advantageous in the global struggle with France.[45] The Irish

---

40 *An humble address to the nobility, gentry and freeholders of the kingdom of Ireland* (Dublin, 1751).   **41** *An answer to the late proposal for uniting the kingdoms of Great Britain and Ireland ...* (Dublin, 1751); N. Archdall, *An alarm to the people of Great Britain and Ireland in answer to a late proposal for uniting these kingdoms shewing the fatal consequences of such an UNION to the constitution, laws, trade and manufactures of both Kingdoms: how destructive to the Protestant religion established in Ireland and how little beneficial to England* (Dublin, 1751).   **42** Archdall, *Alarm to the people ...* , pp 5-6, 8, 22, 31, 34.   **43** J. Hill, *From patriots to unionists: Dublin municipal politics 1660-1840* (Oxford, 1997), p. 119; *Policy and justice* (Dublin, 1755).   **44** Kelly, 'Origins', p. 247.

MP and economist Arthur Dobbs supported this point of view, but the fact that he did not publish his thoughts is indicative of his realisation that, the impact of the money bill dispute notwithstanding, it was unlikely to be received favourably in Ireland.[46] The strength of public antipathy to a union was underlined in November–December 1759 when the conjunction of a number of factors, including an advertisement for Postlethwayt's *Britain's commercial interest* in the Dublin press, precipitated a rumour that a union was imminent. This had no basis in fact, but a protesting mob several thousand strong gathered in College Green on 22 November and 3 December 1759, and compelled a number of prominent MPs to swear 'a solemn obligation never to consent to a union'.[47] This was an exceptional event, but there were other less dramatic indicators in the 1760s and early 1770s to illustrate that Irish public opinion was firmly against a legislative union with Great Britain.[48]

Paradoxically, public discussion of the subject increased rather than diminished. This was a by-product of the increased instability of British, Irish, Anglo-Irish and Anglo-American politics from the 1760s. In the specific context of Irish and Anglo-Irish politics, the decision to end the undertaker system of parliamentary management that had existed for nearly half a century and the more assertive demands of the re-invigorated patriot interest for constitutional and political concessions, many, particularly in England, were attracted by the concept of union as a means of strengthening the Anglo-Irish nexus. Given this inclination, it was both logical and inevitable that the strong demand articulated in the late 1770s by a coalition of patriot MPs, Volunteers and municipal activists for the dilution of the traditional mercantilist restrictions should prompt the most significant initiative since 1709 to bring about an Anglo-Irish union. Fearful of the implications of any loosening of either the commercial or constitutional bonds that fastened the kingdom of Ireland, the prime minister, Lord North, who was persuaded that this was the way forward, made the lord lieutenant, the earl of Buckinghamshire, aware of his preference in the autumn of 1777.[49] Buckinghamshire's conclusion that it was a 'utopian scheme' that should not 'be seriously deliberated upon [until] ... peace is restored' ensured that nothing came of the prime minister's suggestion, but

45 Ibid., pp 249-50. **46** Some thoughts in relation to an union of Britain and Ireland, *c.*1751; A short essay to shew the expediency ... of an incorporating union, *c.*1751, PRONI, Dobbs papers, D162/58, 59. **47** This episode is described by S. Murphy, 'The anti-union riot of 3 December 1759' in O'Brien (ed.), *Parliament*, pp 49-68 and Kelly, *Flood*, pp 72-4. **48** Kelly, 'Popular politics'. **49** North to Buckinghamshire, 13 Oct. 1777, NLI, Heron papers, Ms 13035/13.

the combination of intensified demands for 'free trade' and the politicisation of the Volunteers meant that the government found the appeal of union irresistible by the summer of 1779: 'nothing but a union', Lord George Germain, a former chief secretary of Ireland and now secretary of state for the colonies, observed, 'can serve both kingdoms.'[50] Guided by such perceptions, and aware that there was some support in aristocratic and official circles in Ireland, a decision was taken by an *ad hoc* cabinet committee in August 1779 'that a union between Ireland and England was to be agitated and settled if possible'.[51] In order to determine if it was indeed 'possible', soundings were taken which indicated that a union had highly placed proponents. However, it was also clear that the balance of opinion was strongly averse. The MP for County Wexford, George Ogle, expressed his personal antipathy with characteristic vehemence when he likened the suggestion to 'the murder of my country'.[52] Others expressed more moderate opposition, but the impracticality of the suggestion was underlined by the former chief secretary, Sir George Macartney; sent to Ireland to assess the public mood in the winter of 1779–80, he concluded that 'the idea of a union at present would excite a rebellion'.[53]

Macartney's further observation that 'without a union how vague and loose is the connection of Ireland with England' highlights the increasing conviction in the corridors of power in Britain and Ireland that a union was now essential if the Anglo–Irish connection was to be maintained. The number who shared this conviction grew appreciably in the hothouse environment of the late 1770s, but they misunderstood Irish patriotism. Like the commonwealthmen and others who had argued most strongly for a union in the first decade of the eighteenth century, their object was equality of rights not separation. Given that the American colonists had until recently employed not entirely dissimilar rhetoric only to embrace the option of full independence from the mid-1770s, such misunderstanding was not entirely unexpected. At the same time, it is ironic that opinion in both kingdoms should have changed so completely over the seven decades since the Irish parliament had openly solicited an Anglo–Irish union. That this was so is a measure of London's unwillingness to treat Irish protestants as equals arising out of their conviction that imperial authority must be firmly located in Britain, and their instinctive fear that if metropolitan

50 Buckinghamshire to Heron, 29 Mar. 1779, NLI, Heron papers, Ms 13047/6; Germain to Buckinghamshire, 7 Aug. 1779, BL, Mackintosh collection, Add. Ms 34523 f. 187.   51 Kelly, 'Origins', pp 251–2.   52 Library of Congress, Cavendish's parliamentary diary, xvi, 212–13.   53 Kelly, 'Origins', pp 253–4; Macartney to North, 8 Jan. 1780 in Bartlett (ed.), *Macartney in Ireland*, p.325.

authority was diluted, it would encourage escalating demands until separation inevitably ensued. In other words, the effort of Irish patriots to achieve
commercial and constitutional equality with Britain was fundamentally at
odds with the understanding of the Anglo-Irish relationship held in Britain.
It may not be the case (contrary to what I have previously suggested)[54] that
British politicians did not perceive a difference between equality and loss of
control, but they certainly believed in occupying the ascendant position. This
was possible until 1782 because of the existence of an extensive corpus of
mercantilist and constitutional law (Poynings' Law and the Declaratory Act)
that ensured Irish commercial and legal rights were subordinated to those of
England. Once they were repealed, as was largely the case from 1782, London
had to reconceptualise the Anglo-Irish relationship. The practical options
(since acquiescence in separation was unacceptable) were to accede to the
arrangement of equals, long articulated by Irish protestants, or to inaugurate
some new subordinate arrangement. The only option canvassed was a type of
union; a legislative, 'foederal' or commercial union were proposed.[55] This was
impossible as long as Irish patriotism remained vibrant, as the efforts to promote a union in 1779–80 amply illustrate, but the wish for such a solution did
not diminish. At the same time, since a union could only be achieved if there
were enough supporters in both kingdoms to ensure its acceptance in their
respective parliaments, the current disposition of Irish public opinion
rendered this unlikely in the near future. However, Irish protestant opinion
did change, and the 1790s witnessed support for union appreciate in Britain
and Ireland. The pace at which this occurred varied, not least because the
issues that exerted most profound influence differed. But in both jurisdictions
union emerged as a realistic option; for those who favoured retaining a
connection with Britain, it was the only practical alternative to separation
when the 'legislative independence' conceded in 1782 was deemed incom-
patible with a strong Anglo-Irish relationship.

III

The concession to the Irish parliament of the right to make law unconfined
by the restrictions of Poynings' Law and the Declaratory Act did not give
rise to any public discussion of the option of a union, because of the realisation that to do so would exacerbate an already difficult situation. Ministers

---

54 Kelly, 'Origins', p. 253.   55 See, generally, J Kelly, *Prelude to Union: Anglo-Irish
politics in the 1780s* (Cork, 1992); Kelly, 'Origins', pp 254–8.

and officials on both sides of the Irish Sea were disturbed by events in Ireland in the early 1780s, but having fortuitously seized the political initiative with the fall of North's government in March 1782, the patriot leadership in Ireland ensured that the constitutional 'settlement' of 1782 corresponded more closely to their aspirations rather than to what ministers in London believed appropriate. Thus there was no 'final adjustment', defining the respective rights and responsibilities of both kingdoms, though outline sketches for economic and 'foederal' unions were tentatively promoted from government quarters.[56] These sketches sought to mitigate the implications of legislative independence arising out of the conviction that the Anglo-Irish connection could not long survive if it was fixed to such insecure constitutional foundations. This pessimistic conclusion contrasted sharply with the optimism that characterised Irish attitudes at the same time, but events in the early to mid-1780s associated with popular demands for renunciation, parliamentary reform and protecting duties reinforced the conviction of those charged with the maintenance of the Anglo-Irish nexus that union was the only solution. The duke of Rutland, lord lieutenant of Ireland between 1784 and 1787, articulated this conclusion vividly in 1784 when he observed that 'without an *union* Ireland will not be connected with Britain in twenty years'.[57] Conscious that any attempt to promote a union settlement that trespassed directly on the recently acquired legislative authority of the Irish parliament was doomed to failure, the prime minister William Pitt opted instead for a scheme to bind Great Britain and Ireland together in a commercial union. The basic idea, derived from Adam Smith and, and to a lesser extent Lord Shelburne, was to integrate Britain and Ireland economically and commercially and to inaugurate financial contributions from the Irish exchequer to imperial expenditure. The latter objective was strongly resisted in Ireland where it was interpreted as vitiating the financial authority of their legislature, but the storm this generated was modest when compared with the howls of outrage that greeted a subsequent stipulation that laws regulating trade and navigation should be identical in both jurisdictions and that the Irish parliament should enact 'all' such laws approved at Westminster. Already perceived in some quarters as the custodian of legislative independence, Henry Grattan hastened the eclipse of Pitt's ambitious and imaginative scheme when he condemned it as 'an incipient and a creeping union'.[58]

56 Kelly, 'Origins', pp 254-5; Kelly, *Prelude*, pp 32-56.   57 Rutland to Pitt, 16 June 1784 in Lord Mahon (ed.), *The correspondence between William Pitt and the Duke of Rutland* (London, 1890), p. 19.   58 *The parliamentary register, or history of the proceedings and debates of the House of Commons of Ireland 1781-97*, 17 vols (Dublin,

If the rejection of Pitt's proposed commercial union indicated the antipathy to the very idea of a union in Ireland, the response at Westminster
illustrated that support for union continued to swell in Britain. Whereas
Irish proponents (they included the chief commissioner of the revenue John
Beresford, the attorney general John Fitzgibbon and the chief justice of the
common pleas Marcus Patterson)[59] maintained a discreet public silence in
1785, the issue was openly debated in Britain. Few on the government side
felt at liberty to support the idea of a legislative union publicly, but (liberated
from the responsibilities of office) the former prime minister, Lord North,
and cabinet minister, Lord Stormont, indicated that they favoured such an
arrangement.[60] Equally consequential, influential pressure groups like the
Chamber of Manufacturers, alarmed by the prospect of economic competition from Ireland, urged a legislative union in preference to Pitt's
commercial union. This further eroded opposition in commercial and
political quarters to union, though the suggestion of Josiah Tucker that a
'real union' might be proposed with greater prospect of success in fifteen
years indicated that more perspicacious observers realised that this was
unlikely in the immediate future.[61] Nothing suggested that Irish opinion was
likely to undergo a rapid change of heart.

Despite this, union remained the subject of public comment. Pamphlets
were published in Dublin on the matter in the late 1780s, but while the Irish
parliament's refusal to be guided by Westminster during the Regency crisis
strengthened the desire of British politicians and commentators to implement an Anglo–Irish union as an alternative to 'separation', there was no
equivalent shift in attitudes on the western side of the Irish Sea. As the
1790s began, the unionist constituency in Ireland remained small and
quiescent; its British equivalent was more restless but there was nothing to
suggest that its hopes were any closer to realisation than they had been five
or ten years earlier. Irish political opinion continued in effect to possess a
veto on union; if its attitude on this matter remained constant, then there
was no prospect of its becoming a reality no matter how warmly strategists
like Sir John Dalrymple might aver that it would secure the two kingdoms
against any hostile 'confederacy' that might emerge in Europe by enriching
them militarily, economically and aesthetically.[62]

1782-1801), v, 356.   **59** Tyrone to Beresford, 15 June 1785 in *Beresford corr.*, i, p. 268;
Patterson to Townshend, Townsend papers, 15 Dec. 1785, BL, Add. Ms 38497 ff 74-
5; H. Grattan, *Memoirs of the life and times of Henry Grattan*, 5 vols (London, 1839-
46), i, 294-5.   **60** *The parliamentary history of England from the Norman conquest to
1803*, 36 vols (London, 1804-20), xxv, 848.   **61** [J. Tucker], *Reflections on the present
matter in dispute between Great Britain and Ireland* (London, 1785), pp 33-4.   **62** J.

The first indications that Irish protestant opinion was not as resolutely anti-unionist as its rhetoric in the 1770s and 1780s suggested were provided in 1792 when the subject of admitting catholics to the political process was raised. For atavistic historical as well as for current ideological reasons, this proved a profoundly difficult issue for those who had recently come to define themselves as the 'protestant ascendancy'.[63] If they were unable to prevent or unwilling to come to terms with the implications of admitting catholics to the political process, they had to identify some means of neutralising its impact. In effect, Irish protestants were faced with the options of accepting that the price of preserving their right to make law for Ireland in an Irish parliament was to allow catholics a say in determining the composition of the lower house of that parliament or of acceding to a union and the loss of their legislature because this was the only practical means to preserve their 'monopoly of pre-eminence' once London had determined that catholic enfranchisement was a strategic necessity. Indeed, both Pitt and Henry Dundas specifically advised that they should 'lay aside their prejudices [and] forego their exclusive pre-eminence' but protestants were fearful that enfranchisement was just the first step on the road to 'emancipation' and to the inevitable transfer of control of the structures of power to their hereditary enemies – Irish catholics.[64] In 1778, when the issue being debated was the right of catholics to possess property, it had 'been insinuated' that protestants 'might deem it necessary' to press for a union 'as a protection against the numbers and formidable influence of the Roman Catholicks'.[65] This did not happen, not least because the concessions offered then and in 1782 were tailored to ensure that catholics could not exercise political influence.[66] However, enfranchisement possessed unavoidable political implications – so unavoidable in fact that some conceived it as part of a devious plot by ministers 'to bring about a union with England.'[67] The

Dalrymple, Hints respecting a union with Ireland, 8 July 1790, NLI, Melville papers, Ms 54/35 and BL, Miscellaneous papers relating to Ireland 1770-90, Add. Ms 35919, f. 33ff.   **63** For a discussion of the meaning of this term, see J. Kelly, 'The genesis of Protestant ascendancy' in O'Brien (ed.), *Parliament*, pp 93-127 and W.J. McCormack, *The Dublin paper war of 1786-1788* (Dublin, 1993).   **64** Dundas to [Westmorland], 26 Dec. 1791, NA, Westmorland papers, carton 1 no 29; Memorandum of the conversation ... with Mr Dundas ... on 21 and 22 Jan. 1793 in the presence of Mr Pitt, NLI, Melville papers, Ms 54A/74. For a consideration of the evidence upon which the claim of protestant fear that enfranchisement was just a prelude to further constitutional concessions, see J. Kelly, 'Conservative protestant political thought in late eighteenth-century Ireland' in S. Connolly (ed.), *Political ideas in the eighteenth century Ireland* (Dublin, 2000), pp 209-13.   **65** Buckinghamshire to Germain, 24 June 1778, NLI, Heron papers, Ms 13036/12.   **66** Specifically, they were prohibited from purchasing land in parliamentary boroughs (Kelly, *Flood*, circle of Lord Westmorland, the lord lieutenant, was predominantly conservative in political outlook, but his observation that 'the leading people' no longer greeted the suggestion 'with disapprobation' is indicative. His report to Pitt in April 1793 that the subject of union 'is generally talked of by the Protestants with a sort of acquiescence, [when] two years ago a man would have been insulted for a mention' merely highlight the fact that the prolonged controversy over admitting catholics to the franchise in the early 1790s had prompted a fundamental shift in attitude among Irish protestants on the subject.[68] It was still insufficient to cause William Pitt, who signalled in November 1792 that a legislative union was his preference, to propose such a measure. Having experienced the bitter taste of defeat when his scheme for a commercial union was lost in 1785, the prime minister concluded that Irish opinion had not moved far enough to guarantee the acceptance of a union and, for this reason, that 'Ireland ... must yet continue a government of expedients.'[69] However, it did mean that mainstream political opinion in both kingdoms was in broad concert on this issue for the first time and that the prospects of a union in the foreseeable future were better than at any time in over a century.

Once the immediate crisis over catholic enfranchisement had passed, discussion on the subject of union diminished. However, positions had shifted irrevocably and as the political temperature rose in the mid-1790s, and catholic emancipation pushed its way onto the political agenda during the stormy Fitzwilliam viceroyalty, the frequency with which reference was made to a union in public discourse emphasised that this was a viable political option with real support. In the case of long time unionists like the earl of Clare and the earl of Ely, events strengthened their conviction that union was in the self-interest of 'every man of power'; in other instances, this conviction was newly acquired.[70] It is impossible to establish with any confidence the levels of political and public support for a union at this point, but the *Dublin Evening Post* reported in 1795 that as many as eighty MPs were supportive, which suggests that the unionist constituency was particularly fast growing among the political elite.[71] The replacement of the volatile Fitzwilliam by the cautious Camden eased the anxieties that caused many in Britain as well as Ireland to perceive union as the optimal way

p. 304).   67 Kelly, 'Popular politics';   68 Westmorland to Pitt, 28 Nov. 1792, NLI, Union correspondence, Ms 886, ff 17-26; Westmorland to Pitt, 18 Apr. 1793, PRO, Chatham papers, 30/8/331 ff 124-5.   69 F. Bickley (ed.), *The diary of Sylvester Douglas*, 2 vols (London, 1928), i, 35.   70 A. Kavanaugh, *John FitzGibbon, earl of Clare* (Dublin, 1997), p. 311; Ely to Abercorn, 3 Apr. 1795, Abercorn papers, PRONI, T2541/ 1B3/5/16.   71 *Dublin Evening Post*, 18, 21 Apr. 1795.

forward, but mounting concern that Ireland was in danger of becoming permanently alienated from Great Britain ensured that, in the words of a leading Irish whig, 'a legislative union ... [w]as the only certain means of avoiding' a divisive 'alienation of affection'.[72]

In this context, the emergence of a formidable revolutionary movement that aspired to achieve its goal of an independent Irish republic by insurrection in the second half of the 1790s strengthened the appeal of a union among mainstream and conservative interests in both kingdoms. Lord Clare vividly captured the anxieties of the latter when he deemed a union as the only escape from the prospect of a repetition of 'the scenes of 1641 ... and the country again desolated by every species of savage enormity'.[73] Clare's vision was essentially repressive; others saw in union an opportunity to create a more inclusive political framework in Ireland and a mutually advantageous Anglo–Irish nexus. Thus though Brigadier General John Knox justified the recourse to 'military coercion to subdue the people' as the first step to a union, he also recommended the parallel concession of parliamentary reform and Catholic emancipation.[74] George Dallas from Newtownards, County Down, observed in September 1797 that union was 'the surest means of subduing the [French Revolution] principles now prevailing', but he was equally confident that it would have a positive long-term effect in 'improving the condition of the people; of extending the resources; and strengthening the interests of both countries'. Dallas was not just persuaded of the merits of an Anglo–Irish union; he cited opinion in support of his view that there never was 'a crisis so favourable to the project'.[75]

Pitt did not agree. He had neither the inclination nor the time to revise his approach to the government of Ireland. At the same time, the conviction that a union was in their interest deepened among Irish protestants as news of arms raids, and assassinations, and rumours of 'open rebellion' proliferated.[76] There was even speculation at the highest political level that it might feature in the lord lieutenant's speech opening the 1798 session of parliament, and when this did not happen the confident expectation was that it would be proposed in 1799.[77] This conjecture proved accurate,

72 Ponsonby to Fitzwilliam, 18 Sept. 1795, Sheffield City Library, Wentworth Woodhouse Muniments, Fitzwilliam correspondence, F30/45; P. Jupp, *Lord Grenville* (Oxford, 1985), p. 264.   73 Clare to Camden, 28 Aug. 1796, CKS, Camden Papers, U840/0183/6); Kavanaugh, *FitzGibbon*, p.329; Clare to Mornington, 20 Apr. 1797, BL, Wellesley papers, Add. Ms 37308, f. 34.   74 Knox to Pelham, 19 Apr., 28 May 1797, BL, Pelham papers, Add. Mss 33103, f. 382, 33104 f. 139.   75 [Dallas] to [Dundas], 20 Sept. 1797, NLI, Melville papers, Ms 54A/111.   76 Hewetson to [ ], 16 Nov. 1797, Beinecke Library, Osborn collection, Hewetson file.   77 Stewart to Abercorn, 9 Nov. [1797], PRONI, Abercorn papers, T2541/1B2/ 2/31; J. Greig,

because the outbreak of formal rebellion in Ireland in late May catapulted Ireland to the top of the political agenda. Pitt determined that a union should be concluded at the earliest opportunity.[78]

IV

When chief secretary Castlereagh assessed the state of Irish opinion in July 1798, he was disappointed to observe 'no strong disposition in the public mind' to favour an Anglo-Irish union.[79] Others concurred, but there is no sense in which either political or public opinion in Ireland had experienced a sudden change of heart on the subject in the summer of 1798.[80] The experience of rebellion so dominated the horizon of most protestants in the autumn and summer of that year that their instinctive desire to punish those who had taken up arms against the state took precedence over everything else.[81] For some, probably a minority, the rebellion reinforced them in their unionism. The Church of Ireland clergyman, Charles Warburton, maintained in July that the Protestant population had divided three ways: 'there is a violent party who talk of nothing but *extermination*, another speaks of total *disqualification* and a third (more sensible party) seems to think an union the only measure that can possibly afford peace and security'.[82] Warburton's own inclinations predisposed him to the 'sensible party', but some who were expected to respond likewise were hesitant. Their reasoning varied. The Marquis of Waterford, who was personally 'satisfied that nothing but a union co[ul]d secure Ireland', was doubtful if the country was 'yet ripe for it'. Lord Shannon was reluctant to 'declare ... himself' unless he was sure 'gov[ernmen]t would lay their shoulders to it'. Lord Kilwarden felt likewise, whilst from among the ranks of those who were less sure similar sentiments were common.[83] The stance of ideological conservatives, including a large section of the Orange Order, contributed in no small way to the storm of popular opposition generated in the guilds and corporation

(ed.), *The Farington diary*, 3 vols (London, 1922-4), i, 228.   **78** Bolton, *Union*, pp 53-60; Geoghegan, *Union*, pp 10-16.   **79** Castlereagh to Camden, 9 July [1798], CKS, Camden papers, U840/C98/2; see also Cooke to Auckland [14 Aug. 1798] in A. Malcomson (ed.), *Eighteenth-century Irish official papers*, ii (Belfast, 1990), p. 293. **80** List of those favourable to a union, *c.*Dec. 1798, NLI, Union correspondence, Ms 887, ff 23-32, sub Marquis of Waterford and Lord Kilwarden.   **81** Kelly, 'Popular politics', pp 263-4.   **82** Warburton to Bentinck, 11 July 1798 in *Eighteenth-century Irish official papers*, ii, 188.   **83** List of those 'favourable' and 'doubtful' to a union, *c.*Dec. 1798, NLI, Union correspondence, Ms 887, ff 23-38.

of Dublin in the winter of 1799-1800.[84] The Irish parliament also rejected the suggestion that they should even consider a legislative union with Great Britain when it was first mooted in January 1799. It is tempting then to conclude that Irish protestant public and political opinion was opposed to an Anglo-Irish union when the situation was far less clear-cut. The disposition of ideological conservatives provides a case in point; the Orange Order certainly declined to support a union but it was induced to make this stand in order to ensure organisational unity; many lodges declined the instruction.[85] Furthermore, many of the most important voices of conservatism – Sir Richard Musgrave and Patrick Duigenan most notably – were vigorous proponents of union.[86] Their support was inevitably predicated on its being proposed upon 'protestant principles', which caused both the Irish executive and the British government serious problems. They believed that catholic emancipation should follow a union, but they shrewdly ensured that this did not become a major public matter and it did not prevent the measure's passing.[87] Moreover, there is nothing to suggest that combined or separately the Rebellion, the immediate prospect of the abolition of the Irish parliament or the fear of further catholic empowerment prompted significant leaching from the ranks of Irish unionists. Quite the contrary; sixty to seventy eminences described as 'favourable' and 'doubtful' on lists compiled at Dublin Castle in November and December 1798 suggests that the level of identifiable support for union was at an unprecedented high. The knowledge that 'their old government' was no longer capable of providing for their 'safety and protection' persuaded many that 'nothing but a union can secure Ireland to Great Britain.'[88] This was insufficient to guarantee parliamentary approval as the votes on 22 and 24 January amply attest. However, when Dublin Castle exerted itself, as it manifestly did from the spring of 1799, it not alone secured approval of the measure, it more than held its own in the contest for public opinion.[89] Indeed, such were the majorities it enjoyed in 1800, it probably spent more money and promised more patronage than was necessary.[90] It was certainly true then that there was more public and political support for a union in

---

84 Kelly, 'Popular politics', pp 266-71.   85 H. Senior, *Orangeism in Ireland and Britain 1795-1836* (London, 1966), chapter 5.   86 Musgrave described himself as 'a warm advocate for the union' (Musgrave to Percy, 15 Jan. 1799), NLI, Musgrave papers, Ms 4157, p.7; Duigenan was 'ready to go all lengths in its support' (NLI, Ms 887 f. 29). George Ogle who spoke against a union in the House of Commons declared his support (ibid., f. 27).   87 NLI, Ms 887, f. 27; Geoghegan, *Union*.   88 Carlisle to Auckland, 30 Aug. 1798 in *Auckland corr.*, iv, pp 51-2; NLI, Union correspondence, Ms 887, ff 23-38. 89 Kelly, 'Popular politics', pp 274-9.   90 Between them, Bolton, *Union* and

Britain and Ireland than there had been at any moment in the previous history of the two islands and it was accordingly the optimal moment to attempt such a long-debated constitutional change.

Geoghegan, *Union* provide a thorough account of patronage commitments.

4

Union failed, union accomplished: the Irish union of 1703 and the Scottish union of 1707

Allan Macinnes

That union with Ireland was rejected in 1703, while that with Scotland was accepted at Westminster in 1707, seems to bear out the anglo-centric aphorism 'what England wants, England gets'. The constitutional subordination of Ireland in the eighteenth century was reaffirmed not just by further rejections of union in 1707 and 1709, but by the emphatic imposition of the Declaratory Act in 1720. State formation in the three kingdoms was not resolved as union all round until 1801. On the one hand, the historiography of union is undoubtedly tinted in Irish eyes by the subsequent severing of sovereignty from the third decade of the twentieth century. On the other hand, notwithstanding the move towards devolution, the Scottish perspective has tended to remain bifocally British. Yet, the political process during the reign of Queen Anne was shaped not only by polemics, patronage and party in all three kingdoms, but by an appreciation of union in a transatlantic context. Moreover, this context had significant non-anglocentric ramifications. Arguably for the Scots, the condition of Ireland was the dog that did not bark during the polemical debates on union from 1703 to 1707, not least because of the spin-doctoring necessary to counteract issues of constitutional subordination. Conversely, for the Irish contemplating union with Britain in the later eighteenth century, the Scots were the dogs that barked too loudly.

I

Given that the Irish union of 1703 failed while the Scottish union of 1707 was accomplished, the historiographic imbalance in favour of the latter can

be taken to reflect a major as against a minor theme for British state formation. However, dismissive treatment of the failed union of 1703 is warranted
only from an anglocentric perspective.[1] Perceptive Irish historians have set
this episode within the ongoing context of Irish unionism from the
Cromwellian conquest of 1650 to the parliamentary incorporation of 1801.
They have also demonstrated convincingly that the Irish dimension to the
Scottish union has been as much neglected as sidelined by the historiographic constructs of British identity in vogue since 1707. The failed union
of 1703 was the exclusive project of the English interest in Ireland, not an
endeavour to engage either catholics or protestant dissenters in state
formation.[2] Conversely, the temptation to view the successful Scottish union
of 1707 as an inclusive British project must bear in mind the contemporary
strictures against the Court Party led by James Douglas, duke of Queensberry. As the chief proponents of parliamentary incorporation, they were
castigated as 'little more than the English interest in Scotland'.[3]

The accomplishment of Scottish union can be attributed to various
influences. Diplomatic brinkmanship, military intimidation and political
manipulation on the part of the English ministry of Queen Anne was
compounded by economic defeatism, financial chicanery and, above all,
political ineptitude within the Scottish Estates. The relative significance of
economic and political factors in bringing about a parliamentary incorporation has divided Scottish historians into unionist and nationalist camps;
this division has proved contentious, introspective and exotic. The economic
arguments for union, largely presaged on enlightenment post-1707, were
essentially issues of political economy brought about by Scotland's growing
dependence on England during the 1690s as the commercial prospects of
small European nations were constricted by mercantilism.[4] Nor does a

---

1 W.A. Speck, *The birth of Britain: a new nation 1700-1710* (Oxford, 1994), pp 49, 98-
118; D. Hayton & D Szechni, 'John Bull's other kingdoms: the English government of
Scotland and Ireland' in C. Jones (ed.), *Britain in the First Age of Party, 1680-1750: essays
presented to Geoffrey Holmes* (London, 1987), pp 241-80; J.G. Simms, 'The establishment
of the protestant ascendancy 1691-1714' in T.W. Moody & W.E. Vaughan (eds), *A new
history of Ireland*, iv (Oxford, 1986), pp 1-30.   2 Kelly, 'Origins', pp 236-63; J. Smyth,
'"Like amphibious animals:" Irish protestants, Ancient Britons 1691-1707', *Historical
Journal* (1993), pp 785-96.   3 W. Ferguson, *Scotland's relations with England: a survey
to 1707* (Edinburgh, 1977), pp 186-8. Queensberry's concluding parliamentary
statement on 25 March 1707, that the Anglo-Scottish Treaty of Union would prove a
visionary act of statesmanship – *Acts of the Parliament of Scotland*, xi (1702-7), ed. T.
Thomson, (Edinburgh, 1824), p. 491 – has traditionally obscured the views of historians
(albeit not as much as politicians) about its making.   4 T.C. Smout, 'The road to
Union' in G. Holmes (ed.), *Britain after the Glorious Revolution, 1689-1714* (London,
1969), pp 455-67; R. Mitchison, *Lordship to patronage: Scotland 1603-1745* (London,

longer seventeenth-century perspective support the contention that an incorporating union was the inevitable, far less the complementary, outcome of the regal union of 1603.[5] Arguments supporting the decisive political making of Scottish union carry greater conviction, particularly with respect to its timing in 1706-7 rather than in 1702 or 1705. However, these arguments have accorded primacy to jobbery, manipulative patronage and influence. In the process, constitutional principle has been relegated to a minority concern among the radical opponents of union.[6] The rehabilitation of constitutionalism has not been facilitated either by the continuing nationalist tendency to refute any principled commitment among the proponents of parliamentary incorporation or by the unionist tendency to understate the pragmatism and manipulative political skills of assured advocates of English parliamentary supremacy.[7] Fortunately, Scottish historians have recently restored a more considered, mature and balanced assessment of the accomplishment of union in 1707.[8]

Nonetheless, much revision is still required with regard to process and context. While the discourse of public debate was not necessarily transferred into voting patterns, unpublished letters and diaries confirm that the political process was shaped by the interaction of the polemical and parliamentary debates on union.[9] Indeed, the interplay between polemics, management and principle in the final session of the Scottish Estates is notably underworked. Preliminary analysis of voting patterns and political influences suggests that principle, though undoubtedly a minority pursuit, was not restricted to the non-aristocratic opponents of union. At the same time, patronage and other forms of political influence were exercised both overtly and covertly to shore up support for union rather than to persuade

---

1983), pp 93-160. **5** B.P. Levack, *The formation of the British state: England, Scotland and the Union of 1603-1707* (Oxford, 1987); D. Stevenson, 'The early Covenanters and the Federal Union of Britain' in R.A. Mason (ed.), *Scotland and England 1286-1815* (Edinburgh, 1987), pp 163-81. **6** Ferguson, *Scotland's relations with England*, pp 180-253; P. Riley, *The Union of England and Scotland: a study of Anglo-Scottish politics of the eighteenth century* (Manchester, 1978). **7** P.H. Scott, *The Union of Scotland and England in contemporary documents* (Edinburgh, 1979); J. Robertson, 'Andrew Fletcher's Vision of Union' in *Scotland and England 1286-1815*, pp 203-25. **8** C.A. Whatley, '*Bought and sold for English gold*'?: explaining the Union of 1707 (Glasgow, 1994); T.M. Devine, *The Scottish nation 1700-2000* (London, 1999), pp 1-16. J. Young, 'The parliamentary incorporating union of 1707: political management, anti-unionism and foreign policy' in T. Devine & J. Young (eds), *Eighteenth-century Scotland: New perspectives* (East Linton, 1998), pp 24-52. **9** This paper has drawn heavily on the Loudoun Scottish Collection in the Huntington Library [HL], San Marino, California, on the Argyll Manuscripts in the Inveraray Castle Archives [ICA] in Argyllshire, on the Loudoun Papers and the parliamentary diaries of Colonel William Darlrymple in Dumfries House [DH] in opponents either to abstain from voting or to cross the floor of the unicameral house. English intimidation and public antipathy notwithstanding, primacy in carrying the vote for union through the Scottish Estates must be accorded not to jobbery but to the managerial sophistication of Queensberry and his associates in the Court Party.[10] While the intellectual context of union requires no less serious consideration than the political or the economic, there has been a tendency to lionise political theorists, such as William Molyneux for Ireland and Andrew Fletcher of Saltoun for Scotland, sometimes without taking full cognisance of their limited parliamentary clout.[11] Some penetrating commentary has been applied to the limited engagement between Irish and Scottish political thought between 1703 and 1707.[12] But little has been done to take account of Scottish spin-doctoring, especially in the case of Molyneux's unionist credentials, which were little more than an idealistic aside in his case for the legislative independence of the Irish parliament. A convincing case can be made for Fletcher of Saltoun as a proponent for European confederation as well as British federation.[13] However, his leadership of the constitutional reformers in the Scottish Estates attracted no more than 25 adherents out of the 242 members eligible to attend the last session of 1706-7.

That Scots were conditioned politically, economically and intellectually to adopt dual nationality by 1707,[14] is a neo-whiggish contention that sits uncomfortably with the more erudite analysis of 'the multipolar conflicts of the British nations' which, as the persistence of Jacobitism attests, were by no means resolved by the Scottish union.[15] These multipolar conflicts were

Ayrshire. The material from the private Scottish archives was collated with the generous assistance of successive Major Research Grants from the British Academy. **10** A.I. Macinnes, 'Influencing the Vote: the Scottish Estates and the Treaty of Union 1706-07,' *History Microcomputer Review*, vi (1990), pp 11-25. **11** J. Robertson, 'Empire and union: two concepts of the early modern European political order' in J. Robertson (ed.), *A Union for empire: political thought and the Union of 1707* (Cambridge, 1995), pp 3-37; C. Robbins, *The eighteenth-century commonwealthman: studies in the transmission, development and circumstances of English political thought from the Restoration of Charles II until the war with the thirteen colonies* (Cambridge, Mass, 1959), pp 135-55, 180-4; P.H. Scott, *Andrew Fletcher and the Treaty of Union* (Edinburgh, 1994). **12** J.R. Hill, 'Ireland without Union: Molyneux and his legacy' in *A Union for Empire*, pp 271-96; J. Smyth, '"No remedy more proper": Anglo-Irish unionism before 1707' in B. Bradshaw & P. Roberts (eds), *British consciousness and identity: the making of Britain 1533-1707* (Cambridge, 1998), pp 301-20. **13** J. Robertson, 'Union, state and empire: the Britain of 1707 in its European setting' in L. Stone (ed.), *An imperial state at war: Britain from 1689-1815* (London, 1996), pp 224-52. Fletcher of Saltoun's advocacy of a Scottish Republic, however admirable, was an inconsistent and a solitary pursuit. **14** K.M. Brown, 'Scottish identity in the seventeenth century' in *British consciousness and identity*, pp 236-58. **15** C. Kidd, 'Protestantism, constitutionalism and British identity under not confined to the three kingdoms, however. There is an underappreciated colonial dimension which transcends both Scottish imperial aspirations pre-1707 and the continuing Scottish intellectual commitment to confederation and federation deployed to protect provincial liberties in North America and the Caribbean.[16] The juxtaposition of unionism and colonialism was integral to the political process in Scotland in the second half of the seventeenth century. Simultaneously, alternative structures to union were being worked out in the American colonies. Colonial constitutional modeling, in turn, requires that further reflection must be given to the latent as well as the patent Irish contribution to political discourse during the last session of the Scottish Estates.

II

Regal union of all three kingdoms under the Stuart dynasty was welcomed in Ireland as well as Scotland from 1603. Although the endeavours of James VI and I to effect a complete union between Scotland and England had foundered by 1607, regal union made possible concerted action in London, Dublin and Edinburgh to resolve frontier problems on the Anglo-Scottish borders, between Irish and Scottish Gaels and in the Northern Isles of Orkney and Shetland. Such a frontier policy was only one aspect of the Stuarts' projection of themselves as a British dynasty, a projection that carried over into foreign policy by diplomacy, espionage and armed intervention in the Thirty Years War – and impacted significantly on colonial policy.[17] While trading and colonial ventures were authorised separately from Scotland and England prior to 1707, the Stuarts' exercise of their *ius imperium* ensured that these ventures had a distinctive British dimension. Thus, Scottish colonists were integral to the plantation of Ulster, albeit this plantation was imposed, defined and regulated according to English common law from 1608.[18]

the later Stuarts' in *British consciousness and identity*, pp 321-42.   **16** D. Armitage, 'Making the empire British; Scotland in the Atlantic world 1542-1717,' *Past & Present*, 155 (1997), pp 34-63; N.C. Landsman, 'The legacy of British Union for the North American colonies: provincial elites and the problem of imperial union' in *A Union for Empire*, pp 297-317.   **17** B. Ó Buachalla, *Aisling Gheár: na Stiobhartaigh agus an t-Aos léinn 1603-1788* (Dublin, 1996), pp 148-94; A.I. Macinnes, 'Regal union for Britain 1603-38' in G. Burgess (ed.), *The New British History: founding a modern state 1603-1715* (London, 1999) pp 33-64.   **18** J. Ohlmeyer, 'Civilizinge of those rude partes': the internal colonization of Britain and Ireland 1580s-1640s' in N. Canny (ed.), *The Oxford history of the British empire, volume i: the origins of empire: British overseas empire to the close of the seventeenth century* (Oxford, 1998), pp 124-47; R. Gillespie, 'Explorers,

Colonial policy through the western passage was amenable to a British projection, particularly as the Americas were 'beyond the line' of international regulation in the first half of the seventeenth century.[19] Albeit the Scots never came to dominate a notional English colony in the way the Irish effectively colonised Montserrat in the Leeward Islands, the Scots regarded themselves as independent players in empire, jettisoning the cultural baggage of colonial dependency attributed to the Irish.[20] During the initial phase of American colonisation, there was a declared preference both within governmental and entrepreneurial circles for an identifiable Scottish venture to expand the colonial dominions of the Stuart monarchy. Thus, New England was to be complemented by a New Scotland to bolster the British cause against the French in North America. At the same time, Nova Scotia offered a distinct British alternative to Ulster, in which Scots law would be utilised to implement and direct plantations. Scottish colonial entrepreneurs had one manifest disadvantage, however. Their interests were deemed expendable when their commercial aspirations conflicted with international diplomacy. While the most celebrated instance of this was the Darien fiasco of the 1690s, the discriminatory precedent was actually set over Nova Scotia. Five years after its initial settlement, the plantation was abandoned officially by 1632, as the price of peace exacted from Charles I for his abortive war against Louis XIII of France.[21]

Colonial frustrations in the Americas were only a peripheral irritant, however, as both Scotland and Ireland became progressively disaffected as a result of the attempted imposition of uniformity that resulted from the Stuart's metropolitan interpretation of their British *ius imperium*. In order to protect their revolutionary restructuring in kirk and state, the Covenanting movement in Scotland became committed proponents of confessional confederation with the English, the Dutch or the Swedes. In British terms, the apogee of confessional confederation was the Solemn League and Covenant between the Scottish Estates and the English Parliament. Although

exploiters and entrepreneurs: Early Modern Ireland and its context 1500-1700' in B.J. Graham & L.J. Proudfoot (eds), *An historical geography of Ireland* (London, 1993), pp 123-57.   **19** R.S. Dunn, *Sugar and slaves: the rise of the planter class in the English West Indies 1624-1713* (Chapel Hill, 1972), pp 3-45.   **20** D. Akenson, *If the Irish ran the world: Montserrat 1630-1730* (Liverpool, 1997); N. Canny, *Kingdom and colony: Ireland in the Atlantic world 1560-1800* (Baltimore, 1988), pp 44-59.   **21** G. P. Insh, *Scottish colonial schemes 1620-1686* (Glasgow, 1922), pp 27-39; J. G Reid, *Acadia, Maine and New England: marginal colonies in the seventeenth century* (Toronto, 1981), pp 20-51. The colonial venture which became Nova Scotia (roughly co-extensive with the present Canadian Maritimes) was instigated from 1621 by Sir William Alexander of Menstrie (later earl of Stirling), a noted poet, polemicist and courtier.

Ireland was included within the remit of the Solemn League, this was only done at English insistence. The Scots were reluctant to accord equal standing to a satellite kingdom whose dominant internal confessional confederation was that of the Irish catholics.[22] The co-ordinating confederal agency for British union was the short-lived Committee of Both Kingdoms, which projected itself internationally from 1644 to 1646 as *Concilium Amborum Magnae Britanniae*.[23] Schism between radicals and conservatives within the Covenanting movement was only gradually set aside following the execution of Charles I in 1649. A patriotic accommodation promoted the interests of Charles II, as the covenanted king of Great Britain and, simultaneously, resisted Cromwellian occupation. Accordingly, with the Cromwellian forces triumphant in all three kingdoms by 1651, the enforced union all round was first the commonwealth, then the protectorate of England, Scotland and Ireland. The term Britain was disregarded as an anglicised mark of antipathy to both the Stuarts and covenanting confederation.[24]

The Restoration of Charles II produced a constitutional settlement in all three kingdoms, which revived the Stuarts' British *ius imperium*, but ruled out the confederal conception of a kingdom united by covenanting. However, confederation was redefined in a commercial context, a process facilitated by the resurgence of European mercantilism and, in particular, the imposition of the English Navigation Laws. At the same time, although its political independence had been regained formally, Scotland, like Ireland, operated effectively as a satellite state.[25] In both countries, overtures for union with England featured as debating issues of political economy. Scotland had no equivalent to Sir William Petty who promoted union with England in order to facilitate social engineering, if not ethnic and cultural assimilation, through the transplantation of peoples.[26] Nonetheless, proposals for union in the Restoration era cannot be explained simply as the

22 A.I. Macinnes, 'Covenanting ideology in seventeenth-century Scotland' in J.H. Ohlmeyer (ed.), *Irish political thought in the seventeenth century* (Cambridge, 2000), pp 191-220; J.R. Young, *The Scottish Parliament 1639-1661: a political and constitutional analysis* (Edinburgh, 1996), pp 103-4, 132.   23 Dansk Rigsarkivet, Copenhagen, Tyske Kancellii Udenrigske Afdeling, England, A.I, 3. Brevveksling mellem Konghehusene. Breve til Vels med Bilag, fra Medlemmer af det engleske Kongehous til Medlemmer af de danske (1613-89).   24 D. Hirst, 'The English Republic and the meaning of Britain' in B. Bradshaw & J. Morrill (eds), *The British problem c.1534-1707: state formation in the Atlantic archipelago* (Basingstoke, 1996), pp 192-219; A.H. Williamson, 'Union with England traditional, Union with England radical: Sir James Hope and the mid-seventeenth century British state', *EHR*, cx (1995), pp 303-12.   25 A.I. Macinnes, 'Politically Reactionary Brits? The promotion of Anglo-Scottish Union 1603-1707' in S.J. Connolly (ed.), *Kingdoms united? Great Britain and Ireland since 1500* (Dublin, 1998), pp 43-55.   26 Kelly, 'Origins', pp 237-40.

Scottish response to a series of trade crises.[27] Such an explanation not only disregards overtures emanating from England, but neglects the targeted pursuit of colonies as the commercial alternative to union. Scottish colonialism in the Americas mirrored Scandinavian and German endeavours rather than the global ambitions of the Dutch, the French and the English.

Scottish proposals for commercial union with England, first mooted in 1664, were discussed inconclusively by parliamentary commissioners for both countries during 1668. In so far as Charles II instigated proposals for an incorporating union in October 1669, this was essentially a political diversion to facilitate a secret alliance with Louis XIV of France. An incorporating union was seen, on the one hand, as a method of emasculating the English Commons and, on the other, as a means of weaning Scotland away from commercial association and political sympathy with the Dutch, England's principal mercantilist adversary. The commissioners for both parliaments, all nominees of the king, did not actually meet until September 1670, four months after Charles II and Louis XIV had subscribed the Secret Treaty of Dover. As head of the Scottish negotiators, James Maitland, duke of Lauderdale, played up to English concerns that European precedents for regal union – notably Portugal with Castille and Navarre with France – had not necessitated political incorporation. By October, Lauderdale had created the stumbling block that Scots law was to remain unaltered. At the outset of November, negotiations were wrecked when he insisted upon equal Scottish representation in the joint parliament. Charles II offered no public endorsement to the overtures for a commercial union that emanated from the House of Lords in 1674.[28]

Eight months after he wrecked negotiations for union, Lauderdale pursued the alternative of colonialism. Separate charters were procured at

27 M. Goldie, 'Divergence and Union: Scotland and England 1660-1707' in *The British problem*, pp 220-45.   28 BL, Leeds papers, vol. xvii, Eg. Ms. 3340 fos 1-13; D. Douglas (ed.), *History of the Union of Scotland and England by Sir John Clerk of Penicuik* (Edinburgh, 1993), pp 78-81; E. Hughes, 'The negotiations for a commercial union between England and Scotland in 1668', *SHR*, xxiv (1927), pp 30-47; Ferguson, *Scotland's relations with England*, pp 153-7. Discussions in 1668 foundered within six months largely because of English fears over the competitive edge of the Scottish carrying trade, the close Scottish trading links with the Dutch and, above all, the perceived Scottish threat to vested coal and salt interests in the north-east of England. Support for commercial union was also an important power-play by Lauderdale, to establish his supremacy at court as adviser on Scottish affairs. The proposals for union of 1669, which Lauderdale drew up at court, sought fundamental safeguards for Scots law and the church. In return, incorporation required the acceptance of a United Kingdom of Great Britain, commercial integration, fiscal equivalence and truncated Scottish representation in a common parliament.

court licensing Scottish colonisation of American lands, currently delineated as Georgia and Florida, and of the Caribbean island of Dominica, the home of the most violent Carib Indians. His accompanying recommendation in July 1671 was that Scottish endeavours should be concentrated initially on the former venture, which was to enjoy the same rights, privileges and immunities as the neighbouring English province of Carolina. This recommendation was no doubt motivated by an awareness that Spanish suzerainty was less enforceable on the American eastern seaboard than in the Caribbean. In any event, Lauderdale's colonialism apparently bore no more fruit than his unionism. The proposal for a Florida colony was warranted but never implemented in 1679, by which time Scottish aspirations, if not settlements, were being refocused on the Caribbean island of St Vincent.[29]

The Stuart concept of a British empire was reinvigorated in Scotland when James, Duke of York, established his court in Edinburgh during his retreat from the Exclusion Crisis in England. The future James VII & II (like his grandfather, he viewed his latter nomenclature as king of Great Britain) was the only Stuart monarch not to sponsor political incorporation. Admittedly, he had supported Lauderdale's maneuvers in 1670 and the prospects for union were not eradicated from the political agenda. As Scottish governor in place of Lauderdale, James was faced with a report from the Council of Trade in 1681 that the only effective way for the country to cope with mercantilism and growing dependence on English trade was either to seek commercial union or develop overseas colonies. In choosing colonisation over union, James warranted Scottish colonies in South Carolina from 1682 and in East New Jersey from 1685.[30] Of the two colonies, South Carolina was the more transient. This venture, which was ostensibly promoted by Presbyterian nonconformists, actually resulted from extensive commercial networking on the Scottish western seaboard. The Scots planters along the Ashley River were based at Stuart's Town, named in honour rather than in defiance of their royal patron. They insisted on separate administration according to Scots law rather than incorporation with the English colonial government. This uneasy relationship, which

29 National Archives of Scotland, Ogilvie of Inverquharity papers per Messrs. Lindsay, Howe & Co., W.S., GD 205/40/13/3-4; Society of Antiquaries papers, GD103/2/4/42.   30 P.H. Brown, H. Paton & E.W.M. Balfour-Melville (ed.), *Registers of the Privy Council of Scotland*, third series, i-xvi (1661-91), (Edinburgh, 1908-70), vii, pp 651-5, 664-5. Not only had James a long pedigree in colonial government, having been awarded New York as a proprietary colony on its wresting from the Dutch in 1664, but he had been an assiduous and tolerant promoter of Scottish participation in colonising ventures.

sought confederation but was accorded a federal accommodation, was brought to a conclusion by Spanish reprisals which did not end the Scottish venture, but certainly terminated separate constitutional experimentation. While the New Jersey colony had drawn off some planters from South Carolina, this served to enhance and deepen the colonial expertise among a commercial network that drew support from the Highlands as from the north-east of Scotland. Its principal patrons being well connected at court, the plantation around Perth Amboy effectively enjoyed a confederal relationship with the associated English proprietary colony that failed to be sustained beyond the Revolution.[31]

In addition to the federal model that flourished briefly in South Carolina and the confederal accommodation that applied initially in East New Jersey, there were effectively three other models for Scottish colonial engagement prior to the Revolution. Firstly, there were the distinctive Scottish networks in the Caribbean, New England and the Middle Colonies that were sustained by British enterprise and supported by indentured service. However, the Scottish networks were also subject to sustained criticism from the English colonial administration for their clannishness and their connived breaching of the Navigation Laws to benefit their fellow countrymen. Secondly, there were disparate Scottish networks associated with Dutch colonies that had limited prospects for development, as mercantilist competition was constricting the close commercial association the Scots had long enjoyed with the Dutch. Thirdly, there was the lingering desire that Scotland should pursue a separate colony that would still be under the protection of the Stuart dynasty but no more dependent on England than on Spain.[32]

The Revolution effectively constricted these colonial options by transforming a British empire based on the Stuart's royal prerogative into an

---

31 Insh, *Scottish colonial schemes*, pp 67-94; N. Landsman, *Scotland and its first American colony 1683-1760* (Princeton, 1985); L.G. Fryer, 'Robert Barclay of Urie and East New Jersey', *Northern Scotland*, xv (1995), pp 1-17. The colonial venture in South Carolina was led by the irascible Henry Erskine, Lord Cardross and factored by William Dunlop, the future principal of Glasgow University. While East New Jersey was initially promoted by George Scott of Pitlochy, an entrepreneur of noted presbyterian sympathies, the principal patrons were the Drummond brothers, James, earl of Perth and William, Lord Melfort, who were catholic converts and Robert Barclay of Urie, the most prominent Scottish Quaker. 32 The monitoring of Scottish engagement with the American colonies by the British court and English government can be followed through the seventeen volumes covering the period 1574-1708 in the *Calendars of State Papers, Colonial: America and the West Indies*, W.M. Sainsbury, J.W. Fortescue & C. Headlam (ed.), (London, 1880-1916). John Locke's exclusive views of civil society (accepted whig ideology after the 'Glorious Revolution) were fundamentally grounded

English empire subject to constitutional oversight by parliament. At the same time, Scots were markedly disadvantaged in both the British Isles and the colonies by reinforced Navigation Laws. The British court under William and Mary could no longer endorse Scottish colonial ventures without the support of the English parliament, a situation that led to a build up of commercial frustrations that culminated in the Darien fiasco. Initially, the Darien colonial venture was a commercial confederation of Scottish, English, Dutch and Hanseatic commercial interests, intended to rival the English East India Company. However, William's need for parliamentary supply, his desire to appease Spain and the expendable nature of Scottish interests as he sought to broker a military alliance against Louis XIV, conspired to reduce Darien to a separatist endeavour. Albeit funded as a national enterprise, as a commercial compact between God and the Scottish people, surveying and provisioning were equally deficient. While English polemicists declared open season in ridiculing the audacity of Scottish enterprise, Spanish tenacity in the region was wholly underestimated. Indeed, the Darien fiasco, which came to grief on the Panama Isthmus in 1700, was in no small measure due to misplaced British – not just Scottish disrespect for Spain as 'the sick man of Europe.'[33]

The political fall out from Darien was the mobilisation of public opinion within Scotland against the Court which imperilled the continuation of regal union. The commercial impact was a critical but not crippling loss of venture capital (around £400,000 sterling). The failure of the Scots to break out of the mercantilist prison made them more reliant on access to English domestic and colonial markets. The models for colonial development, in turn, became models for British state formation. The Scots preferred confederation or a federal arrangement, the English were intent on incorporation. Undoubtedly, the Darien fiasco deepened the national sense of defeatism that facilitated the English drive for parliamentary incorporation. Nonetheless, the polemical debates as well as the legislative sparring on union demonstrate that ongoing commercial contacts with the American colonies also bolstered Scottish confidence to oppose incorpora-

in the Carolinas which served as the main colonial testing ground for British constitutional experimentation.   33 [R. Mackenzie], *A full and exact account of the proceedings of the court of directors and council-general of the company of Scotland trading to Africa and the Indies, with relation to the Treaty of Union now under the parliament's consideration* (Edinburgh, 1706); C. Storrs, 'Disaster at Darien (1698-1700)? The persistence of Spanish imperial power on the eve of the demise of the Spanish Habsburgs', *European History Quarterly*, xxix (1999), pp 5-38; D. Armitage, 'The Scottish vision of empire: intellectual origins of the Darien venture' in *Union for Empire*, pp 97-118.

tion. The search for separate Scottish colonies which came to grief at Darien was the culmination of not one, but three, generations of transatlantic entrepreneurial endeavour. Arguably, such Scottish engagement in empire ensured that the making of union involved issues of principle on both sides and, at the same time, rehabilitated the importance of political economy in effecting the United Kingdom of Great Britain.[34] From a colonial perspective, the accomplishment of parliamentary union signposted a collective crisis of political will among Scots to pursue a separate commercial agenda, not an entrepreneurial lack of ambition. The British nature of the empire was reasserted through Scottish networks within an English governmental framework. The realities of British state formation were expressed appositely on 9 May, eight days after the Treaty of 1707 became operative as 'a perfect and entire union'; Governor Handasyd of Jamaica was notified by the Council of Trade and Plantations 'that Scotchmen are thereby to be looked upon for the future as Englishmen to all intents and purposes whatsoever.'[35]

III

The union of 1707 had seemingly accorded the Scots the status to which the anglican ascendancy in Ireland had aspired. Nonetheless, the protestant establishment in Scotland had long been uneasy about too close a political analogy being drawn between the constitutional standing of both countries. Despite the formal reaffirmation of its political independence at the Restoration, Scotland, like Ireland, had undoubted colonial associations from its effective operation as a satellite state of England over the next three decades. The Scottish and Irish parliaments, like the Caribbean colonies, awarded a substantive annuity from its excise to Charles II for life, awards that obviated the need for regular parliaments to vote supply. While the continuity of military governors-general and colonial administration has been well attested with respect to Ireland, Scotland became a training ground for the oppressive use of the militia as well as regular forces.[36] The brief interlude during the 1680s when the Scots were proactive players in colonialism was terminated by the removal and exile of James VII & II at

34 T.C. Smout, 'The Anglo-Scottish Union of 1707: The economic background', *EHR*, second series, xvi (1963-4), pp 455-67; A.M. Carstairs, 'Some economic aspects of the union of parliaments', *Scottish Journal of Political Economy*, ii (1955), pp 64-72; J. Mackinnon, *The Union of England and Scotland: a study in international history* (London, 1896), pp 240-72.   35 *Calendar of State Papers, Colonial* (1707), p. 431.   36 A.I. Macinnes, *Clanship, commerce and the house of Stuart 1603-1788* (East Linton, 1996), pp

the Revolution. The issue of incorporating union was resurrected on the British political agenda by a Convention of Estates from which most Jacobites had absented themselves in the spring of 1689. Such Scottish lobbying, though ostensibly an ideological mark of whig solidarity in Britain, was primarily driven by the military threat from Jacobitism which did not abate until 1691. In like manner, the manifest threat from Jacobitism had revitalised the desire for union among the English in Ireland. Scottish lobbying for union, moreover, facilitated the Convention turning itself into a parliament that had the exclusive powers to commission bilateral negotiations. Of greater constitutional significance was the unshackling of court control over the Scottish Estates. The Claim of Right, issued by the Convention in April 1689, stressed the fundamental, contractual nature of the Scottish state by deposing James rather than following the English fiction of abdication. Giving teeth to the parliament that commenced in July was a radical group known as 'the Club', which was intent on delaying a final political and ecclesiastical settlement to ensure permanent and purposeful consultation between the court and the Scottish Estates. In turn, politicians favourable to the court used the prospect of union as a ploy to divert the Club from root and branch constitutional reform.[37]

Incorporating union, despite the lack of parliamentary endorsement after 1689, continued to be espoused by a handful of political careerists, most notably Sir James Dalrymple, Master of Stair, who wished to cast off his former association with the Scottish regime of James VII & II. As secretary of state, he demonstrably endeavoured to maintain a quiescent Scotland that would not detract from William's continental pre-occupations. A by-product of this unionist careerism was his stage-management of the exemplary massacre of a small Jacobite clan – the MacDonalds of Glencoe in February 1692. No less insidious was the growing intrusion of successive English ministries into the running of Scotland since the reinvigorated Scottish Estates were no longer subservient to the wishes of the court. Such English intrusion effected the unwarranted postponement of the Scottish Estates on the accession of Queen Anne, to ensure that the more pliable privy council reaffirmed Scottish commitment to the war against France.[38]

124-42; S.S. Webb, *The governors-general: the English army and the definition of empire 1569-1681* (Chapel Hill, 1979), pp 445-59.   37 E.W.H. Balfour-Melville (ed.), *An account of the proceedings of the estates in Scotland 1689-1690*, 2 vols (Edinburgh, 1954), i, pp 42, 50-109; P.W.J. Riley, *King William and the Scottish politicians* (Edinburgh, 1979), pp 7-8, 27-33, 48-54, 160-2; Kelly, 'Origins', pp 240-3. The Club, which included Fletcher of Saltoun among its membership, was drawn mainly from the Estates of the gentry and burgess rather than the nobility.   38 A.I. Macinnes, 'Slaughter under trust:

This unwarranted intrusion severely prejudiced efforts at Court to revive incorporating union, which William of Orange had encouraged continuously without ever being prepared to devote the time and energy required to carry the policy through. Doubts over the succession after Anne and the continuance of a Jacobite court in exile recognised by Louis XIV threatened to turn the current War of the Spanish Succession into the War of the British Succession. Union would close Scotland as a back door to England, while the influx of Scottish placemen into the lords and commons would expedite the Court's management of both houses. Despite initial rejection in the commons in March 1700, moves towards incorporation were revitalised when Queen Anne appointed commissioners for both parliaments who met in October 1702. Continuing resentment against intrusive English ministries coupled with Scottish insistence on reparations for Darien ensured that the four months of negotiations were unsuccessful.[39] The Scottish Estates also remained antipathetic to the East India Company, which continued to earn a drawback on customs from all goods re-exported to Scotland. As well as mobilising English parliamentary opinion against Darien, the revitalised Company had lent two million pounds at 8 per cent interest to further William's war effort. A shared aversion to the Company's parliamentary influence in England can be conjectured from Irish legislation hostile to beneficial drawbacks following the rejection of union in 1703. The Irish parliament specifically penalised the Company by imposing a duty on calicos from the outset of 1704.[40]

Notwithstanding its political bite on the issue of drawbacks, the Irish parliament was not prepared to challenge the act of settlement, which the English parliament imposed unilaterally in favour of the House of Hanover

clan massacres and British state formation' in M. Levene & P. Roberts (ed.), *The massacre in history* (Oxford, 1999), pp 127-48; W. Ferguson, 'The making of the Treaty of Union of 1707', *SHR*, xliii (1964), pp 89-110. **39** National Library of Scotland, Saltoun papers, Ms 17498, fo 73; HL, Loudoun Scottish collection, box 18/LO 8600, box 20/LO 9532, box 39/LO 92832; Speck, *Birth of Britain*, pp 44-5. **40** LO 8600, box 20/LO 9532, box 39/LO 92832; Speck, *Birth of Britain*, pp 44-5; HL, Loudoun Scottish collection, box 3/LO 7171, box 48/Lo 10102. As this loan was partially to be reimbursed through taxes on salt, it is apposite to note that only one amendment to the articles of union was carried from the floor of the Scottish Estates during the last session of 1706-7 – that to extend the exemption of domestically produced salt from the equalising of tariffs. From the salt tax of the 3s. 4d. per bushel currently payable in England, 2s. 4d. out was earmarked to repay the debt due to the East India Company, which had its exclusive trading privileges confirmed until 1711. Accordingly the Scots tariff remained at 1s. per bushel (DH, Parliamentary memorandums of Colonel William Dalrymple, 1706-7, A 817/2, p. 98). Scottish MPs in the new British parliament successfully argued that the drawback on goods exported to Scotland by the Company in 1701. Despite the Irish parliament declaring any endeavour to impeach the act as treasonable in 1703, the English still rejected its overture for union.[41] In marked contrast, the Scots did not lack confidence either to question the act or to play the Jacobite card to leave the issue of the succession unresolved. Anglo-Scottish antipathy, which reached its contemporary nadir from the first news of the Darien fiasco in 1700, was compounded by a legislative war. Scottish retaliation to the act of settlement was two-pronged. The 'act anent peace and war' provided for an independent Scottish foreign policy on Anne's death. The act of security threatened to dissolve the regal union unless the sovereignty of Scotland, the power of its parliament and the freedom of its religion and commerce were secured from English interference by Anne's successor. At the same time, those within the court party who were continuing covertly to treat for union with the English ministry were told peremptorily to desist.[42] Instead of the placatory gesture counselled by Anne, the English were not persuaded to share 'the imperium Britannicum that they had usurped'. Scottish retaliation was trumped by the alien act of 1705 and by the mobilising of troops on the Borders and across the North Channel in Ireland. Along with the threat of subjecting the Scots to the same punitive tariffs as foreigners was an invitation to treat for incorporating union.[43]

The understated issue during the legislative war was the relative standing of the Irish parliament. Molyneux's *The case of Ireland* had been provoked by overt English interference post-Revolution; this interference had damaged the wool trade, asserted the jurisdictional superiority of the Lords at Westminster and threatened the redistribution of forfeited Jacobite

should be struck off from December 1707 as inconsistent with Union (DH, Parliamentary notes of Colonel William Dalrymple, 1707-8, A 817/3, pp 59-60). India Office Records, Court Minutes, 22 July1702-19 April 1705, B/47, p. 238. I am obliged to Dr Andrew Mackillop, my colleague in the History Department at the University of Aberdeen, for this latter reference.   41 Hill, 'Ireland without Union' in *Union for Empire*, pp 288-9; Smith, 'Like Amphibious Animals', pp 795-6.   42 [G. Ridpath], *Proceedings of the Parliament of Scotland begun at Edinburgh, 6th May 1703. With an account of all the material debates which occur'd during that session* (Edinburgh, 1704). The Court Party, in a feeble attempt to regain the political initiative, sponsored the wine act, which maintained French links despite the current English trade embargo. Tensions with England were generally aggravated by a largely fabricated Jacobite plot, which was supposed to implicate Scottish politicians across the party spectrum. This 'Scotch Plot' was investigated judicially by the House of Lords without reference to the Scottish Estates (HL, Loudoun Scottish Collection, box 20/Lo 9532, /Lo 9536-7; ICA, bundle 17/3).   43 *History of the Union of Scotland and England*, pp 81-5; P.W.J. Riley, 'The Union of 1707 as an episode in English Politics', *EHR*, lxxxiv (1979), pp 498-527.

estates. His passing assertion, that Ireland was as separate and distinct a kingdom as Scotland from England, instigated a polemical debate which initially differentiated the independence of Scotland from that of Ireland, but then challenged the sovereignty of Scotland in relation to England as an imperial monarchy. Such were Scottish antipathies to covert English interference post-Revolution that pamphlets advocating English claims of suzerainty were publicly burned by the hangman in Edinburgh, while published rebuttals were remunerated by the Scottish Estates. The controversy was further fuelled by Fletcher of Saltoun's publication of his animated conversations with critics of Molyneux, notably with George MacKenzie, earl of Cromartie and consummate Scottish trimmer, and Sir Edward Seymour, an unapologetic saboteur of the Irish wool trade and a noted Scotophobe to boot. Fletcher's published account made much of the constitutional and economic slavery of Ireland. Having been in the vanguard of those adamant that the Scottish Estates assert themselves over the subservient court party as well as the intrusive English ministry, his particular design was to solidify the support of young nobles loosely attached to the confederated opposition.[44]

The slavish dependency of the Irish parliament was reiterated specifically or, more usually, in coded references to Scotland being open to 'the influence of foreign councils' by not just Fletcher, but diverse members of the Scottish Estates throughout the legislative war. At the outset of the parliamentary session in May 1703, James Hamilton, duke of Hamilton and nominal leader of the confederated opposition, welcomed Queen Anne on her accession to the independent imperial crown of Scotland. He later warned the Estates that unless they insisted upon royal assent, which was still being withheld from the act of security in August 1704, they 'were like

---

44 W. Ferguson, 'Imperial crowns; a neglected facet of the background to the Treaty of Union of 1707', *SHR*, liii (1974), pp 22-44; C. Kidd, *Subverting Scotland's past. Scottish whig historians and the creation of an Anglo–British identity* (Cambridge, 1993), pp 33-50; J. Robertson, 'An elusive sovereignty; The course of the Union debate in Scotland 1698-1707' in *Union for Empire*, pp 198-227. The English Tory, Sir Christopher Musgrave, was also party to these conversations. In polemical terms, their publication influenced further Irish involvement when Henry Maxwell, an Ulster parliamentarian, joined the debate, proposing that Ireland be incorporated into England on the same footing as Wales. Warning against incorporation that concentrated political and economic power, Fletcher was less than convinced that the political economy of Wales had benefited from its incorporation into England. Fletcher's standpoint, that Scotland should only engage in union along federalist lines, was endorsed by Robert Molesworth, who had chaired the committee of the Irish Commons which had instigated the failed Union of 1703 (Smyth, 'No remedy more proper' in *British consciousness and identity*, pp 314-18).

an Irish parliament who could act nothing but what was concerted in England'. Determined to avoid the fate of Ireland as an English dependency, the Scottish Estates were not averse to asserting their distinctive liberties by imposing mercantilist restrictions on the importation of salt, livestock, dairy produce and victuals from Ireland as on the re-export of Irish wool. The Irish bore the brunt of Scottish retaliation to the alien act when a naval blockage was imposed on the North Channel in September 1705.[45] Simultaneously, Hamilton, who had to suffer the defection of the New Party or Squadrone Volante (the flying squadron of ambitious opportunists) in the course of the legislative war, sold the pass over the English invitation to treat for incorporation. In a fit of pique with the confederated opposition – which included not only his country party, stocked with disappointed placemen, the constitutional reformers headed by Fletcher of Saltoun and the Jacobites who also masqueraded as cavaliers or tories – he surprisingly moved that the queen appoint both sets of parliamentary commissioners. In the three months of passive negotiations that commenced in April 1706, the only reported discourse of substance was over the size of Scottish representation in the British parliament. Although not always cogniscent about the details in the articles presented to the queen in July, the public reception in Scotland was overwhelmingly hostile to union. Indeed, there was no guaranteed majority in favour of incorporation when the Scottish Estates met that October to implement the Treaty.[46]

45 [Ridpath], *Proceedings of the Parliament of Scotland*, pp 5, 11, 13, 26, 28-9, 31, 36, 46, 48, 57, 68-70; DH, Parliamentary notebook of Colonel William Dalrymple, 1704-5, A 817/1, pp 16-7, 62, 75-6, 91, 137-9, 161. The increasingly irascible Fletcher of Saltoun, who was currently touting the King of Prussia as a monarch more sympathetic to Scottish calvinists than the Lutheran Elector of Hanover, was the sponsor of this mercantilist discrimination. 46 G. Lockhart of Carnwath, *The Lockhart papers; Memoirs and correspondence upon the affairs of Scotland from 1702 to 1715*; A. Aufrere (ed.), 2 vols (London, 1817), i, pp 150-7; *Memoirs of the Life of Sir John Clerk of Penicuik Extracted by Himself from his Own Journals 1676-1755*, J.M. Gray (ed.), (Edinburgh, 1892), pp 58-63; DH, Loudoun papers, 'Green Deed Box'; bundle 1706/January-September; HL, Loudoun Scottish collection, box 4/LO 7259, box 13/LO 8314, box 14/LO 7171, box 18/ LO 8329, box 19/LO 8478-9, /LO 8496, box 20/LO 7637, box 33/ LO 8675, /LO 9114. While there was a general British recognition that regal union was no longer an option, there was no immediate prospect of incorporating union all round that would involve all three kingdoms in an expansive British empire: *The queen and empress, and her three kingdoms one empire: or, brief remarks upon the present, and a prospect of the future state of England, Scotland and Ireland, in a happy union* (London, 1706).

IV

As the Scottish Estates embarked on what turned out to be their last, critical session, the English ministry had several distinct advantages. They were clearly intent on an incorporating union; they were prepared to use the resources of the Treasury to facilitate Scottish politics of influence; and they could rely on the support of key Scottish politicians whose thirst for power was enhanced by their lucrative playing of the English marriage market.[47] Incorporation also offered a viable way out of the mercantilist prison reaffirmed by the alien act, a theme taken up by Scottish merchants resident in London, especially those with interests in colonial plantations. The removal of protective tariffs through free trade, though putting Scottish manufacturing and extractive industries at risk from English competition, opened up unfettered access to the English colonies. On the Scottish side, John Spreull from Glasgow, the city which was the main beneficiary of the transatlantic trade, led a vigorous rebuttal of Scottish vulnerability to the alien act on a global scale, a rebuttal which was reinforced by an attack from within the Scottish merchant community on the Anglo-Scottish trading houses in London. The dubious prospect of free trade was not 'a sufficient equivalency for our sovereignty, independency and laws'. A communication of trade through commercial confederation would allow the Scots to harmonise rather than subordinate their economic regulation to English interests.[48] While there was a broad consensus against an incorporating union among the Scottish Estates, there was no agreed alternative with variations ranging from a federal executive to confederal legislatures. Moreover, there was considerable confusion in defining what was meant by federal or confederal constitutions. While the former term could be applied strictly to subordinate assemblies within a British parliamentary framework, this was a model of limited currency. Federation tended to be defined as separate parliaments holding a British executive to account, while con-

47 Ferguson, *Scotland's relations*, pp 232-69; Riley, *Union of England and Scotland*, pp 254-338. 48 T.C. Smout, *Scottish trade on the eve of Union 1660-1707* (Edinburgh, 1963), pp 261-75; [G. Ridpath], *The case of Scots-men residing in England and in the English Plantations* (Edinburgh, 1703); J. Spreull, *An account current betwixt Scotland & England balanced together with an essay of a scheme of the product of Scotland, and a few remarks on each* (Edinburgh, 1705); *A letter concerning trade from several Scots gentlemen that are merchants in England, to their countrymen that are merchants in Scotland* (London, 1706); *Answer to a letter concerning trade sent from several Scots gentlemen, that are merchants in England to their countrymen that are merchants in Scotland* (Edinburgh, 1706); D. Black, *An essay upon industry & trade shewing the necessity of the one, the conveniency and usefulness of the other and the advantages of both* (Edinburgh, 1706).

federation tended to relate to a supervisory body, similar to the Committee of Both Kingdoms in the 1640s, which harmonised differences between separate executives and legislatures in Scotland and England.[49]

The months between the conclusion of negotiations by the parliamentary commissioners and the reconvening of the Scottish Estates were marked covertly (by concerted political action involving the court party and the English ministry) and overtly (by a polemical deluge). The key to these covert operations, which continued piecemeal into the last parliamentary session, was selectivity in the payment of pension arrears, in the placement of posts and in expounding key articles of the Treaty in order to shore up support in the court party and to secure the commitment of the Squadrone Volante.[50] At the same time, the inveterate polemicist and none too secret agent, Daniel Defoe, was despatched to Scotland to propagate the mutual benefits from partnership through union. Defoe claimed that it was imperative that Scotland was part of a British incorporation; he extolled the advantages for Scottish commerce of free access to English and imperial markets; and he countered religious scruples and other national prejudices standing in the way of the Treaty being ratified.[51] The Scots were not necessarily committed to a British constitutional settlement any more than

---

49 Robertson, 'An elusive sovereignty' in *Union for Empire*, pp 213- 15; *The trimmer: or some necessary cautions concerning the Union of the Kingdoms of Scotland and England; with an answer to some of the chief objections against an incorporating union* (Edinburgh, 1706); D. Brown of Dolphinstone, *A scheme proposing a true touch-stone for the due trial of a proper union* (Edinburgh, 1706); *The smoking flax unquenchable; where the union between the two kingdoms is dissected, anatomized, confuted and annulled* (1706); A. Bruce, *Discourse of a cavalier gentleman on the divine and human law, with respect to the succession* (1706). Queensberry, as queen's commissioner, only added to this confusion in his opening speech to the Scottish Estates in October 1706,when he asserted that the Treaty with England was 'to secure a perpetual union of Confederacy upon just and equall terms advantageous to both the Kingdoms' (DH, Loudoun papers, A 1131/8). **50** DH, Loudoun papers, 'Green Deed Box' bundle 1706/August-December; Lockhart of Carnwath, *The Lockhart papers*, i, pp 262-72; *Calendar of Treasury Books, xxi-ii (1706-8)*, W.A. Shaw (ed.), (London, 1950-2), xxi-ii, pp 36, 300-1, 352; xxi-ii, pp 78-9, 112-19. A slush fund of £20,000 was made available to Queensberry, some of which was assigned to clandestine operations involving agent-provocateurs of dubious provenance, such as John Ker of Kersland who moved from the extremes of militant covenanting to Jacobitism. Probably the most blatant case of selective patronage arose from the demands emanating from John Campbell, duke of Argyll, before he committed himself irrevocably to union. He wanted not only to be indemnified and reimbursed for his past services as queen's commissioner in 1705, but over 45 military and civil places of profit, which he demanded principally for himself and then for his kinsmen and political associates. Only when he was assured that his demands were being met did he depart from London in October 1706 (ICA, bundles 69/1, 144/1). **51** Mackinnon, *Union of England and Scotland*, pp 240-64; K.P. Penovich, ' From 'Revolution Principles' to they were convinced that parliamentary incorporation was the best guarantee of economic prosperity. Scottish concerns to be informed of Dutch and French standpoints on the Treaty of Union had led the privy council to authorise the translation and publication of the *Haarlem Courant* and the *Paris Gazette* from the outset of 1706. In turn, support within Scotland for alternative European confederation led Defoe to uphold British incorporation over alliance with the Dutch or the French.[52]

A coalition with the Dutch had real attractions for the Scots. Not only were the United Provinces Scotland's foremost trading partner until the 1690s, but the Scots had also served for as long and more extensively in the Dutch colonial service as they had in the English. The Dutch were deemed to operate a more cost-efficient colonialism based on commerce rather than plantations. The Scots could further benefit from Dutch expertise in developing deep-sea fishing as an alternative national venture to colonialism. At the same time, the constitutional structure of the United Provinces was deemed more supportive of distinctive Scottish interests, particularly presbyterianism. A league with France was commended as a commercial revival of the 'auld alliance' which would rival English trade on a global scale. Notwithstanding the expulsion of the Huguenots since the 1680s, France was not deemed absolutely hostile to protestant allies. Notwithstanding the persuasiveness of these polemical arguments, there was no evidence that the Dutch were prepared to confederate with the Scots, while an alliance with France primarily served Jacobite interests. Polemics further anticipated the debates by frequent references to international examples which appeared to preserve distinctive sovereignties – notably the Swiss Confederation and the Polish–Lithuanian commonwealth among contemporary regimes, the duchy of Burgundy in the later middle ages and the Greek republics in classical times. Indeed, Defoe's implacable opponent, James Hodge, forcibly made the point that breakaways from incorporating unions, notably Sweden from Denmark in the sixteenth century and Portugal from Spain in the seventeenth, had advanced their wealth as nations rather than consigned them to poverty as provinces. The discriminatory and prejudicial treatment of

Union: Daniel Defoe's intervention in the Scottish debate' in *Union for Empire*, pp 228–42. On the political level, Defoe was to retain a watching brief that the Court Party did not accept any material alterations or amendments to the Treaty that would breach the financial reparations agreed as the equivalents. Any such breach would open the door to the Treaty being questioned or impeded in the English parliament. **52** HL, Loudoun Scottish collection, box 43/LO 10045; [D. Defoe], *The advantages of Scotland by an incorporating union with England, compar'd with these of a coalition with the Dutch or league with the French* (1706).

dissenters, American colonists and, above all, the Irish, reinforced religious, commercial and political doubts about incorporation at the dictate of the English ministry. Defoe shared a general recognition with his sympathisers and detractors among Scottish polemicists that the Treaty did not entail the absolute surrender of Scottish sovereignty. Should ensuing British parliaments breach fundamental safeguards for the presbyterian establishment, education, Scots law and local government, Scotland would be reduced from partnership to the satellite status of the Irish which would, in turn, imperil the continuance of union.[53]

While the debate had effectively narrowed from the desirability of British over European affiliations, major questions remained prior to the last session of the Scottish Estates. Not least, given that the proposed scale of Scottish representation – 45 MPs and 16 Lords – was little more than one-twelfth of the total membership of the new British parliament, would an incorporating as against a federal union be more protective of distinctive Scottish interests? Furthermore, the court party was not guaranteed a majority among the 242 members eligible to attend the last session unless the support of the Squadrone Volante was secured. In this situation, the English ministry persuaded Queensberry to utilise the services of William Paterson, founder of the Bank of England in 1694, originator of the Darien Colony of 1698-1700 and inventive propagandist. Paterson's despatch from London in September was not generally welcomed within the court party. He had seemingly recanted his involvement in Darien as a separate Scottish venture with a proposal for a Council of Trade that would promote Scottish commerce within a British context. He even claimed to have formulated the negotiated articles of the Treaty. After his arrival in Edinburgh, he asserted that his intention in promoting Darien was always to effect British incorporation. During the legislative war, however, he had certainly flirted with the confederated opposition, albeit, he affirmed, only to flush out their antipathy to union. A pamphlet published under the pseudonym 'Philiopatris' had resurrected his proposal of 1700 for a Council of Trade, but now as a separate entity on the Dutch model, in order to give Scots free and

53 DH, Parliamentary memorandums, A 817/2, pp 53-4; P. Abercromby, *The advantages of the Act of Security compared with these of the intended union founded on the revolution principles publish'd by Mr Daniel De Foe* (1706); *A seasonable warning or the pope and king of France unmasked* (1706); *An essay on removing rational prejudices against a union with England* (1706); [J. Hodge], *The rights and interests of the two British monarchies with a special respect to an united or separates states. Treatise III* (London, 1706); [F. Grant], *The patriot resolved* (1707); L. Dickey, 'Power, commerce and natural law in Daniel Defoe's political writings' in *Union for Empire*, pp 63-96.

uninterrupted commerce with the American plantations of all European powers. The riches which would flow would be sufficient 'to preserve such of the representatives of this nation in the love of liberty of their country, and antidote them against that pernicious and contagious foreign influence'.[54] This rhetoric, which was in keeping with the Molyneux-inspired castigations of the English ministry in the Scottish Estates during the legislative war, was now to be spun in favour of union just as a new Scottish publication of the *Case for Ireland* was being sold in Edinburgh. Indeed, primarily because of Paterson's spin-doctoring, Molyneux's writing was to play a part in the making of the Anglo-Scottish union that was as significant, if less celebrated, than its role in the American Revolution.[55]

Paterson's spin-doctoring is recorded in five letters written between 7 September and 15 October, which were immediately published to rebut putative arguments of the confederated opposition.[56] He begins with a denunciation of any leagues and confederacies (other than incorporation) proposed between Scotland and England; a secondary theme was his dismissal of any continental constitutional analogy. Federal union was not an acceptable middle way between confederation and complete union. Nor could the Claim of Right of 1689 be seen as a safeguard against incorporation, as this fundamental law was passed by a Convention of Estates which sought an united British parliament. Notwithstanding this gloss on the Convention's proposal for union as a consultative device to turn itself into a full parliament, Paterson's arguments were virtually repeated on 29 October by the lord chancellor, James Ogilvie, earl of Seafield, who presided over the Scottish Estates as a far from impartial speaker. In rebutting the claims of William Johnstone, marquis of Annandale, that an incorporating union was contrary to the Claim of Right, Seafield ridiculed Annandale as a disappointed placemen who had switched his support from incorporation in 1702 to federal union by 1706. Paterson had been no less vituperative in concluding his first letter with an admonition to the confederated opposition that their reprinting and promotion of Molyneux was misguided. Thus,

54 DH, Loudoun papers, 'Green Deed Box', bundle 1706/September; 'Philiopatris', *An essay concerning inland and foreign, publick and private trade; together with some overtures, shewing how a company of national trade, may be constituted in Scotland, with the advantages which will result therefrom* (1704); Armitage, 'Scottish vision of empire', pp 113-14.   55 P. Kelly, 'Recasting a tradition: William Molyneux and the sources of *The case of Ireland ... stated*' in *Irish political thought in the seventeenth century*, pp 83-106; J. Kelly, *Prelude to Union: Anglo-Irish politics in the 1780s* (Cork, 1992), pp 13-15.   56 BL, W. Paterson, *Treatises on the Union* (transcribed London, 1708), Add. Ms. 10403; printed in *The writings of William Paterson*, 3 vols, S. Bannister (ed.), (London, 1859), iii, pp 5-25.

Molyneux's passing aspiration in favour of union became the essence of his *Case for Ireland*. The real desire of Molyneux and 'all the Protestants in Ireland' was not further to separate, but to have nearer union with England. There was a vast difference between the Protestant interest in Ireland and 'the present scribblers against the Union' in Scotland. The former believed that a more complete communication of government, trade and privileges would increase their people, their commerce and their prosperity. The latter contended that complete union would carry away people, trade and wealth from Scotland. Accordingly, 'nothing in the world can be a greater argument for the Union of this Kingdom, than the present practise, sense and disposition of Ireland'. Again, Patterson's spinning brought a parliamentary dividend when John Ker, earl of Roxburghe, spoke in favour of incorporation on 2 November. Part of the group of young nobles whom Fletcher of Saltoun had sought to influence during the legislative war about the constitutional and economic slavery of Ireland, Roxburghe and his associates had, nonetheless, joined the Squadrone. He now affirmed that as long as Scotland continued as a separate state from England, the Scots would be but 'absolute slaves' and their government in thrall to English ministries. Scottish divisions and animosities in government could only be overcome and, simultaneously, the happiness of the nation through riches and liberty could only be secured 'by an incorporating union'.[57]

57 BL, Add. Ms 10403, first letter pp 1-3, 9-11, second letter pp 13-7; DH, Parliamentary memorandums, A 817/2, pp 27-8, 34-6. Paterson's third letter pointed out how well Wales had thrived since incorporation with England, claiming that the principality's foreign trade was greater than that of Scotland and it was to pay more in land tax than Scotland would be obliged to under the Treaty. At the same time, the parallel economic decline of Cornwall was attributable not to incorporation but to the falling demand for tin! The sparse representation of Scotland was countered with reference to the land tax, when Paterson demonstrated that Scotland had a more generous representation in the new British parliament than Wales or any other district of England except Cornwall, whose representation was directly linked to its former stannic wealth. Paterson's case was elaborated in the Scottish Estates on 7 January 1707, when it was admitted on behalf of the commissioners for the Treaty that Scottish representation was 'greater then we could pretend to have it by any rule' whether based proportionally on land-tax, customs and excise or population (BL, Add. Ms 10403, third letter pp 19-20, 28-30; DH, Parliamentary memorandums, A 817/2, pp 125-6, 142-4). Patterson's fourth letter suggested that the Scots were to benefit greatly from the capital equivalent, particularly the reparations afforded for winding up the Company of Scotland trading to Africa and India which had promoted the plantation of Darien. However, he omitted to mention that the sum advanced from the English treasury was slightly less than the £400,000 venture capital lost in Darien and that reparations were only one aspect of the capital equivalent - together with payment of Scotland's public debts, compensation for standardising the coinage and Scotland's inclusion in England's

As Roxburgh's speech confirmed, the decisive support of the Squadrone for the Court Party was delivered timely. The recorded vote on the first article on 4 November revealed 116 *for* and 83 *against*. During the five months the Scottish Estates were in session, the legislative passage of the union required sophisticated political management on the part of Queensberry and his leading associates in the court party, particularly with respect to such procedural business as the length and frequency of speeches, the order of voting for articles and the acceptance of relatively minor alterations and insubstantial amendments; the latter aspect was notably required to secure acceptance of fiscal palliatives. The confederated opposition, which was reduced to staged protests, filibusters and unrequited requests for adjournments, had all but imploded on the ratification of union on 16 January 1707, when 110 voted for and 68 against. Hamilton's ineptitude left him leading a political rump from which the Jacobites absented themselves in order to reaffirm their commitment to extra-parliamentary protest to terminate the union.[58]

national debt. Moreover, the sum advanced from the English treasury, which was to be repaid from higher Scottish taxes post-Union, carried compound interest of 6 per cent whereas the Darien investors were only to receive simple interest of 5 per cent on their stock and nothing for loss of property and shipping. His fifth letter, which extolled the commercial advantages that would accrue to Scotland from free access to English and colonial markets, revived his proposal for a Council of Trade, as a British national endeavour, that would offer the Scots further opportunities for making 'valuable acquisitions in America' (BL, Add. Ms 10403, fourth letter, pp 37-8, 41-3, fifth letter, pp 45-8, 53-4). Patterson's spinning certainly contributed to the strong voting in favour of free trade. But there was considerable scepticism and cross-voting on other economic issues, particularly when it became evident by 3 December that the customs and excise to be raised in Scotland in the first year after the union was not likely to amount to more than £123,000 – less than that raised in 1700 and less than a third of the capital equivalent. It was also admitted that foreign trade was not likely to advance more than £40,000 per annum in the first seven years of union. Nonetheless, the prospect of some reparations for Darien served as a powerful inducement to shore up support for union (*A state of the publick revenues and debts of England, together with a scheme of the sums of money allowed to Scotland by the treaty of union in name of equivalent* (Edinburgh, 1706); D. Black, *A short view of the trade and taxes of Scotland, compar'd with what these taxes may amount to after the union, even tho' our trade should not augment one sixpence* (1706). **58** DH, Loudoun papers, 'Green Deed Box', bundle 1706/October-December; HMC, *Report on the manuscripts of the Earl of Mar & Kellie*, 2 vols (London, 1904), i, pp 284-375; Lockhart of Carnwath, *The Lockhart papers*, i, pp 146-7, 167-77, 196-215, 221-3.

V

Having routinely passed through the English parliament in February, the Anglo-Scottish Treaty of Union came into force on 1 May 1707. Its accomplishment, rather than that of a federal or lesser union, was welcomed from the pulpit by Francis Hutchinson, the future anglican bishop of Down and Connor, as a perpetual incorporation. Its reception was less fulsome among the anglican ascendancy in Ireland. Jonathan Swift was especially aggrieved that England in 1703 had spurned the loyal protestants in Ireland, but from 1705 had successfully courted a country which could not be trusted for its presbyterianism and its Jacobitism.[59] Disaffection in Scotland towards the Treaty was soon enhanced by administrative dismantling; by breaches in both the spirit and letter of the union with respect to reserved areas in the church and law; and by delays in honouring fiscal palliatives. Of particular significance was the decision in the first British parliament to abolish the Scottish privy council, which had played a vital role in securing union by monitoring dissent within the country; reserving troops reinforcing Berwick and Donaghadee; and intimidating the episcopalian clergy in northern Scotland as Jacobites opposed to the Hanoverian succession. Ostensibly abolished to integrate local government throughout the United Kingdom, the privy council was sacrificed to electoral appeasement. With the first British general election looming in 1708, the Squadrone did not wish that the court party would gain any managerial advantage from their continuing control of the council. Growing resentment with the running of Scotland post-union actually led to a concerted effort by the court party and the Squadrone to terminate the treaty, which lost narrowly to proxy votes in the Lords in 1713.[60] The major beneficiaries of administrative dismantling and political disaffection were undoubtedly the Jacobites who mounted two serious challenges to the British establishment in 1715 and 1745. The suppression of Jacobitism led to the importation of measures used to entrench the anglican ascendancy in Ireland: these measures were carried to

59 F. Hutchinson, *Sermon preached at St. Edmund's-Bury on the first of May 1707 being the day of thanksgiving for the Union of Scotland and England* (London, 1707); Smyth, 'No remedy more proper' in *British consciousness and identity*, pp 301-2. The legislative war of 1703-5 had been reported in *Impartial Occurrences* and the making of the Treaty from 1706 in the *Dublin Gazette*. 60 DH, Parliamentary notes, A 817/3, pp 3, 38-43, 56-9, 60-3, 88-92; DH, Loudoun papers, 'Green Deed Box', bundle 1706/October-December; HL, Loudoun Scottish collection, box 23/LO 8831, /LO 8868, box 33/LO 9116, box 42/LO 9347, box 43/LO12573; *Reasons for dissolving the treaty of union betwixt Scotland and England in a letter to a Scots member of parliament, from one of his electors* (London, 1713).

extremes in the north of Scotland after the Forty-Five, most notably in the Highlands where state terrorism carried more than a hint of ethnic cleansing.[61] With such pervasive doubt and division, the case for the continuation of union remained a major polemical topic in the first half of the eighteenth century. Conversely, the extension of union to Ireland and especially the American colonies remained a maverick pursuit.[62]

Notwithstanding renewed grievances about English distrust provoked by Scotland's omission from the Militia Act of 1757 and resurgent desires for county and burgh reform in the 1780s, British national identity was promoted assiduously as patriotism and prosperity imbued by a common commitment to liberty and protestantism. Leading figures of the Scottish Enlightenment came to view themselves as the moral guardians of the British constitution established at the Revolution and consolidated by the Treaty of Union. Part of this guardianship was a reawakening interest in union all round which harmonised with contemporaneous British critiques of mercantilism that argued forcefully for the repeal of commercial restrictions on Ireland. Simultaneously, surveys of empire contrasted the integral partnership claimed for the Scots with the restricted access and impact of Ireland.[63] The extent to which there should be full legislative and commercial union with Ireland moved from the academic into the political arena following the American Revolution, when Irish radicalism and constitutional instability was perceived as a threat in England. Scots featured in two key initiatives undertaken under the auspices of William Cavendish-Bentinck, duke of Portland, erstwhile lord lieutenant of Ireland. In 1782, William Ogilvie promoted a scheme for union along federal lines – albeit he received

61 Macinnes, *Clanship, commerce and the House of Stuart*, pp 203–5, 210–17.   62 *A proper project for Scotland in a humble address to the peers for using their unitary application in the ensuing Parliament for having the union dissolv'd* (Glasgow, 1722); *An expostulatory address to the nobility and freeholders of Scotland shewing the monstrous folly as well as the ingratitude of the present unnatural rebellion, and the intended dissolution of the union by the arguments drawn from the antient constitution and present situation of that Kingdom. By a gentleman of that country* (London, 1745); Sir A. Murray, *The true interest of Great Britain, Ireland and our plantations: or, a proposal for making such an union between Great Britain and Ireland, and all our plantations, as that already made betwixt Scotland and England* (London, 1740).   63 A. Ferguson, *A sermon preached in the Ersh language to His Majesty's First Highland Regiment of Foot commanded by Lord John Murray at the Containment in Camberwell on 18 December 1745* (London, 1746); M. Postlethwayt, *Britain's commercial interest explained and improved, in a series of dissertations on several important branches of her trade and police ... Also the great advantage which would accrue to this kingdom from an union with Ireland* (London, 1757); J. Campbell, *A political survey of Britain: being a series of reflections on the situation, lands, inhabitants, revenues, colonies and commerce of this island*, 2 vols (London, 1774).

little encouragement from Irish parliamentarians. John Bruce, as keeper of the state papers, was subsequently commissioned to prepare a two volume report on the Anglo–Scottish union in order to establish favourable precedents for the political union of Britain and Ireland.[64] Scots also featured as collectors of historical documents relating to Britain and Ireland. These were not just harmless antiquarian pursuits but part of the cultural conditioning for eventual union.[65]

The threat perceived in England during the 1780s was compounded in the next decade by the French Revolution when Ireland, like Scotland prior to 1707, was seen as the back door to invasion from France. However, it was not until moves commenced in Westminster in support of catholic emancipation that the anglican ascendancy was convinced that incorporating union was a more attractive option than power sharing in Ireland. The relevance of the Scottish experience to the Irish situation was a constant subject of contention. Scottish pretensions to a partnership were thrown into sharp relief by the main thrust of debate – whether England's treatment of Scotland since 1707 manifested 'the fostering hand of a natural parent, or the cold neglect of a step-mother'. That Scotland's economic potential had been blunted rather than fulfilled by union was a theme taken up by Ulster critics. Robert Orr enhanced his political critique with reference to the reforming agenda of Fletcher of Saltoun and, more immediately, to his sympathetic association with the United Irishmen.[66] The Scottish reaction to the French Revolution, while less nationalist than the

---

64 Kelly, *Prelude to Union*, pp 44–9; J. Bruce, *Report on the events and circumstances, which produced the union of the kingdoms of England and Scotland*, 2 vols (London, 1799).   65 Sir J. Dalrymple, *Memoirs of Great Britain and Ireland* (London, 1790); E. Marshal, *The history of the union of Scotland and England: stating the circumstances which brought it to a conclusion, and the advantages resulting from it to the Scots* (Edinburgh, 1799). Daniel Defoe's highly partial history of the making of the Treaty of 1707 was reissued as D. De Foe, *The history of the union between England and Scotland* (London, 1786). In addition to a collection of germane original papers and an introduction in which the consequences and probability of a like union between Britain and Ireland were considered, the volume was prefixed with the life of Daniel Defoe by the Scottish historian, George Chalmers.   66 Kelly, 'Origins', pp 258–63; E. Cooke, *Arguments for and against an union, between Great Britain and Ireland, considered* (Dublin, 1798); J.J.W. Jervis, *A letter addressed to the gentlemen of England and Ireland, on the inexpediency of a federal union between the two kingdoms* (Dublin, 1798); Colonel Tytler, *Ireland profiting by example: or, the question, whether Scotland has gained, or lost, by an union with England, fairly discussed. In a letter, from a gentleman in Edinburgh, to his friend in Dublin* (Dublin, 1799); W. Johnson, *Reasons for adopting an union, between Ireland and Great Britain* (Dublin, 1799); R. Orr, *An address to the people of Ireland, against an union* (Dublin, 1799).

Irish, was arguably no less radical. The Scottish Friends of the People and
their later offshoot the United Scotsmen maintained fraternal links with the
United Irishmen, which made them subject to oppressive reprisals by a
reactionary British state who deployed show trials, selective executions and
transportation to Australia. Prominent in this British reaction was Henry
Dundas, the supreme political manager of Scotland, who was an assiduous
parliamentary promoter of legislative union with Ireland from 1799. His
political clients and associates were to the fore among Scots arguing this case
both at Westminster and in the country, based on the reputedly
advantageous experience that Scotland had enjoyed since 1707,
notwithstanding breaches of the Treaty and Jacobite reprisals.[67] In this
light, the eventual accomplishment of union for Ireland within two years can
be seen as a reactionary British endeavour. At the same time, the patriotic
and progressive connotations of incorporation for the British public have
left tangible legacies, notably Union Street as the main commercial artery in
the city of Aberdeen.

67 H. Dundas, *Substance of the speech of the Right Hon. Henry Dundas, in the House of
Commons, Thursday, February 7, 1799, on the subject of legislative union with Ireland*
(London, 1799); G. Elliot, earl of Minto, *The speech of the Lord Milton, in the House of
Peers, April 11, 1799, on a motion for an address to His Majesty, to communicate the
resolution of the two houses of Parliament, respecting an union between Great Britain and
Ireland* (London, 1799); S. Douglas of Glenbervie, *Speech of the Right Honourable
Sylvester Douglas in the House of Commons on Tuesday, April 23, 1799; on seconding the
motion of the Right Honourable Chancellor of the Exchequer, for the House to agree with the
Lords in an address to His Majesty, relative to a Union with Ireland* (Dublin, 1799);
Captain C. Kerr, *Strictures upon the union betwixt Great Britain and Ireland ... particularly
detailing the advantage derived to Scotland from her union with England* (Dublin, 1799).

5

Acts of union and disunion: Ireland in Atlantic and European contexts

James Livesey

The Acts of Union of 1707 and 1800 are obvious topics for the 'New British' or 'Atlantic' history. Investigating the creation of British identity, along with the resistance to that process, has been the dominant research agenda for scholars in this area ever since Pocock made his plea for a new subject.[1] The 'war of the three kingdoms' had provided the main focus for this work, but Colley's provocative study encouraged more attention to be paid to the 'long eighteenth century'. Recent volumes have generally sought to capture the extension of British identity outside the island of Britain and have stressed the importance of the Irish example to understanding the fortunes of Britishness.[2] The dramatic events of the 1790s, including the Act of Union, are also beginning to be treated from this perspective.[3] While this new approach does generate valuable insights, the meaning and importance of the Irish Act of Union is misapprehended when viewed solely through this optic. Through closer analysis we can see that the two acts of union, but especially that of 1800, were local responses to problems faced by all European states in the eighteenth century, not just the

1 J.G. Pocock, 'British history: A plea for a new subject' in *Journal of Modern History*, xlvii (1975), pp 601-21. 2 R. Asch (ed.), *Three nations – a common history? England, Scotland, Ireland and British history c.1600-1920* (Bochum, 1993); S. Ellis & S. Barber (eds), *Conquest and union: fashioning a British state 1485-1725* (London, 1995); A. Grant & K. Stringer (eds), *Uniting the Kingdom? The making of British history* (London, 1995); B. Bradshaw & J. Morrill (eds), *The British problem c1534-1707: state formation in the Atlantic archipelago* (Basingstoke, 1996); L. Brockliss & D. Eastwood (eds), *A union of multiple identities: the British Isles c.1750-c.1850* (Manchester, 1997); B. Bradshaw & P. Roberts (eds), *British consciousness and identity: the making of Britain 1533-1707* (Cambridge, 1998); T. Claydon & I. McBride (eds), *Protestantism and national identity: Britain and Ireland c1650- c.1850* (Cambridge, 1998). 3 J. Smyth (ed.), *Revolution, counter-revolution, and the Union: Ireland in the 1790s* (Cambridge, 2001).

Atlantic islands. Edinburgh and Dublin were not the only cities in which privileged representative assemblies, and the elites that staffed them, had to work out their relationship to monarchies that were increasingly impatient of intermediary bodies.[4] The political and institutional options faced by the British state and by the Dublin parliament in the 1790s can be usefully illuminated by comparison with those of the Belgians, Austrians, Poles and Russians. Across Europe, venerable institutional arrangements, and the political cultures that sustained them, came under pressure after the 1760s, and the results of those pressures were remarkably similar.

THE ACT OF UNION IN BRITISH AND ATLANTIC PERSPECTIVE

One of the major attractions of a comparative approach, be it Atlantic or European, to understanding the acts of union is the difficulty faced in integrating the various acts within national histories. It is awkward to make an event that extinguishes the national political institutions into a constitutive element of the emergence of the nation. In consequence Scottish historiography downplays the significance of the union of 1707 and narrates the history of the nation in spheres outside politics.[5] The union is similarly external to the narrative of local Irish affairs, but this has not stopped the production of fine institutional and political histories of the events. Irish political history circles around the union but rarely uses the union to explain its features. The origins of the union do not suffer from this problem; Geoghegan's recent revision of Bolton's work shows how fruitful the high political approach can be to understanding the genesis of the union itself.[6] However, general histories cannot make the union constitutive of local developments, except in a negative way. Even Foster's fair-minded history of Ireland only devotes three pages to an analysis of the local effects of the union.[7] There is a surprising lack of analysis of the economic effects of the transformed political status of Ireland.[8] Having debunked the political

4 For an overview of these kinds of relations in eastern Europe, see M. Raeff, *The well-ordered police state: social and institutional change through law in the Germanies and Russia 1600-1800* (New Haven, 1983). 5 A good example is T. Devine, 'The Union of 1707 and Scottish development' in *Scottish Economic and Social History*, v (1985), pp 23-40. 6 Geoghegan, *Union*; Bolton, *Act of Union.* 7 R. Foster, *Modern Ireland 1600-1972* (London, 1988), pp 289-91. 8 R. Weir, 'The Scottish and Irish unions: the Victorian view in perspective' in S. Connolly (ed.), *Kingdoms united? Great Britain and Ireland since 1500: integration and diversity* (Dublin, 1999), p. 59. An exception is F. Geary, 'The Act of Union, British-Irish trade and pre-famine deindustrialization' in *Economic History*

rhetoric of 'planned underdevelopment', economic historians have been largely content to let matters lie.[9] The inability to locate the union within the complexities of the development of social, economic and cultural life in 'these islands' leaves it still to be understood within the categories of nineteenth-century politics.[10] The point here is not that nobody but unionists sees the union as a 'good thing' (the other option is as a 'lost opportunity') but that we lack the context and categories to understand the meaning, nature and effect of the union as part of historical process.[11] Irish historians, who have produced a compelling array of tools for the interpretation and contextualisation of nationalist historical self-understanding, have not been so active in revising and renewing categories of historical explanation that might comprehend the union as anything other than a political option.

'New British' and 'Atlantic' histories offer better grounds than the national histories of Scotland and Ireland from which the two acts of union might be understood. There are sufficiently compelling parallels between them to support the notion of a common context. In both 1707 and 1800 Britain was in conflict with France against French hegemony in Europe. The needs of war and the imperative for civic peace drove processes of organisation of the islands to resist 'universal monarchy', be it that of Louis XIV or of republican France. John Bruce's account of the 1707 union, produced in order to illuminate the issues at stake in the 1790s, made the continuity explicit:

> The union, by consolidating the strength of Great Britain, and by giving equal opportunities to the subjects of every description for the exercise of industry, has not only enabled Great Britain to add to its political and commercial influence, and to preserve the balance of power in Europe for a century, but when that balance has ceased to be upheld by the continental powers, to maintain its own power and trade against the unprincipled Republic of France, now sweeping before it the venerable fabrics of ancient arts and civilisations.[12]

Review, xlviii (1995), pp 68–88.   **9** L.M. Cullen, 'Irish economic history: fact and myth' in *The formation of the Irish economy* (Cork, 1969), pp 113–5; C. Ó Gráda, *Ireland: a new economic history 1780–1939* (Oxford, 1994), pp 307–8.   **10** The point is developed in D. Johnson & L. Kennedy, 'The union of Ireland and Britain 1801–1921' in D.G. Boyce & A. O'Day (eds), *The making of modern Irish history* (London, 1996), pp 34–70.   **11** J. Loughlin, '"Imagining Ulster:" The north of Ireland and British national identity 1880–1921' in Connolly (ed.), *Kingdoms united?*, pp 109–22.   **12** [J. Bruce], *Report on the events and circumstances which produced the union of the kingdoms of England and Scotland*, 2 vols (London, 1799), i, p. 402.

Scottish insistence on separately recognising the Hanoverian succession
and Irish inability to contain local opposition within the constitution drove
the imperial centre to impose new political arrangements in both cases. Pitt
made this analogy explicit in his speech in favour of the union and he was
simply restating the common wisdom in London.[13] Nor was the assertion of
the needs of the imperial state a contingent event. Local politicians had been
well aware in both Scotland and Ireland that any domestic settlement would
have to respect and include the larger and more powerful neighbour. Grattan
had been particularly anxious to stabilise the relationship between the
Dublin parliament and the London executive from 1782 and, as Pitt again
pointed out, the attempt to formalise economic relations in 1785 underlined
the necessary interconnections.[14] The analogy of Ireland to Scotland allowed
proponents of union to argue that just as Scotland had flourished when it
abandoned its imperfect parliamentary tradition and been absorbed in the
more developed tradition of English liberty, so too would Ireland.[15] Clearly
the strategic need for the expanding British state to integrate elements of its
dominion explains some of the rationale for both Scottish and Irish acts of
union. Yet the needs of the emerging British state hardly offer the widest
access to the logic of British history. When doing British history it is tempting to see the islands only from the perspective of one of the few institutions
which necessarily adopted a genuinely inclusive perspective, the London
cabinet. Objections to using this frame are almost too obvious. Seeing the
agency in 'New British' history as that of the needs of a putative British
Atlantic state, and so state elite, is exactly what the critics of such a history
have most objected to from its first conceptualisation.[16]

However, British statesmen were not the only people using the 'British
Isles' context to explicate the meaning of the proposed union in 1800. The
pamphlet debate was also riddled with references to the 1707 example. The
cabinet itself republished Defoe's contributions to the earlier debate and
produced a compendium of the constitutional arguments of 1707.[17] The
use of the Scottish example went far beyond these state actors. The fate of
Scotland under the union became a central image through which political

13 *The speech of the Right Honorable William Pitt in the British House of Commons,
January 31 1799* (London, 1800), p. 10.   14 Pitt, *Speech*, p. 18.   15 [Bruce], *Report*, i,
p. 376. On the extinction of the Scottish constitutional tradition, see C. Kidd, *Subverting
Scotland's past: Scottish whig historians and the creation of an Anglo-British identity 1689-
1830* (Cambridge, 1993).   16 K. Brown, 'British history: a skeptical comment' in Asch
(ed.), *Three nations*, pp 117-27.   17 D. Defoe, *The history of the union between England
and Scotland* (Dublin, 1799); G. Lockhart, *Memoirs concerning the affairs of Scotland from
Queen Anne's accession to the throne to the commencement of the union in May 1707* (Dublin,
1799); [Bruce], *Report*.

opponents expressed themselves. Moreover the languages of politics used to debate the Scottish measure (ancient constitutions, conquest theory, regnal status within composite states and ecclesiastical polity) were made relevant to Ireland and were used to structure the local debate.[18] Proponents of union argued that Scotland had flourished as a direct result of the union of 1707 and its subsequent participation in the English ancient constitution: opponents denied this and claimed that the union had merely opened Scots to English disdain.[19] Joshua Spencer's pamphlet is a good example of how the Scottish exemplar illuminated the Irish discussion.[20] Spencer used a characteristic mixture of enlightenment social science and British ancient constitutionalist rhetoric to argue against the union. He even made a classic alignment of civic virtue with the ancient constitution of the country in his argument that the United Irishmen had been defeated through the efforts of the Irish political nation itself; 'it was to protect and maintain the present constitution of Ireland that the astonishing spectacle of the Irish yeomanry was displayed'.[21] Both opponents and proponents of union converged on a British language of politics informed by previous British experience.

It proved impossible to sustain the imagined equivalence of the Scottish and Irish kingdoms in the creation of a composite monarchy of the British Isles or the strained fiction of equal ownership of the 'ancient constitution.' Even figures who attempted to use this rhetoric, like Cooke, were driven to admit the curious position of Ireland as a dependent kingdom. He argued that 'in the situation which Scotland held previous to the union does Ireland stand at present, except that the crown of Ireland is by express statutes of declaration and recognition perpetually annexed to and dependent on the crown of England.'[22] This asserted, in effect, that Ireland did not have an imperial crown and so lacked sovereignty. Other commentators were less polite in undermining the pretensions to constitutional propriety in the

18 For those languages see J. Robertson (ed.), *A union for empire: political thought and the British union of 1707* (Cambridge, 1995) and W. Ferguson, 'Imperial crowns: A neglected facet to the background of the Treaty of Union' in *SHR*, lii (1974), pp 22-44. On composite monarchies, see G. Koenigsberger, '*Dominium regale* or *dominium politicum et regale*' in *Politicians and virtuosi: essays in early-modern history* (London, 1986); G. Koenigsberger, 'Composite states, representative institutions and the American Revolution', *Historical Research*, cxlviii (1989), pp 135-53; J.H. Elliot, 'A Europe of composite monarchies' in *Past and Present*, cxxxvii (1992), pp 48-71.   19 A. Tytler, *Ireland profiting by example, or the question whether Scotland has gained or lost by union with England fairly discussed* (Dublin, 1799); M. Weld, *No Union! being an appeal to Irishmen* (Dublin, 1798).   20 J. Spencer, *Thoughts on an union* (Dublin, 1798).   21 Spencer, *Thoughts*, p. 29.   22 E. Cooke, *Arguments for and against an union between Great Britain and Ireland considered* (Dublin, 1798), p. 15.

union debate. An anonymous pamphleteer rejected the whole language of 'constitutionality' and 'sister kingdoms' as an illusion, an unfortunate consequence of unwitting extension of English ideas to where they did not apply:

> If we had granted independence to the most wretched, ill-governed and dependent colony on the surface of the globe; if we had dignified with the name of sister kingdom a settlement of English who had neither subdued nor gained the country they inhabited ... should we be totally exempt from the folly or the fault of the planter whose ideas we had bewildered and confused?[23]

Making an analogy between the terms of Scottish union and the condition of Ireland was, in the mind of this pamphleteer, an insult to the Scots: 'in the Scottish union I am at a loss to discover any circumstances of resemblance to the present measure, besides the accidental union of the two crowns on the same head. Was Scotland a colony of ours? Was Scotland planted and watered by our hand? Had it grown and flourished under our protecting shade?'[24] Even less hostile commentators could not bring themselves to participate in the use of these languages of collective identity. An address to the catholics of Ireland urging support for the union despaired over the use of the language of constitutionalism; 'I have heard a great deal said about our political constitution, independent legislature, and many things of this nature, and that nothing should induce us to surrender these blessings – good God, how long are we to be amused, or rather abused, with names and forms.'[25]

The example of Scotland was of limited use to understand the issues of the Irish union. Ireland was a dependent kingdom not an imperial crown and therefore it was impossible to understand the union as the conjunction of two constitutional traditions. The very language of ancient constitutionalism was a total anachronism in any case. The United Irishmen had taught a generation to articulate their politics in terms of rights and abstractions rather than around concrete traditions of political behaviour.[26] The idea of an ancient constitution was under tremendous strain even in Britain. In the aftermath of the 1707 union and particularly after Britain's

23 *Considerations upon the state of public affairs in the year 1799: Ireland* (Dublin, 1799), p. 12.   24 *Considerations*, p. 27.   25 *Union or separation* (Dublin, 1798), p. 6.   26 K. Whelan, 'The republic in the village: the United Irishmen, the enlightenment and popular culture' in *The tree of liberty: radicalism, catholicism and the construction of Irish identity 1760-1830* (Cork, 1996), pp 59-96.

victory in the Seven Years War, the notion of a particular English liberty that had been extended to Scotland became incredible.[27] The American conflict in particular had driven Scots to argue that British liberty had nothing to do with the English constitutional tradition.[28] The old languages were simply inappropriate to the political life of such an extensive empire. The union simply made no sense as the accession to British liberty by a constituent element of the once composite monarchy.

IRELAND, SCOTLAND AND THE END OF THE ANCIEN RÉGIME

The Atlantic or 'New British' frame is insufficient of itself to rescue us from an ideological or politicised understanding of the union. Instead we have to see how the Atlantic history, in which Ireland and Scotland undoubtedly participated, relates to and forms part of general European history. When we turn our attention toward continental Europe, we can see the Act of Union of 1800 not as the second of two moments in the creation of the United Kingdom but as one of a plethora of European territorial dismemberments and integrations performed between 1770 and 1815.[29] Between those dates the most spectacular territorial revision was the disappearance of Poland. However Poland was not alone in suffering this fate. All of the Netherlands, both Austrian and United Provinces, were conjoined to France during the height of the Napoleonic empire. The Holy Roman empire, like Poland, ceased to exist and Italy was completely reorganised. The map of Europe would not be as fluid again until the aftermath of the First World War.

One of the forces that drove the territorial re-organisation was the French Revolution and resistance to it. Ireland was particularly affected by French developments. The Irish Act of Union would have been impossible had the United Irishmen succeeded in aligning the country with revolutionary France. Other innovations were also driven by the actions of the revolutionary state. However, it would be a mistake to replace a history driven by the British state with one driven by the French. The French Revolution did not cause the crisis in the international system and the

27 J. Robertson, 'Universal monarchy and the liberties of Europe: David Hume's critique of an English whig doctrine' in *A Union for empire*, pp 349–73. 28 A. Skinner, 'Adam Smith and America: the political economy of conflict' in R. Sher & A. Smitten (eds), *Scotland and America in the age of the enlightenment* (Edinburgh, 1990), pp 148–62. 29 The best synthetic account of this process is F. Venturi, *The end of the Old Regime in Europe 1776-1789*; ii: *Republican patriotism and the empires of the east* (Princeton, 1991).

political elements that comprised it. Rather the Revolution was itself caused
by such instability.[30] It is often forgotten that the French were the fifth
European people to revolt in the 1780s following in the footsteps of the
Genevans, Poles, Dutch and Belgians. In all of these polities, crisis emerged
from increased tensions between the executive, be it crown or stadtholder,
the privileged representative bodies, from aristocratic *sjem* to Paris *parlement*
and a new force called 'public opinion'. The outcomes of these crises were
variable, ranging from the complete collapse of Poland to the revolutionary
transformation of France, but they all had one common feature. In every
case the old corporate representative bodies, guardians of the 'constitution',
were eliminated. Monarchs seemed to be most threatened by the revolutionary crisis, but many monarchs survived it. No corporate bodies survived,
unless one includes the British parliament. A new politics of nations could
comprehend opposed notions of legitimacy and legality, of authority and
democracy (indeed these polarities would be constitutive of nineteenth-
century politics) but the new politics could not and did not find a role for ·
local representative institutions.

Belgium, or more properly the Austrian Netherlands, illustrates the
dynamics of this period and their relevance to Ireland particularly well. Up
to 1780 the ten provinces of the Austrian Netherlands were a museum of
medieval constitutional forms and corporate privileges. The ancient constitutions were not disturbed by radicals and revolutionaries but by the
emperor, Joseph II. In 1780, he began a programme of modernisation that
climaxed in 1787 in a wholesale reorganisation of the judicial system. The
revolution of 1789 in Brabant was a deeply conservative reassertion of local
and specific traditions, of a piece with the politics of 1782 in Ireland. Exactly
the same dynamic was generated in Belgium as that in Ireland as the initial
movement of resistance to the central power split into conservative and
reforming wings. The effect of the revolution was to make the defence of
the ancient constitutions against the despotism of monarchs irrelevant. By
1792 the political options for Belgians were between the monarchy and
democracy. They either had to accede to the Austrian or the French model
for a modern polity. The ancient constitution had become an irrelevance and
the old structures, estates, courts, and the *joyeuse entrée* that defined them a
museum piece. Belgian inability to stabilise their politics and to reconcile
themselves to their viable political options meant that they would eventually

30 Paul Schroeder argues strongly that the instabilities in the international system were
a major cause of domestic unrest; P. Schroeder, *The transformation of European politics
1763-1848* (Oxford, 1994), pp 1-52.

suffer the same fate as Poland, absorption into the territory of the local power. The parallel with Ireland is almost exact. In both cases defence of the constitution became politically untenable but the inability of local elites to create new political options would spell the end of their political independence.

We can gauge how quickly the politics of privileged bodies collapsed in Ireland through an examination of the changes of the idioms through which political opinion was expressed. In 1792 the 'constitutional idiom' was alive and well.[31] Tone's arguments in favour of catholic emancipation were staged within a venerable language of political reform.[32] Adherence to the principles of the French Revolution did not at that point demand abandonment of the local and specific languages of British liberty. Tobias Molloy, a United Irishman, had not 'recorded any event in the moral and political world, so superlatively astonishing to the mental eye at first sight, or so rationally interesting on sober reflection, as the late Revolution in France', but what drew his rational interest was the analogy he found between 1688 and 1789.[33] For Molloy the goal of reform was to have Ireland an 'imperial, independent, sister kingdom' and so to enhance the 'happiness and rational liberty enjoyed individually and collectively, publicly and privately, by Britons and Hibernians.'[34] After 1798 this was not a tenable position or even language. Arguments in favour of the old constitutional order were now about the defence of privilege.[35] Analyses of the situation, be they from left or right, had to be couched in different terms. Andrew Finlay's pro-union argument bluntly posed the options of joining two imperial systems, French or British, and stated that the term under which such issues were discussed was 'that never failing bond of union, *mutual interest*'.[36] This echoed Cooke's comment that the French had set the terms of unity and indivisibility for any polity that hoped to survive in contemporary conditions, 'supposing there were no other reasons which rendered the union of the sister kingdoms desirable, the state of Europe, and especially of France, seems to dictate it'.[37] The implicit comparison with the old corporate states on the continent was also made explicit by Cooke: 'all

31 J. Epstein, 'The constitutionalist idiom' in *Radical expression: political language, ritual and symbol in England 1790-1850* (Oxford, 1994), p. 9. 32 T. Wolfe Tone, *An argument on behalf of the catholics of Ireland in which the present political state of that country and the necessity of a parliamentary reform are considered* (Dublin, 1791). 33 T. Molloy, *An appeal from man in a state of civil society to man in a state of nature* (Dublin, 1792), pp 10-11. 34 Molloy, *Appeal*, p. 257. 35 R. Gower, *Hosier's Hall* (Dublin, 1798). 36 A. Finlay, *A view of the interests of Ireland, as connected with Great Britain or France* (Dublin, 1803), p. 14. 37 Cooke, *Arguments*, pp 12-13.

writers have agreed in condemning what is called *imperium in imperio*. It is this vice of constitution which has annihilated Poland, where every senator was a sovereign and has enslaved the Seven United Provinces, where every province was a sovereign.'[38] The constitution had ceased to be the keystone of political discourse and become a vice.

The most brilliant interpretation of the project of union from this perspective was William Drennan's. Drennan completely understood that the logic of military competition was driving the creation of ultimately similar unitary states in Britain and France: 'in the uniform habit of cursing and mimicing the French Revolution, your inverted order ends where it began, by decreeing the unity and indivisibility of the empire'.[39] Drennan explained that the essence of the union was extinguishing the intermediary bodies. He argued in a complex and dialectical style that the union would eventually frustrate its own ends. Union would destroy union; 'he will take the middle term out of the Irish constitution and will leave nothing but king and people, the monarch seen only through the medium of military rule, and the people having no other object to which they can ascribe their grievances, but the crown'.[40]

The Irish parliament was a privileged representative body and fell victim to the same dynamics that eliminated the Genevan small council, the council of ten in Venice or the *joyeuse entrée* in Brabant. In all cases any ground between the claim by societies to represent themselves, expressed as public opinion and eventually as nationalism, and the claim to authority of central states disappeared. The privilege of local authority was no longer credible, all authority was now imperial or national. Tellingly, though William Pitt argued that the Irish parliament enjoyed sufficient sovereignty to agree to union, he did not think it sufficiently sovereign to negotiate it.[41] Ireland's parliament was considered as the provincial legislature for an element of the polity, not as a truly sovereign body. Such a reversal of status was very common in the revolutionary decades. The most dramatic example was the disappearance of the republic of Venice in 1797. This would have been unthinkable ten years before; indeed the republic had been the longest existing political institution in Europe. However, its constitution was neither monarchical nor popular and so it could be literally traded away as the elements of the European political system sought to stabilise their relationships. By 1800 the Irish parliament had become an anomaly. It represented neither the nation nor the monarch and so was unacceptable to

38 Ibid., p. 20.   39 W. Drennan, *Letter to the Right Honourable William Pitt* (Dublin, 1799), p. 4.   40 Ibid., p. 19.   41 Pitt, *Speech*, pp 36–8.

both. The only real political question was what would replace it, either a new revolutionary regime or some sort of incorporating union.

Viewed from this perspective the partiality of the union becomes its most important element. Here indeed is what the Scottish comparison explains. The example of the 1707 act of union, made in a very different time and with different strategic ends in view, was the model for Ireland. That first union had not sought to make a new nation and neither would that of 1800. Only sovereignty was transferred; local social, legal, religious and educational structures were all left in place. The alternative would have been to mimic the absorption of Poland into Austria, Prussia and Russia, or indeed that of Wales into England. However, the model of union which had created Britain was more important than the contemporary or medieval examples. Therefore Irish civil society would be largely unaffected by the transformation of the polity, just as Scotland's had been.

CONCLUSION

By seeing the Act of Union of 1800 in both Atlantic and European contexts, we can see more clearly its distinctive features. A result of the revolutionary changes to the European states' system, the Irish Act of Union nevertheless took the form of the closer integration of an element of a multiple or composite monarchy. Sovereignty was transferred, but nothing else. If we reposition the Irish Act of Union in this way as the disestablishment of a privileged corporate body, rather than the loss of national representation, we can recognise why Repeal could be an effective political slogan while never being a political programme. Repeal of the union was impossible as the kind of corporate society that underpinned the old institutions could never be recreated. In political memory the Irish parliament could become the sovereign body it never was and the model for a sovereign body to be. Union, ironically, aided the project of nationalism by eliminating the keystone of a corporate order.

6

Camden and the move towards union
1795-1798

Gillian O'Brien

'Ireland must be our province if she will not be persuaded to a union.'[1] There was little novel in the idea of a union between Britain and Ireland. It had been sporadically suggested since Cromwellian times but advocates of union had been unable to generate the necessary support for such a measure. Demands for union between the kingdoms had never coincided. In Ireland, calls for union climaxed with an appeal to Queen Anne in 1707. This was casually dismissed. In the last quarter of the eighteenth century, the British government recognised union as the safest means of managing the sister kingdom; however, Irish patriot opinion refused to countenance any such notion.[2] As the 1790s progressed, the Irish administration found it increasingly difficult to handle the series of financial and security crises that threatened the stability of the country. These problems peaked with the outbreak of rebellion in May 1798. Rebellion terrified the Irish protestant political elite and infuriated the politicians in Westminster. This combination of fear and indignation offered the prime minister, William Pitt, the opportunity to advance an act of union with the support of both administrations. The 1798 rebellion was the catalyst but events in 1796 and 1797 had moved the political elites in both countries inexorably towards union.

John Jeffreys Pratt, second Earl Camden, was appointed lord lieutenant of Ireland in March 1795, replacing Earl Fitzwilliam. Sandwiched between Fitzwilliam and Cornwallis, both imposing viceroys, Camden's time in Ireland has been overlooked by historians. Fitzwilliam's dramatic and turbulent lord lieutenancy has been the subject of an impressive number of studies.[3] Cornwallis, Camden's successor, was responsible for quashing the

---

1 Lord Bayham (later Earl Camden) to R. Stewart, 4 Feb. 1793, *Castlereagh corr.*, i, pp 156-9. 2 Kelly, 'Origins'; Lecky, *Ire.*, v, pp 120-50. 3 Lord Ashbourne, *Pitt: some chapters of his life and times* (London, 1898), pp 180-229; J.H. Rose, 'Pitt and

1798 Rebellion and facilitating the union between Britain and Ireland. Camden's career was neither sensational or glorious; he was not an innovator, nor was he the 'most decided character in public or private matters'.[4] Nevertheless, his contribution towards defining Anglo-Irish relations is significant since it was during his tenure of office that the first real steps were taken leading to the Act of Union.

The controversial circumstances of Fitzwilliam's recall made the prompt appointment of a successor of paramount importance if control of the Irish administration was to be maintained. In the space of six turbulent weeks, the old guard had been changed, new liberal appointments made, peerages pledged and the promise of a favourable hearing of catholic grievances given. The self-appointed defenders of the protestant interest in Ireland regarded Fitzwilliam's appointment as an act of betrayal; Pitt had sacrificed Ireland for his own advantage, allowing the Portland whigs to use Ireland as their private playground in return for supporting his government. In the circumstances, with Britain engaged in war with France, this appeared a reasonable compromise. What had seemed a sensible and pragmatic solution during 1794 was no longer an option. A loyal, and hopefully subservient, ally was required. Pitt characteristically looked to an old friend to take on this task and his attention focussed on Camden who had attended Cambridge with the prime minister and was a junior lord of the treasury. Camden appeared an ideal choice. He had previously been considered for the post in June 1794 during Westmorland's lord lieutenancy.[5] More importantly, Camden's loyalty to Pitt was unquestioned and he was recognised as a capable if unimaginative administrator. He had publicly declared in 1785 that Ireland should be dependent on England:

> Ireland, more especially the Protestant part of it, will come at last to understand that free and independent as she is, she can never hope to enjoy that freedom or independence without the protection of England unless she shall choose to ask it upon her knees from France.[6]

Earl Fitzwilliam' in *Pitt and Napoleon* (London, 1912), pp 20-36; R.B. McDowell, 'The Fitzwilliam episode', *IHS*, xvi (1966), pp 115-30; E.A. Smith, *Whig principles and party politics. Earl Fitzwilliam and the whig party 1748-1833* (Manchester, 1975); McDowell, *Ireland*, pp 445-61; D. Lindsay, 'The Fitzwilliam episode revisited', in Dickson *et al.* (eds), *United Irishmen*, pp 197-208; D. Wilkinson, 'The Fitzwilliam episode, 1795: a reinterpretation of the role of the Duke of Portland', in *IHS*, xxxiv (1995), pp 315-39. **4** Lord Essex to Lord Lowther, 10 Mar. 1806 in HMC, *Manuscripts of the 1st Earl of Lonsdale*, 13th Report, appendix vii (London, 1893), p. 174. **5** Camden to R. Stewart, 28 June 1794, *Castlereagh corr.*, i, pp 159-60. **6** Camden to R. Stewart, 25 Aug. 1785,

He was also known to be pro-union and, while Fitzwilliam's recall was not prompted by a desire to bring about a union, it could only be advantageous for Whitehall to have a man in Dublin who supported the maintenance of strong ties with Britain.

The Fitzwilliam episode highlighted shortcomings in the relationship between Downing Street and Dublin Castle. Fitzwilliam was condemned by Downing Street for having made decisions, taken action and proposed legislation without first consulting London. Camden reluctantly agreed to replace Fitzwilliam. He feared that the urgency of the appointment coupled with 'the real state of Ireland not being known, and the sentiments of the English cabinet not being completely decided, as to the future measures to be pursued' would render him at a disadvantage as the new lord lieutenant.[7] To prevent any confusion over Camden's role in Ireland, the home secretary, Portland, composed a carefully drafted twelve-page letter that was received by the new viceroy before he left for Ireland. Camden was to be the voice of the British government in Ireland and was to consolidate the position of lord lieutenant. Portland assured him that it would never be necessary that 'a Lord Lieu[tenan]t should commit himself for the responsibility of any measure which must undergo Parliamentary discussion'. Downing Street, not Dublin Castle, would direct Irish policy. Catholic emancipation would not be granted but some concessions were advised; the idea of establishing a catholic college was enthusiastically encouraged.[8] The Protestant Ascendancy required much support and reassurance; Portland suggested that this could be delivered if Camden arrived in Ireland using 'firm and decided language' and promptly established his loyalist credentials. It was relatively simple to deal with the issues that concerned the privileged elite who had suffered during Fitzwilliam's tenure – they were easily satisfied as many of their grievances could quickly be remedied. Other groups would not be placated so swiftly since their demands would not be met. Camden attempted to conciliate Fitzwilliam's supporters. While those who had been promoted would lose their positions of influence, the new lord lieutenant was to avoid unnecessary alienation of these men and make efforts to win their acquiescence, if not their approbation. Finally, and perhaps most surprisingly, Camden was warned to be sensitive when dealing with the question of the 'Irish cabinet'. Portland warned that the cabinet was thought unconstitutional and 'subversive of English government and of the unity of the British empire'.[9]

quoted in Bartlett, *Fall and rise*, p. 319.   **7** Camden to Pitt, 7 Mar. 1795, CKS, U840 0142A/1.   **8** Maynooth College was established in June 1795.   **9** Portland to Camden, 26 Mar. 1795, CKS, U840 0142A/3.   **10** H. Grattan to [Laurence], 11

The 'Irish cabinet' did not exist in any legal sense. Unofficial as it was, the self-appointed members regarded themselves as forming a cabinet as real as that in Whitehall. The men who comprised the 'cabinet' were formidable figures. They effectively managed the day-to-day running of the country and heavily influenced the disposal of patronage, causing Henry Grattan to complain that 'the patronage of the crown is engrossed by a cabal.'[10] The most significant members of this 'cabinet' or 'cabal' were John Beresford, the chief revenue commissioner; John Foster, the speaker of the house of commons; John Fitzgibbon, Lord Clare, the lord chancellor; Sir John Parnell, the chancellor of the exchequer; and Charles Agar, archbishop of Cashel.[11] They greeted Camden's appointment with cautious approval. It was regarded as a vindication of themselves; they had objected to Fitzwilliam and he had been recalled. The new lord lieutenant was regarded as a facilitator of their own ends and as such they approved him. Support was guaranteed only if Camden accepted the role that they had designated for him – a figurehead; signing documents, relaying messages between Dublin and London and hosting lavish banquets. Mindful of Portland's warning, Camden refused to acquiesce in all the demands of his 'cabinet' and they were regularly reminded that ultimately their privileged positions relied solely on the good opinion of the lord lieutenant and the ministers in London. Camden's uneasy relationship with the men who formed his government in Ireland greatly influenced the effectiveness and direction of his administration and as a consequence impacted heavily on the relationship between England and Ireland in the years prior to union.

Within weeks of Camden's arrival in Ireland, it was apparent that the promise of active support from Whitehall would not be kept. Pitt had little interest in Irish affairs, as Camden noted in a letter to the prime minister; 'you candidly acknowledged to me ... that Ireland occupies little of your thoughts'.[12] Instead, Camden relied heavily on the advice of his chief secretary, Thomas Pelham, who proved a valuable ally. An experienced and effective administrator, he had served in Ireland under Lord Northington

Dec. 1796, McPeake papers, PRONI, T3048/A/10. **11** Beresford had been chief revenue commissioner since 1780. He had been removed from office by Fitzwilliam in January 1795 but was reinstated by Camden in March of the same year and remained in that position until 1802. Foster was speaker of the Irish House of Commons, 1785-1800. Fitzgibbon, later earl of Clare, was Irish lord chancellor from 1789 until 1801. Sir John Parnell was chancellor of the Irish Exchequer between 1785 and 1799; Charles Agar was archbishop of Cashel from 1779 until he was appointed archbishop of Dublin in 1801. **12** Camden to Pitt, 6 May 1796, quoted in McDowell, *Ireland*, p. 520.

in 1783-4, but his chief advantage to Camden was his popularity among the groups that combined to make up the Irish and British political communities. However, Pelham suffered bouts of ill health and spent much of his time in England. He repeatedly asked to be replaced but Camden, anxious to retain his service, argued 'there is no person so agreeable to me and whose services will be so advantageous to the public'.[13] Pelham agreed to remain as chief secretary, but continued to spend many months in England. While Camden lamented these long absences, his presence in London provided the Irish administration with immediate access to British ministers. In December 1797, he was permanently, if not officially, replaced by Camden's step-nephew, Lord Castlereagh. Despite his illness and his public requests to retire, Pelham's contribution to Camden's administration was invaluable.

By the summer of 1795, it had become apparent that Camden was required to be far more than a mere mouthpiece for Pitt and his government. Whitehall remained silent when advice was requested. In Ireland, Camden found himself without allies. Many in parliament and beyond were hostile to his presence and those who accepted him did so with reservations. His closest advisor, Pelham, though a diligent correspondent, was absent from Ireland. These factors ensured that the consolidation of British control in Ireland would prove Camden's most arduous task. A delicate balancing act was necessary and Camden soon found himself accountable to two distinct groups, one in Whitehall, the other in Dublin Castle and College Green. Camden was obliged to concede some control to the powerful 'Irish cabinet' while his official masters ignored his requests and gave little practical guidance in times of crisis.

I

The American War of Independence, beginning in 1776, impacted heavily on the army in Ireland. As a consequence of the thirteen colonies' revolt, many soldiers were ordered from Ireland and stationed overseas. The Volunteers were established as a response to this and were intended to protect Ireland from any possible invasion. Never officially sanctioned by the Irish administration, the Volunteers were a formidable private army, funded and commanded by the protestant elite. The Volunteers soon developed far beyond their original purpose and played a significant part in the patriot movement that achieved legislative independence in 1782. After the French

13 Camden to Pitt, 18 Nov. 1795, Chatham papers, PRO HO, 30 8 326/48.

declaration of war on Britain in February 1793, troops were again assigned overseas but this time there would be no Volunteers. They had proved too independent in the past and Camden refused to countenance the idea when it was proposed by Lords Mountjoy and Carhampton.[14] Rather Camden relied on the largely Catholic militias, established in 1793, and later the yeomanry, a force whose formation Camden had initially opposed but upon whom he came to rely during the crisis at Bantry Bay in 1796.[15]

Military matters were the focus of many dispatches that passed between England and Ireland. Official political and military communications between London and Dublin were rare; letters sent from Dublin regularly went unanswered. Camden was critical of such neglect, writing to Pitt in July 1795:

> I wish only to remind you of not only your engagement but that of all your colleagues that intelligence should be sent to the Ld Lt of Ireland regularly whenever it arrived. I did not request this in order to satisfy my own curiosity but I then considered it as a respect done to the Office to have such communication made to it. I am now convinced of its propriety and indeed necessity.[16]

The relationship with the English military and naval commands was far worse than that with Whitehall. Regiments were summoned to England at a moment's notice with little regard for the defence of Ireland. Following complaints, George III's son, Fredrick, duke of York, promised to improve communication between the British army and Irish administration:

> I am thoroughly sensible of the propriety and necessity of giving the Lord Lieutenant ... the earliest intelligence of any proposed change or alteration in the troops in Ireland, and will take care that you shall be regularly informed in future.[17]

Vague efforts were made to boost the morale of the army in Ireland. A visit by York was mooted in autumn 1795 and again in spring 1796.[18] However,

---

14 Camden to Pelham, 3 Oct. 1795, Pelham papers, BL, Add. Ms 33101/306; Cooke to Auckland, 3 Sept. 1796, Auckland papers, BL, Add. Ms 34454/59. 15 A. Blackstock, *An ascendancy army: the Irish yeomanry 1796-1834* (Dublin, 1998), pp 55-74, 171-2; T. Bartlett, 'Defence, counter-insurgency and rebellion: Ireland 1793-1803', in T. Bartlett & K. Jeffrey (eds), *A military history of Ireland* (Cambridge, 1996), pp 265-8. 16 Camden to Pitt, 13 July 1795, Chatham papers, PRO, 30 8 326/34. 17 Duke of York to Pelham, 18 Apr. 1795, Pelham papers, BL, Add. Ms 33101/175. 18 Camden to Pelham, 10 Sept. 1795, Pelham papers, BL, Add. Ms

such plans came to nought. Until the arrival of the French off Bantry Bay, communication between the Admiralty Office and Dublin Castle was almost non-existent. Under the constitution of 1782, Ireland was free to establish its own navy; instead the Irish government contributed towards the maintenance of the British one.[19] For this contribution, Ireland received little protection in the 1790s. Vice-Admiral Kingsmill, commander-in-chief of the fleet based in Cork, was requested to keep in constant contact with the Dublin administration. He failed to do so and Camden was forced to write to Earl Spencer, then First Lord of the Admiralty, reprimanding the conduct of the vice-admiral.[20] The lack of interest shown by Whitehall, the military command and the admiralty stemmed from their preoccupation with war on continental Europe. Throughout Camden's viceroyalty, Britain was in constant danger of suffering a catastrophic defeat at the hands of the French and the cabinet's attention was firmly focused on developments across St George's Channel rather than across the Irish Sea.

While Camden's physical appearance might be 'sufficiently military', William Drennan questioned 'whether his mind be so'.[21] Indeed, Camden was not a military man, and this deficiency was brutally exposed as the military situation in Ireland deteriorated. Without guidance from England, he relied exclusively on the advice of his generals. However the Irish military command rarely presented a united front. Consistency was lacking in the erratic leadership of the Irish army; in the three and a half years of Camden's administration, four men held the position of commander-in-chief. The incumbent at the time of Camden's appointment was the elderly and uninspiring figure of General Robert Cuninghame. Cuninghame was anxious to resign the command, claiming 'his sight is so much impaired it is with difficulty he can get through the business of the day. His limbs are so weak, he is not fitted for active service.'[22] Camden was reluctant to remove Cuninghame, arguing that though 'his age and his habit might render him unfit for a command that called for much personal activity', his knowledge of the military in Ireland and his loyalty to the administration made him a valuable asset.[23] Cuninghame remained an unenthusiastic and disgruntled commander-in-chief until October 1796 when General Simon Luttrell,

33101/264; Duke of York to Pelham, 22 Mar. 1796, Pelham papers, BL, Add. Ms, 33101/390. **19** Malcomson, *Foster*, p. 394. **20** Camden to Spencer, 27 Dec. 1797, CKS, U840 0170/14; Camden to Portland, 16 Dec. 1796, PRO HO 100/62/362. **21** W. Drennan to M. McTier, [end of May] 1797, *Drennan-McTier letters*, ii, p. 316. **22** Cuninghame to Camden, 9 May 1795, encl. in letter from Camden to Portland, 9 May 1795, PRO HO 100/54/108-9. **23** Camden to Portland, 9 May 1795, PRO HO 100/54/108-9.

Lord Carhampton, replaced him. Carhampton's nomination had been approved only because Pitt and his advisors had led Camden to believe that Carhampton's tenure would be brief, and that he would be replaced within weeks by one of two experienced generals, David Dundas or Sir Ralph Abercromby.[24] This was not feasible; in the midst of a savage and damaging war, Pitt was not about to dispatch a valuable military commander to Ireland. Carhampton was unpopular, provoking many complaints about his behaviour and attitude. With Carhampton commanding the troops, Camden alleged that he had 'experienced ... a want of precision and detail in business which is much wanted in this country and ... the country feels it also'.[25] More seriously, Edward Cooke, under-secretary in the civil department, observed 'it is unfortunate, but true, that Lord Carhampton had different opinions about the defence of Ireland and the conduct of war from every officer in the whole army'.[26]

Criticism of the army command was not confined to the commander-in-chief. The conduct of the senior generals provoked exasperated outbursts. Clare wrote to Lord Auckland, exclaiming 'we have an exotic plant at Limerick ... Lt-General Edward Smith, a mad Methodist ... We have some other military exotics ... Major-General Fawcett, Major-General Eustace (the wits call him useless) and Major-General Amherst.'[27] Edward Cooke dismissed the senior commanders of the Irish army; 'Lord Carhampton, quick, but flighty, unexperienced, unsystematic ... Dalrymple ... unwieldy, ... incapable of great exertion. Smith, busy, confused, wild, mad.'[28] Upon hearing of the proposed removal of Lieutenant Generals Dalrymple, Hamilton and Crosbie, York commented to Pelham 'between ourselves I don't think they will be any loss to you'.[29] With such difficulties within the Irish command, it is not surprising that Camden looked beyond Ireland when seeking the appointment of a new commander-in-chief.

As early as January 1797, Charles, Marquis Cornwallis' name was linked to the position of commander-in-chief of the Irish army. Dublin Castle approached Whitehall requesting Cornwallis' appointment 'if the state of affairs in England will allow it'.[30] There was little hope that Whitehall would

24 [Pelham] to [Duke of York], 22 Sept. 1796, Pelham papers, BL, Add. Ms 33113/47.   25 Camden to Portland, 30 Jan. 1797, PRO HO 100/67/35-40.   26 Cooke to [Pelham], 3 Feb. 1797, Pelham papers, BL, Add. Ms 33103/130.   27 Clare to Auckland, 14 Jan. 1797, Sneyd papers, PRONI, T3229/1/12.   28 Cooke to [Auckland], 9 Feb. 1797, Sneyd papers, PRONI, T3229/2/22.   29 Duke of York to Pelham, 4 Oct. 1797, Pelham papers, BL, Add. Ms 33105/159.   30 Pelham to Lake, 6 June 1797, Pelham papers, BL, Add. Ms 33104/185; Pelham to Dalrymple, 7 June 1797, ibid 33104/199; W. Drennan to M. McTier, [end of May] 1797, *Drennan-McTier letters*, ii, p. 316.

order their pre-eminent general to Ireland at a time when the war against the French was going badly. In Ireland speculation mounted and rumours circulated, some alleging that Cornwallis was to be lord lieutenant. Lord Waterford claimed that 'all the letters from England' carried the news that Camden was to be replaced by Cornwallis.[31] And there were grounds for such surmising. Camden believed that the situation in Ireland was such that it would benefit from having the roles of commander-in-chief and lord lieutenant united and he wrote personally to Cornwallis pressing him to accept this dual role. Cornwallis refused. Whitehall disregarded Camden's suggestion, content to leave the lord lieutenant with the task of overcoming growing discontent within the military[32].

The true extent of Irish military incompetence was revealed by the attempted French invasion in December 1796. Edward Cooke blamed the British military command, asking 'what is to become of [Ireland], if men of experience refuse to serve where their talents are wanted?'[33] Senior military commanders in the British army were in a privileged position; they could, in almost every case, chose where they wanted to serve. Until the French appeared at Bantry Bay, the Irish command was an undesirable position. After December 1796, Ireland attracted a sudden interest; it had now become a potential theatre of war. Sir Ralph Abercromby consented to serve in Ireland as commander-in-chief in November 1797. This announcement was greeted with enthusiasm; one of the leading generals in the British army, he had served with distinction in the West Indies. However, like Fitzwilliam, his Irish career was short-lived and notorious. On 26 February 1798, Abercromby issued his 'General Order' which attacked discipline within the army.[34] This order prompted a lengthy letter from an otherwise taciturn Pitt; he deplored Abercromby's actions, complaining that his order 'almost amounts to an invitation to a foreign enemy' and that it was 'likely either to break their [the army] spirits, or to alienate their affections'.[35] Camden described the order as 'most injudicious and almost criminal' but he was loath to remove Abercromby, reasoning correctly that there was no one of his calibre available to replace him.[36] However, Abercromby, who

31 Waterford to Madam ——, 29 May 1797, Windham papers, BL, vol. xxxvi, Add. Ms 37877/68.   32 Camden to Cornwallis, 1 June 1797, CKS, U840 0179/3; Cornwallis to Camden, 1 June 1797, CKS, U840 0179/4; Camden to Portland, 30 Jan. 1797, PRO HO 100/67/35-40.   33 Cooke to [Auckland], 9 Feb. 1797, Sneyd papers, PRONI, T3229/2/22.   34 General Order, 26 Feb. 1798, James, Lord Dunfermline, *Lieutenant General Sir Ralph Abercromby*, (Edinburgh, 1861), pp 93-4.   35 Pitt to Camden, 13 Mar. 1798, NLI Ms 886/249-51.   36 Camden to Pitt, 17 Mar. 1798, NLI Ms 886/253-6.

only reluctantly assumed the command of the troops in Ireland, exploited the furore as an opportunity to resign.[37] Ireland was plunging swiftly towards a military crisis and was, once again, without adequate military leadership. General Gerard Lake, commander of the army in the North, and responsible for the notorious 'dragooning' of Ulster during 1797, was grudgingly appointed in his stead. Camden complained: 'he has no combination in his mind, he can comprehend and execute the duty of a province, but when great arrangements are to be considered, his capacity does not extend to them: he becomes very puzzled'.[38] Lake remained in charge of the Irish army until Cornwallis replaced him in June 1798.

II

Throughout 1795, military policy was dictated by concerns about the internal security of Ireland. Reports concerning the increasing activity of Defenders and United Irishmen proliferated during the summer of 1795.[39] Any attempt to keep local violence in check necessitated the division of troops into small units and their dispersal throughout the country. However, pursuing this military policy meant that effective defence of the coastline was near impossible.[40]

As 1796 progressed, the Dublin Castle administration became increasingly concerned about the French threat to Ireland. By June Camden had decided that it was his 'duty to call the attention of the king's ministers to the situation of this country'. There would be little difficulty in quelling an internal insurrection but if the French arrived, Camden claimed that 'a very formidable body of ill-disposed and disaffected subjects would be found to assist and to encourage them'. Dublin Castle was certain that French interest in Ireland stemmed only from a desire to use the island as part of a greater scheme designed to weaken and ultimately defeat Britain. Camden urged Whitehall to provide support to defend Ireland's vulnerable coastline,

37 Robert Brownrigg wrote to Pelham '[Abercromby] does not wish for the situation of the commander in chief in Ireland but if ordered he will undertake the task'; R. Brownrigg to Pelham, 22 Sept. 1797, Pelham papers, BL, Add. Ms 33105/91; Camden to Pitt, 26 Mar. 1798, NLI Ms 886/261-5.   38 Camden to Pitt, 6 June 1798, NLI Ms 886/307-10.   39 See for example, General C. Crosbie, Carrick-on-Shannon to Pelham, 4 May 1795, CKS, U840 0145/14/1; —— to Agar, 27 July 1795, CKS, U840 0149/17/1; A. Wolfe to Sackville Hamilton, 26 July 1796, CKS, U840 00149/9; Downshire to Camden, 27 Oct. 1796, CKS, U840 0160/5; J. Lees, Dublin to [Townshend], 7 Apr. 1795, Townshend letters, NLI Ms 394, 170/22.   40 Bartlett, 'Defence, counter-insurgency', pp 261-5.

arguing that Ireland's security was vital to winning the war against France. Camden hoped that Pitt and his ministers had information indicating that the French had no intention of attacking Ireland: 'the greatest relief to my mind will be to be informed that I have indulged idle speculations'.[41]

By August 1796 it appeared that Camden had not 'indulged idle speculations;' a variety of well placed informants persuaded him that a French invasion fleet would set out for Ireland during the autumn.[42] Additional troops were immediately requested. Such assistance was not forthcoming: somewhat reassured by Whitehall's relaxed approach to his dire predictions, Camden sought to allay the fears of those in Ireland alarmed at the prospect of a French invasion. Camden assured loyalists that Dublin Castle had 'received no intelligence ... to suppose an invasion of this country may probably take place – I believe the King's ministers in England do not entertain that apprehension.'[43] By September such confidence seemed misplaced; reports from England advised Camden that the war between Britain and France would not end without a French attempt on either Britain or Ireland.[44] It is inexplicable that Whitehall ignored Camden's justifiable fears for over three months; yet it epitomises the relationship between Ireland and the British government throughout Camden's viceroyalty. Pitt and his ministers, absorbed by the war with France, were confident that Ireland could successfully defeat any internal threat and had absolute confidence in the great British navy to deter any potential invading force.

The ominous presence of a French fleet off Bantry on the south-west coast of Ireland illustrated the folly of such complacency.[45] Accurate information was slow to filter through; as late as 23 December, Richard Wright, writing to Vice-Admiral Kingsmill, commented that he had 'not learnt what fleet they are, whether friends or enemies'. The Admiralty Office maintained that they could 'not conceive that the enemy has any intention of visiting Ireland at this season of the year'.[46] Ironically the information from the admiralty was sent after the French had arrived at Bantry Bay.

41 Camden to Pelham, 28 June 1796, PRO HO 100/34/139-35.   42 Camden to Pitt, 6 Aug. 1796, CKS, U840 0156A/2.   43 Camden to Dillon, 15 Aug. 1796, CKS, U840 0181/4.   44 Camden to Shannon, 1 Sept. 1796, CKS, U840 0175/5.   45 Information was initially sketchy with regard to the size of the French fleet. James O'Sullivan writing on 22 December believed that 38 ships with 50,000 men were off the south-west coast of Ireland; PRO HO 100/62/389; On 23 December the Surveyor of Bearheaven reported that 73 ships had been spotted off the coast; PRO HO 100/65/210; PRO HO 100/62/399; that same day Dalrymple wrote to Pelham informing him that 25 French ships were headed towards Bantry Bay; PRO HO 100/62/385; On 26 December 1796 Dalrymple received information from a French prisoner that there were 50 boats with 25,000 men on board; PRO HO 100/65/217;

Chaos, disorder and confusion were the hallmarks of the Irish response to the French threat.[47] There was no military force waiting to repel the invaders had they landed and only inclement weather conditions prevented such an eventuality. The naval response was pathetic. The French fleet successfully evaded detection as it crossed from Brest to Bantry. The British naval command had believed that Portugal was the destination of the French Fleet and Admiral Colpoys and his blockade squadron were not ordered to pursue the French. Admiral Bridport, in dock at Spithead, took ten days to prepare for departure to Ireland. When he finally sailed, on 3 January, the French had already abandoned all efforts to land.[48] Francis Higgins, the unscrupulous editor of the *Freeman's Journal* and an active and enthusiastic Castle informant, vividly illustrated the disillusionment and despondency felt by Irish loyalists:

> You ... have never heard anything equal to the outcry made against the English government for want of the protection of a fleet; ... the enemy on the shores; no assistance given, though ... the country might be overrun by the French. The citizens who are strongly attached to the government speak of the neglect in this way 'that Ireland is to look to itself, the hour of danger has come and neither assistance nor relief from an English fleet have been received'.[49]

on the same day Kingsmill wrote from Cobh that 17 ships were in Bantry Bay; NLI mic.P.6799, DeVesci letters; J. Wolfe writing to Lady DeVesci on 29 December estimated the French Force at about 20,00 men; NLI mic. P.6799, DeVesci letters. **46** R. Wright to Kingsmill, 23 Dec. 1796, PRO HO 100/65/210; Major J. Brown to Camden, 23 Dec. 1796, CKS, U840 0170/2; E. Nepean, Admiralty Office to Pelham, 21 Dec. 1796, CKS, U840 0189/12/1.   **47** For example by Christmas day 1796, according to Camden, the army 'was in motion towards the South'. However in letters from Carhampton to Lieutenant Generals Dalrymple and Smith written on Christmas eve the troops were ordered to halt their progress south and on 27 December, after receiving news that the French had not landed, Carhampton wrote to Camden requesting the army's march south be halted. Camden to Pitt, 25 Dec. 1796, CKS, U840 0156A/3; Carhampton to Dalrymple and Smith, 24 Dec. 1796, CKS, U840 0162/5; Carhampton to Camden, 27 Dec. 1796, CKS, U840 0162/5. **48** E. Pellew, 'Indefatigable', to E. Nepean, 17 Dec. 1796, CKS, U840 0189/13/2; Nepean, to Kingsmill, 21 Dec. 1796, CKS, U840 0189/12/2; 'Narrative of the Proceedings of the Squadron under the respective commands of Vice-Admiral Colpoys and Admiral Lord Bridport' [Admiralty Office?], 12 January 1797, CKS, U840 0170/18; T. Bartlett, 'The invasion that never was', in J.A. Murphy (ed.), *The French are in the Bay. The expedition to Bantry Bay 1796* (Dublin, 1997), pp 48-63. **49** F[rancis] H[iggins] to [Edward Cooke], 8 Jan. 1797, NA 620/18/14.

Camden too resented the relaxed arrogance of the British, their absolute confidence in a fleet that was incapable of preventing the French arriving at Ireland.[50] The lord lieutenant was incensed by the fact that only a 'Protestant wind' had saved Ireland from the devastation of a French invasion; Portland, in a letter to the king, referred to the 'peculiar protection of the Divine Providence which still continues to guard that land from the spoiling hand of the invader'.[51] While Ireland's security had been seriously threatened, the lord lieutenant was ignored by the admiralty, disregarded by the British army and treated with disdain by Whitehall.

III

While the political and military repercussions of the events of December 1796 have frequently been discussed, the financial impact of Bantry Bay and its influence on the Anglo-Irish relationship are ultimately more important.[52] Throughout 1796 the Irish exchequer experienced financial difficulties but it had not been necessary to seek substantial loans from Britain. At the close of December 1796, however, the Bank of Ireland declared it had less than £20,000 at its disposal and on Christmas Eve Camden demanded £50,000 as an immediate loan.[53] The appearance of the French off Bantry exacerbated the problems faced by the troubled Irish treasury. Within days of their arrival, John Parnell travelled to London in the hope of securing a loan of one million pounds.[54] He met with little positive response; it was not until 2 January, after the immediate crisis had passed, that Pitt agreed to dispatch £50,000 to Ireland.[55] Pitt's naïve belief that this loan, combined with the failure of the French to land, would alleviate any 'fears of a run on the bank' proved to be ill-founded.[56] One

50 'Narrative of the Proceedings of the Squadron under the respective commands of Vice-Admiral Colpoys and Admiral Lord Bridport', [Admiralty Office?], 12 Jan. 1797, CKS, U840 0170/18.   51 Portland to George III, 7 Jan. 1797, quoted in Aspinall (ed.), *George III*, ii, p. 533.   52 See for example J.A. Froude, *The English in Ireland in the eighteenth-century*, (London, 1874), iii, pp 156-219; P. B. Bradley, *Ireland in the days of Napoleon and Wolfe Tone*(London, 1931); E.H. Stuart Jones, *An invasion that failed; the French expedition to Ireland 1796* (Oxford, 1950); M. Elliott, *Partners in revolution. The United Irishmen and France* (London, 1982), pp 77-123; M. Elliott, *Wolfe Tone. Prophet of Irish independence* (London, 1989), pp 300-33; Murphy (ed.), *The French are in the Bay.*   53 Camden to Pitt, 30 Dec. 1796, CKS, U840 0156A/6; Camden to Pitt, 24 Dec. 1796, CKS U840 0156A/3.   54 Camden to Pitt, 29 Dec. 1796, CKS, U840 0156A/5.   55 Portland to George III, 1 Jan. 1797, Aspinall, *George III*, ii, p. 532; Pitt to Camden, 2 Jan., ibid, p. 532, ft.   56 Pitt to Camden, 2 Jan. 1797, Aspinall, *George III*, ii, p. 532.

banker stated that the threatened French invasion had caused 'the stoppage of the banks, the annihilation of all credit, trade and commerce, in short I might call it a general bankruptcy'.[57] Camden, anxious to prevent a complete collapse of the economy, petitioned the prime minister 'to pay such a sum to the Bank as shall enable them to enliven trade, that it may not appear to the French that their appearance off the coast has had so serious an effect as it really has produced'.[58] But the situation continued to degenerate and by April 1797 the Bank of Ireland's reserves had dwindled to £8,000; with this news, all hope of Ireland recovering from this financial crisis without British assistance evaporated.[59]

Camden wrote wearily to Pitt at the end of February 1797 telling him that £630,000 was required by 25 March in order to pay the troops. Otherwise the consequences would be dire; 'the salvation of this country … completely turns upon this money being sent'.[60] By the second week of March, there was still no reply. In dismay Camden insisted upon the 'very urgent necessity' of financial assistance from Britain.[61] On 13 March an exasperated Camden dispatched Edward Cooke to London to plead the case of Ireland.[62] Cooke did not meet with immediate success; it took until the beginning of May before a loan was promised to Ireland.[63] Unless this money arrived promptly, Camden feared that 'a mutiny [would] probably be the consequence'.[64] This loan would soften though not solve the financial problems. Less than three weeks, later Camden was hoping for another £500,000 to be sent to Ireland.[65]

Why did it take so long for Pitt to respond positively to Camden's pleas? He did not simply dismiss requests from Ireland for money. Throughout the period when Camden was bombarding Westminster with information about a possible French invasion and entreaties for troops and money, Pitt was fighting a war on continental Europe, a war largely financed by vast loans supplied by the British government to her continental allies. At the outbreak of hostilities between Britain and France, Britain had remained firmly attached to the gold standard, and Edmund Burke had sharply criticised the French policy of printing paper money as need dictated. However, early

57 J. Colclough, Tintern to Caesar Colclough, Neufchatel, 1 May 1797, PRONI, McPeake papers, T3048/C/18.   58 Camden to Pitt, 31 Jan. 1797, CKS, U840 0156A/8.   59 Camden to Pitt, 25 Apr. 1797, CUL, Add. 6958/2141.   60 Camden to Pitt, 23 Feb. 1797, CKS, U840 0156A/11.   61 Camden to Pitt, 9 Mar. 1797, CKS, U840 0156A/12.   62 Camden to Pitt, 13 Mar. 1797, CKS, U840 0156A/13. 63 Pitt to Camden, 2 May 1797, CUL Add. 6958/2144.   64 Camden to Pitt, 6 May 1797, NLI Ms 886/185-7.   65 Camden to Pitt, 19 May 1797, PRO, Chatham papers, 30/8/3326/175.

1797 saw a change to that policy. The arrival, close to Fishguard, of a paltry
group of French soldiers, many of them ex-prisoners who had been
recruited while in jail, under the command of the seventy-year-old Colonel
William Tate, was sufficient to cause a run on the Bank of England. The
raid was a disaster with the French troops rounded up by local men within
hours of their disembarking. The significance of the expedition lay in the
fact that once again the British navy had been exposed. Twice in three
months, French ships had evaded not only capture but also detection by the
supposedly invincible British navy. The panic instigated by the French
landing forced Britain off the gold standard with the Bank of England
obliged to suspend cash payments to those with deposits, thus ensuring that
whatever intentions Pitt and his government had of sending cash to Ireland,
it was now almost impossible to do so.[66]

How then did the appearance of a French fleet in Bantry Bay affect the
relationship between the Irish administration and the British government?
The crisis marked a significant turning point in Anglo-Irish relations. The
arrival of the French ships proved beyond doubt that the French navy could
rival the British. It also demonstrated that the French were serious about
invading Ireland and the inadequate military response in Ireland confirmed
fears that the security of Ireland could not be guaranteed should an invading
force land. In the aftermath of Bantry Bay, the prince of Wales wrote to
William Pitt: 'the value and importance of Ireland cannot be adequately
estimated or sufficiently prized, and its loss or separation would be the most
mortal blow that this kingdom could receive'. He believed that Britain
should do all in her power to prevent the French from landing in Ireland and
the outbreak of civil war in the country.[67] Many agreed. On 23 March, the
British house of commons debated the state of Ireland. In response to a
powerful and scathing attack on the government by the leader of the
opposition, Charles James Fox, Pitt justified British involvement in Irish
affairs:

> may there not be circumstances which justify the interference of the
> executive government with Ireland? ... Can it not interfere in and
> control the conduct of the Lord Lieutenant...? As to the Lord
> Lieutenant and his ministers, the power remains in this country to
> control them and advice may be offered to the executive government
> on that point.[68]

66 J. Ehrman, *The younger Pitt: the consuming struggle* (London, 1996), pp 5-16.   67
Prince of Wales to Pitt, 8 February 1797 in A. Aspinall (ed.), *The correspondence of
George, prince of Wales* (London, 1965), iii, p. 313.   68 *Report of debates in the House*

The power did remain in Britain to control the lord lieutenant and this power was increasingly used in the period after Bantry Bay.

Now completely dependent on financial aid from Britain to support a weakened economy and to pay for military protection, the vaunted independence the Irish Protestant elite once possessed had now vanished. The Irish houses of parliament believed that the British government interfered too frequently in Irish internal affairs and made a mockery of the legislative independence that had been hard-won in 1782. There was much resentment of the Catholic relief acts passed in 1792 and 1793: the political community believed that they had been duped into agreeing to the 'false and mistaken policy of Great Britain in 1793.'[69] Such concessions to Catholics eroded confidence in the British government and by 1797 the conservative Protestant elite were frightened and isolated. They were forced to look to themselves for protection even more then they had done in the past. The United Irishmen had failed to rise in rebellion, but the arrival of the French in such numbers and the subsequent incompetence displayed by the administration and the army proved a vital propaganda victory for the radicals; it convinced many that the French would return and this time contribute to a successful United Irish rebellion.

As Ireland moved toward rebellion, Camden noted that 'military measures are so connected with the politics of the country that the Ld Lt [*sic*] ought to be a military man and really to command the army of which he is nominally the head.'[70] This incongruous position was the chief reason behind Abercromby's resignation because 'a military character used to command cannot submit to be under the command of a person in my situation and the country cannot be saved without a military character of experience and ability being sent here'.[71] This was not the first time that there had been tension between the positions of lord lieutenant and commander-in-chief. In 1776 the lord lieutenant, Harcourt, wrote to the prime minister, Lord North that he found it intolerable staying in Ireland while the commander-in-chief usurped the viceroy's powers.[72] With the outbreak of rebellion on 23 May 1798, the embodiment of commander-in-chief and lord lieutenant in the one person became inevitable. On 6 and 7

of Commons of Ireland in session 1796-7 to which are annexed debates in the British Parliament upon Mr Fox's motion, touching the state of Ireland (Dublin, 1797), p. 226. **69** Fitzgibbon to Auckland, 18 May 1795, PRONI, Sneyd papers, T3229/1/9.   **70** Camden to Pitt, 26 Mar. 1798, NLI Ms 886/261-5; Camden to Pitt, 7 April 1798, ibid, 269-71.   **71** Camden to Pitt, 23 Mar. 1798, NLI Ms 886/257-8.   **72** Harcourt to North, 13 Sept. 1776, *Harcourt papers*, x, pp 183-5. My thanks to Tom Bartlett for this reference.

June Camden dispatched two secret letters to the prime minister, reiterating his argument for uniting both posts. In the circumstances, this was 'an arrangement upon which might depend the salvation of Ireland and her connexion [*sic*] with Great Britain'.[73] Pitt agreed. Camden received a letter relieving him of his position and appointing Lord Cornwallis. Camden's aspiration had finally become a reality but he was 'hurt at the very great speed with which the measure of my retirement from Ireland is accompanied' which he feared would be misconstrued as a slur on his lord lieutenancy.[74] To guard against criticism, Camden was offered a position as a member of the cabinet – albeit without office – on his return to England. It was also proposed that he be promoted to the position of Marquis and he was made a knight of the garter.[75]

In a recent study of the Irish act of union, Geoghegan describes Camden variously as 'unsuitable', 'an inappropriate viceroy', 'a liability' and 'an embarrassing reminder of the old Anglo-Irish relationship'. There is perhaps some justification for such claims but it is erroneous to suggest that Camden contributed little to preserving the strong connection between the two kingdoms. Geoghegan argues that Camden's hasty departure from Ireland stemmed more from Pitt's urgent desire to replace him with 'a conciliatory figure' than a response to Camden's politically astute requests to be replaced by a military man.[76] Given the circumstances of Cornwallis's appointment, in the midst of rebellion, it is hardly surprising that decisions once taken were acted upon with haste.

IV

Lord Charlemont, former commander of the Volunteers, dismissed Camden, commenting 'Instead of a viceroy, [he] is in effect no more than a vice-Pitt.'[77] Such an appraisal is unfair. Camden had been appointed as the king's representative in Ireland and it was fully anticipated that he would do as he was bid and act in accordance with British interests at all times. The

---

73 Camden to Pitt, June 1798, PRO, Chatham papers, 30/8/326/318; Camden to Pitt, 6 June 1798, NLI Ms 886/307-10.   74 Camden to Pitt, 16 June 1798, CKS, U840 0156A/44; Camden to Pelham, 19 June 1798, BL, Pelham papers, Add. Ms 33105/441; Camden to Elliot, 15 June 1798, BL, Pelham papers, Add. Ms 33105/431; Camden to Pelham 15 June 1798, ibid /433.   75 Pitt to Camden, 27 June 1798, CKS, U840 0190A/8/1; Pitt to Camden, 29 June 1798, CKS, U840 0190A/8/2; Camden, Berkely Square to Pitt, 29 June 1798, CKS, U840 0156A/45. 76 Geoghegan, *Union*, pp 13-20.

reality was not so straightforward. Soon after Camden's arrival in Ireland, the lord chancellor, Lord Clare remarked:

> it is essential to the peace of this country that all parties should be satisfied of the determination of the British government to maintain and defend the remnant of political strength which is left in the hands of the Protestants of Ireland. I hope that such is their determination, else they never can preserve this country to the British Empire.[78]

For three years Camden strove to 'maintain and defend the remnant of political strength' possessed by loyal Irish protestants. Anxious to secure the protestant interest and bind Ireland closer to Britain, Camden soon realised that this could not be achieved by acting as Whitehall expected. Isolated, Camden relied on manipulating political and military powers in Ireland, in an effort to maintain order in the country. Hampered by a lack of troops and cash, he addressed the security and economic crises with enthusiasm and vigour. He made repeated requests to combine the positions of commander-in-chief and lord lieutenant.[79] The longer Camden remained in Ireland, the more convinced he became that union was the only method available to 'preserve' Ireland 'to the British empire'. By May 1798 he had completed much of the groundwork necessary for union.

Cornwallis' appointment was the first overt move towards union; since the close of 1796, practical reasons encouraged a union. With Ireland virtually bankrupt and forced into the humiliating position of relying on Britain for funds, the question of how to facilitate such funding was raised. In general, loans from Britain were given in the form of Bank of England notes. This created difficulties, especially after Britain came off the gold standard, as English bank notes became unacceptable to the Bank of Ireland. Demands for specie were regularly refused as the Bank of England was unwilling to part with its depleted cash reserves.[80] A union would negate

77 Charlemont to Halliday, 26 July 1795, *Charlemont*, ii, p. 265.   78 Clare to Auckland, 18 May 1795, PRONI, Sneyd papers, T3229/1/9.   79 See for example Camden to Cornwallis, 23 May 1797, CKS, U840 O179/3; Camden to Pitt, 1 June 1797, CKS, U840 O156A/19; Camden to Pitt, 7 April 1798, CKS, U840 O156A/30; Camden to Pitt, 6 June 1798, CKS, U840 O156A/39; Camden to Pitt, 15 June 1798, CKS, U840 O156A/43.   80 Pelham to Camden, 30 Jan. 1797, BL, Pelham papers, Add. Ms 33103/107; Cooke to Pelham, 20 Mar. 1797, CKS, U840 O153/15; Dalrymple, Cork to Pelham, 30 Mar. 1797, BL, Pelham papers, Add. Ms 33103/305; Parnell to Camden, 5 July 1797, CUL Add. 6958/2185; G. Rose, 8 July 1797, BL, Pelham papers, Add. Ms 3314/349; G. Rose to Pelham, 12 July [1797], BL, Pelham

such difficulties as bank notes would be equally acceptable on either island. Union was the object of Cornwallis's mission, Pitt commenting that he 'must ... as soon as possible have in view some permanent settlement which may provide for the internal peace of the country and secure its connection with Great Britain ... by an union'.[81]

Though many of the Protestant elite regarded the idea of union with trepidation, and in some cases hostility, it had become unavoidable. So long ignored by the British parliament, the 'protestant establishment' were cautious about accepting assurances that it would be to their advantage to consent to a union with Britain.[82] Yet, faced with a security and financial disaster, union was the obvious solution. It bound Ireland to Britain and afforded Whitehall complete control. Ireland was permitted to keep some vestiges of independence; the retention of the viceregal court was merely symbolic. For the first time in over a century and a half, the British government was in a position to garner sufficient support on both sides of the Irish Sea to guarantee the passage of an act of union. Camden, an enthusiastic advocate of union, had succeeded in putting what had long been promoted privately on the official agenda. Despite his best efforts, Ireland had proved a reluctant and troublesome province; it was now time to 'persuade her to a union.'[83]

Camden returned to England and took his seat in the house of lords where he was unobtrusive and rarely participated in debates. However, his absence from Ireland did not diminish his interests in the country and he maintained contact with many in the Irish administration.[84] His letters regularly advanced the prospect of a union between Britain and Ireland; when Foster made it known that he would not be a supporter of a union, Camden immediately wrote to him in an attempt to persuade him of its merits.[85] In the house of lords he spoke in two debates and strongly endorsed the proposed union, arguing that by a union with Britain Irish politicians would be 'engaged in ... important concerns, instead of having to deliberate upon mere local questions' – a reference, no doubt, to the powerlessness he had often felt during his period as viceroy in Ireland. Camden concluded his speeches remarking, 'I have always been a friend to

papers, Add. Ms 33104/360.   81 Pitt to Camden, 11 June 1798, CKS, U840 0190A/7.   82 J. L[ees] to Auckland, 10 April 1797, BL, Auckland papers, Add. Ms. 34454/2210.   83 Camden to Robert Stewart, 1793, quoted in L. Hale, *John Philpot Curran; his life and times* (London, 1958), p. 141.   84 Camden to Shannon, 8 Feb. 1799, CKS, U840 0175/10; Camden to Clare, 8 Feb. 1799, CKS, U.840 0183/13; Cooke to Camden, 7 May 1799, CKS, U.840 081/1.   85 Camden to Foster, 25 July 1799, CKS, U.840/01845/5.

this measure.'[86] He was not alone. Despite many setbacks, by June 1800 there were sufficient 'friends to the measure' to ensure the passing of the Act of Union.

---

86 Camden, 21 April 1800, *The parliamentary history of England*, vol. xxxv (London, 1819), p. 180; Camden, 19 Mar. 1799, ibid, vol. xxiv, p. 685.

7

The union and the importance of public opinion

Daniel Mansergh

Accounts of the passage of the Union written over the last hundred and fifty years, notably those by Bolton, Lecky, and most recently Geoghegan, have tended to focus mainly on the high political transactions which led to, accompanied and enabled it. It is my aim to broaden these analyses into a new area by shifting away from the pecuniary and ideological motivations of individual parliamentarians, grandees and governmental figures and looking instead to the issue of how the battle over the Union was fought outside parliament.

This topic was partially addressed by Bolton, though only from a governmental point of view.[1] In the course of 1798, over 200 pamphlets based around the subject were published, ranging in length from under ten to over two hundred printed pages.[2] Many went into multiple editions. Authors with even a moderately high public profile, like the former United Irishman William Drennan, could sell 1,500 copies of a single work.[3] In addition, the newspapers of the day shook off the restrictions of the rebellion period to enter with enthusiasm into the debate.[4] Two specialist papers went into short-lived production, the *Anti-Union* (on two separate occasions and in different formats) and the *Olio*.[5] Marquis Cornwallis, the head of the Irish administration, suffered some criticism in British governmental circles for

---

1 Bolton, *Union*, p. 76. 2 I am much indebted to the work of W.J. McCormack, *The pamphlet debate on the Union between Great Britain and Ireland 1797-1800* (Dublin, 1996). McCormack lists more than 300 items; many, however, cannot be counted as relevant for my purposes, including single-sheet publications, works only published in Britain, textually identical but separately listed reprints, musical compositions and reprints of older works. 3 Drennan to McTier, 27 Feb. 1799 in *Drennan-McTier letters*, ii, p. 147. 4 B. Inglis, 'O'Connell and the Irish press', *IHS*, viii (1952-3), pp 1-27. 5 *The Anti-Union* (Dublin, 1798-9) and *The Olio or anything-arian miscellany* (Dublin, 1800).

allowing such an explosion of print agitation to occur with fairly few restrictions[6], though banning material that was not explicitly rebellious would probably have simply played into opposition hands. Nor was extra-parliamentary activity restricted to the printing business; for certain crucial phases of the Union period, the opposition organised, and the government attempted to stifle, large-scale and threatening displays of public hostility to the government's project.

The first rumours that a union was under contemplation by the British government began circulating in Ireland in the autumn of 1798, and the first distinct phase of public activity based around the question ran from then until the meeting of parliament in late January 1799, when the measure was effectively defeated in the Irish house of commons. Official preparation for a pro-union publicity campaign had been hopelessly inadequate. Cornwallis was a military man and not a politician by temperament. He had restricted himself to briefing only a handful of leading peers, MPs, borough magnates and Catholic notables on the government's intention.[7] His second-in-command, the chief secretary Lord Castlereagh, though he was later to show himself a skilled parliamentary manager, remained notably *blasé* throughout the union period when considering the need to cultivate public support. He believed that public sentiment was only of relevance to the Castle in the sense that it conceivably might affect the votes of a minority of parliamentarians.[8] Only one prominent official exhibited any real concern over the gathering public storm against the union and the uses to which the opposition might put it: the hugely experienced under-secretary at the civil department, Edward Cooke. But Cooke was effectively marginalised by the viceroy, who regarded him as an ally of the ultra-protestant 'Orange' faction in Irish politics, and thus an enemy to his conciliatory anti-rebellion policies.[9] Cooke faced an uphill task in persuading the Castle to put any significant effort into orchestrating a pro-union campaign. As late as November 1798, with the meeting of parliament only two months away, we find him writing desperately to Castlereagh that the viceroy was 'gradually letting the public mind slip away from him'.[10] Indeed, the discredited Cooke probably only got the job of managing any kind of publicity effort because nobody else at the Castle was showing the remotest interest in stimulating one.

So far as the print war was concerned, the opening salvo was fired by Cooke himself, with his deceptively impartial title of *Arguments for and*

6 Buckingham to Grenville, 7 Dec. 1798 in *Fortescue*, iv, pp 404-5.　7 Lecky, *Ire.*, v, pp 158-61, 168, 180.　8 Castlereagh to Portland, 1 Feb. 1799, *Castlereagh corr.*, ii, pp 149-53.　9 Bolton, *Union*, pp 58, 68.　10 Cooke to Castlereagh, 9 Nov. 1798, *Castlereagh corr.*, i, pp 431-3.

against a union between Great Britain and Ireland considered.[11] The result was a deluge of anti-union replies of varying quality, eagerly snapped up by the waiting public. Cooke's pamphlet was received with acclaim by some English readers, including the former viceroy, the marquis of Buckingham. But Cooke's piece appeared too late: as Buckingham wrote, 'there is hardly a man in Ireland who has not already made up his mind'.[12] Moreover, Cooke's approach alienated his Irish, as opposed to English, readers, especially given that he himself was of the latter nationality. Take this extract from the pamphlet:

> When ... one of the states desirous to form a union is inferior in point of civilisation, agriculture, commerce, manufactures, morals, manners, establishments, constitution; and the other state is eminent and superior to all the world in these advantages, it is evident that a union ... must be more beneficial to the former ... Now in many of these particulars we acknowledge and lament the inferiority of Ireland: our civil and religious discontents, jealousies and distur-bances; the conspiracies, the insurrections, the rebellions which have disgraced us; proclaim our defects in civilisation and policy. [13]

Unsurprisingly, Cooke's piece was seized on by opponents as an insult to national pride. Instead of 'giving a tone' to the union's supporters, it provided its literary enemies with quotations for two months to come.[14] One early response angrily told Cooke that 'you write as an Englishman to Englishmen. I write, and speak, and FEEL as an Irishman.'[15] The impression was cultivated that the union was 'the most barefaced, undisguised attempt at our honour, dignity and character as a nation ... that has ever been yet attempted'.[16]

In these early months of the union period, over twice as many anti-union as pro-union pamphlets were produced, a striking number of the anti-union works being structured as replies to Cooke. Moreover, the Castle's intended propaganda piece stimulated prominent public and private bodies to meet and declare their stance on the measure. Only the Corporation of Cork, a body largely controlled by two pro-union magnates, came out in support.[17]

---

11 [E. Cooke], *Arguments for and against an Union between Great Britain and Ireland considered* (London, 1798). 12 Ibid. 13 Ibid., pp 25-6. 14 Castlereagh to Wickham, 19 Nov. 1798, *Castlereagh corrs.*, ii, p. 8. 15 P. Rudd, *An answer to the pamphlet entitled* Arguments for and against an Union (Dublin, 1799), p. 19. 16 W. Smyth, *First letter to a noble lord on the subject of the Union*, 2nd edition (Dublin, 1799), p. 4. 17 Bolton, *Union*, p. 93.

In Dublin, the most extreme sectors of anti-union struggle (the lawyers, the loyalist aldermen of Skinner's Alley, the bankers, the merchants and the Corporation) all declared their opposition.[18] The Orange Order was only narrowly prevented from doing so by patrician leaders anxious not to allow it to become internally split by political controversy. For the present, the leadership's policy of neutrality prevailed, though nobody was in any doubt as to the real sentiments of the Order's grass roots, though only much later, in 1800, did individual lodges resort to declaring themselves to be opposed to a union and deeply discontented with the Grand Lodge.[19] But anti-union partisans intended to make better use of anti-union public sentiment than simply confining themselves to seeking hostile declarations, given that these could be ignored with impunity by both the government and most parliamentarians.

There was no formal centre for anti-union agitation at this point, in contrast to the pro-union efforts, which were increasingly orchestrated from the Castle. A voluble and high-profile role was assumed from the start by the Irish Bar. Nearly half of the anti-union pamphlets produced up to February 1799 were ascertainably written by barristers. The *Anti-Union* newspaper, launched in December 1798, was also largely the initiative of the lawyers Bushe, Plunket, Goold, Smily and Wallace, though the senior whig MP Henry Grattan also contributed.[20] From the government's perspective, the most damaging aspect of the lawyers' activity was their readiness to encourage disloyalty in the irregular military as a reaction to the union in order to undermine it. William Saurin, a distinguished and previously pro-government northern barrister, was active in November and December 1798 in persuading the lawyers' yeomanry corps to set an example to other such units by declaring themselves, in their military capacity, opposed to the union.[21] Fortunately for the government, sufficient of Saurin's colleagues objected to this tactic to prevent the attempt in December.[22] The following month, Saurin was only prevented from renewing his efforts by threats from Castlereagh that he would be stripped of his numerous crown-conferred professional distinctions.[23] Saurin's disrespect for government knew few bounds: he humiliated the lord chancellor, the earl of Clare, by marching into the earl's court of chancery while it was in session and proceeding to collect signatures to an anti-union petition from six out of the seven king's

18 Ibid., pp 81-2.   19 Lecky, *Ire.*, v, p. 353.   20 J. O' Flanagan, *The Irish Bar*, 2nd edition (London, 1879), pp 143-5.   21 Cooke to Castlereagh, 8 Nov. 1798, *Castlereagh corr.*, i, p. 429; Cornwallis to Portland, 5 Dec. 1798; *Castlereagh corr.*, ii, p. 35.   22 Cornwallis to Portland, 5 Dec. 1798, *Castlereagh corr.*, ii, p. 37.   23 Portland to George III, 7 Jan. 1799 in Aspinall, *George III*, iii , p. 177.

counsel present.[24] Nor was he by any means the most extreme of his profession, as the published account of the Bar meeting in December makes clear.[25]

By the time parliament convened on 22 January 1799, the lawyers' tactic of inciting the yeomanry to take a political stand against union began to bear fruit. A serious confrontation arose in mid-January when Sir William Worthington, commander of Dublin's Liberty Rangers yeoman corps, ordered his men to parade under a banner reading 'For our own King and the Constitution of Ireland' the day before parliament convened. Only the threat of disbandment prevented the demonstration.[26] Lord Donoughmore's Cork legion soon after produced an anti-union address, with worrying lack of regard for the wishes of their pro-union patron. A northern corps indicated that they would refuse to undertake military duties.[27] The parliamentary defeat for the union at least had the temporary advantage for the viceroy of suspending the prospect of a serious crisis of loyalty in the government's Irish allies. In the immediate aftermath of January, Cornwallis and Castlereagh were anxious to allow the public debate to fade away rather than immediately reintroducing the question, as many in Britain wished.[28]

If the government were surprised by the vehemently hostile public response to union in the early period of debate, they were soon taking steps to ensure that they were not outflanked again. In tandem with their efforts to secure extra support in parliament, the Castle orchestrated an elaborate campaign to curry public support. Castlereagh obtained £5,000 of British secret service money for the purpose of paying pro-union writers and printers, who were now offered monetary or professional inducements to continue writing.[29] William Smith, for example, who produced no less than five pamphlets in favour of the measure, became solicitor general in 1800 and a Baron of the Exchequer in 1801.[30] In addition, the pro-union speeches of British political giants like William Pitt, Auckland, Henry Dundas, Temple and Minto were printed and distributed in vast numbers at the public expense.[31] It is impossible to judge with certainty the impression that these works made. William Smith's *Address to the people of Ireland* went

24 O'Flanagan, *Irish Bar*, pp 124-7.   25 *A report of the debate of the Irish Bar on Sunday the 9th of December, on the subject of an Union* (Dublin 1799).   26 *Cornwallis corr.*, iii, p. 29n; Buckingham to Grenville, 19 Jan. 1799 in *Fortescue*, iv, p. 445.   27 Blackstock, *An ascendancy army: the Irish yeomanry 1796-1834* (Dublin, 1998), pp 181-2.   28 Castlereagh to Portland, 14 Apr. 1799, *Castlereagh corr.*, ii, pp 273-5.   29 Castlereagh to Wickham, 2 Jan. 1799, *Cornwallis corr.*, iii, p 27.   30 DNB (entry for Sir William Cusack Smith), pp 563-4.   31 McCormack, *Pamphlet debate*, pp 86, 93, 97, 98.

through six Dublin editions and indications are that it was widely read;[32] 10,000 copies of Pitt's speech were allegedly printed.[33] On the other hand, many of these publications were distributed free outside Dublin, so multiple editions may not be a good indication of popularity. The anglican bishop of Meath pointed out to Castlereagh that hundreds of government pamphlets were lying unread in post-offices all over Ireland.[34]

The policy of deluging the provinces with pamphlets was complemented by a campaign to secure the signatures of leading provincial notables to pro-union petitions.[35] The aim was to change the impression created by the uproar of late 1798 and early 1799 that the nation was united in opposition to union; instead, it was suggested that while Dublin might be violently opposed, the rest of the country was quietly favourable. If successful, this effort to cultivate the provinces would destroy the ability of noisy Dublin's lawyers, corporation and yeomen to claim a national voice.

The Castle's tactics in this second phase of the union period, extending to the end of 1799, seemed successful. Government-sponsored works outnumbered anti-union pamphlets. Public uproar seemed virtually to disappear, though this was partly due to uncertainty over whether or when the union might be reintroduced, and whether Cornwallis was even to be permitted to continue as viceroy. Despite the steady progress of draft union terms through the British parliament, many clung to the belief that the January victory would prove decisive.[36] The government's relative success at this juncture lay not with their own efforts but with a change in tactics by their opponents. The days of leaderless and spontaneous opposition to the union were ending. The speaker of the Irish house of commons, John Foster, was now generally accepted as the leader of a loose anti-union parliamentary coalition. For most of his career a government figure, Foster showed little inclination to encourage ostentatious displays of public opposition outside parliament; indeed he had been an avowed opponent of extra-parliamentary agitation of any kind throughout the 1790s.[37] Foster's whig allies, the Ponsonby brothers, were similarly inexperienced in the art of cultivating and deploying public support; they accepted Foster's leadership as the price for the aura of respectability he brought to the move-

32 Ibid., pp 96-7.   33 J. Foster, *Speech of the right honorable (sic) John Foster, Speaker of the House of Commons of Ireland, delivered in committee on Thursday the 11th day of April, 1799* (Dublin, 1799) pp 3-4.   34 *Castlereagh corr.*, iii, pp 26-27; undated memorandum by O'Beirne, bishop of Meath.   35 Bolton, *Union*, pp 126-56.   36 Drennan to McTier, 22 Oct. 1799, *Drennan-McTier letters*, ii, p. 525; Foster to Sheffield, 20 Mar. 1799, PRONI, *An Anglo-Irish dialogue: A calendar of the correspondence between John Foster and Lord Sheffield 1774-1821*, p. 30.   37 Malcomson, *Foster*.

ment.[38] In the aftermath of 1798, and the bitter vilification the Irish whigs had received from loyalists for their alleged ambiguous attitude to the rebellion, the Ponsonbys may have felt such respectability essential to the success of the anti-union effort in parliament. Some whig figures favoured a more aggressive harassment of the government out of doors. But of their principal leaders, Grattan was at this point an invalid in Britain,[39] Curran was being shunned by the respectable for his defence in court of the most prominent United Irish leaders,[40] and neither was actively courted in the anti-union movement at this point. The elderly Charlemont was painfully aware that 'the silence of the country' was Dublin Castle's greatest asset, but his health was deteriorating, and he died in August.[41] With Foster disengaged from public activity, and with government deliberately discouraging any impression that the union's reintroduction was imminent, the momentum built up by the union's opponents in earlier days was allowed to slacken.

The winter of 1799-1800 was therefore a rude awakening for the anti-union leaders. Not only did the Cornwallis administration enjoy the absolute support of the British government, but the union would be aggressively reintroduced, and the government this time appeared to have a safe parliamentary majority. Foster's tactic of confining opposition to parliament had failed dismally, and his leadership of the movement was abruptly terminated.[42] Grattan returned from convalescence in Britain, and it was partly under his influence that the whig and radical elements of the anti-union coalition attempted to reinvigorate fading popular anger against the union. When parliament, as anticipated, rejected a motion opposing union, a large aggregate anti-union meeting of the leading citizens of Dublin, including a substantial deputation of catholics, was assembled and addressed by John Philpot Curran, the prominent whig lawyer best known for his courageous defence of the United Irish leaders. His words on the occasion are testimony to the desperate importance that was attached by the opposition to public expressions of support:

> Our only road to safety [remains] the unanimity of the people. The
> capital [has] nobly set the example. If the country [follows] the
> example, Ireland [can] not be lost. The projected surrender of

38 Buckingham to Grenville, 1 Feb. 1799, *Fortescue*, iv, p. 462; Buckingham to Grenville, 8 Feb. 1799, ibid., p. 469; Buckingham to Grenville, 13 Feb 1799, ibid., p 470.   39 H. Grattan (ed.), *Memoirs of the life and times of the Rt. Hon. Henry Grattan*, iv, pp 437-8. 40 Grattan, *Memoirs*, iii, pp 421-2.   41 Charlemont to Haliday, 2 Feb. 1799, *Charlemont*, ii, p. 345.   42 Cornwallis to Portland, 18 Jan. 1800, Castlereagh to Portland, 18 Jan. 1800, Castlereagh to Portland, 20 Jan. 1800, *Cornwallis corr.*, iii, pp 165-7.

Ireland [will] be defeated ... Without our own ardent co-operation, what can we hope from our friends in parliament; with all their virtues and their talents, what barrier can they form without our own assistance; at the best an uncemented wall, destitute of that connection which nothing but support can give, it must soon be overwhelmed in the overbearing tide of corruption.[43]

This last phase of the union period, the first half of 1800, saw a brief flurry of the activity that had occurred early the previous year. Anti-union pamphleteering recovered to equal the production of the Castle's ongoing propaganda campaign. The *Anti-Union* newspaper, having been allowed to lapse in March 1799, was relaunched as *The Constitution; or Anti-Union Evening Post*. The new format, carrying daily British, European and provincial news as well as the compositions of opposition writers, was capable of acting as a substitute for standard newspapers in a way that its predecessor had not. By the volume of advertising it attracted, one can judge that it proved both profitable and popular. Handbills circulated urging the yeomanry to resist the union forcibly, one suggesting that 'No government can wrest the parliament from 60,000 armed and tried men.'[44] The radical lawyer and associate of the Emmet family, Robert Holmes, having already had one pamphlet suppressed in 1799 for seeming to advocate a total separation of Ireland and Britain,[45] now issued another which asserted to the yeomen that it was their constitutional duty to declare their sentiments as a body on the subject of union.[46] Meanwhile, Foster, Downshire and the Ponsonbys made use of their extensive connections among the landed gentry to encourage the convocation of large-scale anti-union county meetings in 26 of the 32 counties of Ireland in order to explode the Castle myth that the provinces acquiesced in the Act.[47] Given the fact that much of the country was still under martial law in the aftermath of 1798, this was a deliberately provocative action, though the Castle cautiously refrained from banning the meetings. Even the anti-union borough owners joined the lurch towards populist tactics by finding seats in parliament for a number of extremist anti-union lawyers, some of them, like Peter Burrowes, with well

43 *The speech of Henry Grattan esq. on the subject of a legislative Union with Great Britain; the resolutions ... at an aggregate meeting held on the 16th of January last; the celebrated speech delivered on that occasion by John Philpot Curran, esq. ...* (Dublin 1800), pp 27-8. 44 Cornwallis to Ross, 21 Jan. 1800, *Cornwallis corr.*, iii, pp 167-8.   45 Drennan to McTier 15 Jan. 1799, *Drennan-McTier letters*, ii, p. 45. The banned pamphlet was [R. Holmes], *A demonstration of the necessity of a legislative Union of Great Britain and Ireland* (Dublin, 1799).   46 [R. Holmes], *An argument addressed to the yeomanry of Ireland* (Dublin, 1800).   47 Lecky, *Ire.*, v, pp 347-8n, 354n.

known United Irish connections.[48] Orators like Burrowes, Saurin, and Curran made eager use of their seats in parliament to do what they could not safely do in print or at large meetings: in thinly veiled language, they urged displays of popular resistance to the union, even going so far as to argue that the use of violence would be legally justifiable.[49]

For a brief period, this campaign seemed to yield results. Cornwallis wrote a number of panicky letters early in 1800 desperately requesting a faster influx of British troops to restore the impression that government was in control.[50] But as early as 14 February, Cooke was reporting that the opposition had failed to provoke large-scale popular resistance.[51] Little occurred thereafter to suggest that the decisive action would take place anywhere other than in parliament; despite increasingly desperate clamour from the opposition benches, the union swept successfully through all its stages.

With this necessarily brief overview of the trends in public activity during the union period completed, one might ask what importance we should assign to the role of public opinion in the act's passage. It has been suggested that expressions of public opinion were essentially irrelevant to the processes of parliamentary and governmental decision making in the eighteenth century. Members of the Irish parliament, after all, were not usually dependent on public approval for the retention of their seats and offices.[52] However, in relation to the union period, we might legitimately ask why, if this analysis is correct, the government lavished over £10,000 on the production of pro-union literature, and why anti-union leaders turned so determinedly towards agitation of the public in the first half of 1800.[53]

One clue is provided in the language used by both sides in stating their case. Anti-union arguments did not rest simply on the effect a union might have on the economy, the catholic question, reform or other such issues, as we would expect if their object was simply to sway the opinions of parliamentarians. Many pamphlets also sought to delegitimise any union that

48 Castlereagh to Portland, 29 Jan. 1800, *Cornwallis corr.*, iii, p. 174, Cornwallis to the Bishop of Lichfield and Coventry, ibid., p. 247.   49 W. Saurin, *An accurate report of the speech of William Saurin, esq., in the House of Commons, on Friday, the 21st of February 1800* (Dublin, 1800), pp 4-8; Lecky, *Ire.*, v, pp 413-6.   50 Cornwallis to Portland, 21 Jan. 1800 and 27 Jan. 1800, *Cornwallis corr.*, pp 168 and 173.   51 Cooke to Grenville, 14 Feb. 1800, *Fortescue*, vi, p. 128.   52 G. O'Brien, 'The unimportance of public opinion in eighteenth-century Britain and Ireland', *ECI*, viii (1993), pp 115-27.   53 Apart from the £5,000 mentioned already as requested by Castlereagh, Cooke was in 1801 still requesting £4,400 to discharge printer's bills (Wilkinson, 'How did they pass the Union'). We can add to this the pension given to Theobald McKenna of £300 a year (McDonagh, *Viceroy's post-bag*, pp 52-3). There were probably other costs of which we simply are not aware.

might be passed, arguing that parliament was not competent to enact a union, that any attempt to implement it would be fundamentally unconstitutional, and that hence popular refusal to accept the act would be justifiable and legal.[54] Others asserted that the parliament was being bought by government corruption, and that a union passed by such corrupt methods would not be legally binding.[55] Conversely, government writers argued strongly that parliament was competent to enact legislation of any nature whatsoever and denied the allegations of corruption, while asserting that any resistance to a parliamentary act of union would constitute a rebellion as illegal as that of 1798.[56] The pro-union and anti-union standpoints here were paradoxical: opponents of the union defended the Irish parliament from extinction by asserting its constitutional limitations, supporters sought to abolish it by denying those limitations.

The implications of the argument over the limits of parliament's powers were serious. From the start, anti-unionists severely doubted whether parliament was capable of resisting the vast lure of the government's patronage resources, and the setback received by the union in January 1799 amazed all but the parliamentarians themselves. The object of the anti-union agitators had thus been to stir up a public storm of such violence that either parliament, or government, or both, would be intimidated into abandoning the act. By denying the legitimacy of the union, if it passed, its opponents wished to frighten both parliamentarians and government leaders with the spectre of violent resistance. Consider the following words by Colonel O'Donell, who had commanded a Mayo militia regiment with impeccable loyalty during the 1798 rebellion:

> Should the legislative independence of Ireland be voted away by a parliament which is not competent thereto, I shall hold myself discharged from my allegiance ... I will join the people in preserving their rights: I will oppose the rebels in rich clothes with as much energy as I ever have done the rebels in rags.[57]

O'Donell was by no means alone in using such extreme language: frequent incitements to armed resistance were delivered in parliament, where they

---

54 I. Weld, *No Union! Being an appeal to Irishmen*, 3rd edition (Dublin, 1798), pp 28–9. 55 [Holmes], *Argument addressed to the yeomanry*, pp 30–1. 56 W. Smith, *The substance of Mr William Smith's speech on the subject of a legislative Union between this country and Great Britain delivered in the House of Commons on Thursday, January 24th, 1799, and now reduced to the form of an Address to the people of Ireland*, 4th edition (Dublin, 1799), pp 26, 37, 42–3. 57 *A report of the debate in the House of Commons of Ireland on Tuesday and Wednesday the 22nd and 3rd of January 1799* (Dublin, 1799), p. 76.

could not result in prosecution, and even in print, where they could.[58] Such firebrand orations, however, have seldom received much credence in the histories. Bolton, for example, pointed to the military service of Plunket and O'Donell against the rebels in 1798, and asserted that 'it was sheer bluff for them to pose as leaders of an Irish war of independence.'[59]

Bolton's interpretation here is flawed. It is true that men like O'Donell could ill afford to partake in armed resistance to the government that safeguarded their interests, especially in the aftermath of the bloodiest civil conflict in Irish history. But neither could the British government in the midst of the French revolutionary wars jeopardise its position by risking the emergence of yet more Irish discontent, especially from the political classes that had previously been loyal. Pitt's avowed aim in pursuing a legislative union was, after all, a stabilisation of the security situation in Ireland.[60] If the anti-union leaders were bluffing, so too were the government, and the opposition repeatedly showed themselves more than willing to play with fire. They did so under the assumption, almost certainly correct, that given a convincing show of force, the British government would be forced to back down. Even if they did not, the probability existed that Irish MPs would absolutely refuse to risk their own security and property by pursuing a scheme for destabilisation, whatever pecuniary rewards might be offered to them.

With reference to the unimportance of public opinion, the government or the parliament or both had indeed been forced to act contrary to their own wishes due to the power of some form of mobilised public pressure in at least three instances in the twenty-five years prior to the union. These three cases were those of the volunteer pressure for free trade and an independent legislature, the assembling of the Catholic Convention in 1792–3, and the furious public reaction to Orde's commercial bill in 1785. The tradition invoked during the Union period by many anti-union leaders was explicitly that of the Irish volunteers; the volunteer era was the formative political experience for many of them. The most obvious target of their rhetoric was the Irish yeomanry. The yeomanry was in many respects a body strikingly similar to the old volunteer one. Both were largely Protestant in makeup, locally raised, officered by the gentry, and territorially based. In some cases, the personnel were identical, or from the same families.[61] Anti-union writers and speakers deliberately identified the two, making liberal

---

58 Ibid., pp 40, 42, 49, 53.   59 Bolton, *Union*, p. 111.   60 W. Pitt, *The speech of the right hon. William Pitt in the British House of Commons on Thursday, January 31 1799* (Dublin, 1799), pp 25-6.   61 Blackstock, *Ascendancy army*, pp 75-92.

reference to the events of 1782[62] and strongly emphasising the 'heroic' defensive roles played by both the volunteers during the American war and the yeomanry and militia in 1798.[63] If the anti-union side could emulate the patriot party of the 1770s and 1780s by bringing forward the yeomanry as a paramilitary wing of their movement, they would have an armed body of 57,000 with which to bolster their claim to speak for the nation.[64] This would have made a very considerable impression on both parliament and government, especially given the unreliability for various reasons of the other irregular military forces in Ireland, the British and Irish militias.[65] Regular forces, incidentally, amounted to only 32,000 in Ireland in 1799, and Pitt ideally wished to be able to reduce that figure in the interests of the wider war effort.[66]

Potentially alongside or separately from the yeomanry, the Dublin mob threatened to play its part in events. There was a precedent in 1759 of rioters invading the Irish parliament in response to rumours of an impending attempt at union.[67] Not dissimilarly, in January 1800, a mob including many yeomen attacked the carriages of pro-union MPs and attempted to throw them in the Liffey. In response, and with some of the government's allies in parliament quailing at this threat to their bodies, Cornwallis was forced to order extra British troops into Dublin.[68]

In the end, the union passed quietly. Barring isolated units, the yeomanry never assumed a political role, and the mass of the lower classes outside Dublin remained seemingly uninterested in the union issue, with Cornwallis guessing, probably rightly, that they hated both the government and the opposition equally.[69] The opposition had failed to overcome a number of stumbling blocks in their ambition to recreate the victory of 1782. Despite superficial similarities to the Irish volunteers, the yeomanry was an easier body for the government to control. The government had the power to remove the captain of any troublesome corps, or even to disband a unit altogether, with a consequent loss of status and lucrative income for all concerned.[70] This ability would have been of little use had the yeomanry staged a unified show of defiance, but it did enable Cornwallis to make some

62 J. Collis, *An address to the people of Ireland on the projected Union* (Dublin, 1799), pp 6-7.   63 J.W. Jervis, *A letter addressed to the gentlemen of England and Ireland on the inexpediency of a federal Union between the two kingdoms* (London, 1798), pp 37-8.   64 Grattan, *Memoirs*, v, p. 31n.   65 *Cornwallis corr.*, iii, pp 74-8, various correspondents including Portland, Dundas and Ross, March 1799.   66 Grattan, *Memoirs*, v, p. 31n. All figures apply to 1799.   67 H. Calkin, 'For and against an Union', *Eire-Ireland*, iv (1978), pp 22-3.   68 Cornwallis to Ross, 31 Jan 1800, *Cornwallis corr.*, iii, p. 175.   69 Cornwallis to Ross, 2 July 1799, *Cornwallis corr.*, iii, p. 111.   70 Blackstock, *Ascendancy army*, pp 55-74.

useful examples when faced with isolated displays of disobedience. Anti-
union leaders were left in no doubt of the serious consequences of acting
alone in encouraging military insubordination. The most high profile victim
of the government's ruthlessness was the marquis of Downshire, Ireland's
most influential borough magnate, who had calculated unwisely that his
immense power in parliament and elsewhere rendered him immune from
government censure. He circulated an anti-union petition around his Down
militia, and promptly found himself disgraced, dismissed from his offices
as colonel of the militia unit, privy councillor and governor of County
Down, the last office being gifted instead to a loathed political rival (Castlereagh's father) for good measure.[71]

As well as the practical difficulties of giving the anti-union movement a
threatening militant aspect, much has often been made of the heterogenous
political nature of the anti-union alliance. Foster and Downshire, while
possibly appealing to the more conservative sections of the yeomanry, were
loathed by Catholic activists and radicals. It is indeed striking how quickly
United Irish writers dissociated themselves from the movement once Foster
assumed its leadership. Many washed their hands of the struggle altogether
with the passage by the Irish parliament, with substantial anti-union support, of the Indemnity and Rebellion Bills of 1799. By 1800, many radical
pamphleteers, though still opposed to the union, were advising their readers
not to lift a finger to prevent it.[72] Conversely, Foster was extremely reluctant
to be associated with Grattan,[73] who had still not completely shaken off
allegations that he had been in collusion with the United Irishmen prior to
1798.[74] The loyalist yeomanry may not have reacted well to Grattan's exhortations, whatever his popularity in Dublin, and the entry of Curran into
parliament was exceptionally difficult to swallow for those who had suffered
property destroyed or friends and relatives killed or injured in 1798.[75]

More important than any of these factors was the fact that the government entered fully into the battle for public opinion in marked contrast to
their conduct during the volunteer era. In contrast to the situation in the
early 1780s, the opposition was not left to cultivate the public without
challenge. Anti-union assertions on economic issues, on the catholic
question, even on the very nature of Irish national identity, were challenged

---

71 Bolton, *Union*, pp 191-2.   72 *A letter to the Irish parliament on the intended bill for
legalising military law* (Dublin, 1799); *An address to the people of Ireland showing them why
they ought to submit to an Union* (Dublin 1799).   73 Castlereagh to Portland, 18 Jan.
1800, *Cornwallis corr.*, iii, pp 166-7.   74 R. Mahony, 'The pamphlet campaign against
Henry Grattan in 1797-99', *ECI*, ii (1987), pp 149-66.   75 Cornwallis to Bishop of
Lichfield and Coventry in *Cornwallis corr.*, iii, p 247.

in every detail by pro-union writers, and the opposition's internal divisions were relentlessly exposed. The enormous Castle propaganda campaign instilled sufficient doubt and division to prevent the emergence of a truly national opposition to the union. It would be inaccurate to assert that the pro-union activists secured an ideological victory, since the majority of the Irish people of most social classes remained unenthusiastic about the act. Ultimately, the Castle only needed to achieve an ideological stalemate to suffocate the populist efforts of their opponents.

The narrative of the union's passage has usually been related with the emphasis lying very heavily on events in parliament and government. Contemporaries were acutely aware that the determining events might occur outside, not inside, the parliament building. The anti-union movement aimed to bring the debate out of the house of commons and into the streets. Historians should emulate them.

8

Marriage against inclination:
the union and caricature

Nicholas Robinson

The caricaturists were contemporary witnesses of events. What did they make of the union campaign and its aftermath? And to what extent is their witness a useful source of historical evidence?[1]

An anonymous print, *Union between England & Ireland!!* (Plate 1), published in London by William Holland on 20 February 1799,[2] is offered at the outset to suggest that their insights were, typically, neither morally uplifting nor particularly nuanced. As this material is analysed under our contemporary historical and art-historical microscopes, we should remember that the caricaturists of the day, as with today's cartoonists, were as likely to be thinking of nothing more profound than the vulgar fun of it all, exposing, as one writer has put it, 'a plump backside for a coarse laugh'.[3] Fairness and complexity are readily sacrificed for the rewards of the one-liner that may amuse the audience but does less than justice to the facts. But the prints do offer extensive commentary on political life and, as Diana

1 For an analysis of the development of caricature during the reign of George III, see D. Donald, *The age of caricature* (New Haven and London, 1996); see also [R. Godfrey *et al.*], *English caricature 1620 to the present* (London, 1984); N.K. Robinson, *Edmund Burke: a life in caricature* (New Haven and London, 1996). For a discussion of prints in general as a reliable source of historical evidence, see B. Maidment, *Reading popular prints 1790-1870* (Manchester, 1996). 2 Listed in the British Museum's *Catalogue of political and personal satires*, published in eleven volumes between 1870 and 1954, as 9462A (hereafter: BM 9462A). The *Catalogue* describes 17,391 prints (up to 1832) preserved in the Department of Prints and Drawings; the last seven volumes, in particular, by M. Dorothy George, constitute a meticulous and erudite work of scholarship extensively mined by every writer since. This image is from the Nicholas Robinson collection, Trinity College Dublin Library, ref. 137 (hereafter: TCD, NR coll. 137). 3 Godfrey, *English caricature*, p. 7. The word 'cartoon' (in the sense of a humorous drawing) was put into circulation later, by John Leech in *Punch*, 1843.

Donald points out, 'most comic draughtsmen are ... no more than the unselfconscious vehicles of majority opinion'.[4]

While London was, overwhelmingly, the source of caricature prints, a trade was beginning in Dublin that would flourish into the 1820s based largely on pirating and plagiarising the London publications. An undated copy (reversed) of Plate 1 was published by Del Vecchio of 26 Westmorland Street, entitled *John Bull enjoying Grauna*,[5] in which John Bull observes contentedly, *How Sweet's the Love that Meets Return!!* That very few caricatures remain today bearing Del Vecchio's publication line underscores their ephemeral nature, with prints from the top end of the market, part of a luxury trade, more likely to survive. Donald argues that 'satirical prints of the reign of George III must have permeated the national consciousness far more widely and deeply than has been suspected'.[6]

In essence, caricatures can be a valuable source for the historian, but they can also be misread as we try, two centuries later, to interpret the immediacy of the artist's response: to spot the characters, identify the incidents, penetrate the satirical allusion, decode the short-hand artistic conventions. Roy Porter, noting that historians have tended to relegate visual material to an illustrative or confirmatory role, has urged that these prints should be analysed not just as 'evidence' but as 'art' with its own conventions for expressing moral messages.[7]

This review of caricatures on the union begins with English and, indeed, Scottish perceptions, for if the material comes from London many prints have a Scottish bite.[8] Isaac Cruikshank[9] had arrived from Edinburgh in or about 1783 and had become a leading caricaturist by the 1790s, while James Gillray's father was also a Scot. Some artists, such as Thomas Rowlandson,[10]

4 Donald, *Caricature*, p. 22.   **5** An impression is in the Prints and Drawings Collection of the National Library of Ireland (hereafter: NLI coll.); not recorded in the BM *Catalogue* (hereafter: BMX), though as the BM collection continues to grow, it does not necessarily follow that an impression is not to be found there. BMX prints are like precious truffles to historians of caricature, and much snuffling takes place in American collections such as the Library of Congress, the Lewis Walpole Library attached to Yale, and the Huntington Library, California. TCD and NLI contain many BMXs of Irish subject matter or origin.   **6** Donald, *Caricature*, p. 21.   **7** Noted in Maidment, *Popular prints*, p. 24. See Porter, 'Prinney, Boney, Boot' in *London Review of Books*, 20 March 1986, pp 19-20 and 'Seeing the past' in *Past and Present*, February 1988, pp 186-205.   **8** Of some 3,420 prints recorded in the BM *Catalogue*, vols. vii and viii (1793-1810), only a tiny handful, literally measured in ones and twos, come from each of Bath, Brighton, Cambridge, Glasgow, Manchester and Newington. Dublin, too, is a modest source as are Edinburgh, Paris, and (for copies published in the periodical *London und Paris*) Weimar.   **9** (1764-1811), George Cruikshank's father.   **10** Born July 1756 in Old Jewry, the son of a London wool and were Londoners; others whom we cannot place include the ubiquitous Anon. One of these, active on the union issue, worked for the radical printseller and publisher William Holland, and executed aquatints such as Plate 1. Holland had been convicted and imprisoned in 1792 for publishing seditious material, *The Times* expressing its pleasure 'that some stop is at length attempted to be put to the sale of those scandalous prints which have long disgraced the windows of our public streets'.[11] So if there is a dearth of biographical details, this is not the sort of trade whose practitioners are afforded informative obituary notices – Holland, as it happens, being an exception.[12]

John Wardroper has written that the work of Isaac Cruikshank

> neatly demonstrates what was true of many caricaturists: they made use of passing events in a detached and perhaps cynical way; but as they had always to aim at winning a wide response, everything they did had to look to a body of opinion. It is for this reason that caricatures are one of the most sensitive, as well as much the liveliest, guides to the many-sided truth of past times.[13]

We must not, however, be carried away by notions of detachment and independence, or that each separate work could be 'untrammelled by cant of politics or good taste, shaped only by the artist's inspiration and the need to appeal to the contemporary eye'.[14] These artists – to put it bluntly – were often character assassins, pedlars of downright lies and, more dangerous, of credible half-truths, instinctively oppositionist but, in the propaganda battles that flared from time to time, guns for hire. Even the great Gillray was for hire, though his sly ambiguity made him a dangerous man to choose.

If union was the preoccupying issue in Ireland at the turn of the century, it vied in London with other pressing concerns (some indicated in *A Week's Amusement for John Bull*:[15] Plate 2): the new income tax; the war with France; a bad harvest; the rising price of bread and food riots. It vied, too, with passing fancies like that of the Prince of Wales and the Duke of York for the Misses Gubbins of Bath; a horserace at Newmarket between *Hambletonian* and *Diamond* (*Hambletonian* won by half-a-neck); Richard Brinsley Sheridan's stage success *Pizarro*; a madman's attempt to assassinate the king at Drury Lane Theatre (affording further extravagant displays of

silk merchant.   **11** Donald, *Caricature*, p.147.   **12** *Gentleman's Magazine*, 1816: M.D. George, *English political caricature*, i (Oxford, 1959) p. 175.   **13** J. Wardroper, *The caricatures of George Cruikshank* (London, 1977) p. 8.   **14** Wardroper, *Cruikshank*, p. 8.   **15** [Charles Williams] published 27 March 1799 by S.W. Fores; BM 9366; TCD, NR coll. 1017.

loyalty by Sheridan); and Lord Belgrave's attempt to suppress Sunday newspapers. These, as well as Irish affairs, are some of their customers' preoccupations addressed by the London printsellers in 1799 and 1800.

An anonymous print (Plate 3)[16] reveals William Pitt's Irish plan in the context of the war with France. John Bull, ironically skittish, is '*tired of all the old Jigs*' and wants something new – '*something stilish, and grand*'. '*I will endeavour to please you if I can*', responds Pitt, '*what do you think of this – it is a grand serious-movement called the Deliverance of Europe, or Union with Ireland.*' The flamboyant attire of Henry Dundas, secretary of state for War, and the accoutrement he wields, remind us that if the caricaturists seemed to have it in for the Irish, then Scottish speech, customs and supposed characteristics were equally ridiculed.[17]

Irish affairs had been, spasmodically, the subject of caricature in London since legislative independence in 1782. For instance, in *A Whisper Cross the Channel*,[18] Charles James Fox is accused of fomenting trouble in Ireland by urging on a firebrand earl bishop of Derry. Pitt's commercial propositions for Ireland, being controversial domestically, received due satirical attention.[19] The regency crisis of 1788–89 not only revealed difficulties inherent in the constitutional arrangements between Britain and Ireland – John FitzGibbon warning the Irish house of commons grimly that union was the alternative to Ireland's following Great Britain 'implicitly in all regulations of imperial policy'[20] – but afforded ample opportunity for satire as the Irish parliamentary delegation, with comical mistiming, arrived in London on the king's recovery to offer the prince of Wales an unrestricted regency of Ireland. 'Just in time to be too late' gibed one of the caricaturists, William Dent.[21] And there were bound to be hostile prints in reaction to rebellion in Ireland in 1798, though some purported to show John Bull's good-natured puzzlement,[22] and emphasis was placed on the dangers posed by revolutionary France and the imagined role of the whig opposition with their francophile sympathies.

---

16 Perhaps by T. (or F.) Sansom, *John Bull learning a New Movement against the next Campaign*, published 21 March 1799 by S.W. Fores; BM 9364; TCD, NR coll. 142. 17 H.M. Atherton, *Political prints in the age of Hogarth* (Oxford, 1974), pp. 210-16. 18 James Sayers, published 1 August 1785 by Thos. Cornell; BM 6805; TCD, NR coll. 720.   19 It is surprising not to find prints reflecting the agitation in 1800 by the English woollen manufacturers who feared the union would provide dangerous competition from Ireland.   20 R.B. McDowell, 'Parliamentary independence 1782-9' in *New history of Ireland*, iv, p. 285.   21 For an account see N. Robinson, 'Caricature and the Regency crisis: an Irish perspective' in *ECI*, i (1986), pp. 157-76. 22 e.g. Anon., *What do you want, Paddy??* published 9 April 1798 by W. Holland; BMX; TCD, NR coll. 117.

Fox, 'Citizen Fox', was a prime target, excoriated as a character witness for Arthur O'Connor at the Maidstone trial of 1798. Gillray's treatment of the whigs' evidence at the trial, and of O'Connor's subsequent admission of guilt, was one of the most damaging caricatures of the age.[23] Now, in December 1798, in *Horrors of the Irish-Union* (Plate 4), Gillray borrows that phrase, 'a whisper across the Channel', to accuse him of further mischief.[24]

'Hip! my old Friend Pat!' calls Fox, *'... a word in your Ear!... dont you see that this damn'd Union is only meant to make a Slave of you! – do but look how that cursed Hag is forging Fetters to bind you ...'* (he is referring to the youthful matriarch Britannia; for some time she and John Bull have been the two most famous visual images employed to conjure up British nationalism. Now, with prints like this, Gillray and others are creating equivalent – if less flattering – Irish images for their customers).[25] *'... rouse yourself Man! raise all the Lawyers & spur up the Corporations. Fight to the last drop of blood, & part with the last Potatoe to preserve your Property & Independence.'*

Pat is confused: *'– why – by St Patrick its very odd now! for the old Girl seems to me, to be offering me her Heart & her Hand, & her Trade & the use of her Shelalee to defend me into the bargain!'* (we note how Britannia has stamped on the viper of discord) *'– by Jasus, if you was not my old friend, Charley, I should think you meant to bother me with your Whisperings ...'*

The allusion to the hostile resolutions of the Irish bar on 9 December and of Dublin Corporation on 17 December 1798 reflects the acuteness of Gillray's political antennae.[26] His representation of union as *'Security Trade & Liberty'* is unusually sympathetic to Pitt in these prints, and it is not irrelevant that he had been in receipt of a secret government pension since November 1797.[27]

To a print he had made in July 1798, Gillray had later added the words *'No Union'* to the battlecry, *'Erin go brách'* of an Irish chief said to be *'drawn from life at Wexford'*.[28] Isaac Cruikshank's charge is more specific: his

---

23 *Evidence to Character*, published 10 October 1798 by J. Wright; BM 9245; TCD, NR coll. 8. Even the death of his cousin Lord Edward FitzGerald is laid at Fox's door by Gillray: *Nightly Visitors at St Ann's Hill*, published 21 September 1798 by H. Humphrey; BM 9244; TCD, NR coll. 115.   24 Published 24 December 1798 by H. Humphrey; BM 9284; TCD, NR coll. 123. Several prints, including this, were copied in reduced size for *London und Paris* by C. Starcke (or Starck) who worked in Weimar *c.*1790–1810.   25 This is an ongoing process: Paddy might be rebellious and hostile, but in a few years time with the threat of Napoleonic invasion he will become, briefly, *'honest Pat'*, giving the French a *'warm welcome'*. Later in the century Sir John Tenniel and others will continue the process.   26 Bolton, *Union*, pp 78, 82.   27 Donald, *Caricature*, p. 175.   28 Perhaps Gillray is merely adding to the shelf life of a print that has dated: *Portrait of an Irish Chief*, published 10 July 1798 by H. Humphrey; first state BMX; TCD, NR coll. 112; later state BM 9236.

THE PLATES

Plate 1 Anon. (perhaps after G.M. Woodward): *Union between England & Ireland!!*
Published 20 February 1799, by W. Holland.

Then, as now, caricaturists were adept at turning the serious political issues of
the day into vulgar fun.

Plate 2 [Charles Williams]: *A Week's Amusement for John Bull.* Published 27 March 1799 by S.W. Fores.

At a time of crisis in Britain and Europe, developments in Ireland vie with other pressing concerns and passing fancies, as William Pitt presents his bill of fare.

Lord love ye my good Masters—do give us
something new—I'be tired of all the
old tho'—I knows the March
to Paris by heart, and as for
Indemnity for the Past, and
Security for the future, they are
as easy to me as my A.B.C. I want
something stilish, and grand

I will endeavour to please you
if I can, what do you think of
this—it is a grand serious-
movement called the
Deliverance of Europe,
or Union, with— Ireland

Pub March 11. 1799 by S.W. Fores N.º 50 Piccadilly

Edes of Caracatures Lent out for the Evening

JOHN BULL *learning a* NEW MOVEMENT *against the next* CAMPAIGN.

Plate 3 Anon. (perhaps Sansom): *John Bull learning a New Movement against the next Campaign.* Published 21 March 1799, by S.W. Fores.

Union with Ireland — the key to saving Europe, mocks the artist — is proposed by Pitt in the context of the long drawn out war with France. John Bull's cynical request for a new tune ridicules a ministerial assertion (made five years earlier) that Paris was ready to be marched upon.

Plate 4 James Gillray: *Horrors of the Irish-Union.* Published 24 December 1798, by H. Humphrey.

Behind Britannia's back, Charles James Fox incites 'Pat' – an unflattering Irish version of John Bull developed by Gillray and others –

Plate 5 Isaac Cruikshank: *Peep of Day Boy's Preventing an Union by adding Fire to the Sun!!!* Published 2 March 1799, by S.W. Fores.

Irish bulls abound when the Irish are being caricatured. Here, '*adding Fire to the Sun*' is seen as '*an Irish Method of throwing Cold Water on a Subject*' as William Pitt's irradiated face is dragged off to the bonfire by a lawless protestant mob.

Plate 6 John Cawse: *The Inside of a School*. Published 7 February 1800, by S.W. Fores.

Given his long absence from the commons, Fox is represented here as the school truant whose punishment is to stand on *Lists of Traitors* and embarrassing *Reports of the Secret Committee* that reveal the activities of his cousin Lord Edward FitzGerald, James Coigly and Arthur O'Connor. Meanwhile, Pitt coaches a new boy on the spelling of a valuable word, '*Pension*'.

Plate 7 Anon.: *A Trial for A Rape!!!* Published 8 February 1799, by W. Holland.

Fox, with Richard Brinsley Sheridan as his tipstaff, presides over a Jacobin court in which Hibernia lays charges against Pitt. Sir Francis Burdett, a champion of prisoners, must now assume the task of gaoler; fellow whigs around the table are, no doubt, both prosecution and jury.

Plate 8 Anon: *The Rival Managers*. Published June 1799, by W. Holland.

Pitt and Sheridan are seen as theatrical impresarios, each anxious to assert the superiority of his own company. The impecunious whig Sheridan invokes 'Mr Reynard my Property Man,' to vouch for their finances, while Pitt thinks his productions (including the pantomime 'Union for Ever,' in which he plays Harlequin) 'would make your best Tragedies and Comedies appear mere Farce.'

Plate 9 Isaac Cruikshank: *The Union Coach*. Published 4 June 1799, by S.W. Fores.

Cruikshank depicts his compatriot Henry Dundas as guard on Pitt's coach to Westminster, dispensing nuts to the subservient Scottish MPs comfortably settled within. The nutshells he scatters to the *'quarrelsome'* Irish members who have gullibly accepted seats in the basket behind.

Plate 10 Isaac Cruikshank: *An Irish Union!* Published 30 January 1799, by S.W. Fores.

John Bull, a good-natured yokel, is not at all clear about Pitt's intentions, as his hand is joined with that of his hostile Irish counterpart. The flamboyant Dundas, a noted distributor of patronage to the Scots, recalls the Scottish union, and *'how many made the siller [silver] frae that time to this'*.

Plate 11 Anon: *Paddy's escape from the Union Net.* Published February 1799, by W. Holland.

News from Dublin, that the plans for union were threatened with failure is received rather more philosophically by a pipe-smoking John Bull than by the dismayed Pitt.

A FLIGHT ACROSS the Herring Pool.

Plate 12 Isaac Cruikshank: *A Flight Across the Herring Pool*. Published 20 June 1800, by S.W. Fores.

As Hibernia (right) laments the emptying of Dublin's parliament house, Pitt entices newcomers to the 'Imperial Pouch' while Dundas, multiple holder of office, perches smugly on his own very considerable perquisites.

The image carries the following text within the illustration:

'I will have some more,'

Isaac Income!!

Really M.r Bull notwithstanding you have done me the Honor of placing me at the head of your table to day—You, I must declare all thoughts of an intended Union—your Family is so very large, & so enormously expensive, that, after my small Dowry will scarcely suffice Master Income alone for one meal—besides I understand there are less a small part of your numerous Family, & that you have several tumor hopeful still in the Nursery.

What is that lubberly headed fellow about there?' Cant you take what comes to your share like the rest of the Family, why you swallow more than all the rest put together, Miss Hibernia will be frightened at your prodigious Stomach and break off the connection !!

Dont be so boisterous, there is enough for us all.

Plate 13 Isaac Cruikshank: *Miss Hibernia at John Bulls Family Dinner.!!* Published 18 March 1799, by S.W. Fores.

The suspicions voiced by James Moore O'Donel MP, and others, 'that Ireland was coveted as a new untapped source of revenue' are supported by Cruikshank's image of the many appetites to be satisfied at John Bull's table. Hibernia takes fright, fearing 'my small Dowry will scarcely suffice Master Income alone for one meal …'

MISS HIBERNIA AT JOHN BULLS FAMILY DINNER!!

The Union Coach

Pubᵈ By Mᶜ Cleary Nᵒ¹ Nassau Sᵗ

Plate 14 Alexander McDonald: *The Union Coach*. Published (?) 1799, by W. McCleary.

In pirating Cruikshank's print (Plate 9), McDonald has added the burly figure of the anti-unionist barrister John Egan haranguing the departing coach. Others now portrayed in the basket are (?) Castlereagh, the earl of Clare, (?) William Beresford, archbishop of Tuam, and Charles Agar, archbishop of Cashel.

THE RIVAL ORATOR'S

Plate 15 Anon: *The Rival Orator's*. Published [Dublin], (*c*.1800).

The threatening lunge of John Egan, on the left, perhaps more skillful as duellist than orator, is countered by Dr Patrick Duigenan. Fellow lawyers and MPs, they held passionately opposing views on the union.

Plate 16 Alexander McDonald: *Union Fishery.* Plate 2d. Published (*c.*1800), by W. McCleary.

McCleary's publications were, for the most part, social in character. Rather more daring is this political print showing the hook-nosed archbishop of Cashel, Charles Agar, fishing with other bishops for preferment. Agar duly landed Dublin, which became vacant in October 1801. Castlereagh (left) looks for a '*Place*'; beside him Henry Grattan goes for '*no union*.'

Plate 17 [?Alexander McDonald]: *The Union — No Grumbling.* Published [?1800], by W. McCleary.

'Is this the reward of my Loyalty!' cries an opponent to union, an order dangling from his lapel, as he and another are assailed by Pitt and his lieutenant, Dundas, determined to put down resistance from whatever quarter.

NO BRIBERY BILLY.

Plate 18 Anon: *No Bribery Billy*. Published [Dublin], (*c.*1800).

Trampling underfoot Edward Cooke's pro-union pamphlet, both loyalist and croppy reject Pitt's outstretched purse, and offer their own form of inducement.

Judging in this a cast of utmost moment will darken all the conquests he has won. "Reverse.

LOYALTY REWARDED

Plate 19 Anon: *Loyalty Rewarded*. Published [Dublin], (c.1800). The original sketch, in the National Library of Ireland, has been attributed to James Henry Brocas.

Prints, like pamphlets, played their part in the propaganda war. Here anger, and devotion to the speaker, John Foster (whose likeness she clasps as a shield) is the response attributed to Hibernia, who will admit of '*No Union but Union of Irishmen*'.

Plate 20 'W.S.': *Ways & Means or Vox Populi!!* Plate to *Hibernian Magazine*, 1 February 1800.

The viceroy, Cornwallis, accompanied by the ambitious prelate Agar, comes to inspect the process of garnering support, as the elegant Castlereagh (fifth from right) solicits signatures from '*respectable persons*' outside a prison.

Plate 21 Anon: *Union Street – or ease and Plenty* (detail). Published [Dublin], (*c*.1800).

In a great city reduced to sloth and decay, a goat finds grass on the plinth of King William's statue outside Trinity College, in this grim vision of post-union Dublin.

The Death of ERIN!!

Plate 22 Anon: *The Death of Erin!!* Published (*c.*1800), by (?M.) Williamson, Dublin.

John Philpot Curran leads the pall-bearers, and Grattan and Foster the mourners, as their beloved constitution of 1782 is laid to rest. Gravediggers in the distance are Clare and Castlereagh.

Plate 23 Anon: *Carrying the Union* (detail). Published March 1800, by W. Holland.

In a print that epitomises the theme of 'marriage against inclination', Pitt and Clare, eluding St Patrick and others in pursuit, carry off the beautiful and tragic bride Hibernia. Her harp sinks slowly beneath the waves of the Irish Sea.

Plate 24 Anon., 'Dennis O'Doody of Drumcondera' (probably after John Nixon): *The Triumphal Entry of the Union into London, 1801* (detail). Published 1 January 1801, by W. Holland.

Even St Patrick is forsaking his own 'nate little Kingdom' for another, teases the author of this elongated aquatint, probably the Irish artist Nixon. The saint is part of a motley procession winding towards Westminster.

Plate 25 James Gillray: *The Union Club* (detail). Published 21 January 1801, by H. Humphrey. First state.

A famous print (and in such demand that the plate had to be reworked), this shows the whigs – who had strongly opposed the union – drowning their sorrows at a grand function in the new Union Club in Pall Mall. Perched on the table, the earl of Moira raises a bumper and James across to clasp the hand of Earl Clermont. They and others wear shamrock to indicate their Irishness. The prince of Wales has disappeared beneath the table, and in the foreground the duke of Norfolk anticipates next morning's hangover.

Plate 26 James Gillray: *Integrity retiring from Office!* Published 24 February 1801, by H. Humphrey.

Gillray contemptuously contrasts the dignified exit of Pitt's cabinet with the rabble-rousing response of the Opposition. The artist's secret government pension, however, almost certainly stopped on Addington's coming to power.

Plate 27 Anon: *The Friends of Liberty, and the people, driving the great mangy mungrel Dog home to his own kennel.* Purports to be published in London, 14 April 1801.

In what is probably an Irish print, the artist takes malicious satisfaction in Clare's discomfiture as his hopes for English office evaporate.

Plate 28 John Cawse: *John Bull Shewing his Intended Bride the Parliament House!*
Published 30 April 1800 by W. Hixon.

John Bull (long employed in English caricature as the embodiment of national character) reassures a dismayed Hibernia that with the old House at Westminster '*quite alter'd—new touch'd up*' to accommodate their union, they shall live '*as happy as the Flowers in May!*'

firebrands are a lawless protestant mob, *Peep of Day Boy's Preventing a union by adding Fire to the Sun!!!* (Plate 5),[29] as the sun, with Pitt's irradiated face, is dragged off to the bonfire to wild exhortations. Across the channel stands Fox, at *Holy Head*, accused again of fomenting trouble.

Having virtually seceded from the commons in 1797, Fox's opposition to the union was expressed in private and in Whig Club speeches.[30] This is a pity: as the most caricatured figure of the age, any public utterances on the subject would have ensured lively coverage in the prints;[31] so there was a brief flutter when he turned up for a debate in February 1800 on Bonaparte's offer for peace.[32] The artist John Cawse (Plate 6)[33] gives Fox the role of a schoolroom dunce being punished for his truancy, and put to stand on a pile of embarrassing documents, such as reports on '*Ld. E. Fitzgerald*' and '*O'Conner's Confession*'. While Dundas admonishes the '*sulky boys*' Sheridan and Sir Frances Burdett to '*Haud yere Tongues*', Pitt with his *Plan for an union* is coaching a new scholar to spell the word pension: '*be a Good Boy & you shall be rewarded ...*'

Meanwhile, if Fox is slow to attend parliament, 'the anonymous Holland aquatinter' is happy to see him preside as judge in *A Trial for a Rape* (Plate 7),[34] with Sheridan his tipstaff, as Hibernia lays charges in a Jacobin court against Pitt, charges that cause some clucking among fashionable ladies in the gallery. One of them, with delicate ambiguity, advances a view of Pitt's sexual orientation that is to be found occasionally in the prints, confiding in her companion: '*I took him to be a different kind of man.*'[35]

Of the whigs assembled in the print, only Sheridan and George Tierney (seen at the bottom right-hand side) opposed the union in the debates.[36] Sheridan, speaking on the subject five times during 1799,[37] is one of *The Rival Managers* (Plate 8) in a print published by Holland that June.[38] This is another example of how in caricature 'the verbal invades the graphic to construct the overall image'[39] though here it is the text that supplies nearly all the fun. Pitt and Sheridan are rival impresarios, each talking up the

29 Published 2 March 1799 by S.W. Fores; BM 9351; TCD, NR coll. 140.   30 George, note to BM 9284.   31 Robinson, *Burke*, p.194.   32 L.G. Mitchell, *Charles James Fox* (Oxford, 1992), p. 106.   33 *The Inside of a School*, published 7 February 1800 by S.W. Fores; BM 9515; TCD, NR coll. 161. See also G.M. Woodward/John Cawse, *The Ghost of St Stephens*; published 27 January 1800 by W. Hixon; BM 9511; TCD, NR coll. 158: Pitt, terrified at what he takes to be Fox's ghost in the commons, drops from his hand a speech on the union.   34 Published 8 February 1799; BM 9347; TCD, NR coll. 34.   35 See J. Ehrman, *The younger Pitt*, iii (London, 1996), pp 93-7.   36 George, note to BM 9347.   37 F. O'Toole, *A traitor's kiss* (London, 1997), p. 353.   38 Anon., BMX; TCD, NR coll. 148.   39 As Maidment has put it, *Popular prints*, p. 9.

superiority of his own company. Sheridan had been since 1776 manager of Drury Lane Theatre; his anti-union outfit, he now asserts, is the better conducted theatre: *'As to our Finances – ask Mr. Reynard, my Property man! – and as to Loyalty where you have touch'd with a pencil, I have made use of the Trowel, Sir!!'* This mocks the ultra-loyalist speeches Sheridan had incorporated in his new play *Pizarro*, adapted from a German drama, *The Spaniards in Peru*. It was proving a smash hit. *'This evening'*, says his poster, *'will be performed for the 60th Time the Gold Mines of Peru or a new way to pay old debts ...'* Dorothy George has dryly observed that 'such exuberant and profitable loyalty from a needy Foxite was open to misconstruction.'[40]

Meanwhile Pitt, since 1783, had been impresario of another great institution, named in his poster as *'Theatre Royal P[arliamen]t Street.'* *'This Evening'*, it announces, *'will be performed the favourite Comedie of Tax upon Tax or the way to grow rich / the Characters by select Performers. End of the Play a grand Spectacle called Peace in Perspective! to which will be added the last Pantomine* [sic], *called Union for Ever. Harlequin in Ireland. The part of Harlequin by the Manager.'* *'You must not pretend to compare your Company with mine, Sir,'* he admonishes Sheridan. *'A chosen few! Methodical Actors; never want the word – Know their cues, dashing Performers! – why, Sir, the Pieces I bring forward, would make your best Tragedies and Comedies appear mere Farce.'*

One of Pitt's dashing performers, his chosen few, was Henry Dundas, who had moved the address on the reading of the king's message in January 1799, and who was seen by the London caricaturists as Pitt's lieutenant in the project. Gibes at the greed and subservience of Scottish MPs, and Dundas's skills in controlling them, are to be found in prints such as *The Union Coach* (Plate 9), made by their fellow Scot, Cruikshank, in June 1799.[41] Driven off to Westminster by Pitt, the gullible Irish members experience the agonies of travelling in the basket.[42] *'I don't much relish this Union Coach'*, complains one, *'the Guard told us the back seats were the best, by Shaint Patrick the front ones must be bad enough then!'* (Irish protestants, too, invoked St Patrick in caricature). *'Why Sawney[43] seems Perfectly comfortable in the inside,'* replies his companion, and from within comes confirmation: *'Why this is quit warm & cosey canna ye haud yere tongues ye Bullocking Bulls!!'* *'Hoot mon'*, asks another, *'is this the way to the Treasury[?]'* Dundas is the guard, with blunderbuss and a bag of nuts to

---

40 *English political caricature*, ii, p. 45.   41 Published 4 June 1799 by S.W. Fores; BM 9394; TCD, NR coll. 149.   42 Agonies which Pastor Moritz had described in 1782: George, note to BM 9394.   43 This nickname for the Scots, generally perjorative, derived from 'Alexander.'

keep his compatriots happy. '*I ken the way well enough,*' he replies and adds, for the benefit of the Irish: '*There's the shells for you, ye quarrelsome crew.*'

In an earlier Cruikshank print (Plate 10),[44] a hostile, suspicious Pat is asked to join hands in friendship with John Bull, while Dundas seeks to reassure him by reading '*a little aboot the same Business in my ain country*' from a *History of Scotland.* John Bull, who had started life in 1712 as a literary character, came later in the century to embody in prints the English national character,[45] and of particular interest is how Cruikshank handles John Bull's reaction here: '*This may be Nation good Fun – but dang my buttons if I know what it is about! & Cousin Paddy dont seem quite clear in the Case neither.*' Cruikshank signals what he believes are Pitt's underlying intentions; a man standing by – possibly his private secretary Joseph Smith, of the Treasury – is ready with the *Wet Blankets* of income tax.

If Cruikshank's John Bull reflects public confusion, it is perhaps not surprising that Holland's John Bull, a pipesmoking countryman, seems quite unperturbed by *Paddy's escape from the Union Net* (Plate 11), a print of February 1799 reflecting the news from Dublin.[46] '*I declare that obstinate Irishman has broke my Net,*' complains Pitt, '*just when I thought I had compleated the job ...*' '*Good bye, Billy, honey,*' replies Paddy ('honey' is one of those words, like 'arrah' and 'by Jasus' that alert us that the speaker is Irish), and he adds, with no great prescience: '*old birds are not caught with chaff.*'

Dundas, too, is taken aback by the stout resistance they encounter. As one of Pitt's seconds in a fight with Hibernia (proclaimed as *A Grand Battle between the Irish Hen and the English Bantam*),[47] he marvels, '*What an obstinate cheeld o' th' Deel she is. I thought it would be only come and kiss me, and the Lassie would do it!*' Urged by her seconds, Sheridan and Henry Grattan, and by St Patrick (poised in the heavens above with the laurels – or, more precisely, the shamrock – of victory), Hibernia strikes a belligerent pose to confront an opponent who shows little stomach for the encounter, and scoffs: '*You stand up to me, no, no, I know a thing or two better than that!*'

A subsequent print emphasises, however, that Pitt's grim tenacity was not to be underestimated.[48] Dundas, at his side, urges care as he tries to rope a

44 *An Irish Union!*, published 30 January 1799 by S.W. Fores; BM 9344; TCD, NR coll. 145. 45 Atherton, *Political prints*, p. 97. 46 Anon., BMX; TCD, NR coll. 150. See also Isaac Cruikshank, *A New Irish Jaunting Carr. The Tandem – or Billy in his Sulky*, published 20 February 1799 by S.W. Fores; BM 9348; TCD, NR coll. 143. 47 Anon., published 11 February 1799 by W. Holland; BMX; TCD, NR coll. 144. A copy (see fn. 56) is BM 9372. 48 [Isaac Cruikshank], *Slender Billy and Hopping Harry*, published 12 February 1800 by W. Hixon; BM 9517; TCD, NR coll. 154.

wild Irish bull. '*Gently – Paddy – Gently*,' soothes Pitt, '*don't look so furious, it's all for your good depend upon it – only let me throw this small cord over your <u>Horns</u> that I may lead you to your Brother Johny, where you & he will live in Clover ...*' But the union noose is one of taxation, and Pitt's aside is ominous: '*... if once I lay my Clutches on you I'll bring that high spirit of yours down till you kneel on your marrow Bones.*' '*I ha been a drover this mony a year*,' observes Dundas, '*but the Deel swell me Gif e'r I saw sic a stirk as this, a' my scots Beasts are as tame as Lam's I can either lead or drive them Just at Pleasure.*'

Dundas features in caricature as a distributor of patronage to the Scots and as a pluralist, a multiple holder of office. Secretary of state for War, he was also treasurer of the navy and chairman of the influential Board of Control, his position there being virtually that of a secretary of state for India.[49] In June 1800, as he and Pitt encourage *A Flight Across the Herring Pool* (Plate 12)[50] – and demonstrate that old birds can, after all, be caught with the chaff of place and pension in the '*Imperial Pouch*' – Dundas perches on his own very considerable perquisites, as Governor of the Bank of Scotland, Commissioner of Chelsea Hospital, Custos Rotulorum for Middlesex, and several besides. '*Come on my little Fellows*', says Pitt to the Irish MPs, '*– there's plenty of room for you all ...*' Hibernia laments that Dublin's parliament '*... will look like a Walnut shell – without a Kernel*'.

Westminster's problem was the opposite: space had to be found to accommodate the new members. In a print by Cawse, John Bull '*Shewing his Intended Bride the Parliament House*' (plate 28)[51] promises that the old house '*will be quite alter'd – new touch'd up ...*' Seeing Hibernia's agitation, John Bull continues: '*dont let them Persuade you that you'l make a bad Match of it – bless your jolly good humour'd Countenance we shall live as happy as the Flowers in May!!!*'[52]

---

49 Cruikshank had satirised Dundas as *A Specimen of Scotch Modesty* in playing twelve separate roles; published 5 February 1798 by S.W. Fores; BM 9169. See, too, Richard Newton, *Tria Juncta in Uno*, published December 1797 by Newton; BM 9052. For his influence in Indian affairs, see James Gillray, *The Board of Controul. Or the Blessings of a Scotch Dictator*, published 20 March 1787 by R. Phillips; BM 7152. Dundas, finding the burden almost unsupportable, had tried in April 1800 to set a date for resignation from the War Department and as treasurer of the navy: Ehrman, *Pitt*, p.357.   **50** Isaac Cruikshank, published 20 June 1800 by S.W. Fores; BM 9543; TCD, NR coll. 15.   **51** John Cawse, *John Bull Shewing his Intended Bride the Parliament House*, published 30 April 1800 by W. Hixon; BMX; TCD, NR coll. 156. The architect James Wyatt found space by cutting into the walls of St Stephen's chapel next door: Ehrman, *Pitt*, p.357.   **52** In another print by Cawse on the same theme, Hibernia looks rather more demure and acquiescent as Parson Pitt publishes the '*Banns of Union*': *John Bull ask'd at Saint Stephens!!!*, published 20 April 1800

Dismayed by her intended quarters, Hibernia is shocked at what she sees around John Bull's dinner table (Plate 13),[53] as the head of the household remonstrates with an especially greedy member of the family, *Isaac Income*: '*... Miss Hibernia will be frightened at your prodigious Stomach and break off the connection!!*' At the far end of the table she is trying to do just that, fearing '*... my small Dowry will scarcely suffice Master Income alone for one meal ...*' (Also to be fed are *Abraham Hat Stamp*, *Simon Soap Tax*, *Hannah House Tax*, *Tommy Tile Tax*, *Patty Paper Stamp*, *Harry Heraldry*, *Walter Window Tax*, and *Polly Powder Tax*, and – says Hibernia – there are '*several Junior branches still in the Nursery*'). Income tax, introduced in 1799, was deeply resented, and one of the Irish arguments against union – put by James Moore O'Donel MP – was that 'Pitt's maladministration of war-time finance had bled Britain white, and that Ireland was coveted as a new untapped source of revenue'.[54] Some of these London prints clearly echo O'Donel's view. In *Party's Not Agreed*,[55] Pitt's vision of happiness ('*I will make you Rich & give you plenty of money & provide for your Children*') is rudely dismissed: '*... by Jasus what do you want of me: are you not after starving your own Country and Bringing them to Beggary ...*' While expressing some sympathy for the anti-union position, the main intent of the caricaturists is to underscore English domestic discontent.

What of the plates being produced in Dublin? Apart from examples of original work considered below, and the inevitable piracies,[56] some older images are adapted for present purposes, as in the case of *The Botching Taylor Cutting his Cloth to Cover a Button*.[57] In a print of the same name, George III had been ridiculed in 1779 for his hobby of button-making; on the advice of his fellow tailor, the earl of Bute, he is shown reluctantly slicing off *Ireland* from a length of cloth (as he had already sliced *North America*) in pursuit of this hobby.[58] Now Pitt is the tailor, Dundas and Clare his advisors, as again the shears are poised to cut the cloth between *Great Britain* and *Ireland* – the unintended consequence of Pitt's plan, claims the

by S.W. Fores; BM 9532; TCD, NR coll. 160. **53** Isaac Cruikshank, *Miss Hibernia at John Bull's Family Dinner!!*, published 18 March 1799 by S.W. Fores; BMX; TCD, NR coll. 340. **54** Bolton, *Union*, p.112. **55** Anon., published 14 May 1800 by J. Aitken; BM 9535; TCD, NR coll. 163. **56** e.g. Anon., *A Grand Battle between the Irish Hen and the English Bantam*; plate to *Hibernian Magazine* [1 May 1799]; BM 9372, a copy (reversed) of the print noted earlier in fn. 47. **57** [? Alexander McDonald], undated, c.1799, published by [William] McCleary, 21 Nassau Street [Dublin]; BMX; coll. Neptune Gallery, Dublin. In examining this print I am grateful for the assistance of Rosemary Baker. **58** 'John Simpson', published 27 December artist. Where Lord North had occupied a place in the original design, a new figure now stands with the length *North America* in his hand; it could be George III, or it could be his viceroy, Cornwallis who had surrendered at Yorktown, and who is portrayed confusingly like the king in some of the prints.

Other Dublin publications, like *The Union Coach* (Plate 14),[59] are copies, but with variations: in it the figure of the barrister John Egan has been added, haranguing the departing coach to the annoyance of Clare, who calls to Dundas, '*Guard thi[s] is a troublesome fellow he wants to stop us.*' A cleric facing forward wishes he were in Beresford Place (a conventional way for caricaturists to identity their speakers) and he is, perhaps, the Hon. William Beresford, archbishop of Tuam since 1794. Sitting opposite him, with hook nose, is the archbishop of Cashel, Charles Agar,[60] while the man at the back, also a portrait, is probably the chief secretary, Viscount Castlereagh.

Although a plagiarism of Cruikshank's print (Plate 9), it is signed (the initials AMD on the coach stand for Alexander McDonald or MacDonald) and bears the publication line of William McCleary of 21 Nassau Street. Printsellers like McCleary catered to the demands – and reflected the prejudices – of their customers. Dublin prints, many of them vulgar, were for the most part social rather than political in character.[61] Dabbling in politics was unusual – rash political flirtations would be bad for business – but in this exceptional case might be undertaken profitably, because protestant Dublin, with its barristers and merchants, was caught up in the union contest, and decidedly partisan. So to show the barristers and MPs John Egan and Patrick Duigenan as *The Rival Orator's* (Plate 15) is merely a bit of fun.[62] Many members of the overstocked bar went into politics and, to quote Geoffrey Bolton, 'as a rule began their careers in opposition, which allowed more scope for facile eloquence and left the way open for the Government to persuade them to its side when a suitable vacancy occurred.'[63]

1779 by 'James Tomlinson' (both names thought by George to be fictitious); BM 5573. **59** Alexander McDonald, undated, published (?) 1799 by W. McCleary; BM 9395; coll. Neptune Gallery, Dublin. **60** An engraved portrait of Agar, after George Dance, is in the National Portrait Gallery, Heinz Archive, London. **61** Typical would be the amusing caricatures rendered by Henry Brocas junior (in the manner of the Dightons) of the military stationed in Dublin, that James Sidebotham of Sackville Street published and McCleary pirated. **62** Anon; BMX; NLI coll. [impression reproduced is from coll. Neptune Gallery]. **63** Bolton, *Union*, p.81. According to the *Belfast Newsletter*, 67 lawyers sat in the Irish Commons, of whom 42 were in active practice. John FitzGibbon (later earl of Clare) began his political career – as Bolton puts it – 'as an assailant of the hapless Lord Lieutenant Buckinghamshire'. To remind us what a small world it was (and in which the

The arch-protestant Patrick Duigenan of Trinity College and MP for Armagh would occasion an extraordinary intervention by George III; a proposal in January 1801 that Duigenan be asked by the new archbishop of Armagh to resign his seat, in order that one could be found for the Irish chancellor of the exchequer Isaac Corry, so infuriated the king that he proposed to 'apprize the Lord Primate of the ill effect it would produce'.[64]

The primate, William Stuart, a son of the famous earl of Bute and translated from St David's, had been appointed in 1800 by the king in preference to Irish aspirants. A more daring political statement is made by McCleary and his artist McDonald in depicting Agar of Cashel and some fellow bishops fishing for preferment (Plate 16), Agar in the centre casting to become primate.[65] To the right is the other cleric (? William Beresford) spotted in the basket of *The Union Coach* (Plate 14), here carrying his bishop's mitre. Castlereagh (left), the young chief secretary, is fishing for a place, while Grattan hopes for '*no union*', and Pitt, hoping to catch Hibernia, is himself being snared by the Devil.

As the contest intensifies, McCleary's prints become increasingly hostile and anti-Castle, alleging vote-buying and coercion. In *Political Jugling, or Sqwire Piper Giving his Vote*,[66] Castlereagh solicits the signature of '*Darby Drone Esqr*', a blind piper in ragged clothes who '*cant see any hurt I do my country*', while the Devil at Castlereagh's side is doling out coins. Pinned to the wall is a dubious '*List of the noble-men & Gentlemen who have signed for the Union*'. Others, clearly not freeholders, wait in line. Emboldened, perhaps, by the vote in the Irish house of commons in January 1799 (but not so far as to risk a publication line), the same artist had envisaged *Union between England, Ireland and Scotland*[67] to be a communal gallows, on which are hanged Dundas, Pitt and Clare, holding hands. They are despatched by Egan, while John Foster in his speaker's robes encourages him to '*Pull away*.' However, in *The Union – No Grumbling* (Plate 17),[68] the caricaturist

caricaturists operated), Buckinghamshire's daughter Amelia Anne Hobart married Castlereagh.   **64** Bolton, *Union*, p. 210. A colourful entry in the *DNB* notes that Duigenan was the son of a Leitrim farmer, Ó Duibhgeannáin, who had intended him for the Catholic priesthood 'until the boy's abilities were perceived by the Protestant clergyman of the parish.' Though an able lawyer, the verdict of R.B. McDowell and D.A. Webb is that 'he contributed more to the entertainment than to the education of Dublin:' *Trinity College Dublin 1592–1952* (Cambridge, 1982), p. 66.   **65** [? Alexander McDonald] *Union Fishery*. Plate 2d; undated, published *c.*1800 by W. McCleary; BMX; coll. Neptune Gallery, Dublin. Agar landed Dublin, which became vacant in October 1801.   **66** [? Alexander McDonald], undated, published *c.*1800 by W. McCleary; BMX; coll. Neptune Gallery, Dublin.   **67** [? Alexander McDonald] undated, no publication line, published (?) 1799 [? by McCleary]; BMX; coll. Neptune Gallery, Dublin.

concedes that Pitt has taken charge, and Dundas, assisting '*Billy the Grinder*' with the grindstone, calls out: '*Down Down Orange and Croppy lye down.*' One of those being coerced, wearing an order on his lapel, cries '*Murder! Is this the reward of my Loyalty?*' *No Bribery Billy* (Plate 18), rejecting bribery, offers its own form of coercion and, Edward Cooke's pamphlet being trampled underfoot, indicates how much opposition is coming from loyalist quarters.[69]

Anger, and devotion to the speaker, John Foster, are the themes of *Loyalty Rewarded* (Plate 19):[70] clasping as her shield a likeness of her hero, a grim and pugnacious Hibernia will admit of '*No Union but Union of Irishmen*' and resists the threatening advances of George III, who has already shackled an impoverished Scot. As with Britannia, Hibernia's is the voice of patriotic exhortation, and when one of the pro-unionists, Lord Minto, argued that 'local affection' could be expanded to include the two islands, he added: 'the true patriot will prefer the solid and real happiness of his country to its metaphysical identity'.[71]

Caricaturists tended to enjoy the crude and scatological. The lord chancellor, Clare, suffers indignity to his office and person when mocked as '*the terrified unionist*' who is confronted on his way to the privy by its occupant, a ghostly rebel wielding a pike.[72] Two snarling tomcats on the wall behind mirror this confrontation with their '*arguments for and against a union*'. To help him with his necessary business, Clare has been carrying leaves torn from a document '*Irish ... Independence 1782 ...*' which now flutter to the ground, and, in his pocket and marked '*Waste Paper,*' the '*Bill of Rights*' offers a further supply.

The barrage of loyalist criticism of Cornwallis's viceroyalty is reflected in the Dublin prints.[73] In a tableau to *The Union Olio*[74] (an aptly named hotchpotch of local opposition), he is the pike-carrying soldier labelled '*A*

68 [? Alexander McDonald] undated [? 1800], published by W. McCleary; BMX; TCD, NR coll. 850. **69** Anon., undated, no publication line; BMX; NLI. coll. **70** Anon., undated, no publication line; BMX; NLI coll. See also *The Children of Erin Seeking Protection from their Foster Father, a plate to Hibernian Magazine* [1 April 1799] BM 9368, NLI coll.; and *The Mad Music Master*, in which Pitt attempts to cajole and coerce a duet from Scotland's bagpipe and Hibernia's harp. The new tune is *Union* but the decrepit highlander prefers to turn back the page to *Over the Water to Charley*, while she prefers *My own Dear Somebody*, her harp being decorated with the mace and head of Foster: Anon., undated [c. 1799], and without publication line (probably Irish), BM 9697; NLI coll. **71** McDowell, in *New history of Ireland, iv*, p.364. **72** Anon., *The Apparition*; undated, no publication line; BMX; NLI coll. **73** Described, for example, in Geoghegan, *Union*, pp 31-34, 64-65. **74** Anon., frontispiece to *Hibernian Magazine* [1 February 1799]; BM 9346; NLI coll. Among

Turn Coat', whose intervention, at once admirable and politically unfortunate, in the affair of the yeoman Hugh Whollaghan, is remembered with bitterness. Charged with murdering an unarmed civilian, the yeoman – against the evidence – had been acquitted by court martial. Cornwallis, furious, had Whollaghan dismissed from the yeomanry, and directed that the presiding officer, the earl of Enniskillen, and his colleagues should not sit on any future court martial.[75]

In a plate to the *Hibernian Magazine* of 1 February 1800 (Plate 20), Cornwallis (looking not unlike his monarch)[76] is seen arm-in-arm with the ambitious prelate Agar, proclaiming: '*this great object accomplished by any means, I shall then retire from Public Business!!*' Some of the means he has in mind are illustrated; the town-crier is looking for '*a few Hundred persons of any Description*' who will be paid to sign for a union or can scratch their mark. Towards the right, in front of a prison, the elegant figure of Castlereagh is collecting signatures from '*respectable persons*' such as the man coming forward in leg-irons and the disabled beggar beneath.

Archbishop Agar hints at other ways in which help is to hand. ' ... *I've been long <u>troying</u> the due weight of the Clergy in this Diocese*' he says, referring to the crucial support of the Catholic archbishop of Dublin Dr John Thomas Troy.[77] (The link between union and emancipation had become progressively stronger, for, as John Ehrman puts it, 'when the former failed in effect at the first attempt, the latter ... was called in aid of success'.[78] Many catholics, wrote Cooke, 'thought it foolish to oppose a measure which

the tableaux familiar themes include *Young Paddy*, the wild Irish bull that escapes from Pitt's clutches (in this curious image Pitt, in soldier's uniform, reaches over the head of a saddled British lion to shoot at it), while *Billy the Driver* furthers the metaphor of Paddy being harnessed to pull the royal carriage. Both these images were issued as separate prints: *Young Paddy*, BMX; NLI coll., *Billy the Driver*, BMX; NLI coll. For another composite print, see Anon., *The Union*, BMX; NLI coll. In one tableau Castlereagh seeks to bind with a '*union*' chain three men who fight among themselves, and who represent Catholic, Protestant and Dissenter. '*This is a dirty job*,' he says, looking to Cornwallis, '*I expect to be well paid for it*.' Grattan, Curran and Egan are elsewhere depicted supportively; Agar less so, calls for the whipping of a few of '*those refractory lawyers Aldermen and Bankers...all knaves or fools*.' A weeping Hibernia submits her hand to receive the wedding ring of John Bull, whose intentions are spelt out: '*Weighty as my incumbrances are I can still borrow money if you will join in the Securities*.'   **75** Bolton, *Union*, pp 64–5.   **76** 'W.S.', *Ways & Means or Vox Populi!!*, BM 9514; NLI coll. In *Marriage against Inclination, A Step to Separation*, plate to *Hibernian Magazine* [1 April 1800]; BM 9531; NLI coll., the same artist represents George III in a way that is graphically unrecognisable but identifiable from the King's habit of saying '*What – What – What ...*'   **77** The next lord lieutenant, Hardwicke, would find a revenue job for Troy's nephew: Bartlett, *Fall and rise*, p. 273. **78** Ehrman, *Pitt*, iii, p. 496.

was opposed by their enemies the Orangemen'.[79] *'For loyalty they now almost equal Killarney my lord!!'* enthuses an aide, and a local wit expresses the hope '... *that as the Grass will be Growing in the Streets, your Lordship Will make the Fodder Cheap.'*

Echoing this last sentiment, a vision of post-union Dublin is conjured up in *Union Street – or ease and Plenty* (Plate 21),[80] grass on the plinth of King William's statue offering sustenance for a clambering goat. While Daly's clubhouse is decaying, a thatched lean-to behind the pillars of the parliament house promises (an old gibe at the Irish) *'Good dry Lodgin[gs].'*[81]

The obsequies of poor Erin must now be attended to, and in a protestant churchyard (Plate 22).[82] The print appears to be by the same hand, and here a publication line identifies the printseller as Williamson – his initial looks to be M – of 36 Grafton Street, Dublin. In marked contrast to Gillray's mocking print on the collapse of the regency in 1789,[83] there is sympathy for the pall bearers. *'We struggled till the last,'* says John Philpot Curran who leads, *'but the torrent of Corruption bore us down.'* He and a weeping Egan help carry a bier that has been decorated with notices such as *'Liberty and Prosperity'*, *'Constitution of 1782'* and *'Catholic Emancipation'*. Behind Egan, Foster (in his speaker's wig and robes) is also in tears: *'Alas! If we could have kept our Parliament – our Constitution would have lived –.'* *'I told you,'* responds Grattan at his side, *'if you did not put this faction down they would extinguish Ireland.'* Members of the faction referred to are at work in the background with pick and shovel, Clare remarking: *'We have done the deed and now lets sink the Body deep in Earth, least it should rise in Judgement against us.'* *'Twas nobly done my lord,'* replies Castlereagh, *'an artful well put Stroke – there bosted Constitution is no more.'*

For the London caricaturists it was a much jollier, more superficial affair (Plate 23).[84] Nonetheless, the image is of the union as violation, as Pitt and Clare carry off their prize with St Patrick *'and all his wild Irish Pat-riots'* at their heels, among them Foster and Grattan. Mounting the Irish on bulls was an old joke (a nod, no doubt, at the figure of speech), much employed in 1789 at the expense of the Irish regency delegation.[85] Thomas

79 Quoted in Bartlett, *Fall and rise*, p. 249. Cooke was under-secretary for civil affairs, 1789-1801.   80 Anon., BMX; NLI coll.   81 Dublin's supposed decline was later depicted in two contrasting plates by Thomas Rowlandson: *College Green, before the Union*, BM 11851; NLI coll. and *College Green after the Union*, BM 11852; published 7 February 1812.   82 Anon., *The Death of Erin!!* undated (? 1800), published by (?) M. Williamson; BMX; NLI coll.   83 *The Funeral Procession of Miss Regency*, published 29 April 1789 by S.W. Fores; BM 7526; TCD, NR coll. 335; see Robinson, *Burke*, p. 132.   84 Anon., *Carrying the Union*; published March 1800 by W. Holland; BM 9529, TCD, NR coll. 817.   85 See fn. 21 above. The ragged fortune hunter,

Rowlandson, one of the greatest caricaturists but whose political prints (in the words of John Riely) 'make up the least memorable part of his *oeuvre*',[86] offers a print of the pot-boiler category: two bulls on which Pitt and St Patrick are mounted, confront one another; '... *the duece of anything like a union do I see*' complains the saint, '*except their horns being fastened together*.'[87]

An enormous Holland aquatint records *The Triumphal Entry of the Union into London* (Plate 24 – detail). Dated 1 January 1801, its four separate plates have been glued together to create a giant panorama of stage Irishness.[88] St Patrick and his bull are each disconcerted by efforts to detain them, while an old labourer calls out: '*Ah long life to your holy Reverences memory, why will you lave your own nate little Kingdom* ...' Further on, Grattan is borne by two chairmen, and still trying to warn Hibernia that Pitt is a '*false flattering gay deceiver*'. But, suggests the artist, there is a peerage in it for Grattan, too: resting on top of his sedan, along with the Irish harp, is a coronet. Hibernia continues to resist Pitt's amorous attentions – '*Oh, come Sir be aisy – you shall never win my affections by violence!*' – while Clare provides accompaniment on the fiddle, impressed that Billy's '*soul begins to thaw!*'

Thence to *The Union Club* (Plate 25)[89] where the whigs, some with shamrock in their hats to proclaim their Irishness, drown their sorrows at a grand dinner, and Gillray helps perpetuate the myth of how the Irish enjoy a party.

The political drama immediately following the union involved (according to Gillray) another, less edifying outing for the whigs, and was occasioned by George III's adamant refusal to countenance emancipation. *Integrity retiring from Office* (Plate 26), published on 24 February 1801,[90] eulogises Pitt for leading his ministers with dignity from the Treasury. Flourishing his paper, *Justice of Emancipating ye Catholics*, he looks disdainfully at the whig rabble

mounted back-to-front on a bull, was one of Gillray's earliest images: *Paddy on Horse-Back*; published 4 March 1779 by W. Humphrey; BM 5605; TCD, NR coll. 7. See also Anon., *St Patrick Mounted on the Pope's Bull Appearing to the City Sages*, undated [? 1800], BM 9688; NLI coll.   86 Quoted by B. Rix, *Our old friend Rolly* (Toronto, 1987), p. 7.   87 *The Union!*, published 7 January 1801 by R. Ackermann; BM 9696; TCD, NR coll. 171.   88 Anon. (probably after John Nixon) BMX; TCD, NR coll. 836.   89 James Gillray, published 21 January 1801 by H. Humphrey; BM 9699; TCD, NR coll. 168. (The print was so successful that Charles Williams blatantly plagiarised it for his publisher, S.W. Fores: 8 February 1801; BM 9704; TCD, NR coll. 170). The Prince of Wales, having presided, lies unconscious beneath the table. For a detailed analysis of the revellers, see George, note to BM 9699.   90 Published by H. Humphrey; BM 9710; TCD, NR coll. 165. For Pitt's resignation, see also Anon., *The Benediction of St Patrick!!*, published 20 February 1801 by W.

who have gathered to taunt him, with their missiles and rotten fruit. Sheridan menaces with a butcher's cleaver[91] while Tierney beside him, dressed up as a cobbler, prepares to fling another squalid projectile, a dead cat.

Behind Pitt comes a sombre Dundas, a glimpse of tartan waistcoat hinting at his more usual flamboyant attire, then the round face and peer's robes of Grenville, the foreign secretary and (to the left) Spencer, first lord of the Admiralty. Between Grenville and Dundas another Scot emerges, Lord Chancellor Loughborough. It is tempting to read something into the quiet smirk on Loughborough's face, given his Judas role in secretly agitating the king's passion, and given the fact – as Lord Stanhope put it – that 'even the warm admirers (if there be any such) of his Lordship's political career will scarcely ascribe to him any very ardent zeal on the abstract merits of the question'.[92] But Gillray's biographer judges that the artist was 'evidently unaware' of Loughborough's activity.[93]

Pitt's decision to resign had caused bewilderment and, ironically, even as Gillray was producing this plate, the minister was privately having second thoughts. But Henry Addington had given up the speakership to succeed him, and the die had been cast. One virtually certain consequence of Addington's coming to power was that Gillray's government pension was stopped.[94]

A curious print (Plate 27)[95] dated 14 April 1801 and stated to be published in London, provides a suitably disedifying image with which to conclude our inspection, and echoes the missile-throwing scene outside the Treasury. Now Fox, inexplicably absent from Gillray's tableau, joins his fellow whigs, *The Friends of Liberty* and hoists with Sheridan a chamber pot of '*Fox's Mar[tyrs'] Drops*',[96] to shower their disapproval on '*the great mangy mungrel Dog*' Clare, driving him '*home to his own kennel*'. In the distance a gibbet beckons. Still wearing the wig and robes of a lord chancellor, and with an old kettle inscribed '*wool sack*' tied to his tail, he tries to avoid a dead cat that has been flung at his head. It was almost certainly Clare who had broken the news to the king in January that the cabinet was considering afresh the question of emancipation.[97] With an irony bordering on the ludicrous, says his biographer Ann Kavanaugh, he was excluded

Holland; BMX; TCD, NR coll. 167.   91 Recalling earlier depictions of the whigs as e.g. *The Butchers of Freedom*: [James Gillray], July 1788; BM 7352; TCD, NR coll. 910; see Robinson, *Burke*, p.114.   92 Quoted in Ehrman, *Pitt*, p. 498.   93 D. Hill, *Mr Gillray the caricaturist* (London, 1965), p. 103, fn. 1.   94 Hill, *Gillray*, p.104.   95 Anon., *The Friends of Liberty, and the people, driving the great mangy mungrel Dog home to his own kennel*, BMX; NLI coll.   96 The whigs had long been dubbed 'Fox's martyrs' (after John Foxe's much reissued *Book of Martyrs* of 1570), 160 having lost their seats in the general election of 1784.   97 Bartlett, *Fall and rise*, p. 264.

from Addington's 'new no-Popery cabinet' as 'simply too notoriously anti-Catholic'.[98] And having claimed (it was alleged) that he would render the catholics as tame as 'geld cats', the insult now appears to be remembered by the caricaturist, as it would be later by jeering crowds at his funeral procession in 1802.[99]

Embarking on this review one might have expected to find London caricature apathetic to the union question and hostile to the rebellious Irish, while in Dublin anonymous, unattributable prints would rehearse the burdens of colonial oppression, and lament the corrupt attainment of the government's aim. Not all of this proved true and there were unexpected twists and shadings. Few of the Dublin prints were fully anonymous. Some were plates to the *Hibernian Magazine*, others had the publication lines of McCleary or Williamson, or Del Vecchio. If vote buying and coercion are themes, so too is a sense of betrayal – 'the reward of loyalty', as some put it bitterly. Surprisingly little is made of the issue of catholic emancipation.

Nor was caricature in London apathetic, though the union measure had to be seen in the context of other grim concerns. Gillray, obsessed with the war against France, was adamantly in its favour. Others, tired of the war, tired of Pitt,[100] and cynical of his intentions, reflected real anger about the state of the national finances.[101] While the Scottish union might have suited some of his more voracious compatriots, warned Cruikshank, most Irish would rue such a course, and he used the metaphor of the unsuitable match, the marriage against inclination. Some, albeit with a degree of mockery, went further and called it rape. And others, as was evident at the outset, just wanted to make vulgar fun of it all.

98 A. Kavanaugh, *John FitzGibbon, earl of Clare* (Dublin, 1997), p. 373. **99** According to one witness's account some years later: Kavanaugh, *FitzGibbon*, p. 386. **100** As he himself was tired and frequently ill: see Geoghegan, *Union*, pp 130-1, 143-4, 175-7. **101** This mood continued and is reflected in a print [by Charles Williams] of 29 May 1802 in which Hibernia and John Bull view a bronze statue of Pitt on a pedestal composed of his supposed triumphs: income and other taxes, and an '*Increase of National Debt.*' '*Odzooks there's the dear Image, – the promotion of our Union,*' exclaims Hibernia, '*and I suppose that there Writing there, is the account of all his wonderful Works. Why Mr. Bull I thought he was the greatest Man we ever had, but it's all Bodder, why by St Patrick, Mr. O Brien (the Irish Giant) would make six of him:*' *The Brazen Image erected on a Pedestal wrought by Himself*, published by S.W. Fores; BM 9869; TCD, NR coll. 176. For the proposed statue of Pitt see BM 9863 etc. (A bronze statue by Francis Chantrey – was eventually erected in Hanover Square, London.)

ACKNOWLEDGEMENTS

The author, as always, owes much to the custodians of collections for their unfailing helpfulness: Colette O'Daly, then Curator of Prints and Drawings, and her colleagues in the National Library of Ireland; Charles Benson, Keeper of Early Printed Books and Special Collections, Trinity College Dublin; and Antony Griffiths and his colleagues in the Department of Prints and Drawings, British Museum. Thanks are also due to Edward McParland and Brendan Dempsey of TCD, Rosemary Baker, Andrew Bonar Law, Simon Heneage, Viscount and Viscountess Sidmouth, and, especially, to the editors Kevin Whelan and Dáire Keogh, and Katie Keogh of the Keough-University of Notre Dame Centre, Dublin.

For kind permission to reproduce material, the author thanks the Board of Trinity College Dublin, the National Library of Ireland, and the Neptune Gallery, Dublin.

9

Catholic responses to the
Act of Union

Dáire Keogh

'The catholics carried the union; the rest is detail'; so Bartlett concludes
his discussion of the great measure of 1800.[1] Such an aphorism has an
immediate attraction; yet its starkness masks the complexity of the issues
involved, as well as the sense in which the measure passed by virtue of
catholic *passivity* and *compliance*, rather than any conscious activity on their
part. Indeed, one wonders if even the blanket term 'catholic' makes any sense,
in this disturbed period, since there had been bitter divisions within their
ranks since the country fell beneath the French revolutionary spell. Increasingly through the decade, the catholic community was riven between an
aristocratic faction, headed by Archbishop Troy, Lords Fingall and Kenmare,
and the democratic majority, headed by John Keogh, Edward Byrne and the
leadership of the Catholic Committee, United Irishmen and Defenders. An
awareness of such divisions is crucial to any understanding of the largely
quiescent role adopted by the catholics throughout the union debates.

Initially, the factions differed on the appropriate means of advancing
their aims. The aristocrats clung to their traditional view that loyal
petitioning of the crown would merit relief, while the democratic majority
demanded emancipation as a right rather than a reward to be sought
through deferential addresses which had proved ineffectual in the past.
Such differences led to a formal schism within the Catholic Committee in
1791. At that point the bishops and catholic gentry attempted to reassert
their control of the catholic body, but were quickly forced to acknowledge
the new radicalised leadership of the Catholic Committee. Their attempted
reconciliation is best symbolised by Archbishop Troy's appearance at the

1 Bartlett, *Fall and rise*, p. 259.

Catholic Convention at which he declared the bishops 'second to no description of Catholics [in the demand] for emancipation.'[2]

In a sense, however, the deferential stance adopted by the old guard is understandable. Certainly the addresses to the crown may have achieved little, but the loyal demeanour of the catholic community had been their trump card since the 1760s. It was no coincidence that the relief measures of 1778 and 1782 were promoted by London in time of war, when Catholic loyalty stood out in contrast to the adversarial muscle-flexing of Ireland's protestant patriots.

In any event, it was evident that the strained catholic consensus could not be maintained. In February 1793, Britain went to war with France – clearly war was no time for constitutional experimentation(as Grattan acidly observed in 1797, there were two periods in which talk of reform was to be avoided, one was time of war, the other during peace); but as part of the armoury of war, Ireland's catholics were admitted to the county franchise in an attempt to bind them to the constitution. Yet, this concession was accompanied by a raft of counter-revolutionary legislation, including a measure establishing a militia force of almost 15,000 men, and a reactionary Convention Act which outlawed representative assemblies.

This legislation frustrated the work of the various reform movements. The Catholic Committee dissolved itself in 1793, and the Dublin Society of United Irishmen was suppressed in May of the following year. In this way the catholic community was left without an effective voice. One might have expected the hierarchy to champion their cause, but little support came from that quarter. In public, at least, the catholic bishops maintained their traditional stance, that loyalty alone brought results; indeed this stance was reinforced by the advice of their greatest mentor Edmund Burke. The bishops reminded the people that the various relief measures had been granted by the king's goodness, not through any sense of right. So just as loyalty had brought rewards, so too, intemperate or treacherous actions might result in the re-imposition of the penal laws. The ostentatious loyalty of the bishops did not go un-rewarded. In 1795 the Royal College at Maynooth was established by a grant from the crown in a cynical, and ultimately successful, attempt by the Castle to bring the catholic hierarchy on board. From that point the bishops remained silent in the face of increased tyranny and oppression, while excommunicating Defenders and United Irishmen, thus, as Watty Cox put it, sending a 'man to the devil for loving his country.'[3]

2 Troy to T. Bray, 8 Dec. 1792, Cashel Diocesan Archive (CDA).   3 W. Cox, *Irish Magazine*, Mar. 1815.

II

The rebellion of 1798 represented the realisation of the worst predictions of Burke and his Irish episcopal disciples as the summer's carnage claimed twenty thousand lives. Bishop James Caulfield of Ferns, whose detestation of the radical elements of the Catholic Committee was already well known, expressed caustic satisfaction at the defeat of the rebels. Following the execution of John Hay and his United Irish companions, he hoped that 'they will now see the differences between their principles and mine.'[4]

Such considerations, however, were of little consolation. Despite the overwhelming loyal display of the bishops and priests during the rebellion, the well publicised activity of clerics amongst the rebels was sufficient to feed interpretations of the rising as yet another 'popish plot', hatched under the weasel watchwords of 'reform' and 'emancipation'. Memories of the massacres of 1641 were revived; once more loyalists rallied to the call for revenge, giving rise to a backlash as vicious as the rebellion itself.

Significantly, it fell to the bishops to lead the defence of the general catholic body. The Catholic Committee was already dissolved, while the leading catholic radicals, tainted by their association with the United Irish cause and rebellion, were forced underground. In their absence, Troy became the acknowledged voice of Irish catholics, an ironic development which placed him in an unenviable position, given his conspicuous loyalism throughout the decade.

Troy's immediate task was to counter the polemical attacks in print, but of greater concern was the overwhelming fear and insecurity felt by catholics for their future which Caulfield attributed to 'their crazy union, that had caused more disunion throughout this country, than it had ever perhaps experienced before'.[5] Troy was particularly concerned at the revenge the orangemen had begun to inflict on the catholic community. The burning of the chapel at Ramsgrange, County Wexford, on 19 June was the first of sixty such incidents over the next two years. Rumours spread that chapels were to be permanently closed, priests were murdered with impunity, several were attacked and loyalists were reported to have boasted that 'there would not be a priest alive in County Wexford in twelve months time.'[6] Neither were the laity secure; apart from personal assaults, there was a real fear for the security of their property.

Amongst the protestant community, too, there was a sense of vigilance and fear. The rebellion illustrated their precarious circumstances and many

4 J. Caulfield to J. Troy, 3 July 1798, Dublin Diocesan Archive (DDA). 5 J. Caulfield to J. Troy, 6 Sept. 1798, DDA. 6 J. Caulfield to J. Troy, 10 Oct., 10 Nov.,

accepted the sectarian interpretation given to events. This spin was illustrated graphically in a tract entitled *A fair representation of the present political
state of Ireland*, published by the rabidly anti-catholic Patrick Duigenan,
dubbed the 'Black Doctor' by the radical press. In it the author pointed to
the inherent unreliability of catholics, claiming that the rebels were not only
sanctioned but commanded to fight by their priests. In this he echoed his
recurrent theme of the 'necessary connection between popish supremacy in
spirituals, with its tyranny in temporals'.[7] Catholic relief was a mistake – the
Irish protestant ascendancy needed to be fortified by a renewal of the penal
laws.[8]

Duigenan was not alone in this interpretation, as others echoed his views.
John Foster commented that 'The demons of every sort have escaped from
their cells when the padlocks were taken off the papists fetters.'[9] Lord Clare
wondered if 'the King's ministers [would] ever be taught to feel the insanity
of letting loose the popish barbarians of Ireland, lay and ecclesiastical, upon
the property and respect[ability] of Ireland?'[10] Lord Kerry recalled 'how
happy was the country whilst the rod of iron was held over them [roman
catholics]'. Fear, then, was common to both catholic and protestant communities. This poisonous atmosphere facilitated the passage of the union.[11]

III

In this way the rebellion provided the opportunity to press the union.
Throughout the eighteenth century, the problem of managing Ireland had
perplexed successive governments. The truculent undertakers had given
way to resident viceroys, but in a paradoxical way the legislative independence achieved by the Irish parliament in 1782 put the question of union
firmly upon London's agenda. Obviously public opinion in Ireland would
not hear of it, but its possibility was acknowledged by many, including the
presbyterian William Drennan who as early as 1785 identified the future of
Ireland in reform, separation or legislative union.

The relief act of 1793 which gave catholics the vote advanced a possible
union as an attractive option to hardline sections of protestant opinion, as

17 Dec. 1798, DDA.   7 P. Duigenan, *An answer to the address of the Rt Hon. Henry
Grattan to his fellow citizens of Dublin* (Dublin, 1798).   8 J Biggs-Davidson & G.
Chowdharray-Best, *The Cross of St Patrick; the catholic unionist tradition in Ireland*
(Bucks, 1984), p. 91.   9 J. Foster to Sheffield, Sept. 1798, PRONI, T3465/108.   10
Clare to Auckland, 2 Apr. 1800, PRONI, T3456/1.   11 Kerry to Landsdowne, 12
Apr. 1800, cited in Bartlett, *Fall and rise*, p. 243.

articulated in the parliamentary debate by FitzGibbon who rightly identified this concession to catholics as a serious threat to protestant ascendancy; 'if the principle is once yielded ... it goes directly to the subversion of all civilised government'.[12] The significance of conceding the vote is difficult to exaggerate. Lecky believed that the act (which increased the electorate by 30 per cent, or 30,000) 'revolutionised the whole system of government in Ireland', arguing that the measure was more significant than O'Connell's victory of 1829 which occupies a 'fictitious magnitude in the public mind'.[13] Just as catholics had used protestant trustees in the penal era, so now they could use protestant MPs to represent their interests – in fact, they continued to do so until the close of the nineteenth century.[14] Equally significant, Pitt, who had long contemplated union, failed to grant catholics full emancipation in 1793. Was this to be a prize held out at a later date or was he fearful that if catholics were admitted to the Irish parliament there would be no possibility of carrying the union?

In any event, Pitt chose the rebellion as the moment to pursue his great plan. Fear was the means – King George approved of 'using the present moment of terror for frightening the supporters of the Castle into a union' – and Lord Carysfort stressed the importance of acting 'while the terror of the late rebellion is fresh.'[15] Within this context, Marquis Cornwallis arrived as viceroy in June 1798 with the dual mandate of suppressing the rebellion and promoting legislative union. Cornwallis was known to be sympathetic to the catholic cause – he had refused the command of the Irish army in 1797 because of the government's failure to consider further emancipation. In this sense, his appointment was itself an indication of their cabinet's open mind on the catholic question. This liberal reputation made him attractive to catholics, particularly Archbishop Troy who saw him as their only guardian against orange fury; the bishop of Cork, Francis Moylan, fulsomely described him as 'the saviour of Ireland'.[16] Within ultra-loyalist circles, he was jeered as 'Crop-wallis' on account of his policy of conciliation.

Cornwallis did not have complete freedom of action. He favoured a broadly based union, arguing that 'England must now make a union with the Irish nation instead of making it with a party in Ireland'.[17] There was,

12 *The speech of the right honourable John, Lord Baron FitzGibbon ... delivered in the House of Peers on the second reading of the Bill for the relief of His Majesty's roman catholic subjects*, 13 March 1793 (Dublin, 1798), pp 21-2; see A. Kavanaugh, *John FitzGibbon, earl of Clare* (Dublin, 1997), pp 262-81. 13 Lecky, *Ire.*, iii, p. 141, 148. 14 Biggs-Davidson, *Cross of St Patrick*, p. 63. 15 Carysfort to Grenville, 15 Aug. 1798, *Fortescue*, iv, p. 280; Cornwallis to Pitt, 20 July 1798, *Cornwallis corr.*, ii, pp 364-5 cited in Bartlett, *Fall and rise*, p. 245. 16 Moylan to Marshall, 26 July 1799, *Castlereagh corr.*, iii, pp 364-5. 17 Cornwallis to Pitt, 8 Oct. 1798, *Cornwallis corr.*,

however, no possibility of this. While Pitt had originally favoured an inclusive union, political realities ruled this out. At the highest level, King George had set his mind against emancipation in 1795, following Fitz-Gibbon's line that such a measure would violate his coronation oath. Similarly, he believed that the Act of Union with Scotland had preserved for all time the Act of Uniformity and other acts maintaining the protestant establishment. In this way, any admission of catholics to parliament was precluded by the existing union.[18] On a more pragmatic level, the numbers game dictated that the catholic question be avoided. There was fear of opposition to tinkering with the Test Acts in England; there was also a sense that the rebellion could not be seen to have succeeded in winning concessions and other concerns.

In sum, the best chance the union had was that it be introduced in a bald fashion, offering Ireland's protestants a barrier against further catholic threats. Cornwallis accepted this policy, believing that the question would be raised again 'in quieter times to the unprejudiced decision of the united parliament'.[19] With this in mind, he embarked on a rather dishonest attempt to sell the union. To the protestants, he sold it as a shield, a guarantee of numerical superiority in the united parliament; to the catholics, he held out union with an implicit promise of full emancipation.

IV

The union debate illustrated the complexity of Irish politics; one has only to look at the bizarre situation where FitzGibbon, champion of protestant ascendancy, and John Troy, catholic archbishop of Dublin, adopted the same line. Even more incredible were rumours in January 1799 that the leading opponents of the measure, John Foster and George Ponsonby, offered the catholics 'everything' provided they joined the anti-union camp.[20] The catholics however remained unmoved. In public, at least, they made no attempt to oppose the motion. On one level, as Edward Cooke observed, it made no sense for them to side with their arch enemies, the Orange Order. In the past loyalty had brought results; now at this critical moment, with their reputation in tatters, they chose, as Castlereagh put it, 'to play their game thro' government rather than the opposition'.[21]

ii, pp 415-16.   18 Biggs-Davidson, *Cross of St Patrick*, p. 68.   19 Cornwallis to Portland, 5 Dec. 1798, *Castlereagh corr.*, ii, pp 35-6.   20 Bartlett, *Fall and rise*, p. 252. 21 Castlereagh to Portland, 28 Jan. 1799, PRO HO 100/85/160.

On another level, the catholics had minimal attachment to the protestant parliament in College Green and whatever relief measures had been granted were conceded grudgingly at London's insistence. In this respect, too, they continued Burke's line that it was the ascendancy, the Castle junto, which was their real enemy, not the king or the London government. As Burke put it, the English government had 'farmed out Ireland, without the reservation of a pepper corn rent in power or influence', thus depriving Ireland's catholics of the protection of the British parliament.[22] Such sentiments lay behind Bishop Thomas Hussey's remark that he would prefer a union with the 'Beys and Mamelukes of Egypt than being under the iron rod of the Mamelukes of Ireland'.[23] One catholic pro-union pamphleteer placed the misery of Ireland's catholics firmly at the door of the ascendancy:

> [The penal laws] never found an advocate out of Ireland; they were discredited in appeals to Westminister ... lenity came from abroad and harshness was the immediate and natural propensity of our own government! No unfavourable omen for the meditated change, no light inducement to prefer the usual composition of the British legislature to the native rule, recommended by volumes of coercive laws ...[24]

Other considerations encouraged catholics to support the measure. Some like Arthur O'Leary, the veteran pamphleteer, believed that union would end all religious disqualification and national jealousies.[25] Critics point to bribes – both Gormanston and Fingall had their Jacobite titles confirmed by the crown. Kenmare became an earl and Troy received generous compensation from the crown for chapels damaged by loyalist outrage. That in itself was remarkable – previous rebellions were followed by confiscation and penal legislation, but Troy secured compensation!

It would be misleading, however, to exaggerate Troy's achievement. Indeed, throughout the union debate, the bishops adopted a deferential stance towards the Castle administration which stands in stark contrast to their aggressive confidence during the discussions prior to the establishment of Maynooth.[26] Compromised in 1798, the hierarchy was forced to make

---

22 E. Burke to T. Hussey, 9 Dec. 1796, *Burke corr.*, ix, p. 165. 23 T. Hussey to J.B. Clinch, 10 Jan. [1799], Madden Mss, TCD, 873/197. 24 T. McKenna, *Memoirs on some questions respecting the projected Union of Great Britain and Ireland* (Dublin, 1799). 25 A. O'Leary, *Address to the parliament of Great Britain*, cited in Biggs Davidson, *Cross of St Patrick*, p. 99. 26 D. Keogh, *'The French disease.' The catholic church and radicalism in Ireland 1790-1800* (Dublin, 1993), pp 68-89.

concessions on the question of the royal veto on episcopal appointments and the provision of a state payment of the clergy. Certainly the bishops were aware of precedents in Russia and Prussia. Although the Canadian system was repeatedly held up as an appropriate model, yet such interference in the church had been strenuously resisted since it was first mooted by Thomas Lewis O'Beirne when he had served as private secretary to Portland, the viceroy, in 1782.[27]

In the wake of the rebellion, however, the resolve of the catholic hierarchy was weakened. Burke, who had consistently warned the bishops against such truck with the Castle, was dead while the catholic gentry had confessed to the viceroy their 'anxious wish' to render the clergy less dependent on 'the lower orders'.[28] Within this troubled context, the hierarchy gave their guarded approval of the government proposals, in the knowledge, perhaps, that their implementation would be prevented by the opposition of either the Holy See or the protestant ultras who would do all in their power to prevent any establishment of the catholic church.

Although a combination of circumstances decided that these proposals would proceed no further, yet the concession of the point illustrated the vulnerability of the hierarchy. An exasperated Troy, chastised by Rome for his part in such independent action, confessed to a Dominican confrere;

> We all wish to remain as we are, and we would do so were it not that too many of the clergy were active in the wicked rebellion or did not oppose it ... If we had rejected the proposals in toto, we would be considered here as rebels ... If we agreed to it without reference to Rome, we would be branded as schismatics.[29]

V

Remembering that Cornwallis was attempting to sell the union to the protestants as protective of their interests, it was imperative that the catholics would not appear too enthusiastic about the measure. In fact, catholic indecision and divisions ensured that this would not happen. The remnant of the Catholic Committee met at Fingall's Dublin home on 15 December 1798 to consider an appropriate response. The absence of the radicals was immediately apparent – Troy referred to the gathering as 'respectable

27 T.L. O'Beirne to Castlereagh, Nov. 1800, *Castlereagh corr.*, iii, p. 400. 28 Cornwallis to Portland, 5 Dec. 1798, *Castlereagh corr.*, ii, pp 35-6. 29 J. Troy to J. Concanen [spring 1800], DDA.

persons, gentry and the principal merchants of the city'.[30] William Bellew was angry that the catholic question was not to be addressed. Significantly he was called to the Castle days later to be reassured by Cornwallis – but the outcome of the meeting was to be discussed again at a subsequent meeting 'of a more general description of roman catholics'.[31] That gathering was equally indecisive.

The catholic leadership met again in February 1799, in the wake of the initial defeat of the union. During a seven-hour debate, a letter was read from the bishops urging the body 'to wait patiently for that kindness and relief which it was manifest that the English government had always shewn'.[32] The meeting condemned the actions of the handful of 'violent and democratic Catholics' who had come out in favour of Ponsonby's anti-union stance. Again, for pragmatic reasons the meeting decided not to present a formal petition in favour of union, but rather to remain quiet. Archbishop Troy informed Castlereagh:

> The general opinion of the meeting was, that the catholics as such ought not to deliberate on the union as a question of empire, but only as it might affect their own peculiar interests as a body; and on this it was judged inexpedient to publish any resolution or declaration at present.[33]

Clearly a formal catholic petition in favour of union would weaken the government's hand and make it difficult to sell the measure as protective of the protestant interest. This reality was immediately apparent to the bishop of Ferns:

> I consider the case, the time and the circumstances exceedingly delicate and tender. Union is looked for; in order to obtain it the Ascendancy is not to be irritated, but rather to be kept in tolerable good humour, but that point gained, I am persuaded in my own mind we shall be better off than ever. For the ruling powers are convinced, that the late unfortunate and wicked rising was not on the part of catholics, a rebellion against the King, but against the Protestant Ascendancy and orangemen. Persuaded as I am of the good and honest intentions of government on both sides of the channel, I would not press or urge any measure that can tend to defeat or obstruct government in the way to the main point.[34]

30 Troy to Castlereagh, 24 Dec. 1798, *Castlereagh corr.*, ii, p. 61.   31 *Faulkner's Dublin Journal*, 18 Dec. 1798.   32 Buckingham to Grenville, 13 Feb. 1799, *Fortescue*, iv, pp 469–71.   33 Troy to Castlereagh, *Castlereagh corr.*, ii, p. 61.   34 Caulfield to

So while there was no formal petition for union on behalf of the catholic body, there were petitions from various catholic bodies. Troy busied himself behind the scenes promoting the measure. In February 1799 he enlisted the support of Bishop Matthew Lennan of Dromore to ensure the re-election of Isaac Corry, chancellor of the exchequer and leading champion of union in the Commons. Through the efforts of the catholics, who stood together like a 'Macedonian phalanx', Corry was re-elected to his seat for Newry – this event was described by Biggs Davidson as 'an opinion poll on the union'.[35] Significantly Corry lost his seat in the first general election to the imperial parliament but the event shows the potential of a well marshalled catholic electorate and justified FitzGibbon's prescient comment in 1793 that whoever controlled the forty shilling freeholder controlled the kingdom.

Bishop James Lanigan signed a petition in Ossory, and Troy encouraged Caulfield to present a petition on behalf of the catholics of Wexford. Caulfield obliged and the address, couched in loyal rhetoric, lamented the folly of the rebellion, but saw in the union:

> the most beneficial effects to both kingdoms, by increasing their wealth, resources and security, by destroying religious animosity and giving permanent success to both countries, to effectively oppose the attempts of foreign and domestic enemies.[36]

Similar resolutions were signed by bishops Bray (Cashel), Dillon (Tuam), Sughrue (Kerry), Cruise (Ardagh), Coyle (Raphoe), French (Elphin), MacMahon (Killaloe) and Bellew (Killala), while Thomas Hearn signed in Hussey's absence. The tenor of the Raphoe address was particularly penitential. Referring to 'the baneful seeds of the French rebellion', it lamented the rising;

> especially such of our own religion as have ungratefully and in direct opposition to the principles of our holy religion enlisted under the *laborum* or standard of the most unnatural and ever to be reprobated rebellion.[37]

In many dioceses the priests sent priests from parish to parish promoting similar resolutions which were published in the press. There was, however, a fear amongst the bishops that their intervention would be unhelpful –

Troy, 15 July 1799, DDA.   **35** Biggs-Davidson, *Cross of St Patrick*, p. 96.   **36** *Belfast News Letter*, 19 Nov. 1799.   **37** Pro-union address of the roman catholics of Raphoe, 3 Dec. 1799, NA 620/49/6.

Bishop Patrick Plunkett observed that in matters of politics 'it becomes us rather to follow than lead'.[38] The archbishop of Cashel reiterated these sentiments to Thomas Pelham, claiming that 'if we act in any ostensible capacity in the business of union, either by a personal signature to an address in favour of it, or otherwise, in my humble opinion, instead of serving the cause we may injure it'.[39]

At another level, Castlereagh commissioned Theobald McKenna, the veteran catholic pamphleteer, to write a tract in support of the union. *His Memoirs on some questions respecting the projected union of Great Britain and Ireland* (1799), held out a stark warning:

> unless the servants of the crown mean ... to include a settlement under the head of religious difference completely co-extensive with the grievance, then will an incorporation of the legislatures be found a measure bad for Ireland, but if possible worse for Britain.

VI

It would, however be mistaken to believe catholics were unanimous in support of union – on the contrary a significant number opposed the measure but were unwilling or unable to oppose it. From Cork, Leonard McNally reported in January 1799:

> The orange and the green were making rapid approaches towards each other ... The respectable catholics are determined not to come forward on the question of union in a body, though individually they are to a man against it.[40]

The renegade Franciscan Denis Taaffe was arrested in March 1799 and charged with the publication of a seditious paper, the *Shamroc*, which the *Dublin Journal* believed was designed to produce disloyal results under the mask of anti-unionism. Then there was Daniel O'Connell – deist, yeoman, United Irishman – and his famed address to the meeting of Dublin catholics (January 1800) in the Royal Exchange in which he urged his audience not to 'sell their country for a price' and instead called on them to prefer the

---

38 P. Plunket to Castlereagh, 29 Oct. 1799, *Castlereagh corr.*, iii, pp 226–7. **39** T. Bray to T. Pelham, 11 July 1799, *Castlereagh corr.*, ii, pp 244–5; Troy to Castlereagh, *Castlereagh corr.*, ii, p. 61. **40** 'J.W.' [McNally], 2 Jan. 1799, cited in Lecky, *Ire.*, v, p. 211.

current dispensation to a union with emancipation. At the same meeting a resolution declared that 'even if there were advantages in the giving up of an independent legislature, they would be only the bounty of the master to the slave'.[41]

One unionist pamphlet, written by George Cooper, asserted that catholic opposition centred on Dublin and was confined to 'a few discontented individuals who assume the voice of the whole catholic body'.[42] The *Anti-Union*, begun in December 1799, mentions three local catholic declarations against the union. Bishop Caulfield complained of James Edward Devereux and Philip Hay 'leading the wise men of New Ross' in presenting an independent address. Lecky repeats this and during the Home Rule debates Gladstone asserted that there were substantial bodies of catholics against the measure.[43]

Amongst the bishops, too, Dr John Young of Limerick was immovable in his opposition to what he called the annihilation of Irish independence.[44] There were rumours, too, that the bishops had been bribed(an accusation refuted by Castlereagh in the union debate) while Hussey believed that the people regarded the higher clergy as 'hateful and contemptible', 'willing slaves under government and instruments ever disposed to keep their people under the harrow'.[45]

VII

In any event the union was carried – the catholics carried the union; the rest is detail. But did they? Certainly their passivity allowed it to pass. As Cornwallis observed 'in the late political contest on the measure of the union ... [catholics] certainly had it in their power to have frustrated the views of government, and throw the country into utmost confusion.'[46]

Still, the narrow union, the protestant union was flawed – it was, in Cornwallis's phrase, a union with 'a party in Ireland' as opposed to the Irish nation.[47] The exclusion of catholics and royal intransigence prompted the resignation of Pitt in February 1801, but the failure to address the issue undermined the prospects of the measure. McKenna's prophecy was fulfilled – the measure proved disastrous for Britain, transforming the catholic question into the Irish question.

41 *The Constitution: or Anti-Union Evening Post*, 14 Jan. 1800. 42 G. Cooper, *Letters on the Irish nation* (London, 1800), p. 197. 43 Biggs Davidson, *Cross of St Patrick*, p. 101. 44 J. Young to T. Bray, 30 Dec. 1798, CDA. 45 T. Hussey to J. Carroll, Baltimore, 29 Sept. 1799, Baltimore Diocesan Archive. 46 Cornwallis to Portland, 1 Dec. 1800, *Cornwallis corr.*, iii, p. 307. 47 Cornwallis to Pitt, 8 Oct. 1798, *Cornwallis corr.*, ii, pp 415-16.

10

Writing the union

Claire Connolly

'[The Union must be] written-up, spoken-up, intrigued-up, drunk-up, sung-up, and bribed-up.'[1]

'Oh that mine enemy would write a book.'[2]

This chapter examines the fierce paper war fought in Dublin and London between the end of 1798 and the start of 1801 and its implications for the ways in which Anglo-Irish relations could be written about. The proposed Act of Union between Great Britain and Ireland was the focus of debate and the views quoted above come from opposite sides of the argument. Despite a disparity in political outlook, however, each view places writing at the sharp end of (respectively) the pro- and anti-union campaigns, depicting innovations in textual practice as potentially productive of an altered political future. In what follows, I consider just how 'writing up the union' worked, especially in relation to early nineteenth-century modes of cultural production. I do not offer a history of the debates, opting instead to select some of the dominant metaphors and see how they operate according to certain textual manoeuvres and strategies. In so doing I hope to show how the meanings of Ireland's relationship with its nearest neighbour shift in relation to such stylistic concerns as language and genre.

The first quotation is the privately stated opinion of under-secretary Edward Cooke, who made good this injunction in his adroit financial management of Dublin Castle's pro-union paper campaign. McCormack's recent researches in the bibliography of the pamphlet debate have amassed

1 E. Cooke to W. Eden, Baron Auckland, 27 Oct. 1798, quoted in Geoghegan, *Union*, p. 21. 2 [Charles Kendal Bushe], *Cease your Funning; or, the rebel detected*, 3rd edition (Dublin, 1798).

new evidence (chiefly from account books in the Public Record Office, Kew) showing how Cooke paid writers and booksellers to 'write up' the union.[3] Geoghegan has further shown how Cooke was left with an embarrassing number of debts to pay in the immediate aftermath of the union in respect of the various government bribes or 'engagements' – including a substantial amount of printer's bills.[4] This discovery of 'Cooke in the books' (as McCormack puts it) coincides with the fact that Cooke was the author/editor of one of the earliest pro-union publications, *Arguments for and against a union*, described elsewhere by McCormack as 'Dublin Castle's spearhead contribution to the paper war' and as 'the opening shot in a serious pamphlet war'.[5]

A riposte to *Arguments for and against a union* – entitled {*The Union*} *Cease Your Funning* – quickly followed, taking as its epigraph the second of the above quotations. This pamphlet purports to think of the union propositions as a joke, surely ironic in tone and intent. Linking *Arguments for and against a union* to Jonathan Swift's *A Modest Proposal*, the pamphlet claims to discern a duplicitous rhetoric: 'The stile [*sic*] consists altogether in the art of supporting in a strain of grave irony the opposite of the opinion which you mean to establish.'[6] The author (probably Charles Kendal Bushe)[7] declares himself convinced that the *Arguments* are, both in tone and content, the product of 'either a member of the Opposition or an absolute United Irishman'.[8] The accusation cleverly rests on two central contentions in the *Arguments*, that Ireland's distance from the seat of power and its subsidiarity to Britain in all practical matters make an incorporative union essential. By asserting Irish dependence on Britain, Bushe claims, the *Arguments* reproduce 'the mere cant and fabrication of the United Irishmen'.[9] He concludes with a call for the author, 'a concealed United Irishman' who has 'jesuitically assumed the style and character of a loyal Englishman', to be prosecuted.[10]

3 W.J. McCormack, 'Between Burke and the Union: reflections on PRO: CO 904/2', in J. Whale (ed.), *Edmund Burke's Reflections on the Revolution in France: New interdisciplinary essays* (Manchester, 2000), pp 60-93. 4 Geoghegan, *Union*, pp 205-6. 5 W.J. McCormack, *The pamphlet debate on the Union between Great Britain and Ireland, 1797–1800* (Dublin, 1996), pp 7-20 (p. 9); McCormack, 'Between Burke and the Union', p. 70. 6 *Cease your funning*, pp 3-4. 7 McCormack, *Pamphlet debate*, p. 35. Bushe was himself to enter the ranks of fiction, as a source for the depiction of the lord chief justice in Maria Edgeworth's novel of public life, *Patronage* (1814). See M. Butler, Introductory note to *Patronage. The novels and selected works of Maria Edgeworth*, 12 vols (London, 1999), vi, xi. 8 *Cease your funning*, p. 4. 9 Ibid., p. 11. 10 Ibid., p. 7, 44-5.

By claiming to prove that not only the language but the content of the pro-union proposals are revolutionary in intent, Bushe not only creatively misreads but bears down on and pressures the original proposition, bringing it into uncomfortable proximity to the more recent Irish usages of 'union'; most especially the political merger of Irish people otherwise divided by class or creed called for by the Society of United Irishmen. The proximity of these different registers of 'union' can be seen in John FitzGibbon, earl of Clare's, descriptions of the dangers posed by 'the Irish union' and 'the mystic union' of the United Irishmen.[11] Taking my cue from such over settings of the language in which the union was proposed, I wish to suggest that close attention to the language in which the union is couched might enable new readings of the political arrangement on offer.

The union debates put into words, and indeed onto the statute books, many hitherto unstated (if shared) assumptions, and, in the process, opened up a space for dissent. Castlereagh, chief secretary to the lord lieutenant throughout the union period, took care to ensure that 'at all times the union was presented as a treaty'. In what was undoubtedly a conscious echo of the 1707 union with Scotland, Ireland's new relationship with Britain was to be expressed in legal articles rather than in 'mere clauses'.[12] Such concerns underline the ways in which Ireland's entry into the new relationship mark a shift into a newly legalistic and technical concern with its status. In Edmund Burke's last letter on Irish affairs, written in 1797, he insists that the most fruitful way to improve Anglo-Irish relations was not to reform the law or to pass acts of parliament, but to influence the 'mind of the ruling power' which he contrasts to the letter of the law:

> Men do not live upon blotted paper. The favourable or the hostile mind of the ruling power is of far more importance to mankind, for good or evil, than the black letter of any statute.[13]

The union, however, goes against this Burkean model and places faith in 'blotted paper'. It thus makes the inclination of the monarchy (what Edmund Burke calls the 'disposition of the ruling power') visible as the assertive and so recently aggressive force of the state. In these terms, it is possible to read the Act of Union as a piece of legislation which offered a

11 *A compleat refutation of the statements of Lord Moira respecting Ireland; being the entire speech of the earl of Clare, lord chancellor of Ireland, in the House of Peers of that kingdom, Monday, February 19, 1798* (London, 1798), pp 14-17. 12 Geoghegan, *Union*, p. 102. 13 Burke, 'A letter on the affairs of Ireland, written in the year 1797' in M. Arnold (ed.), *Irish affairs: Edmund Burke* (London, 1881), p. 381.

problematic answer to a connection which many contemporary observers would have preferred not to call into question.

According to McCormack, who has produced the authoritative bibliography, the pamphlet debate around the union gave rise to 'more than 250 separate publications'.[14] But, beyond this number, it is difficult to ascertain how widely individual publications were read, by whom, or where. Some speculation is possible and potentially fruitful. McCormack suggests, for example, that John Milliken, one of the leading publishers, 'gathered together sets of union pamphlets and sold them as intellectual furniture for post-union country-house libraries.'[15] But any such exercise in book history risks ignoring wider reading patterns as they took shape within what was still a predominantly oral culture. The rhetorical skills discussed above are at least in part explicable as a product of the professional training of the many barristers who took the anti-union side. Considered in this light, it may seem that the union debates took place at some remove from popular politics, not least the recent realities of the revolution of 1798. The United Irishmen, too, were concerned with print culture and its circulation, however, and, in the words of one report, 'every species of literary mischief is resorted to and circulated at an extraordinary expense to every part of the kingdom and amongst all the lower orders of people'.[16]

Some traces of the popular perception of the union debates can be found in the writings of two contemporary women authors, Sydney Owenson and Mary Leadbeater. In Sydney Owenson's *Patriotic Sketches in Connaught*, she produces the first of these paradigmatic instances of 'heard' accounts of the union:

> A few days back, I met with two peasants who were making complaints of the oppression they endured. A gentleman asked them if they thought they were worse off since the union. They replied, 'they had never heard anything about the union, and did not know what it meant.' After some further questions, they were asked 'if they did not know there was now no Irish parliament. They replied, that all they had heard was, that the parliament-books were sent away, and that the good luck of the country went with them. So full is the heart of the Irish peasant of his own grievance, and so little is his head troubled about public affairs.[17]

14 McCormack, *From Burke to Beckett*, p. 442; McCormack, *Pamphlet debate*. 15 McCormack, 'Between Burke and the Union', p. 64. 16 A. Charles Murphy to Dublin Castle, 10 Apr., 1794 quoted in N. Curtin, *The United Irishmen: popular politics in Ulster and Dublin 1791–1798* (Oxford, 1998), p. 174. 17 S. Owenson, *Patriotic sketches of*

In her *Annals of Ballitore*, written some years later and offering a view from a Quaker community in county Kildare, Mary Leadbeater reports on how 'amusing' it was during the period 1800-1 'to hear the country-folk discussing the great political question of the day; they seemed to think that parliament was a great book which had been removed from Dublin to England'.[18] Both writers depict a general alienation from and indeed unconcern for the business of the union, and further suggest that this distance is perceived specifically in relation to its technical and bureaucratic aspects. More generally, in conceiving of parliament as a volume ('a great book'), these accounts underline the fundamentally written and textual basis of the new arrangement.

Parliamentarians themselves were less sure that the union was conceived of solely as an administrative measure. Richard Lovell Edgeworth deplored the iron hand of government in the management of the affair: 'I am a unionist, but I vote and speak against the union now proposed to us,' he wrote, giving as his reason that 'It is intended to force this measure down the throats of the Irish ... the good people of Ireland ought to be *persuaded* of this truth, and not be dragooned into submission.'[19] The presence of Lord Cornwallis in Ireland, acting uniquely as both lord lieutenant and commander in chief of the army, was a daily reminder of this conjunction of parliamentary and military powers. Perhaps it was a loss of faith in the powers of persuasion and indeed public discussion altogether that suggested to Richard Lovell Edgeworth the measure of leaving the House just before the bill was passed, taking a group of anti-unionist MPs which included Henry Grattan with him.[20]

As such gestures might suggest, the union debates were, from their inception, alert to questions of argumentative style and rhetorical position. Anti-unionists sought to annex language of revolution and counter-revolution and to characterise the proposed act as an innovative and speculative response to troubled times. *The Anti-Union* in its first issue declared itself modelled on *The Anti-Jacobin*, explicitly asserting that 'the success of the Union, now under discussion, is intimately connected with the triumph of Jacobinism, Rebellion, and French fraternity.'[21] Taking upon itself the task of 'repelling so monstrous an innovation', *The Anti-Union* associates the

Ireland, written in Connaught, 2 vols (London, 1807), i, 121n.   18 Mary Leadbeater, *The Leadbeater papers: the annals of Ballitore*, 2 vols (London and Dublin, 1862), p. 284.   19 Letter to Erasmus Darwin, 31 Mar. 1800; *Memoirs of Richard Lovell Edgeworth, Esq. begun by himself and concluded by his daughter, Maria Edgeworth*, 2 vols (London, 1820), ii, p. 252.   20 *Memoirs of Richard Lovell Edgeworth*, ii, p. 254.   21 *The Anti-Union*, 27 Dec. 1798, p. 1.

pro-union campaign with deceit and cunning.[22] The short lived journal ran a regular feature called 'Lies of the Week', usually designed to show up reports of sectarian violence as hollow and baseless rumours.

Contending that the union partook of the revolutionary tenor of the events it sought to forestall, John Foster (leader of opposition to union in the Irish house of commons) called for a calmer conduct of Irish affairs: 'When republics and republicans are described as violating every principle of moral rectitude, it behoves kings, and the representatives of kings, to secure the admiration of the world by magnanimity and moderation.'[23] The suggestion is that the proposed union disturbed the existing order and, more particularly, that by seeking to replace and thus calling into question the constitutional arrangement which the rebels had so recently attacked and loyalists so fiercely defended, the union had the potential to turn the recent past upside down. This served to recast 1798 in a new and uncongenial light, and had the odd effect of making such a staunchly ascendancy figure as Foster the spokesman for a view of the insurrection as unfinished business.

Even while he insists that 'Enthusiasm, though it may desolate a country, is, from its violence, of short duration', Foster strives to cope with its recent legacy in Ireland. He characterises political vehemence as a faith-ridden position to be dispersed by the light of reason, and proposes instead an enlightenment view of the past as that which while tending towards betterment necessarily rests on a memory of violence:

> Every respecting man must recognize, in the deplorable extent of religious animosity, the true and exact features of short-lived enthusiasm, operating on minds depraved by superstition the most unworthy and intolerant. And I defy any man to point out, in the luminous pages of GIBBON, VOLTAIRE, ROBINSON, and HUME, a single instance where a Civil War has not had the effect of giving a country a more determined aspect, and a more dreaded character – look at Rome under Marius – Sylla – Pompey – Caesar – Antony – Augustus – and look likewise at modern France – and the scholar, the stateman, and the philosopher, will see the force and weight of this observation.[24]

22 *The Anti-Union*, 27 Dec. 1798, p. 2.   23 [John Foster], *The commercial system of Ireland reviewed and the question of union discussed in an address to the merchants, manufacturers, and country gentlemen of Ireland*, 2nd ed. (Dublin, 1799), p. 96. For the attribution of authorship, see McCormack, *Pamphlet debate*, p. 36.   24 *Commercial system*, pp 98-9.

This call to take the long historical view from which a balance will naturally re-establish itself derives in part from the writings of Burke on France, India and America. This is made evident when Foster actually cites Burke's speech on conciliation with America, removing the word America and replacing it with Ireland.[25] Yet a similar language could be deployed to opposite ends. Lord Minto, a friend of Burke's who shared his views on America, and who helped him prepare the case against Warren Hastings, contemplates separation from Britain (presented as was common as the only alternative to full Union) in luridly revolutionary terms:

> An Irish, democratic republic, or rather anarchy, must be the first and instant consequence of our separation. – Let any man then, attached to the British constitution – let any one, who is fond of order and security in society, or even afraid of the extremes of disorder – let any one, who would shrink from universal plunder, confiscation, and murder, with all the nameless miseries, wretchedness, and guilt which are but the particulars of that aggregate, called anarchy; let any man, I say, who has the slightest concern for the human race and its happiness, a spark of love for his country, or even a common and vulgar solicitude for his own and his children's security, reflect for a moment on the triumphant establishment of a democratic anarchy in Ireland.[26]

These calls on an active spirit of public affection rooted in familial and parental ties sound a distinctly Burkean note and help illustrate how, even if 'his name disappears to a large extent from the increasingly heated debates on Irish affairs which culminated in the union of 1801,'[27] Burke's language did not. Minto quotes Burke more directly in his warning that 'it is part of our own tenement that is in flames, and we come into absolute contact with this pestilent contagion.'[28] This reprises the Burke of the *Reflections on the Revolution in France*, who tells his young correspondent in Paris that although 'The beginnings of confusion with us in England are at present feeble enough,' there is no security in the face of France's 'war with Heaven itself': 'Whenever our neighbour's house is on fire, it cannot be amiss for the

---

25 *Commercial system*, pp 99-100.   26 *An abridgment of the speech of Lord Minto in the House of Peers, April 11 1799, on a motion of address to His Majesty, to communicate the resolutions of the two Houses of Parliament respecting an union between Great Britain and Ireland* (Dublin, 1799), p. 16.   27 McCormack, 'Between Burke and the Union', p. 61. McCormack writes of a 'Burke-shaped silence' in Irish affairs 1797-1800' (p. 79).   28 *Speech of Lord Minto*, p. 17.

engines to play a little on our own.'[29] Minto, in bringing the metaphor to
bear on Ireland, explicitly widens the 'our' of the *Reflections* and thus
heightens the immediacy and proximity of dangers Burke himself was more
cautious in applying to the Irish situation. Moreover, there is a performative
aspect to Minto's inclusive pronoun: he speaks as if union were already a
fact, assuming Ireland's role within 'the British constitution' and invoking
that authority even as he calls for its extension to Ireland.

Many anti-unionists sought to associate union with subtlety and sophis-
try. John Foster claims that linguistic agility and ingenuity must be put to
the service of union whereas the existing arrangement makes plain – 'glaring
and palpable' – sense. Yet Sylvester Douglas, writing on behalf of the government, could accuse the opponents of union of wishing to 'induce us to
shut our eyes against history, and wander with them in the obscure mazes
of theory and speculation.'[30] Attempting to halt speculation on all sides,
Thomas Brooke Clarke insists that writing of one kind or another cannot
alter what is the inevitable political future:

> For after tropes and figures have been let off without number, after
> torrents of eloquence have been poured forth, much paper blotted,
> and much ink spilt, – RECOURSE MUST BE HAD AT LAST, EITHER TO
> A SEPARATION, – OR TO A UNION.[31]

There is a strong sense on all sides of union as an event for the present,
evincing a responsibility towards posterity. This is connected on the anti-
union side with the idea that the present parliament is the legitimate one,
and that its authority, rather than that of any past arrangements, must hold
a shield against the deceitful future. Invocations of the stable wisdom of the
present or the certain future prove troubled, however, beset as much by their
own contradictory rhetoric as by external disagreement or danger. Thus
Foster is reluctantly forced back to the past:

> The reader's wishes cannot exceed my anxiety to get over this
> retrospective view of our national occurrences, but I do assure him,

---

29 E. Burke, *Reflections on the Revolution in France* (London, 1986), p. 92.   **30** *Speech of
the Right Honourable Sylvester Douglas in the house of commons, Tuesday April the 23rd
1799, on seconding the motion of the Right Honourable the chancellor of the exchequer for the
House to agree with the Lords in an address to His Majesty relative to a union with Ireland*
(Dublin, 1799), p. 4.   **31** *Dean Tucker's* Arguments on the propriety of an union
between Great Britain and Ireland; *written some years since and now first published in this
tract upon the same subject, by the Rev. Dr. Clarke* (Dublin, 1799), p. 19.

that a knowledge of past occurrences will be a necessary shield against the canting hypocrisy and plausible treachery of a minister.[32]

There are others exceptions, too, to this absence of historical reference, most notably the firebrand speech made by Lord Clare in the Irish House of Lords when proposing the measure and the answer penned by Henry Grattan. In his response, Grattan accuses Clare of national defamation: 'The idea is to make your history a calumny against your ancestors in order to disenfranchise your posterity.'[33] Thus begins a point-by-point refutation of Clare's historical arguments, in order to show that 'Ireland had a parliament from the beginning, and that the legislature was not of the Pale, but of the nation.'[34]

Such comments indicate that the debates have the potential to release a wider discussion as to what 'Ireland' means in the period. Josiah Tucker's 1780s discussion of union, reprinted with approving comments by Edward Cooke in 1798, takes on the accusation that 'an union would extinguish Ireland' and calls for more semantic exactitude: 'The name may remain, and surely it will not extinguish the people and the soil; though it may meliorate both.'[35] Tucker separates out name, people and soil. This kind of fine linguistic discrimination leads to a sense that power is arbitrary, and the feeling that Ireland is ruled from a distance which is both geographical and more broadly geopolitical is actually enhanced by the language employed by apologists for the union. Patrick Duigenan, for instance, described by Geoghegan as 'the narrow-minded MP for Armagh' and 'no friend to the catholics',[36] wrote of how:

> the present connection between Great Britain and Ireland is such as has no parallel in the history of the world: it contains in it anomalies heretofore unknown to the law of nations, and the seeds of dissolution; these anomalies must be corrected; and these seeds must be effectually prevented from striking root; which can be only effected by an incorporating union of the two kingdoms.[37]

32 *Commercial system*, p. 20.   33 H. Grattan, *An answer to a pamphlet, entitled* The speech of the Earl of Clare, on the subject of a legislative union between Great Britain and Ireland (Dublin, 1800), p. 1.   34 Grattan, *Answer*, p. 2.   35 [E. Cooke] *Arguments for and against a Union between Great Britain and Ireland considered*, 2nd ed. (Dublin, 1799), p. 42   36 Geoghegan, *Union*, pp 33, 75.   37 *Speech of Patrick Duigenan LLD in the Irish House of commons, Wednesday February 5 1800 on the subject of an incorporating union between Great Britain and Ireland* (London, 1800), pp 6-7.

Surrounded as it is by extreme language and shot through with the organic and vital image of 'the seeds of dissolution', Duigenan's promised corrective – an 'incorporating union' – seems ill fitted to the dangers he describes.

Most significantly, perhaps, there is a mounting sense in the debate that the union itself, the substantial legislative fact behind this flurry of argument and speculation, may in fact mean nothing at all, or rather may consist of meaningless words. This provokes a debate as to the relation between words and things, political formula and material change. Prime Minister William Pitt set the tone for much pro-unionist rhetoric when he spoke in the British house of commons of the need for 'fixing that connexion upon a more solid basis'.[38] Fear of a lack of solidity or substance pervades the union debates and it is possible to discern a distinct linguistic interest in supplementing the union. Union has to be supplemented with an adjective, implying not just union but union that actually unites, as in Lord Minto's call for 'perfect union'.[39] There is a desire to put flesh on the union, to give substance and meaning to the words:

> Men unfortunately take words for things. The word republic excites and bears with it the idea of freedom; but examine the thing, and it is a compound of all the elements of tyranny.[40]

This desire to embody or render incarnate the relationship between the two countries can be further contextualised in the light of one of the main metaphors deployed as part of discussions, that of the union as a marriage. A pamphlet entitled *To be, or not to be, a Nation; that is the Question?* quotes from *Arguments for and against an union*, translating its contentions into sexual terms:

> Says he, 'Two independent States, finding their separate existence mutually inconvenient, propose to form themselves into one state for their mutual benefit.' (They find the state of celibacy mutually inconvenient; they, therefore, resolve to take the advice of their friends, and to propose a treaty of marriage, or, in other words, a union.– God grant that they may turn out a happy couple, and that the said union may not terminate in a divorce!).[41]

38 *The speech of the Rt Hon. William Pitt in the house of commons on Thursday January 31 1799* (Dublin, 1799), p. 14.   39 *Speech of Lord Minto*, p. 9.   40 T. Brooke Clarke, *The political, commercial, and civil state of Ireland, being an appendix to* 'Union or separation' (London, 1799), p. 58.   41 *To be, or not to be, a nation; that is the question?* (Dublin, 1799), p. 2.

At stake here is the legal tie of marriage, the 'treaty', which in these judicial terms brings with it a potential ending in divorce. The many songs and ballads which take up these sexualised terms invariably present the relationship in terms of force, as an unwanted or even unnatural sexual coupling, as in this song of 1800:

> The genius of Britain, who long had enjoy'd
> Supreme, as a keeper, Miss Ireland's charms,
> Mad jealous that Miss with Republicans toy'd,
> And seem'd half-inclined to escape from his arms.
> > He swore, in a rage,
> > He'd surely encage
> His mistress's person, and hold it for life;
> > He'd make her his own,
> > His flesh and his bone –
> He'd lawfully wed her and make her his wife.[42]

Reading these and many other such comments alongside contemporary novels of romance and marriage, what is most notable is the omission of any mention of love, or, more strictly speaking, any sense of the contemporary ideology of companionate marriage. Irish national romances such as Sydney Owenson's *The wild Irish girl* (1806) or Maria Edgeworth's *The absentee* (1812) do not then simply reproduce the imagery of union; rather they thicken and intensify that language, creating in the process new and affective political possibilities.

Josiah Tucker's definitive argument in favour of union rules out other kinds of connection between Ireland and Britain, producing the often repeated mantra of 'union or separation'. Thomas Brooke Clarke, who also edited Tucker in the late 1790s, specifically opposes the kinds of alliance found between 'all the new republics' or any kind of loose federal structure: 'NO NOMINAL UNION CAN HOLD OR LAST LONG.'[43] The opposite is 'real' or incorporative union. Foster, like many other anti-unionists, regularly distinguishes between nominal and actual union, insisting 'Let no man tell me that the magic word of union is to inter all our jealousies, heart-burnings, and destructive ill-will. Granted that your countrymen are turbulent – is the best mode of reducing them to subjection, by giving them

---

42 [Song] *On the Union. Air 'The Duchess'* (Dublin, 1800).   **43** Dean Tucker's *Arguments*, p. 39   **44** *Commercial system*, pp 26-7.

something substantial to complain of?'[44] In assuming the voice of simple and honest reason, Foster stresses the novelty of the proposals, referring to 'the wild, and visionary and futile, and treasonable attempt to incorporate the two countries' and arguing that 'If one thing is more likely than another to rekindle the sparks of freedom, it is the tricking, tyrannizing measure of a union. If any thing can re-animate her faded form, it is the vigour which it will inspire.'[45]

The magic word 'union' might moreover be an irritant, as William Parnell endeavours to show when he insists that 'the union is a name, a sound, a fiction; there is no union; the nominal union is only an additional source of discord.'[46] Parnell, attempting to explain the persistence of popular unrest in the Irish countryside in 1804 actually lists the union (alongside the tithe system and United Irish propaganda) as a source of unrest. Parnell worries that the union exacerbates differences, giving presbyterians in particular further cause for dissatisfaction. To further paraphrase Parnell, were there no public discourse of unity, differences would not be so visible: the language of unity rubs salt in the wounds of history, serving to underline rather than erase Ireland's inferior role in the union.

As attentiveness to language becomes itself part of the process of union, new forms were diligently sought out. Anti-unionist mock playbills were produced, advertising performances such as the following:

> At the royal circus near College-Green for the benefit of the Great Mrs Britain on Wednesday February 5 will be performed a grand serio-comic pastichio called The Rape of Ierne, or Fidelity Betrayed.

The playbills further listed such interludes as 'The Scramble; or Every One for Himself'; the performance 'To conclude with a grand display of the new Political Steam Engine; or, Civilising Machine, For Britainizing the Wild Irish. After which there will be a harsh Concert of Woeful and Detrimental Music.' Parts were to be played by actors such as 'Reaycastle' (Castlereagh), taking on the role of 'Ticklepalm'; and 'Queerblack' (Sir John Blacquiere), playing 'Pander'. The role of 'Mrs Dupely' was to be given to Mrs Erin.

In a pro-union ballad called 'Granu Wale', Granu, personifying Ireland, is warned to resist the temptation to 'rehearse the old tale'.[47] But how to find a new way of telling the tale? John Foster felt that 'The consideration of the great subject of union is fitter for a volume than a letter.'[48] From this sense

45 *Commercial system of Ireland*, pp 26-7.   46 [W. Parnell], *Inquiry into the causes of popular discontents in Ireland*, 2nd ed. (London and Dublin, 1805), p. 72.   47 *Granu Wale* [Dublin, 1800].   48 *Commercial system*, p. 4.

that the subject of union places particular demands on available discourse, questions of genre emerge. The sense of pressure on existing resources is still felt by W.J. Fitzpatrick, looking back on the union from the vantage point of the 1850s: 'Oh, that our volume were not an octavo but a folio, in order that we might cull the beauties of those masterly anti-union orations, which in 1799 awakened the echos [*sic*] of the Irish parliament.'[49]

Dominant among the favoured genres, at least retrospectively, is tragedy, especially in the influential accounts of union as a falling away from potential splendour put forward by Sir Jonah Barrington – the title of his *The rise and fall of the Irish nation* is enough to indicate that his is the classic of the genre – and after him William Lecky, Elizabeth Bowen and Edith Mary Johnson, all of whom remember the union as tragic moment in the classical mould. Avoiding this backward look at union, however, there are genres that seemed to make themselves more readily and instantly available, as in the complaint found among many anti-unionists that supporters of the Government were trying to turn 1798 into a gothic horror story. William Parnell, in his 1804 *Inquiry into the causes of popular discontents in Ireland* complains how rational public debate about the consequences of union for Ireland was impossible because 'imaginations ... have been worked up to such a degree of agitation, by poor Sir Richard Musgrave's *Tales of terror*'.[50] The term 'Castle spectre' was regularly applied to both Dublin Castle and to some of its inhabitants, ambiguously described, for example, by John Wilson Croker in 1806 as 'a kind of Deity much worshipped by the wild Irish, and which is supposed to have the power of looking into futurity and telling fortunes.'[51]

One of the most vivid of these tales of terror is found in W.J. Fitzpatrick's rendition of the funeral of John FitzGibbon. Fitzpatrick describes Lord Cloncurry arriving in Dublin on 31 January 1802 after some years of exile and coming upon 'a strange scene' – Lord Clare's funeral. As he watches the remains being drawn through the street, Cloncurry sees people throwing 'a perfect volley of dead cats' at Clare's hearse and later into his grave, in recognition, apparently, of slighting comments Clare had made as to the catholic Irish being no more important than the cats on the street.[52]

'The life of Lord Clare is the history of Ireland,' declares Barrington, seeing in his death a fitting end to the business of union. His rendition of that life readily shapes itself around both novelistic patterns and recent

49 W.J. Fitzpatrick, *The life, times and contemporaries of Lord Cloncurry* (Dublin, 1855), p. 246. **50** Parnell, *Popular discontents*, p. xii. **51** [J.W. Croker] *The Amazoniad; or, figure and fashion: a scuffle in high life. With notes critical and historical, interspersed with choice anecdotes of bon ton*, 2nd ed. (Dublin, 1806), p. 16n. **52** Fitzpatrick, *Cloncurry*, p. 264.

history so that when the climactic moment of union has passed we are told that 'the mind and body [of Lord Clare] became too sympathetic for existence, and he sunk into the grave'.[53] Barrington suggests that the form of the *bildungsroman* (a novel with a strong central plot line which condenses the moral, spiritual, educational and professional development of its protagonist) offers a way of encoding national and historical as well as personal and educational developments.[54] One of the earliest pro-union positions, stated in *Arguments for and against a union*, asked a question of its readers which would sit happily in the pages of an early nineteenth-century novel:

> If any person has a son uneducated, unimproved, and injured by bad habits, and bad company; in order to remedy these imperfections, would it not be his first endeavour to introduce him in the best societies, and introduce him into the most virtuous, the most polished, and the most learned company; and if he could once reconcile himself to such companies, and teach him to relish their conversation, would he not be certain of his son's improvement, and of his finally turning out to his credit and satisfaction?[55]

The focus here on body, movement and travel might be usefully read in term of Ina Ferris's discussion of the travel plot in Irish novels of the same period, which, she says, subject their heroes to a certain *boulversement* or overturning of metropolitan certainties.[56]

The suggestion that Ireland might be introduced to its more mature neighbour who would sit back and watch it grow 'progressively and in time another England' was mocked by the opponents of union.[57] Such a fiction of generational change tries to imply that what is produced by union is new and different, but opponents of the measure insisted on opposing 'young Ireland' to 'old England'.[58] Clark paraphrases these views:

---

53 Barrington, *Rise and fall*, p. 36. The controversial figure of Lord Clare spawned many fictional productions. See for example *Lessons to a young chancellor; or a letter from a mentor to Lord Jeffreys, Baron Petulant, of the kingdom of Barataria* ('Barataria Printed, 1792'), and, for Clare's own attempt at fiction, *No Union! But unite and fall. By Paddy Whack of Dyott-street London in a loving letter to his dear mother Sheelah of Dame-Street Dublin* (Dublin, 1799). **54** Barrington, *Rise and fall*, p. 34. **55** *Arguments for and against an Union*, pp 7-8. **56** I. Ferris, 'Narrating cultural encounter: Lady Morgan and the Irish national tale' in *Nineteenth-century literature* (1996), pp. 287-303. **57** N. Gay, *Strictures on the proposed union between Great Britain and Ireland, with occasional remarks* (Dublin, 1799), p. 20. **58** *Commercial system*, p. 42.

> Flaming PATRIOTS, as they *would* be thought, have called the
> union an act, whereby a youthful and rising body is coupled to one
> old in decay and tumbling into dissolution. Now, in truth, the fact is,
> that it is joining the Irish nation, old in disorder and feeble in itself,
> through those disorders, to one that is vigorous and virtuous. It is the
> union of a child, or rather a pigmy, to a giant, in strength, commerce
> and freedom, for mutual support.[59]

His effort to overturn one metaphor gives way to a riot of others, as age and
body become morality, nature and the unnatural. Even such seemingly
naturalising metaphors as age and health, then, cannot be used to mollify or
assuage doubts; rather, as in this case, they make make the power relations
explicit: 'Those that are well need not a physician, but those than are sick:
and such was our case, very sick indeed, nor yet by any means recovered, nor
ever shall, without a union.'[60]

'The union cannot subsist', commented Sydney Owenson (by then Lady
Morgan) in an essay on absenteeism published in 1825: 'Sin and death have
fixed their peremptory seal of doom upon it.'[61] Nicholas Gay, on the other
hand, thought that the union would 'effectually extinguish' the flames of
rebellion 'and from the ashes will, phoenix-like, arise Ireland regenerate,
born anew, a work to wonder at'.[62] The image derives in part from the idea
of a dead parliament but gains resonance in the context of Lord Clare's
death and funeral procession. In Jonah Barrington's account of one of the
final debates on the topic of union in the soon to be extinct Irish parliament,
he likens the arrival of Henry Grattan on the floor of the house to 'the
appearance of a spectre'.[63] The old and ill Grattan is, for Barrington, a ghost
who calls up the past, in particular the 1782 achievement of legislative
independence which is soon to be consigned to the past and to history.

The union was not so much dead or even dying however as undead.
Sydney Owenson compares the Anglo-Irish oligarchy (in what is itself an
uncannily prescient image given the later history of protestant gothic) to
vampires, feeding on the country they should protect: 'for it was ever, as it
is now, the singular destiny of Ireland to nourish within her own bosom her
bitterest enemies, who, with a species of political vampyrism, destroyed that
source from whence their own nutriment flowed'.[64] Owenson's image of
ravished Ireland helplessly trapped in a cycle of victimhood ('for it was ever,
as it is now') can be further contextualised in terms of the inability of

59 *Dean Tucker's* Arguments, p. 61.   60 Gay, *Strictures*, p. 6.   61 Lady Morgan,
Absenteeism (London, 1825), p. 152.   62 Gay, *Strictures*, pp 19-20.   63 Barrington, *Rise
and fall*, p. 442.   64 Owenson, *Patriotic sketches of Ireland*, i, pp 111-12.

contemporary novelists to understand Ireland in generational terms. The most striking example of this is Maria Edgeworth's *Castle Rackrent* (1800). This fictional text, included by McCormack in his bibliography of the pamphlet debate, testifies to a distinctive concern with stasis and the difficulties of change. Compared to the use of gradual generational change in fictions by British women writers of the period (the novels of Mary Hays or Amelia Opie for example, where daughters regularly redeem their mother's wrongs), it is as if the opposite impulse seems to be at work in the Irish context, where plots of inheritance and history yield instances of a traumatic and raw past returning to haunt the future.

In a novel by Thomas Moore, *Captain Rock* (published in 1824 and said by Daniel O'Connell to be the *Uncle Tom's Cabin* of the Catholic Emancipation movement),[65] the central protagonist vividly describes what he calls the 'unnatural measure' of union which, 'like Frankenstein's ghastly patchwork [is] made up of contributions from the whole charnel-house of political corruption'.[66] For Captain Rock, the union, emerging jointly from the violent conflict of 1798 and the venality of the Irish parliament, is made up at once of the tattered parchment of broken promises and the gory wounds of the recent past, all hung upon a spectral frame:

> The Union, a measure rising out of corruption and blood, and clothed in promises put on only to betray, was the phantom by which the dawn of the nineteenth century was welcomed.[67]

The movement for repeal of the union, to quote Barrington, sprang up as 'a sprite to terrify the English people'.[68] Not just a nineteenth-century ghost story, however, the union is also legible as twentieth-century horror, a fiction of Anglo-Irish relations that has notoriously failed to supply the sense of an ending.

65 O. McDonagh, *The emancipist: Daniel O'Connell 1775–1829*, p. 17; quoted in M. Howes, 'Tears and blood: Lady Wilde and the emergence of Irish cultural nationalism' in T. Foley & S. Ryder (eds.), *Ideology and Ireland in the nineteenth century* (Dublin, 1998), p. 161. See also L. Gibbons, 'Between Captain Rock and a hard place: art and agrarian insurgency', in Foley & Ryder (eds), *Ideology and Ireland,* pp 23–44.   66 [T. Moore], *Memoirs of Captain Rock, the celebrated Irish chieftain, with some account of his ancestors, written by himself* (London, 1824), p. 322.   67 Ibid., p. 363.   68 Barrington, *Rise and fall*, p. x.

11

A queen of hearts or an old maid?: Maria Edgeworth's fictions of union

Willa Murphy

In a 1799 letter to her aunt, Maria Edgeworth describes 'a political print just come out, of a woman, meant for Hibernia, dressed in orange and green, and holding a pistol in her hand to oppose the Union.'[1] The image she seizes on portrays Ireland as the street-wise woman defending her virtue, refusing to surrender herself to the foreign abductor, packing a pistol as insurance against any risk of imperialist rape. Six months later, Edgeworth writes that 'the union would be advantageous to all the parties concerned, but England has no right to do to Ireland good *against her will*,' calling attention again to the image of embattled virtue.[2] It may not be exactly rape against which Edgeworth protests here, but it is certainly a coercive kindness. The Act of Union between Great Britain and Ireland has often been figured as a marriage contract, or sexual coupling, not least by Edgeworth herself, and by her father, Richard Lovell Edgeworth, Maria's literary partner and patriarch. He imagined the political union as 'an identical and equal partnership, such terms as leave no temptation on one side, and no suspicion on the other'.[3] His daughter's Irish works have frequently been read as allegories of literary unionism – imaginative attempts to consecrate the union as a necessary and desirable marriage of equals.[4] Her

---

1 M. Edgeworth to C. Sneyd, 2 Apr. 1799 in A. Hare, *The life and letters of Maria Edgeworth* (London, 1894), p. 68.   2 M. Edgeworth to S. Ruxton, 29 Jan. 1800 in Hare, *Life*, p. 72.   3 R.L. Edgeworth, *The substance of three speeches delivered in the House of Commons of Ireland upon the subject of an Union with Great Britain* (London, 1800), p. 20.   4 S. Deane, *Strange country. Modernity and nationhood in Irish writing since 1790* (Oxford, 1997), describes Edgeworth's novels as attempts to make 'two oppositional elements appear ultimately harmonious with one another,' which succeed only in producing 'an analgesic version of the question of English-Irish relations' (p.30). For another treatment of Edgeworth as literary unionist, see T. Dunne, 'Haunted by history: Irish romantic writing, 1800-1850' in R. Porter & M. Teich (eds), *Romanticism in a national context* (Cambridge, 1989), pp 68-91; for a corrective,

project strives, with almost evangelical zeal, to achieve in the black-and-white pages of fiction a merger that looked rather more doubtful in the murky bogs of County Longford. Edgeworth is, by this analysis, an image consultant for Ireland, attempting to convince English readers that their rough-around-the-edges Irish bride will soften with time, and that the crumbling estate she comes with (called Ireland) has great potential.

But her fiction also contains images of marital union that might complicate this reading. Her Irish tales in particular are full of grotesque couplings, abusive partnerships, failed marriages and divorce. Two years after the Act of Union, Edgeworth herself rejected an offer of marriage from a Swedish gentleman.[5] While we need not make too much of this biographical detail, it is worth noting her reasons for refusing a personal union, in the thick of defending a political one defined in analogous terms. She writes to a friend:

> I have no doubt that my happiness would be much increased by a union with a man suited to me in character, temper, and understanding, and firmly attached to me, but deduct any of those circumstances and I think I should lose infinitely more than I should gain ... I am not afraid of being an old maid.[6]

Edgeworth's fiction reveals certain sympathy with the reluctant virgin of the political cartoon described in her letter, and articulates a shared dread of lost identity in any union of unequal partners. 'I am not afraid of being an old maid' might be taken as a fitting caption for the pistol-packing Hibernia as much as for the pen-wielding reformist of Edgeworthstown.

This is by no means to align Edgeworth with her contemporary Sydney Owenson, later Lady Morgan, a flaming anti-unionist, who denounced the marriage of Great Britain and Ireland as the cause of 'an eternity of woe ... endless cycles of misgovernment and resistance' and a spiral of violence, 'disease and pestilence'.[7] Nor did she believe unequivocally with Jonah

see M. Butler, 'General introduction', *The novels and selected works of Maria Edgeworth* (London, 1999), pp vii-lxxx; M. Myers, 'Deromanticising the subject', in P. Feldman and T. Kelley (eds), *Romantic women writers* (London, 1995), pp 88-110. **5** M. Butler, *Maria Edgeworth: a literary biography* (Oxford, 1972) discusses Maria's friendship with Chevalier Abram Niclas Clewberg Edelcrantz, and his unsuccessful offer of marriage in December 1802; pp 192-6. **6** Quoted in Butler, *Edgeworth*, p. 187. Maria's stepmother Frances Anne Beaufort believed that Maria actually 'was exceedingly in love with him' but sacrificed her own happiness for that of her father and family; see Hare, *Life*, p. 108. **7** Lady Morgan, *Absenteeism* (London, 1825), p. 156.

Barrington that the Act of Union was 'one of the most flagrant public acts of corruption on the records of history, and certainly the most mischievous to this empire', reducing Ireland to nothing more than a 'withered limb' of Britain.[8] Anyone looking for a stubborn critic of the union, in other words, could do better than ransack the pages of Maria Edgeworth. Yet Edgeworth was less unwavering about the union than critical representations of her would suggest. Her father's behaviour during parliamentary debates on the union is emblematic of this ambivalence: he spoke so even-handedly about the pros and cons of the proposed union that by the end of his parliamentary speeches nobody, including himself, knew which way he intended to vote.[9] *Castle Rackrent* echoes this vacillation, when the editor remarks that 'It is a problem of difficult solution to determine, whether a union will hasten or retard the melioration of this country.' And it is precisely in the figure of marriage that this indecision and indeterminacy rests.

Marriage in the late eighteenth century was no longer a straightforward matter of pre-arranged unions based on economic advantage and social profit. It was that, to be sure, but it had increasingly become a matter of love as well as money.[10] During this period, the motives for marriage shift from the concrete ones of rank and real estate to 'the imponderable one of affection'.[11] Jane Austen's characters are typical of this struggle to negotiate a balance between affections and account books, as they scramble to win partners who will satisfy at once the requirements of love-me-tender and legal tender.[12] When that harmony is not found, when a marriage is based upon bounty-hunting on the one hand, or on dreamy passion on the other, Austen rewards the couple with domestic misery. Lady Geraldine in Edgeworth's *Ennui* is another embodiment of the refusal to compromise love or social duty in the decision to marry. She cannot agree to marry the bloodless, calculating Lord Glenthorn, a man who believes 'young women

8 J. Barrington, *Personal sketches and recollections of his own times* (Dublin, 1997), p. iii; *Historic anecdotes and secret memoirs of the legislative union between Great Britain and Ireland* (London, 1809), p. 17. **9** M. Hurst, *Maria Edgeworth and the public scene* (London, 1969); Butler, 'General introduction', pp xxxvi–xxxvii. **10** L. Stone, *The family, sex and marriage in England 1500–1800* (London, 1979) argues that marriage evolved from an economic to an emotional matter during the eighteenth century (p. 392). **11** Stone, *Family*, p. 398. **12** For a discussion of Austen's treatment of the cluster of power, property and passion involved in the hunt for suitable spouses, see T. Tanner, *Jane Austen* (London, 1986); R. Sales, *Jane Austen and representations of Regency England* (London, 1994). Some of Austen's contemporaries, like Oliver Goldsmith, believed that (far from simply reflecting existing marital values), novels were to blame for raising exaggerated expectations of romantic love in marriage.

were divided into two classes; those who were to be purchased, and those who were to purchase'.[13] Glenthorn's outdated notion of his role as husband simply will not do if he hopes to capture the heart of Geraldine: 'I thought it manly and fashionable to be indifferent, if not contemptuous to my wife. I considered her only as an encumbrance, that I was obliged to take along with my fortune.'[14] Maria Edgeworth herself finds that her suitor's obsession with duty does not bode well for any future they might have: 'He says ... he should despise himself if he abandoned duty for any passion. This is all very reasonable, but reasonable for him only, not for me.'[15]

So, too, the political union between Great Britain and Ireland must be a matter, according to the Edgeworths, of passion as well as pounds. The union, argues Richard Lovell Edgeworth, will place Ireland in the heart of empire, and gain for it favoured terms of trade. A renewed economy will transform 'idleness and poverty into industry and wealth'.[16] In the closing lines of *Castle Rackrent*, Maria echoes her father's hope that the union will introduce British manufacturers to an industrially-challenged Ireland. But the Edgeworths also know that this cannot simply be a mercenary union – that spouses should not be chosen, as Lord Glenthorn learns in *Ennui*, 'according to the numeration table – units, tens, hundreds, and thousands, tens of thousands, hundreds of thousands'.[17] In what we might call her Princess of Walesian strategy, Maria Edgeworth calls instead for a 'union of hearts'.[18] Like Edmund Burke, the Edgeworths acknowledge the value of human affections in the management of political affairs, recognising that, as Maria puts it, 'it was bad policy to make people detest the authority which they were bound to obey'.[19] A ruling power operates most effectively that can glide gradually and imperceptibly into the hearts of those governed, becoming inseparable from their habits, traditions and conventions. In custom, writes Richard Edgeworth, 'there is always to be found a power, what the workmen call a purchase, which the skilful legislator can ... apply to useful purposes'.[20] Or, as fellow landowner Elizabeth Smith writes later in her diary: 'What we want to lead [the Irish tenants] to is to consider [the landlord] as their friend, the natural guardian of their rights and their

13 M. Edgeworth, *Ennui* (London, 1992), p. 150.   14 *Ennui*, p. 151.   15 M. Edgeworth to S. Ruxton, 8 Dec. 1802 in Hare, *Life*, p. 113.   16 R.L. Edgeworth, *Speeches*, p. 15. 17 Edgeworth, *Ennui*, p. 150.   18 Recall Diana, princess of Wales, in a 1995 interview on BBC's *Panorama*, claiming that she did not expect to be queen of England but hoped, in good Burkean terms, to be 'queen of people's hearts'. For Edgeworth's 'union of hearts', see Hurst, *Public scene*, p. 37.   19 Quoted in J. Beatty (ed.), *The rebellion remembered: loyal and neutral women's narratives of the Irish rebellion of 1798* (forthcoming), p. 256.   20 R.L. Edgeworth and M. Edgeworth, *Memoirs of Richard Lovell Edgeworth, esq.*, 2 vols (London, 1820), ii, p. 465.

comforts.'[21] The Edgeworths know that without a heart-shaped card to play in Ireland, the Union must fold.

Richard Edgeworth, ever the apostle of enlightenment, looks to science to provide metaphors for such an ideal political union, based on mutual attraction and material gains. 'The two islands,' he writes, must be envisioned as 'mutually dependent – so are the earth and moon; they mutually regulate and enlighten each other.'[22] Again, he asserts that 'the real union of different materials can alone be effected by the mutual attraction of their respective parts; when these parts have once combined they become one body without danger of spontaneous dissolution'.[23] Love, 'the attraction that Newton left out',[24] is the essential ingredient in the Act of Union if it is not to be a recipe for dissolution, or worse, violent explosion.

For the Edgeworths, then, an ideal union involves practical economic gains in the present and enlightenment for a benighted island in the future. 'The sun of reason has ascended too high to be followed by the mists of ignorance,' writes Edgeworth in his arguments in favour of union, 'let it shine on Ireland.'[25] The union is to be the light of openness, truth, reason, plain-dealing, and standard English, one which will dispel forever the counter-enlightenment mists of conspiracy, ignorance, secrecy, reticence, double-dealing, lying, cheating, prevaricating, and popery. 'Good example and good education,' writes Richard Edgeworth, 'will carry off, or prevent the peccant humours that disease [this] country.'[26] In short, a union with Great Britain would pack away all wild and childish Irish things into the cupboard of history. Elizabeth Smith similarly believed in the power of education to overcome Irish social ills:

> Sometimes a perfect glow of happiness comes over me when I think of twenty years hence. We have party and sectarian bigotry to get over however before any great advance can be made. We don't want the rapidity of enthusiasm but the sober conviction of rational intelligence and lending libraries are to be among our tools.[27]

Maria Edgeworth's fiction, with its tales of education and improvement through marriages between the English and the Irish, at one level preaches that the union, like a well-arranged marriage, can only mean improvement for both partners.

21 E. Smith, 28 Feb. 1843 in D. Thomson and M. McGusty (eds), *The Irish journals of Elizabeth Smith 1840-1850* (Oxford, 1990), p. 59. 22 Edgeworth, *Speeches*, p. 16. 23 Ibid., p. 32. 24 T. Stoppard, *Arcadia* (London, 1993), p. 74. 25 Edgeworth, *Speeches*, p. 14. 26 Ibid., p. 17. 27 Smith, *Journals*, 30 May 1842, p. 48.

But the Edgeworths were perhaps not as starry-eyed about the union as their discourse of communing hearts and heavenly attraction might suggest. Lurking behind even the reasoned astronomical and chemical conceits is the risk of eclipse or evaporation of the weaker body in any unequal union. A perfect union was easier to achieve in ether or beaker, or with pen and ink, than on contested Irish soil. As witnesses to the recent fury of 1798, the father and daughter knew only too well that the relationship between Britain and Ireland seemed to follow the laws of the jungle more closely than the laws of physics. A union of hearts might be difficult to realise while Irish hearts were still wild. In this sense, Edgeworth's fiction might be read not so much as presiding over the wedding, but as performing the thankless task of marriage counsellor to a mismatched couple – attempting to convince the unhappy partners to stick it out for reasons of economic and social convenience, with the hope that over time they might learn to love each other. As Richard Edgeworth puts the case, 'the force of England is wanted to restrain the violence of party [in Ireland], and to give time for the revival of better passions, to give time for the effects of knowledge and of increasing property'.[28] Lord Glenthorn's proposal to Lady Geraldine in *Ennui* follows just this formula, striving to convince her to accept him on the rational basis of the partnership's economic and social value, and trust that affection would follow later.

The Edgeworths' cheery predictions about the future mask an anxiety that the union as it stands is hardly a match of equals made out of mutual affection. 'Are not troops stationed in every part of this kingdom to enforce what will formally be law, but what can never be substantially legal till it has been sanctioned by time and acquiescence?,' writes Maria's father.[29] In Burkean terms once more, Richard Edgeworth recognises that affection for the law requires the passage of time to smooth over the violent sources of that law. Time makes crooked governments straight and rough powers plain. Like a sound marriage, a lasting political union depends on partners learning how to forgive and forget past trouble and strife. Love, be it for one's spouse or one's state, requires a necessary degree of amnesia. It is just this forgetting, this passage of time and acquiescence, that the Edgeworths find lacking in Ireland, where the memory of past crimes is too recent and painful. Edgeworth ended up voting against the union in part because he felt it to be a quick-fix measure based on London's desire for stability, rather than on the consolidated will of the Irish people. Beneath their confident theoretical unionism lies an anxiety that, as Cecil Devereux puts it in *Ennui*,

28 Edgeworth, *Speeches*, pp 14-15.   29 Ibid., p. 46.

'in certain political, as well as in certain geometrical lines, there is a continual effort to approach, without the possibility of meeting'. The union of British and Irish hearts might prove itself to be an asymptotic goal; not a little like the mixing, writes Richard Edgeworth, of oil and vinegar.[30]

In the Edgeworths' evolutionary model of history, Britain must wait for Ireland to catch up with enlightened English values, to mature to its potential, to become an attractive partner so that mutual affection will be possible. As Elizabeth Smith has it, the Irish are 'but an emerging people ... We consider them too much as if they were further advanced – more on par with ourselves than it is possible for their intellect to become under many generations.'[31] The structure of the relationship in this liberal whig arrangement stunts the very growth it is intended to promote. Like many premature weddings, the marriage that is meant to solve the individuals' identity problems only succeeds in complicating them. This union of hearts and ascendancy of affection anticipated by the Edgeworths masks a real subservient partnership: Ireland, like many eighteenth-century women, finds that her task is not to be herself, but to make herself attractive and acceptable to her prospective husband. Her success in marriage, in other words, is in direct proportion to her lack of identity. She must be pliable, passive, eager to be moulded into a pleasing shape. In the whig scheme of history, Ireland is treated as unformed raw material, stuck in an earlier developmental stage, a child-bride waiting to be tutored by her older and more experienced English husband. But Ireland's history shows her to be less the pleasing bride than the rebellious wife in the years following the union, which is one of the reasons the marriage failed.

Lawrence Stone insists that with the rise of the companionate marriage, where women became the chosen and not the choosers, 'successful marriage thus depended on the docility and adaptability of the woman, as it had always done in the past, which is one of the reasons that some women were so vociferous in their disappointment and frustration in the eighteenth century'.[32] Stone catalogues the steps to becoming an attractive, desirable wife:

> A young married woman was advised to obey her husband, even if under protest, not to cry, to put on a cheerful expression and not to complain, never to refer to 'the rights of women', to curb her tongue, and to try to avoid a quarrel, not to criticise her husband's friends or relatives, not to keep him waiting, and to be neat and elegant.[33]

30 Ibid., p. 42.   31 Smith, *Journals*, 12 July 1846, p. 100.   32 Stone, *Family*, p. 399. 33 Ibid., p. 400.

Such advice sounds not unlike certain exhortations by reforming land-owners such as the Edgeworths in the years following the Union. Elizabeth Smith in County Wicklow laments: 'Unhappy Ireland, how much have your wild children yet to learn,' warning that she and landowners like her 'will not put up ... with their dirt and their gossiping and their utter carelessness and indifference to our interests.'[34] The preface to *Castle Rackrent* insists that 'When Ireland loses her identity by a union with Great Britain, she will look back with a smile of good humoured complacency on ... her former existence.' But like many marriages, this one was to be less about the heavenly attraction of two equal bodies than about the eclipse of one by the other. It is this loss of identity that Edgeworth herself feared in the prospect of marriage ('I feel I should *lose* infinitely more than I should gain'), a loss which her fiction explores, and which complicates readings of her works as simple unionist allegories.

Edgeworth's novels are full of co-dependent couplings and disastrous duos – subordinate relationships that sap the life out of one to swell the identity of the other. More often than not, the wives in her fiction demonstrate the frustration and disappointment linked to marriage, even those matches ostensibly based on affection. The Jewish heiress Jessica in *Castle Rackrent* marries Sir Kit in the mistaken belief that he loves her. Thady Quirk describes Sir Kit's treatment of her: 'He used to swear at her behind her back, after kneeling to her to her face, and call her in the presence of his gentlemen his stiff-necked Israelite, though before he married her ... he used to call her "my pretty Jessica".'[35] His abuse crescendos to tormenting her with piles of bacon and sausage before locking her away in her bedroom for years, turning the entire household against her as an outsider and alien who 'brought nothing but misfortunes among us'. Like Edgeworth's eloping young female characters, Ireland is too uncultivated and unformed to enter into a true marriage of equals, but marriage is one way of taming and tutoring her. Isabella Moneygawl in *Castle Rackrent* is the embodiment of this identity crisis: she elopes to Scotland with Sir Condy Rackrent in an outbreak of adolescent rebellion, only to discover in her maturity that Condy never loved her and that she was too young to know her own mind. She runs back to her family to try to reclaim her identity, but the novel has her run over by a carriage en route – presumably as punishment for this independent streak.

34 Smith, *Journals*, 22 June 1842, p. 151; 20 Mar. 1843, p. 62.   35 M. Edgeworth, *Castle Rackrent* (London, 1992), p. 80.

These and other marriages represented in Edgeworth's novels explore not the mutual affection between peers, but lopsided partnerships between powerful and powerless figures. Next to marriage, the Edgeworths' favourite image for the relationship between Great Britain and Ireland is that of parent and child. Paternalist landowners like the Edgeworths regarded their Irish tenants as their unruly, unlettered foster children, a wayward and cunning crew always in need of a watchful eye. As the catholic novelist Gerald Griffin has it, Ireland was treated not as a 'sister-island' but as a 'step-daughter', suggesting a relationship of bitter dependence and (if the fate of step-children in his tales is anything to go by) danger and death.[36] The union in this sense becomes a custody case, a calling in of social services to tame a hyperactive Irish child. 'We have not been able to keep the peace amongst ourselves,' writes Richard Edgeworth. 'We have called in England to our aid, to settle our domestic quarrels.'[37] The union is a surveillance operation, a watchfulness by the parent figure to see that the child behaves. And supervision of children was something about which the Edgeworths had much to say in their writings on education.

Like marriage, child-rearing during the eighteenth century took a radical turn towards affection. The influence of thinkers like Rousseau meant that brutal and authoritarian treatment of children was increasingly frowned upon, and replaced by a more permissive, loving regime. A 1798 guide informs mothers that 'the first object in the education of a child should be to acquire its affection, and the second to obtain its confidence'.[38] Parents were advised to gain their authority through love, and to achieve discipline by example.[39] Such guides echo Edmund Burke's advice to politicians during this same period – governing by consent is more effective than by coercion, a regime based on feeling is sturdier than one based on force, sentiment is mightier than the sword.

Like many of their Ascendancy counterparts, the Edgeworths were involved in developing schemes to enlighten Ireland, and so to create a union of open hearts and minds. For them, the Ascendancy's strongest weapon against Irish delinquency was education. The proper instruction of children and tenants would diffuse enlightenment ideals throughout Ireland, and turn Irish hearts of stealth to hearts of truth. The Edgeworth household, as Maria describes it in her *Memoirs* of her father, was an enlightenment experiment, committed to reason, openness and free communication, opposed to all forms of concealment and reticence:

36 G. Griffin, 'The brown man' in *Holland-Tide; or, Munster popular tales* (London, 1827), p. 292. 37 Edgeworth, *Speeches*, p. 15. 38 Quoted in Stone, *Family*, p. 434, from *The Lady's Monthly Museum*. 39 Stone, *Family*, pp 433-40.

Some men live with their family, without letting them know their affairs ...This was not my father's way of thinking. – On the contrary, not only his wife, but his children knew all his affairs. Whatever business he had to do was done in the midst of his family, usually in the common sitting room: so that we were intimately acquainted, not only with his general principles of conduct, but with the most minute details of their every-day application.[40]

Based on his own child-rearing practices, Edgeworth compiled with his daughter their *Guide to practical education*, a twelve-step program for parents who wanted to become more like the Edgeworths. Influenced by the educational theories of Rousseau, Joseph Priestley, David Hartley, and their friend Thomas Day, Richard and his second wife Honora formulated a child-friendly experimental approach to education. Tutored at home, children are encouraged through reward rather than discipline to develop the ability to reason, and to consider everyday activities and events as opportunities for learning everything from scientific to moral principles. Their intention is to produce children who, through affection and encouragement, internalise enlightenment values, and so are eventually free to discipline and monitor themselves. The ideal Edgworthian child operates, in other words, on automatic pilot.

Published the year of the United Irish rebellion, the guide also shows the marks of its genesis in the troubled 1790s. Parents are warned that 'some secret intercourse [might] be carried on between children and servants', a danger 'lessened by [making certain] arrangements in the house'. These arrangements include 'care in a mother or governess to know exactly where children are, and what they are doing every hour of the day'; design of a house that 'make[s] it impossible for them to go without detection into any place which we forbid';[41] separate staircases and passageways for servants; and ensuring that no passageway exists between children's and servants' chambers. The guide encourages a constant scrutiny of children's conversations: 'children who are encouraged to converse about everything ... will naturally tell their mothers if any one talks to them ... they will never be the spies of servants, nor should they keep their secrets'.[42] More often than not in *Practical education*, 'education' is another word for surveillance. In the *Memoirs*, Maria Edgeworth praises her father's constant supervision of his children, which involves keeping 'a register of observations and facts,

40 Edgeworth and Edgeworth, *Memoirs*, ii, p. 15.   41 R.L. Edgeworth and M. Edgeworth, *Guide to practical education* (London, 1798), p. 201.   42 Edgeworth and Edgeworth, *Guide*, p. 200.

relative to his children'.[43] He creates a personal panopticon in his house, keeping 'notes of every circumstance which occurred worth recording.'

Though Edgeworth's code employs enlightenment tenets about the value of affection in the raising of children, it also shares features in common with that movement's adversaries. The new lenient school of bringing up baby, with its Rousseauian assumptions about the natural goodness of the child, did not sit well with all mothers and fathers. English evangelical parents, for instance, guided by a belief in the innate depravity of human beings, scrupulously scanned their children for flickers of original sin, and disciplined them accordingly. Stone describes the relationship towards their children as 'not so much loving as intensely watchful'.[44] While there is no doubt that Edgeworth was fond of most of his many children, it is difficult not to hear echoes of evangelical scrutiny in his parenting advice.[45] The *Guide*, like Maria's didactic tales for children, preaches the value of free expression and exploration in the education of children. But overseeing this autonomy is a close, almost scientific eye, coolly monitoring the progress of the educational experiment. Edgeworth's child rearing is at once permissive and highly intrusive, involving constant superintendence of his children's actions and thoughts to see that all is proceeding according to plan.

The treatment of Irish tenants by parental reformers like the Edgeworths follows a similar code, combining sentiment with surveillance. Elizabeth Smith remarks in her diary that 'It has been my endeavor ... to establish a more affectionate intercourse between us,', but also insists that her tenants 'require constant watching to keep them all in order and up to industry.'[46] For Maria Edgeworth, Ireland is steeped in a threatening secrecy, from Maynooth seminary, whose 'closed doors' and 'concealment' represent 'the dangerous spirit and tendency of catholicism',[47] to those tenants leagued in 'secret rebellion' who are 'so secret and cunning, that no proofs could be obtained against them'.[48] Left to their own devices, the child and the Irish tenant risk falling into the devious ways of secrecy – creating imaginary, superstitious and alternative worlds. The impulse to hide, to evade the eyes of the law and exist in a secret space suggests a desire for autonomy shared by children and by Irish tenants. To shape one's own world and become

43 Edgeworth and Edgeworth, *Memoirs*, ii, pp 184-5. 44 Stone, *Family*, p. 466. 45 Edgeworth is generally considered to have disliked the children from the first of his four marriages, and though Maria (who was born of this first wife) was his close partner, she felt to a certain extent this lack of affection. See Butler, 'General introduction,' pp xiv-xv. 46 Smith, *Journals*, 19 Jan. 1840, p. 6; 28 Oct. 1845, p 83. 47 Quoted in Hurst, *Public scene*, p. 98. 48 Edgeworth and Edgeworth, *Memoirs*, ii, pp 209-10.

master over it is the stuff of which children's dreams are made, as are the dreams of a colonised, disempowered people. It is no surprise that the processes of colonial power generated a culture of concealment in Ireland. When the majority of a population is excluded from public means of expression and protest, those political energies move underground, creating a smouldering underground culture beneath a surface of submission. Nineteenth-century Ireland as a whole was a 'secret society.' Secrecy and strategic silence became mechanisms of survival, and alternative spaces for enacting social and political power. As Lecky noted, 'Ireland's Catholics learned the lesson which ... rulers should dread to teach. They became [adept] in the arts of conspiracy and disguise. Secrets known to hundreds were preserved inviolable from authority.'[49] Secrecy and obstruction was one response of the Irish tenantry to the glaring light of empire, and to intrusive eyes like the Edgeworths.

Written in such a context, the preface to *Castle Rackrent* insists that 'a love of truth ... necessarily implies a love of secret[s],' an assertion that well articulates the double impulse at work in the Edgeworth literary and social project. Like the *Guide*, *Castle Rackrent* is a text concerned with surveillance and secrecy. Thady Quirk's narrative, with its first person confessional style, its nods and winks to the reader, its diplomatic deference to the editor, might be read as an example of the threatening Irish discourse of secrecy. His penchant for eavesdropping, his eye for confidential letters and documents, his tight-lipped posture towards his masters, and his gossipy tone towards his readers, all combine to create the kind of insinuating Irish voice the Edgeworths came to fear. Thady witnesses every detail of the downfall of his masters: he is always 'just within hearing' of private conversations, or happens to catch a glimpse over his son Jason's shoulder of secret documents[50] – but all the while maintains a strategic silence: 'I never said anything one way or the other'; 'I kept my mind to myself'; 'I said nothing' is his constant refrain as the Rackrent family self-destructs.[51] Thady, the eagle-eyed, elephant-eared presence, is every landlord's nightmare, whatever his claims to being a loyal retainer. Wrapped in his great cloak (which, the notes tell us, provides among other things concealment and anonymity to Irish rebels), Thady might be read as not too far removed from those double-dealing tenants who serve their landlords faithfully by day and plot their overthrow by night.

Kathryn Kirkpatrick has recently explored the competing discourses of the text and the glossary of *Castle Rackrent*, the former written by Maria

49 W.E.H. Lecky, *A history of Ireland in the eighteenth century* (London, 1972), p. 50. **50** Edgeworth, *Castle Rackrent*, pp 71; 75. **51** Edgeworth, *Castle Rackrent*, pp 72; 77; 96.

without her father's supervision; the latter written, or at least strongly encouraged and edited by him.[52] Where the original text is generally sympathetic to Thady, the glossary is patronising and suspicious. The glossary itself acts as a supervisor of a potentially dangerous text, correcting and reining in any perceived complicity with the dispossessed, childish and secretive Irish. The glossary aligns clandestine activities not only with the Irish but also with women. A gloss on 'the raking pot of tea' disapproves of these 'stealth[y]' women's meetings, 'the joys' of which depend 'on its being made in secret, and at an unseasonable hour', behind a locked door, amidst much 'giggling and scrambling', and involving the exchange of private letters, pocket-books and gossip about men. The gloss adds that the tradition finds its origins among 'washerwoman and the laundry-maid', or, as it puts plainly, among 'low life'.[53] The glossary bespeaks an anxiety about unsupervised activities, particularly among the Irish lower classes and among women.

The writing of *Castle Rackrent* was one activity that went unsupervised by the all-seeing Richard Lovell Edgeworth. And it is this text that is most complicit with the discourse of secrecy. Despite her reformist rampages against Ireland's furtiveness, Maria Edgeworth knew well the pleasure and power associated with a good secret. In an 1803 letter to a friend, she describes composing stories in secret as 'one of my greatest delights and strongest motives for writing'. Her favourite stories 'were all written whilst my father was out somewhere or other, on purpose to be read to him on his return'.[54] Edgeworth associates a certain freedom and delight with this secret scrawl, this activity hidden from prying eyes, and the succeeding disclosure to her father. The subtexts of Edgeworth's other novels present a similar attraction to the power and pleasure of secrecy, all the while their texts preach against its dangers – Harriet Freke in *Belinda* whose secret cross-dressing allows her to participate in the male world of politics and power; Lord Colambre in *The absentee*, whose disguise allows him to speak and move freely among his tenants and agents, gathering the truth about his estate through a secret identity; Ellinor in *Ennui*, whose secret swapping of her infant son with the future Lord Glenthorn casts the mighty landowners from their thrones and raises up an Irish tenant in their place.

Why, then, all this secrecy in a writer committed to a union of open hearts and minds, and to a marriage of transparency? Though she never married, Maria Edgeworth arguably knew something about a subservient

52 K. Kirkpatrick, 'Putting down the rebellion: notes and glosses on *Castle Rackrent*', *Eire-Ireland* 30:1 (1995), pp 77-90.   53 Edgeworth, *Castle Rackrent*, pp 135-6.   54 Quoted in Butler, *Maria Edgeworth*, p. 288.

partnership in her relationship with her father, who was described by a friend of Maria's as 'father, friend, husband – he was all to her.' Edgeworth once told his daughter that 'no human creature ever saw the heart of another more completely than you have seen mine'. Whether the reverse was true is less apparent. Her father was, in Emily Lawless's later description, an 'autocrat', 'arbitrator and general overseer' of his family, who forced Maria to 'carry on her little pursuits under his direct eye'.[55] Edgeworth reveals that her father required that she present him an outline of each novel before beginning to write. His invention of a margin machine for her writing paper, to keep her margins justified – to keep her colouring within the lines, so to speak – might make a fitting image of his superintendence. 'When not actually guiding her pen', argues Lawless, 'in spirit he hovered over it.'[56] Under his supervision and fostering, Maria's greatest defect, 'a lack of imagination', was raised to a sort of 'solemn duty'.[57] Except, Lawless says, in the case of *Castle Rackrent*, a novel she describes as 'wholly independent and revolutionary.'

The downtrodden Rackrent wives survive their mercenary husbands in part through the power of secrecy. The Jewish heiress Jessica, believed to have secret jewels hidden on her person, closets herself in her bedroom to escape Sir Kit's abuses. When she hears news of his death, she rises from the ashes of illness and a bad marriage to a new independence, takes her share of the property and runs before his body is cold. Isabella Moneygawl learns of Sir Condy's true feelings for her by eavesdropping on the servants. Both women use secrecy as a means of survival and liberation. With Thady Quirk they form part of the subtext of *Castle Rackrent*, which bespeaks the positive power of all those dark Irish mists the Edgeworths meant to dispel.

Secrecy is intimately bound up with identity, with the opacity of human subjects, and can be a source of creative power.[58] Just as the initiation rites of secret societies transform the identity of their members, individual secrets can allow a transcending of one's ordinary boundaries and subjectivity. Maria Edgeworth detected this liberating power when she wrote stories in secret; this same creative power rears its head in her writing. The subtext of Edgeworth's novels is that secrecy empowers and liberates as often, if not more often, than it destroys. As Tony Tanner comments on the

55 E. Lawless, *Maria Edgeworth* (London, 1904), pp 38-40. Echoing Edgeworth's own astronomical conceits, Lawless writes that Edgeworth regarded the women in his life – wives, sisters-in-law, daughters, tenants – as 'so many satellites, revolving gently, as by a law of nature, around the pedestal upon which he stood alone'(p. 38). 56 Lawless, *Edgeworth*, p. 18. 57 Ibid., p. 39. 58 S. Bok, *Secrets: on the ethics of concealment and revelation* (New York, 1984), p. 46.

culture of concealment in Jane Austen's fiction, 'if secrecy is often a painful obligation imposed by the forms of a rigid society, it may also be a strategy against or around them'.[59] Edgeworth's novels suggest that in certain situations it is altogether *reasonable* to be clandestine and secretive. Nineteenth-century Ireland might be one place where survival depended on being reticent and double-dealing, on shifting identity to meet the situation, on telling and keeping secrets. Edgeworthstown House might be another. The presence of secrecy in Irish servants and tenants, in children, and in Edgeworth's fiction itself, might say something about the intensely watchful, conformist society which bred them. To this extent, the light of reason and the darkness of Irish hearts might not be so far apart as the Edgeworth enlightenment experiment would like to insist. Maria Edgeworth's fiction understands something about the confinement of being watched, the frustration of needing to please an exacting partner, and the necessity of secrecy in any union of unequal hearts. For all these reasons, Edgeworth's fiction offers more than simple allegories of literary unionism, but a complex equivocation between enlightenment and obfuscation, revelation and reticence, open hearts and secrets behind closed doors. She is more than her father's daughter, precisely because of her experience as her father's daughter. This is the other union Edgeworth ends up writing about, inhabiting the silent sorrow of lost identity, and the secret spaces where it might be found again. It is a union perhaps best described by a line from the Irish ballad 'She Moved through the Fair':

> The people were saying no two were e're wed
> But one had a sorrow that never was said.

59 Tanner, *Austen*, p. 81.

12

Mr and Mrs England: the Act of Union as national marriage

Jane Elizabeth Dougherty

The Act of Union was consistently depicted as a marriage, with England as the groom and Ireland as the bride, a metaphor which appeared not only in cartoons and popular entertainments, but also in pamphlet literature and parliamentary speeches of the period.[1] In the wake of the union, the marriage metaphor was used to argue for the inclusion of Ireland in the domestic realm of Britain, by those who advocated a liberal 'union of hearts', and was deployed subsequently to advocate Irish separatism, by those who denounced the union as a failed marriage. Indeed, the union as a marriage remains a persistent metaphor; it has become a commonplace in discussions of the union. The use of the marriage metaphor reveals that the union is a contract, which like all marriage contracts represents an anomaly in a contractarian society; the terms of this marriage contract had both discursive and historical implications in the context of the Anglo-Irish relationship.

The union was a heterosexual marriage because it was effected to alleviate the anxiety caused by the French threat to Britain's 'rear end' and because the British tried to end the narrative of Irish nationalism as in a Jane Austen novel. It was a heterosexual marriage because it aimed, in Louise

---

1 Entertainments include two allegedly staged in Dublin: 'At the royal circus near College Green for the benefit of Mrs Ireland on Wednesday January 15th will be performed a grand serio-comic olio called The forced marriage; or the humbugged Islanders,' and 'At the royal circus near College Green for the benefit of the great Mrs Britain on Monday February 3rd will be performed a grand serio-comic pastichio called The rape of Ierne, or fidelity betrayed.' One pamphlet survives from London, entitled *The wedding and bedding, or John Bull and his bride fast asleep, a satirical poem containing an history of the happy pair from their infancy to the present period, with reasons for and means used to accomplish their Union; also The matchmakers matches, with their rueful lamentation for the loss of the bridecake.*

Fradenburg's words, both to preserve and suspend inequality, to admit the Irish to sovereignty in order to establish sovereignty *over* them.[2] It was a heterosexual marriage because it both denied and reified difference; it claimed a fundamental gender difference and a common interest between the two countries. It was a heterosexual marriage because it turned coercion into consent through the forced hegemony known as matrimony. It was a heterosexual marriage because it promised the Irish protection and legitimacy in return for submission, and because it divided the civil society of the United Kingdom into two spheres, the public sphere of Britain and the private sphere of Ireland. It was a heterosexual marriage because it produced the question 'what do the Irish want?' and the British charge that the Irish kept changing the answer. It was, finally, a heterosexual marriage because it blurred the distinctions between self and other, with far-reaching consequences.

Tzetvan Todorov argues that the experience of alterity makes possible only one of two fundamental moves: the coloniser can either conceive of the other as 'human beings altogether, having the same rights as himself', a stance which ultimately leads to 'assimilationism' and 'the projection of his own values on [to] the others,' or he can emphasise 'difference'.[3] Instead, the British authorities who were confronted once again with rebellious colonial others sought to combine both stances: to both assimilate and differentiate the Irish; to invite the other in, in the service of keeping the other at bay. In attempting such a paradoxical move, the prime minister William Pitt, his chief secretary for Ireland Lord Castlereagh, and the chief propagandist for union, Castlereagh's undersecretary Edward Cooke, were proposing – though they did not often like to admit it – what was in essence a marriage contract, a metaphor which could account for the paradoxical nature of the union enterprise. The marriage contract has been defined as a vehicle through which, by their own consent, '[w]omen are incorporated into a sphere that both is and is not in civil society,' a private sphere which 'is part of civil society but separated from the "civil" sphere'.[4] Certainly, the need to gain consent for the union was uppermost in the minds of the pro-unionists, who were at pains to suggest that the proposed Act of Union was a contract between two parties rather than a takeover: that it would come about through consent, not coercion. Yet as Pateman notes of the marriage contract, 'forced or unwilling submission is often treated as consent', a point echoed by those opposed to the union.[5] Richard Brinsley Sheridan, the dramatist and a British MP,[6] argued:

2 L. Fradenburg, *City, marriage, tournament: arts of rule in late medieval Scotland* (Madison, 1991), p. 72.   3 T. Todorov, *The conquest of America: the question of the other* (New York, 1982), p. 42.   4 C. Pateman, *The sexual contract* (Stanford, 1988), p. 11.   5 Pateman, *Sexual contract*, p. 106.   6 Foster notes that Sheridan 'consistently supported

If we are to incorporate any part of the empire, let us hold up the perfidy and fraud of France to the disgust of the world, and let our conduct afford a direct contrast; let no suspicion be entertained that we gain our object by intimidation or corruption; let our union be an union of affection and attachment, of plain dealing and free will; let it be an union of mind and spirit, as well as of interest and power; let it not resemble those Irish marriages which commence in fraud and are consummated in force. Let us not commit a brutal rape on the independence of Ireland, when by tenderness we may have her the willing partner of our fate. The state of Ireland does not admit to such a marriage; her bans ought not to be published to the sound of the trumpet, with an army of forty thousand men. She is not qualified for hymeneal rites, when the grave and the prison hold so large a share of her population.[7]

Sheridan, like many other anti-unionists, rejected the notion that Ireland could freely give her consent to union in the wake of a thwarted rebellion.[8] The consent given by a vanquished nation could only be effected by coercion; in this view, Ireland's consent had no validity because of the 'intimidation' and 'corruption' attendant on the proposal for union.

The pro-unionists argued that because they had sought Ireland's consent, the proposed union was indeed a contract between two equals which would also, paradoxically, make them equals.[9] In so doing, they were seizing on a fundamental anomaly in classic contract theory:

If women have been forcibly subjugated by men, or if they naturally lack the capacities of 'individuals,' they also lack the standing and capacities necessary to enter into the original contract [which makes a civil society out of the state of nature.] Yet the social contract theorists insist that women are capable of entering, indeed must enter, into one contract, namely the marriage contract. Contract theorists simultaneously deny and presuppose that women can make contracts. Nor does Locke, for example, explain why the marriage contract is necessary when women are declared to be naturally

all conciliatory policies towards Ireland, but only in opposing the union did he admit his own Irish identification. Otherwise, [he was] unique in his ostensible ability to jettison Irishness.' R. Foster, *Modern Ireland: 1600-1972* (New York, 1989), p. 180n.   7 C. Coote, *History of the union of the kingdoms of Great Britain and Ireland* (London, 1802), p. 76.   8 Sheridan's reference to abduction shows that his anti-union beliefs did not necessarily indicate, as Foster notes, an identification with Irish cultural practices.   9 Coote, *History of the union*, p. 242.

subject to men. There are other ways in which a union between a man and his natural subordinate could be established, but instead, Locke holds that it is brought into being through contract, which is an agreement between two equals.[10]

Certainly Edward Cooke argued that 'an union presupposes that, when it is completed, the contracting states shall be bound together by the same constitution, laws, and government, and by an identity of interests, and equality of privileges' though he noted that 'we acknowledge and lament the inferiority of Ireland',[11] suggesting that the Act of Union, like the marriage contract, represented a contract between a man – in this case John Bull – and his natural subordinate. Indeed, the 'constitutions, laws, and government' in which Ireland would partake were the constitution, laws, and government of Britain, and as anti-unionist pamphleteers pointed out, Ireland, like any bride, would be acquiescing in the loss of her ability to consent, contracting to give up her right to make contracts. Cooke argued that Ireland would partake in the glories of Britain's constitution and laws through a marriage contract, in which the wife's identity is incorporated into that of her husband. Writing in 1765-9, the authoritative legal commentator Sir William Blackstone noted of the marriage contract that 'by marriage the husband and wife are one person in law: that is, the very being, or legal existence of the woman is suspended during the marriage, or at least is incorporated and consolidated into that of the husband',[12] a legal doctrine known as coverture. Cooke, then, argued for Ireland's incorporation into the civil sphere of Britain through the vehicle of coverture, and presented it as an assimilation of Ireland into civil society, though in fact it represented both Irish assimilation into and the division of the civil sphere.

Critics quickly exposed Cooke's disingenuous attempt to disguise a marriage contract as a standard Lockean social contract. One pamphlet, *To be, or not to be, a nation: that is the question*, pointed out the similarity between entering the marriage contract as a bride and committing suicide. In his parody of Cooke, this anonymous pamphleteer wrote:

> Says he, 'Two independent states, finding their separate existence mutually inconvenient, propose to form themselves into one state for their mutual benefit.' (They find a state of celibacy mutually

10 Pateman, *Sexual contract*, p. 54.   11 E. Cooke, *Arguments for and against an union between Great Britain and Ireland considered* (Dublin, 1799). As countless rebuttal pamphlets pointed out, Cooke's pamphlet presented, almost exclusively, the arguments in favor of a union.   12 Pateman, *Sexual contract*, p. 90.

inconvenient; they, therefore, resolve to take the advice of their
friends, and to propose a treaty of marriage, or in other words, an
union. – God grant that they may turn out a happy couple, and that
the said union may not terminate in a divorce!)[13]

In fact, as the pamphleteer Robert Orr noted, divorce was not possible:

Were a freeman voluntarily to become a slave? Would you not laugh
at the folly of the one, and despise the baseness of the other? Yet such
will be your conduct, if you make an incorporate union. In any other
settlemement, the infringement of the articles is a dissolution of the
compact. But incorporate union annihilates the contracting parties
without the power of revival. It will bind us in an adamantine chain
which we will never break.[14]

Unlike other contracts, but like the marriage contract, the Act of Union was
seen to be irrevocable. It annihilated – albeit in vastly unequal measures –
the contracting parties, because it created a new entity, the United Kingdom, which would retain the 'constitution, laws and government' of Great
Britain. As anti-unionists pointed out, the consent of Ireland to the union
represented the binding of Ireland, in Orr's words, in 'an adamantine chain,'
and as such the union resembled a slave contract. William Drennan,
erstwhile prominent United Irishman, ended his pamphlet on the union by
signing off with 'I am your humble servant, But not yet – your slave – ,'
suggesting that the contract he was being asked to enter was hardly a classic
Lockean one.[15]

Indeed, Drennan believed that the very proposal for union was an affront
to the Irish nation:

The nation that does not feel the debasement of the very proposition
deserves to suffer the prostitution: for certain proposals may be made
to individuals, in which the injury, monstrous as it is, is lost in the
insult: which by the one sex, can be repelled only by a look of
ineffable contempt, and by the other, with a blow – so there are
affronts to nations, on which controversy is contamination; as if we
could be reasoned into making a capon of our country – an eunuch
of Ireland.[16]

13 *To be or not to be, a nation: that is the question* (Dublin, 1799), p. 2.   14 R. Orr, *An
address to the people of Ireland, against an union: in which, a pamphlet entitled* Arguments
for and against that measure, *is considered* (Dublin, 1799), p. 43.   15 W. Drennan, *A
letter to the right honourable William Pitt* (Dublin, 1799), p. 48.   16 Drennan, *Letter*, p.

Drennan concluded that this union proposal 'should be as revolting to the nation, as to the man.'[17] The suggestion that the proposal for union is a homosexual advance is telling (Drennan once called Ireland 'the base POSTERIOR of the world'),[18] as is Drennan's notion that union will make Ireland an eunuch. Drennan was ultimately trying to protect the concept of Ireland as both containing and embodying a public (and political) sphere, much as a man, in the Lockean sense, both possesses and embodies himself; the proposal was insulting precisely because it made clear that the British did not see Ireland as a masculine equal.

The principal provision of the union was, in fact, the abolition of the Irish parliament, which represented both the public (and political) sphere of Ireland and the manifestation of Ireland's claim as a political (and public) entity. The public sphere is always masculine, and thus it was the presence of at least a nominally independent parliament that made Ireland a masculine nation.[19] The proposal for its abolition revealed, as Bartlett notes, 'that the English, so far from seeing [Irish protestants] as partners in and co-equal beneficiaries of the "Glorious Revolution" viewed them as a subject people'.[20] Throughout the eighteenth century, Irish protestants had resisted this conception, preferring to see Ireland not as a colony, but as a 'brother' or 'sister' kingdom to England, with an Irish parliament that was or ought to be co-equal with the English parliament.[21] Drennan wrote that '[i]t is not from ... any consideration of equal relationship to the whole family of the people, that this plan has proceeded.'[22] In making their proposal for the destruction of the Irish parliament, the British were asserting not only their power but their authority, laying bare the fiction of an independent Irish brother or sister parliament and proposing to install another fiction, a marriage, in its place.[23] If the pro-unionists represented this as an invitation to the Irish to be assimilated into the British sphere, the anti-unionists took it as a humiliating sign of their subordination to the English. The marriage contract provides for both assimilation and subordination.

32. In the same vein, Edward Lawless wrote in his anti-union pamphlet; 'this just indignation can never fail to be roused in the bosom of every Irishman, when a proposal, so ruinous, so insulting, so inflaming, is made to this independent kingdom.' E. Lawless, *Thoughts on the projected union, between Great Britain and Ireland* (Dublin, 1799), p. 27. 17 Drennan, *Letter*, p. 33.   18 Quoted in Vance, 'Irish literary traditions and the Act of Union,' in *Canadian Journal of Irish Studies* ii, (1986), p. 36.   19 Pateman, *Sexual contract*, p. 11.   20 Bartlett, *Fall and rise*, p. 34.   21 Ibid., p. 36.   22 Drennan, *Letter*, p. 4.   23 The Irish protestant device of referring to Ireland as a 'brother' or 'sister' kingdom in fact reinforced Lockean notions of possessive embodiment. Encoding the kingdom as female ensured Irish possession, and encoding it as male ensured Irish embodiment. Thus the two conceptions of the 'siblinghood' of the kingdoms were intertwined.

Yet some protestants, and more catholics, were in favor of the union, which offered two of the traditional spoils of wifehood: protection and legitimacy. The protestants were offered protection by the union: they would become part of the majority in the United Kingdom, rather than a beleaguered minority in Ireland. In return, they would surrender their claim to independent masculinity. The catholics were promised legitimacy by the union: the implicit promise of full catholic emancipation, which would at last mean assimilation into the British civil sphere. Moreover, the union promised to give catholics an opportunity to participate in the British empire. In return, they would relinquish their aspirations to independence. Westmorland pointed out to Pitt that 'The protestants frequently declare that they will have an union rather than give the franchise to catholics, and the catholics that they will have an union rather than submit to their present state of degradation.'[24] The promise of catholic emancipation was rescinded because of George III's objection that it violated his coronation oath to uphold the protestant faith, reflecting the extent to which the British constitution remained protestant.

Indeed, the Tory peer Lord Sheffield argued against 'the admission of one hundred wild Irish [into the British parliament.] The intrusion of eighty is rather too much, seventy-five would be sufficient, the present House of Commons is very trumpery and bad enough. I do not think any of our country gentlemen would venture into parliament if they were to meet one hundred Paddies';[25] these were protestant paddies, who presumably would have been seen as less objectionable. Clearly, at least according to this Tory peer, there remained a view of the Irish as savage, inassimilable, and certainly not worthy of political representation. That Sheffield could see eighty Irish members as too much is extraordinary when one considers what a low proportion it represented of the Irish population. As Henry Grattan noted of the union:

> It is not an identification of the people, as it excludes the catholic from the parliament and from the state; it is not an identification of government, for it retains the Lord-Lieutenant and his court; it is not an identification of establishments; it is not an identification of revenue; it is not an identification of commerce, for you have still relative duties, and countervailing duties; ... if it be not an identification of interests, still less is it an identification of feeling and of sympathy. The union, then, is not an identification of the two

24 Bartlett, *Fall and rise*, p. 170.   25 Quoted in Bolton, *Union*, p. 86.

nations; it is merely a merger of the parliament of one nation in that of the other; one nation, namely England, retains her full proportion; Ireland strikes off two-thirds; she does so, without any regard either to her present number, or to comparative physical strength; she is more than one-third in population, in territory, and less than one-sixth in representation. Thus there is no identification in any thing, save only in legislature, in which there is a complete and absolute absorption.[26]

The union settlement ensured that there would be some Irish representation at Westminster, yet as Grattan noted, Ireland was extremely underrepresented in parliament. The marriage contract of the union had not quite completely segregated the 'public' from the 'private'; yet it is worth noting that '[f]ully half of the Irish MPs who sat at Westminster in the period 1801–1820 made no recorded speech in the house and the contribution of the remainder appears to have been insignificant,' suggesting the extent to which the Irish were silenced in England's House.[27] Indeed, the way the Irish operated in the British parliament has been compared by Oliver MacDonagh to the private influence wives exert over their husbands: '[a]t best, such an influence was akin to that of Victorian women over husbands and fathers – not indeed in terms of affection or compassion, but in terms of the domestic miseries that might ensue were they wholly thwarted, maltreated, or abandoned.'[28] The union settlement ensured that the contribution of the Irish 'to the welfare of the nation' would be, like that of women, 'essentially private and always indirect';[29] in the British parliament, they would wield some influence but little power.

The union ultimately meant destruction of the Irish parliament, the masculine public and civil sphere of Ireland. Once the consent for union was given, and the Irish parliament became the only parliament in history to vote for its abolition, the Irish, like all wives, could no longer make contracts. Once the Irish parliamentarians had rejected or accepted the proposal for

26 Quoted in Foster, *Modern Ireland*, p. 283.   27 S.J. Connolly, 'Aftermath and Adjustment' in W.E. Vaughan (ed.), *Ireland under the Union 1801-1870* (Oxford, 1989), p. 6. Anthony Trollope writes in *Phineas Finn*, his novel about an Irish M.P., that 'it seemed to [Phineas] ... that Irish members of Parliament were generally treated with more indifference, than any others. There were O'B——, and O'C——, and O'D——, for whom no one cared a straw, who could hardly get men to dine with them at the club, and yet they were genuine members of Parliament. Why should he ever be better than O'B——, or O'C——, or O'D——? And in what way should he begin to be better?' A. Trollope, *Phineas Finn* (New York, 1982), i, p. 23.   28 O. MacDonagh, 'Ireland and the Union, 1801-70' in Vaughan, *Ireland under the Union*, p. liii.   29 L. Colley, *Britons: forging the nation 1707-1837* (New Haven, 1992), p. 47.

union, the Irish parliamentarians had no say in the union settlement, which Boyce notes was remarkable in that its terms were drawn up solely by the British government and were not the subject of negotiation as the Anglo-Scottish union had been.[30] The terms of the union were presented as 'generous' precisely because the Irish parliamentarians had no say in the union settlement: the terms could be seen as 'generous' because, like any bride, the Irish had given away the right to make future contracts when they contracted into the union. This is the major reason that the union was opposed so bitterly before it was enacted; as Peter Burrowes, the Irish opposition MP, argued, '[i]f an union should pass, I shall be indifferent how many or how few deputies shall be sent from this emasculated country'.[31] Having given up his (masculine) civil freedom, Burrowes embraced political apathy. Henry Grattan was more optimistic, saying in 1810 that '[m]y sentiments remain unchanged. The marriage, however, having taken place, it is now the duty, as it ought to be the inclination, of every individual to render it as fruitful, as profitable, and as advantageous as possible.'[32] With many Irish protestants, who increasingly identified the union with the protestant interest, Grattan saw the union, like a marriage, as irrevocable. Indeed, had the catholics also formally consented to the marriage contract of the Act of the Union, and received the wifely legitimacy they had been promised, they might also have seen it as irrevocable. Instead, the claims of catholics to legitimacy were deferred, and in winning legitimacy for themselves, rather than having it conferred on them, the catholics reclaimed Ireland as a nation – indeed, as their nation. Nevertheless, some prominent catholics, with Thomas Moore, pronounced the achievement of catholic emancipation, and the assimilation of Irish catholics to British civil rights in 1829, as the 'end of [their] politics'.[33]

Through union Ireland became the wife of Great Britain, an anomalous status that was to have grave consequences in both the discursive and historical realms, themselves implicated in each other. Ireland remained, much like women within the marriage contract, both assimilated and different: as Terry Eagleton notes, the British

> treated Ireland at once differently and not differently enough – The Irish were different enough to require a special civil service and apparatus of repression, to be asked to foot the bill for the Famine, and to enjoy a peculiar franchise qualification. But they were alike

30 D.G. Boyce, *Nineteenth-century Ireland: the search for stability* (Savage, 1991), p. 19.
31 Coote, *History of the union*, p. 368. 32 Quoted in J. Fisher, *The end of the Irish parliament* (London, 1911), p. 311. 33 Thomas Flanagan, 'Literature in English, 1801-

enough to have MPs at Westminster in the first place, a privilege
enjoyed by no other British colony, to contribute to the national debt,
and to share with the imperial nation an exchequer, armed forces,
postal services, and a free-trade area.[34]

Eagleton suggests that 'the text of the [Anglo–Irish relationship] is indeci-
pherable' because the two countries are 'at once too near and too far, akin
and estranged, both inside and outside each other's cognitive range.'[35] With
the union, then, an epistemology of Ireland became impossible; the 'Irish
question' of the nineteenth-century became the Freudian question, 'What
do the Irish want?'

Immediately following the union, there were attempts to bring Ireland
into England's cognitive range: there was a burst of interest in Ireland, and
a 'cult of the Celt' swept Britain. Writers like Maria Edgeworth and Lady
Morgan became popular, and with the publication of Edgeworth's *Castle
Rackrent*, George III is said to have observed, 'I know something now of my
Irish subjects.'[36] Likewise, travel writers began to visit Ireland, insisting that
through their observations 'Ireland should become more available and
ordered.'[37] As Glenn Hooper writes:

> J. Curwen explained his interest in 'visiting a country, which,
> although almost within our view, and daily in our contemplation, is
> as little known to me, comparatively speaking, as if it were an island
> in the remotest part of the globe.' The sense that Ireland could be
> historically tied to Britain and yet so alien, so close and yet so imag-
> inatively distant, suggests that while a desire existed to satisfy the
> political difficulties of Ireland once and for all, the British were still
> disadvantaged by not having a substantially complete file on Ireland.[38]

This immediate post-union project failed: the status of Ireland as both
assimilated and different – as Britain's wife – ensured that the 'file' would
never be complete, and that Ireland would remain 'as little known' as 'an
island in the remotest part of the globe'. Indeed, had Ireland been more
remote, it might have been easier to answer the Irish question. While
Edward Said has argued that the self/other split produces knowledge, in the

91; in Vaughan (ed.), *Ireland under the Union*, p. 487.   **34** T. Eagleton, 'Changing the
question,' in *Heathcliff and the Great Hunger* (London, 1995), p. 131.   **35** Eagleton,
Heathcliff, pp 126, 128.   **36** M. Edgeworth, *Castle Rackrent* (ed.) George Watson (New
York, 1991), p. xvii.   **37** G. Hooper, 'Stranger in Ireland: the problematics of the post-
union travelogue', *Mosaic*, xxviii, no. 1 (1995), p. 38.   **38** Hooper, 'Stranger in Ireland',
p. 35.

case of the Anglo–Irish relationship, the union blurred the divide.[39] The
project of the immediately post-union writers was doomed to fail;
Edgeworth and Morgan both stopped writing on Ireland well before their
careers should have ended. In the political realm, as in the cultural realm,
Ireland remained unknowable: Cecil Woodham-Smith notes, in writing of
the Great Famine, that 'in the forty-five years since the union no fewer than
114 Commissions and 61 Special Committees were instructed to report on
Ireland', but that in fact 'Commissariat officers serving in Irish [famine]
relief declared that the English knew as little of Ireland as of West Africa;
in fact they knew less'.[40] Likewise, Anthony Trollope, writing in 1866, has
his Irish hero, Phineas Finn, say to a colleague that '[i]t has often seemed to
me that men in Parliament know less about Ireland than they do of the
interior of Africa'.[41] The absence of a clear self/other split in the Anglo–
Irish relationship[42] – as opposed to something like Abdul JanMohamed's
'manichean allegory' of race in the classic colonial relationship -- and the
epistemological failure in the wake of this split is illustrated by Luke
Gibbons. He notes that at the turn of the nineteenth century:

> a children's toy circulated in the 'Big Houses' of the Irish Ascendancy
> which purported to give the 'British empire at a glance.' It took the
> form of a map of the world, mounted on a wheel complete with small
> apertures which revealed all that was worth knowing about the most
> distant corners of the empire. One of the apertures gave a breakdown
> of each colony in terms of its 'white' and 'native' population, as if both
> categories were mutually exclusive. When it came to Ireland, the wheel
> ground to a halt for here was a colony whose subject population was
> both 'native' and 'white' at the same time. This was one corner of the
> empire, apparently, that could not be taken in at a glance.[43]

The post-union inability to answer the question 'what do the Irish want?'
– the absence of an epistemology of Ireland – had its gravest consequences
during the Great Famine, when the Irish were accorded neither a full
inclusion in the British polity nor the sympathy that might be due to more

39 E. Said, *Orientalism* (New York, 1979).   **40** C. Woodham-Smith, *The Great Hunger*
(New York, 1962) p. 36, p. 122.   **41** Trollope, *Phineas Finn*, ii, p. 178.   **42** JanMohamed
posits that the central trope of the colonial relationship is the 'manichean allegory,'
which is 'based on a transformation of racial difference into moral and metaphysical
difference.' JanMohamed, 'The economy of manichean allegory: the function of racial
difference in colonialist literature' in H. Gates (ed.), *Race, writing and difference*
(Chicago, 1986), p. 80.   **43** L. Gibbons, *Transformations in Irish culture* (Notre Dame,
1996), p. 149.

remote others. The Famine revealed the extent to which Ireland had become a liminal space, betwixt and between categories of self and other, home and abroad, the domestic and the imperial. Irish colonial resistance thus became predicated on the restoration of the self/other split, and so, paradoxically, did Irish colonial participation.

The terms of the marriage contract recur again and again in Victorian-era cartoons, which are both post-union and post-famine: representations of Ireland, concurrent with the return of the physical force tradition in 1848 and becoming more pronounced with the rise of Fenian separatism, are split between the racialised, violent and masculine Fenian and the inert, passive, and weeping Hibernia.[44] In order for the Irish to reclaim masculinity, they had to be violent; in order to restore the self/other split, they had to claim racial difference. Whether this violence took the form of literary revivals or organised rebellions – of imagined and mythologised violence or all-too-real guerrilla warfare – it was the primary means by which Irish colonial resistance took place. Indeed, it is only because of this violence, imagined or real, that we 'know' that Ireland is a colony, because it makes visible the hidden coercion of the national marriage. Likewise, O'Connell's non-violent civil rights movement is considered to be responsible for the rise of romantic nationalism in Ireland, a nationalism which, unlike the patriotism of the pre-union United Irishmen, was based on race, on filiation rather than affiliation.[45] These repeated assertions of an othered identity were often taken by the British authorities to be disguised cries for reform, suggesting the extent to which even armed rebellion could be 'domesticated' in the union relationship. One famous example is Gladstone's admission that it was

44 L. Curtis, *Apes and angels: the Irishman in Victorian caricature* (Washington, 1997). 45 Romantic nationalism is explicitly opposed to a contractarian society. Oliver MacDonagh links O'Connell's romantic nationalism with Teutonic romanticism and its idea of *gemeinschaft* nationalism, which is opposed to *gesellschaft* nationalism, the nationalism of the French Revolution and the United Irishmen of the late eighteenth century: '*Gemeinschaft* tends to be used of an association that is internal, organic, private, spontaneous: its paradigm is the *Gemeinschaft* of marriage, the *communio totius vitae. Gesellschaft* – comparatively new as a word and as a phenomenon – is, on the other hand, usually something external, public, mechanical, formal or legalistic. It is not an organic merger or a fusion but a rational coming together for ends that remain individual.' O. MacDonagh, 'The Age of O'Connell 1830-45' in Vaughan (ed.), *Ireland under the union*, p. 161 n. Romantic nationalism, then, replaces the contractarian version of marriage with one that is mystical, organic, and natural. It is marriage that propagates the race, not marriage in which a woman and a man contract for, respectively, protection and obedience. Eagleton has written that contractarian notions were not necessarily importable to Ireland: 'if the British thought in terms of contract and utility, there was at work in popular Irish attitudes a doctrine of moral economy.' Eagleton, *Heathcliff*, p. 139. Indeed, the catholics of Ireland had signed no contracts, and so were bound by no terms.

the Fenians who inspired him to pursue a policy of Irish reform.⁴⁶ And, indeed, it was Matthew Arnold's attempt to argue for an inclusion of Irish culture in the domestic sphere of Britain – for the union finally to be consummated – that provided the writers of the Irish Literary Renaissance with the materials of cultural nationalism.⁴⁷ Thus did the assertion of a separate, racial, and masculine identity have to be repeated and rehearsed throughout the nineteenth century, as the Irish question remained unanswered.

If Irish colonial resistance sought to restore the self/other split, so too did Irish colonial participation. In the period 1801-20, the union produced Irish protestant silence in England's House, but it was meant to ensure, in Dundas' words, that after the union the voices of Irishmen 'would be heard not only in Europe, but in Asia, Africa, and America'.⁴⁸ Ireland was in a liminal position in the United Kingdom, neither home nor abroad, domestic nor imperial, as evidenced by the simple fact that there is still no name for the inhabitants of the United Kingdom: the inhabitants of the island of Ireland are either completely subsumed into Britishness or completely differentiated into Irishness. Yet their status as both assimilated and different places the Irish, not surprisingly, in much the same relationship to the empire as that of women. Anne McClintock writes:

> [c]olonial women made none of the direct economic or military decisions of empire and very few reaped its vast profits. Marital laws, property laws, land laws, and the intractable violence of male decree bound them in gendered patterns of disadvantage and frustration. The vast, fissured architecture of imperialism was gendered throughout by the fact that it was white men who made and enforced laws and policies in their own interests. Nonetheless, the rationed privileges of race all too often put white women in positions of decided – if borrowed – power, not only over colonised women but over

---

46 Foster, *Modern Ireland*, p. 395.   47 The rise of the domestic – with its extension of the marriage contract into the daily life of the marriage – was itself a mid-Victorian impetus to Irish reform; yet the terms of the original marriage contract had been carefully set to provide for Ireland's subordination. The true assimilation of the Irish into the domestic sphere of Britain – the union of hearts – was thus profoundly threatening, even to its whig proponents, because it called into question the ability of the British authorities to keep Ireland subordinate. This anxiety was all the more acute because the rise of the domestic was so closely linked to Britain's imperial adventure, and an inclusion of the Irish in the domestic space would remove Ireland's liminal status between the 'home' and the 'abroad' of Britain, which allowed for Britain to govern Ireland in its own interest.   48 T. Bartlett, 'This famous island set in a Virginian sea: Ireland in the British empire 1690-1801' in P.J. Marshall (ed.), *The Oxford history of the British empire*, ii (New York, 1998), p. 271.

colonised men. As such, white women were not the hapless onlookers of empire but were ambiguously complicit both as colonisers and colonised, privileged and restricted, acted upon and acting.[49]

Some Irish were enthusiastic participants in the British empire, and did indeed 'have a voice' in the empire, as Dundas had promised; the union can be seen as a way of increasing the pool of available soldiers by allowing for the recruitment of Irish catholics.[50] The Irish became the foot soldiers of the British empire, planting and fighting for the Union Jack in every corner of the globe. An enthusiasm for empire extended even to Irish 'nationalists,' despite complaints that they were not receiving their fair share of the imperial spoils.[51] The Home Rule movement aimed to restore a public, and masculine, sphere to Ireland while retaining Irish participation in empire. Through imperial service, the Irish were offered a chance to restore the self/other split, only with themselves the 'selves' of the colonial relationship. If the Irish were 'abroad' when at home in the United Kingdom, they could be 'at home' when abroad, thanks to the national marriage of the Act of Union.[52]

Writing in 1994, Geoffrey Wheatcroft compared the Anglo-Irish relationship to a bad marriage: 'over the centuries England displayed all the worst male faults: brutishness, exploitation, selfishness, neglect. As a result, Ireland became the eternal wronged woman, sunk in brooding, resentful, vengeful self-pity.'[53] In fact, it has long been a commonplace to describe the Act of Union as a national marriage, a description which is not merely fanciful but exposes the union as a marriage contract, which allowed for the assimilation of Ireland into, and the differentiation of Ireland from, the civil sphere of Britain. That the victorious winners of the Irish War of Independence retained almost wholesale the governmental system forced on them by the British is testimony to the fact that, in agitating for Ireland's independence, the most important goal of Irish nationalists was always the restoration of a public and masculine sphere to Ireland, the dissolution of the marriage contract of the Act of Union of Great Britain and Ireland.[54]

49 A. McClintock, *Imperial leather* (New York, 1995), p. 6.   50 Bartlett, 'This famous island', p. 272.   51 Ibid., p. 273.   52 I have borrowed these terms from Edward Said, who is at pains to include Ireland in his theoretical formulations, but is hamstrung by Ireland's anomalous relationship to the home/abroad binarism of Britain's imperial adventure. E. Said, *Culture and imperialism* (New York, 1995).   53 G. Wheatcroft, 'Disenchanted Isle,' in *Atlantic Monthly* (May 1994), p. 78.   54 In 1912, with Home Rule for Ireland imminent, Andrew Bonar Law 'solemnised the wedding of protestant Ulster with the Conservative and Unionist Party,' in the presence of some 100,000 spectators' at the Balmoral showgrounds. T.P. Coogan, *The Troubles: Ireland's ordeal 1966-1996* (Boulder, 1996), p. 14. The union has still not formally ended.

13

The union and internal security
1798-1799

Ruán O'Donnell

For government supporters the aftermath of the 1798 rebellion provided a deeply unsettling backdrop to the union debate. Assassinations, arms raids, brigandage and quasi-agrarian outrages across the country infused the discussions of the political elite with urgency. The private correspondence of key union protagonists reveals the large extent to which residual insurgency and unrest competed for their attention between December 1798 and August 1800. One legislative manifestation of this concern was the Rebellion Act of March 1799 which addressed highly relevant matters of martial law and prisoner disposal. Although pressing the union was not expected to trigger another rebellion in the absence of massive French aid to the United Irishmen, government circles believed that severe protests could be expected in the metropolis.

On 10 December 1798 Dublin city barristers issued a resolution stating: 'Legislative union of this kingdom & Great Britain is an innovation which would be highly dangerous and improper to propose at the present juncture to this country.'[1] Emphasising timing rather than legitimacy indicated that the most coherent body of anti-unionists in Ireland had seized on security to induce procrastination. This argument had been previously raised by ultra-loyalists concerned that the mooted pairing of union with catholic emancipation would fatally compromise protestant ascendancy. The premise that the disturbed state of Ireland militated against controversial legislation nonetheless reflected genuine concerns in December 1798.[2]

A major bone of contention was whether the supremacy of an imperial parliament at Westminster offered the solution to the seemingly intractable Irish security crisis which had ebbed and flowed from 1793. Effecting union,

1 *Finn's Leinster Journal*, 12 Dec. 1798.   2 For general background to the Union, see Geoghegan, *Union*.

however, threatened to prove so unpopular with both die-hard revolutionaries and orange ultra-loyalists as to exacerbate the situation. A secondary consideration was whether the seething rural unrest would tempt the French to mount a serious invasion. Government supporters had to trust in the prowess of the royal navy to prevent that scenario although some believed that continental enemies might take advantage of the disarray attending the forcing of an unpopular union bill through College Green.[3]

For John Beresford and other conservative backers of the disgraced ex-viceroy Lord Camden, post-rebellion violence demonstrated the failure of the clemency policy directed by Lord Lieutenant Cornwallis from June 1798. Chief Secretary Castlereagh was warned that the union had 'given the almost annihilated body of United Irishmen new spirits, and the Society is again rising like a phoenix from its ashes'.[4] This exaggerated United Irish interest in the fate of what they perceived as an undemocratic, oppressive bastion of sectarian privilege but was correct in one respect: the republican organisation was reviving in late 1798. Few believed that the thousands of rebel veterans pardoned under the Amnesty Act promulgated in October 1798 would honour their oaths of loyalty if the French army arrived in force on Irish soil. Actual and potential republican violence and speculation regarding the attitude of the French Directory towards Ireland provided a compelling subtext to the union debates.[5]

One loyalist, W.A. Crosbie, was appalled by the disorderly behaviour of Dublin's 'Jacobin' lawyers in December 1798 and their willingness to exploit the threat of the 'impending rising.' He claimed that the 'public mind' had been 'very much inflamed' in the capital and that political violence would 'be attributed to the proposing a question of such magnitude at so improper a moment'.[6] Loyalists, according to Crosbie, were 'in a dreadful state, and only less dreadful than a few months ago, as much as private assassination and general plunder and robbery can be called less dreadful than open rebellion'.[7]

Crosbie's pessimism rested on three cogent observations: the amnesty program had 'not had the success it deserved'; political violence posed a threat owing the disaffection of the 'lower Irish ... catholics or presbyterians' and leading United Irishmen remained at large. Arms raids, mail coach

---

3 W. Wickham to Castlereagh, 11 Jan. 1799 in *Castlereagh corr.*, ii, p. 93.   4 J.C. Beresford to Castlereagh, 19 Dec. 1798 in *Castlereagh corr.*, ii, p. 51.   5 J. Stewart to Charlemont, 12 Dec. 1798 in *Charlemont corr.*, ii, p. 342. For United Irish claims to be 'ready on the first opportunity to support the banners of liberty', see memorial of Denis O'Neil, 30 Jan. 1799 in *Castlereagh corr.*, ii, p. 234.   6 W. Crosbie to Duke [of Montrose], 25 Dec. 1798 in *Fortescue*, iv, p. 424. See also Buckingham to Grenville, 7 Dec. 1798, pp 404-6.   7 Ibid.

robbery, jury intimidation and killings provided stark reminders of the inadequacy of the Irish military during and after 1798. The Irish army had proved incapable of defending the country 'against her interior or exterior enemies without the men, navy, or credit of the friendly neighbour of whom she is so jealous'. Union, therefore, was necessary to preserve the status quo of the political establishment in Ireland, even if its enactment produced short term security problems.[8]

Assessing the United Irish threat after 1798 is complicated because their military potential was never revealed owing to the inability of the French allies to effect a full scale invasion. Robert Emmet's rising of July 1803, furthermore, was an improvised contingency intended to enable the plotters to fight another day. The 1803 episode recalled the premature outbreak of the rebellion on 23 May 1798 when the Fitzgerald/Neilson faction commenced unilateral insurrection without French aid lest coercion destroy what remained of the leadership and disarm their followers. As matters transpired, this plan misfired when a government intelligence breakthrough undermined the Dublin-centred plan.

While the United Irishmen were defeated between May and July 1798, the organisation was by no means routed and non-government fatalities in the range of multiple thousands were confined to at most nine of Ireland's thirty-two counties: Wexford, Wicklow, Kildare, Carlow and Mayo and probably also Antrim, Down, Sligo and Meath. Westmeath, Monaghan, Longford, Leitrim, Tipperary, Queen's County (Laois), King's County (Offaly), Kilkenny and county Dublin either experienced major skirmishes or contributed substantial forces to fighting in neighbouring areas. Cork, Queen's County, Louth, Armagh, moreover, were amongst those where less deadly clashes in which scores rather than hundreds of casualties occurred. The sporadic outbreak of rebellion ensured that most county networks were largely intact when the major episodes were finally contained in the last week of September 1798. The tentative figure of 30,000 rebellion fatalities, even if doubled by arrests, summary deportations, executions and flight abroad, represented a small proportion of 280,000 sworn United Irishmen available in May 1798. Munster and west Ulster, where the United Irishmen were very strong in early 1798, were barely affected by the rebellion crisis.[9]

8 Crosbie was exasperated at the sight of 'the greatest villains, bearing commissions of generals in the rebel army, tried and condemned by courts martial, now walking about the streets, and probably hatching new treasons for our destruction.' Crosbie to [Montrose], 25 Dec. 1798 in *Fortescue*, iv, p. 424. See also Sir G. Atkinson to Downshire, 5 Apr. 1799, PRONI, D607/G/147.   9 *Report from the Committee of Secrecy appointed to take into consideration the treasonable papers presented to the House*

Non-mobilisation of rebel forces was a strategy adopted by mid-ranking leaders in the midlands, Munster, Ulster and parts of Connaught to preserve future combat capability. The Simms leadership of the Ulster Directory prohibited armed actions after 6 June 1798 in the absence of the French, even though insurrection was then snowballing in Leinster. Notwithstanding this decision, the technically mutinous behaviour of a minority clique attached to Henry Joy McCracken sparked an Ulster revolt in Antrim on 7 June which gathered momentum from the victory at Saintfield two days later of Down commander Henry Munro. Munro, another ideologically committed and charismatic opportunist, seconded the early promise of McCracken's forces and precipitated the decisive defeat at Ballinahinch on 12-13 June which forestalled a juncture with Leinster and mid-Ulster insurgents.

Like Simms, Tipperary's Hervey Montmorency Morres, veteran of the Russian army and adjutant-general elect of north Munster United Irish forces, inhibited the mobilisation of his subordinates to husband resources for the major invasion he anticipated. Rebels in Westmeath and Longford, over whom he subsequently claimed authority, were only roused at Cloone when the line of march of a French expeditionary force was unexpectedly diverted away from west Ulster towards Dublin by a clash outside Sligo town on 5 September 1798. Morres had earlier prevented heavily organised parts of Tipperary and Limerick from rising en masse, rebels whose militancy had led them to skirmish with state forces prior to May 1798.[10]

Major James Plunkett restrained the Roscommon United men under his control which later exposed him to accusations of treachery when an exile in Hamburg. Plunkett, formerly an officer in the French army, concurred with Morres' initial instincts that Humbert's vanguard did not warrant a full scale turn out. His subordinate officers evidently agreed and made no attempt to supersede him in command, perhaps mindful of the disasters reputed to have befallen their comrades in Leinster and east Ulster.[11] Regardless of the true motives of Simms, Morres and Plunkett, thousands

of Commons of Ireland, on the 17th day of July last ..., second edition (Dublin, 1798), p. 131. See also Cooke to Castlereagh, 20 Dec. 1798 in *Castlereagh corr.*, ii, pp 49-50 and Rev. Hudson to Charlemont, 30 Nov. 1798 in ibid., p. 341. Casualty figures do not take account of the fact that many of those killed in mobilised zones, moreover, were not these committed sworn adherents but unfortunate civilians, refugees and camp followers. 10 Memorial of Citizen Hervey Montmorency Morres ... , n.d., [1798] in *Castlereagh corr.*, ii, pp 92-6. 11 For Plunkett and the tradition of Roscommon involvement at the Battle of Ballinamuck, see M. Gormley, 'Castleplunkett' in *Tulsk parish in historic Maigh Ai. Aspects of its history and folklore* (Tulsk, 1989), pp 82-3; R. Hayes, *The last invasion of Ireland* (Dublin, 1937), pp 208, 276, 295-6.

of their ill-armed adherents and junior officers were shielded from an uneven, unco-ordinated and doomed war of attrition.[12]

   The incidence of rebellion in the summer and autumn of 1798 bore little relation to the numerical strength and militancy of county organisations. Rather, such factors as leadership, the timing of attempted risings, experience of martial law, geography and the outcome of the first major contest were critical to the transformation of desultory skirmishes and arms raids into massed open rebellion. These conditions were not favourable in counties Cork, Waterford, Limerick, Kerry, Donegal and Derry which played very minor roles in the rebellion, inaction which gave rise to assumptions of incompetence on the part of local conspirators. The critical point was that the seditious organisations of strategic maritime counties was preserved to open a front in an international war which the French seemed increasingly likely to win. The real issue after 1798 was whether dormant and damaged networks could preserve enough of their military cohesion and political conviction to offer meaningful support to the French. This was the task of the United Irish Directory which regrouped in Dublin as the union question pre-occupied parliament.

   In hindsight, the rebellion appeared a hopeless effort; yet the government had struggled prior to mid-June 1798 to weather the storm in south Leinster. Dublin Castle also faced challenging risings in north-eastern Ulster, north Connacht and in the midlands and was probably incapable of fending off properly co-ordinated risings. Cornwallis knew that the bulk of the United Irish organisation had survived the rebellion and that virtually all of the minority who turned out to fight had to be amnestied. 1798, therefore, represented a hollow victory which gave the administration no cause for complacency as long as French naval capacity escalated and the war provided Irish republicans with a compelling reason for further resistance. In parts of Wicklow, Wexford, Kildare, Carlow and Dublin, the rebellion which commenced in May 1798 was prosecuted to some extent until February 1804.[13]

---

12 Plunkett's inaction did not endear him to the British authorities or alienate him from high ranking fighting leaders. In March 1799 he was said to have conspired in Bath and Bristol with fellow United Irish exiles Garret Byrne of Ballymanus (Wicklow), Edward Fitzgerald of Newpark (Wexford) and William Aylmer of Painstown (Kildare). Lieutenant-General James Rooke to Anon., 23 Mar. 1799, PRO HO 100/66/421 and Shannon to Boyle, 26 Mar. 1799 in E. Hewitt (ed.), *Lord Shannon's letters to his son. A calendar of the letters written by the 2nd earl of Shannon to his son Viscount Boyle 1790-1802* (Belfast, 1982), p. 183.   13 R. O'Donnell, *Aftermath. Post-Rebellion insurgency in Wicklow 1799-1803* (Dublin, 2000); L. Chambers, *Rebellion in Kildare 1790-1803* (Dublin, 1998); D. Gahan, ' "The Black Mob" and "The Babes in the Wood:" Wexford in the wake of

The union and internal security 1798-1799

A combination of martial law and indifference may well have driven the crowd from the streets of Dublin when the union debates began but the capital was by no means pacified. Most Dublin committees survived the rebellion and were bolstered in late 1798-1799 by released prisoners, amnestied migrants and the establishment of a substantial community of fugitive rebels in the south city. The progressive abandonment of martial law procedures after December 1798 gave conspirators greater freedom of association than they had enjoyed since May; guarded Liffey crossings were re-opened and yeomanry corps were stood down from permanent duty. Edward Cooke was distracted from his Secret Service duties at this important juncture by the difficult task of managing the Castle's pro-union propaganda campaign. Town-Major Henry Charles Sirr, de facto chief of police, was in no position to secure a city teeming with suspects with his small and unreliable staff in the Castle.[14]

II

Senior city radicals were augmented in late 1798 by migrating provincial commanders such as Edward Byrne of Ballymanus (Wicklow), Nicholas Gray (Kildare), Miles Byrne of Monaseed (Wexford) and Morgan Kavanagh (Carlow).[15] Edward Byrne, a former County Committee member, enjoyed the confidence of the outstanding Wicklow rebel groups whom he supplied with munitions and money into 1799. Once bailed, Surgeon Thomas Wright, a founder member of the Dublin United Irishmen, resumed his role as a supplier of cash and war material to guerrilla bands, as did Donnellan, of Baggot Street, one of many building contractors who employed rebel veterans. Master Sweep Horish, notorious for a May 1798 admission that he had donated £200 for the manufacture of pikes, retained the respect of plebeian republicans and had contact with the Wicklow faction led by Michael Dwyer. Armaments belonging to Dwyer's Imaal rebels were periodically serviced by a Hanover Street gunsmith and were replaced in mid-1802 with top quality muskets by the Emmet circle.[16]

the rebellion 1798-1806' in *Jn. Wex. Hist. Soc.*, vi (1990), pp 92-110; C. Dickson, *The life of Michael Dwyer with some account of his companions* (Dublin, 1944); T. Bartlett, 'Defence, counter-insurgency and rebellion: Ireland 1793-1803' in T. Bartlett and K. Jeffery (eds), *A military history of Ireland* (Cambridge, 1996), pp 247-93.   **14** For Sirr's staff see n.d. [1799], NA, 620/52/7; *Dublin Magazine*, June 1799, p. 382 and *Hibernian Journal*, 19 Dec. 1798.   **15** M. Byrne, *Memoirs of Miles Byrne*, 2 vols (Paris, 1863).   **16** O'Donnell, *Aftermath*, chap. 5; NA, 620/49/113, 25 Sept. 1801 and *Freeman's Journal*, 31 May 1798.

Dublin rebel colonels Charles O'Hara, Francis McMahon and Felix Rourke had led city and county insurgent units into battle during the Leinster campaign and remained committed to militant republicanism after 1798. Their links with former subordinates preserved an informal chain of command that was useful for triggering later campaigns in support of the French. Valuable bonds had also been formed during the rebellion with rural officers; this facilitated Dwyer's sojourns in the capital in 1799-1803. The main function of the urban network was to maintain a state of readiness and to provide logistical support to outstanding rebel bands who retained political motivation.[17] City-based republicans remained the conduit for the transmission of orders.

The survival into 1799 of the Dwyer, Mernagh and Dalton groups in Wicklow, the Corcoran/Cody faction in Wexford and Carlow, and the Doorley network in Kildare boosted United Irish morale and provided their agents in Europe with proof of the continued receptiveness of Ireland to invasion. This low intensity warfare otherwise lacked military purpose. Certain groups, specifically those led by Dwyer and Corcoran, were deemed 'dangerous in case of invasion' by the Castle as they could become focal points for mass mobilisation should the French land. Their surprising ability to survive embarrassed an administration that was keen to project an image of social stability to the sceptical pro-union lobby and to initially wary politicians in Westminster.[18]

Dublin cadres also maintained communications with their associates in Irish, British and European cities. An internal and or external attempt on the capital would remain central to any revived insurrection plan, whether or not it was timed to coincide with a French invasion. As in May 1798, Dublin was the linchpin of the United Irish conspiracy and the predictable centrepiece of Emmet's scaled down planning in mid-1803. The harsh realities of the 1798 rebellion had suggested new, tighter, security-conscious modes of operating which further increased the importance of the city conspirators. The amended constitution of May 1795 was abandoned along with once cherished democratic structures which had permitted crippling indecision at command level during the rebellion. This major ideological sacrifice was made in the hope that promised French military assistance would eventually pave the way for republican democracy in Ireland.[19]

17 O'Donnell, *Aftermath*, pp 141, 147 and Madden, *United Irishmen*, iii, p. 349.   18 Henniker to Dundas, 23 Aug. 1801, PRO HO 100/104/71.   19 O'Donnell, *Aftermath*, pp 51-2; J.G. Patterson, 'Continued presbyterian resistance in the aftermath of the rebellion of 1798 in Antrim and Down' in *Eighteenth-Century Life*, xxii (1998), pp 45-61.

The benefits of maintaining the massive pre-rebellion United Irish superstructure did not balance the security risks entailed in its aftermath. The reformed Directory concluded that the pre-rebellion model was obsolete given that the field performance of rebel forces in 1798 was much better than could have been hoped for in an untrained, ill-equipped, popular army. It was certainly far more impressive than the army expected or would publicly admit at New Ross, Arklow and Castlebar. This pragmatic change of direction was aided by the imprisonment or absence of the more doctrinaire ideologues who had guided the evolution of the United Irishmen since 1791. In 1799, the year in which the transition was effected, it could not have been predicted that the Peace of Amiens would free such men to congregate on the continent in 1802. By then overtures from the Dublin Directory had met with a positive French reaction.

The post-rebellion republican leaders differed from those arrested in March 1798. They were entirely unelected, financially unsupported and unaccountable to their subordinates. Members were no longer obliged to pay monthly dues and to elect candidates to parish, barony and county level committees every three months. Rank-and-file United Irishmen were also relieved of the duty of obtaining by purchase, theft or manufacture the weapons needed to prosecute rebellion. The new strategy dictated that the streamlined movement would remain quiescent until the French made good their commitment to campaign in Ireland. No military action would be initiated without a substantial French army presence which would also redress the chronic shortage of armaments and munitions. The arrival of the French in strength would be sufficient to initiate an irresistible, popular uprising in Ireland. Despite public claims to the contrary, this spectre privately haunted Dublin Castle until the naval balance of power shifted decisively at Trafalgar in October 1805.[20]

A new executive was in place by the spring of 1799 under the aegis of Surgeon Wright and other experienced operators who provided the Directory with legitimising continuity. Its membership in May included Robert Emmet, favoured by the strong reputation of his exiled elder brother, Thomas Addis Emmet. The younger Emmet assisted Wright and Kildare rebellion and Austrian army veteran Malachy Delaney in producing a handbook on insurgent tactics. Other leadership figures, such as Hugh O'Hanlon and Henry Baird, had been identified by the authorities by late April and (despite the paucity of evidence against them) were either arrested

20 Wickham to Castlereagh, 1 May 1799, PRO HO 100/86/302; J.W. [McNally] to Downshire, 17 Apr. 1799, PRONI, D 607/G/159.

or forced on the run. This disruption proved little more than a temporary setback and in September 1800 the city leadership was named as Emmet, Wright, Charles O'Hara and John Lawless. They comprised the core of a self-appointed leadership that had come together to promote republican objectives which had remained unchanged since 1795.[21]

The threat posed by outstanding insurgents was frequently discussed in Dublin Castle after 1798. Army district commanders and county brigade-majors of yeomanry were required to submit monthly reports and to have their courts martial decisions ratified in the Castle. Their staff passed on the data in digest form to the Home Office in London. The Irish establishment had grappled with demobilising rebel factions from June 1798 when the tide of the rebellion turned towards the government. The amnesty program was held to be the key to restoring normality as a mechanism to enable the insurgents to disband without fear of prosecution. This averted the prohibitive economic and political consequences of widespread guerrilla campaigns. Clemency did not totally eradicate residual insurgency, however, and conventional military tactics proved useless in combating mountain fighters and the 'babes in the woods'.

III

In December 1798 political violence was clearly increasing rather than diminishing in Wicklow where at least thirty soldiers, loyalists, rebels and civilians were killed. Wicklow, a mere twenty miles south of the seat of government, was home to many key players in the union debate, including Sir John Parnell who lived at Avondale, Henry Grattan at Tinnehinch and Lord Powerscourt, leader of the anti-union bloc in the house of lords. Powerscourt's Enniskerry mansion remained a military outpost in the winter of 1798 and the object of frequent sniping attacks. Wicklow had been

21 Wright was re-arrested in April 1799 and began to inform, albeit not in such a way as to warrant Treason trials. Information of Thomas Wright, 1 May 1799, PRO HO 100/86/301. Lawless (a former associate of the Sheares brothers, Mathew Dowling and William Aylmer), lived in Shankill, south County Dublin in 1797-8. He had close connections with British based republicans and the elusive Belfast emissary William Putnam McCabe. A well placed source, probably Samuel Turner of Newry, reported on 5 February 1799: 'One D[Richard Dillon?], arrested at Oliver Bond's, but now at large, is a member of the new Executive Committee [of United Irishmen] lately chosen in Dublin. One O'H[ara], of Antrim, now a merchant in Dublin, is a great patron of United Irishmen.' *Castlereagh corr.*, ii, p. 225. See also *Saunder's Newsletter*, 15 Mar. 1798; PRO HO 100/86/195-6; M. Elliott, *Partners in revolution. The United Irishmen and France* (London, 1982), pp 243-50.

ravaged by the rebellion and from July its near roadless mountains became the principal haven of the militant factions under General Joseph Holt who rejected the amnesty and awaited the French. The negotiated surrender of Holt on 10 November and killing of Andrew Hackett two weeks later did not lead to the pacification of Wicklow. Well armed and determined rebel groups under Michael Dwyer, James Hughes, Michael Dalton, William Pluck and John Mernagh remained potent into 1799.[22]

The Hughes faction, which specialised in shooting isolated yeomen and concealing their bodies in bog holes, killed an informer and at least three loyalists in late December 1798 and early January 1799 in the Baltinglass area. They also stole £1,600 from the city mail coach, a venture into criminal activity which signalled their abandonment of an ideological basis for armed actions and rendered the gang even less restrained. Hughes' men were mainly rebel veterans from Wicklow, Wexford, Kildare, Dublin and Carlow but included deserters from the 17th Light Dragoons, 5th 'Royal Irish' Dragoons, Clare Militia and Dublin County Militia. Deserters, house burners and those who had killed in cold blood were ineligible for clemency under the terms of the Amnesty Act and were consequently more likely to form part of rebel bands/ brigands. The group of military defectors in Wicklow had split from Holt's main force in October 1798, leading to the formation of gangs led by 'Antrim John' Mooney, Francois Joseph, Barney Collagan and others. These quickly gravitated from the inhospitable and unfamiliar mountains towards Dublin city.[23]

Unlike the brigand gangs, Dwyer, Mernagh and Dalton, survivors of the Leinster campaign and former followers of Holt, rarely admitted non-Wicklow born deserters/ defectors or non-United Irishmen into their ranks. Dwyer distrusted deserters and reputedly executed three Meath militiamen whom he suspected of infiltrating his faction in December 1798. Far from welcoming fugitive strangers, Dwyer was related to many of his long term followers: two of his closest colleagues, Hugh 'Vesty' Byrne of Kirikee and Arthur Devlin of Clone, were first cousins. Another associate, Martin Burke of Donaghmore, was a lifelong friend. A striking feature of the factions led by Dwyer, Mernagh and Dalton was that they never robbed mail coaches and were credited with passing over innumerable opportunities to enrich themselves. By February 1803 the mails had been robbed on sixty-six occasions, not counting failed attempts, and coaches were repeatedly attacked at Galloping Green (Dublin), Newrath Bridge (Wicklow) and Red Gap (Kildare).[24]

22 O'Donnell, *Aftermath*, chap. 1; Carysfort to Grenville, 23 Jan. 1799 in *Fortescue*, iv, p. 449. 23 17 Dec. 1799, Sirr Papers, TCD, Ms 869/5/F36. 24 *Observer*, 6 Feb. 1803.

Dwyer, following Holt's ruthless practice, killed or informed on brigands operating in his area to protect the interests of his harbourers and to distance his activities from theirs. The need to establish this demarcation was illustrated on 24 December 1799 when the North Naas yeoman cavalry arrested 'the desperado who calls himself Captain Dwyer (but whose real name is Leary)'. Although obliged to requisition supplies from loyalist farms, Dwyer and Mernagh often paid for goods taken and raised cash for the purpose by auctioning their personal effects in Dublin's rebel pubs.[25]

Wicklow rebels lessened the desire for retaliation against their supporters and themselves by rarely initiating attacks on soldiers and yeomen after December 1798. Prisoners, if taken, were almost invariably released unharmed unless doomed by their participation in atrocities before or during the rebellion. The rebels all but ceased their once common practice of house burning and confined their movements to the remote districts where they lived. Fewer than fifteen men massed at any one time although many amnestied and unsuspected men could and occasionally were drawn upon in good weather. Post-rebellion insurgents everywhere abandoned the pike, a weapon which required large numbers to be effective, and relied instead upon firearms. Victims of rebel activity in Wicklow were typically informers, state witnesses, loyalist arms holders and those injured in defensive skirmishes. This reactive strategy generated the tacit, if not active, support of local communities and the longevity of Wicklow's rebel groups.

If there was to be a propaganda dividend for United Irish negotiators on the continent, it was important that the routine activities of the outstanding insurgents did not discredit their long term political purpose. The revived Dublin city committees readily supported the Dwyer network with cash and weaponry whilst ignoring the predicament of the criminal Hughes faction. Napper Tandy, Thomas Cloney, Robert Emmet and other high ranking United Irishmen maintained contact with the Dwyer/Mernagh circle in the early 1800s and included them in their plans to spearhead a French-assisted revolution. Tandy was instrumental in ensuring that the Dwyer group did not disband on learning of the Peace of Amiens (1802); an initiative indicative of their importance to the propaganda effort and the serious minded approach of a Wicklow cadre which later assisted Emmet.[26]

---

25 *Hibernian Telegraph*, 3 Jan. 1800. That the gang was composed of former rebels is indicated by the arrest with Leary of Enniscorthy insurgent Darby Logan. Holt betrayed a hated brigand gang led by one Lynch to his yeomen enemies which led to eighteen arrests and Dwyer put several robbers to death in the early 1800s.   26 T. King to Lt.-Col. G. Stewart, 12 Dec. 1802 in Dickson, *Dwyer*, p. 208; Information of Michael Dwyer, 11 Jan. 1804, PRO HO 100/124/26.

Dwyer's was the best known of several Leinster factions to span the period of the rebellion of 1798 and Emmet plot of 1803. Another was led by John and Michael Doorley, veteran officers of the rebellion in Kildare, whose family provided continuous leadership to Lullymore area insurgents from May 1798 until early 1804. Their faction was similar to the Corcoran/ Cody group in that United Irish membership was required and that political objectives seemed important, even if not explicitly addressed or advanced by their day to day activities. Michael Doorley took pains to liaise with the like-minded Mathew Donnellan as late as the winter of 1802–3, leader of a lower profile faction in the Clane area. Contact with other groups with whom co-operation could be expected in the event of a French invasion was highly likely and extended in Doorley's case to insurgents from Carlow and King's County. Dwyer, similarly, often visited rebel comrades in Carlow town, north Wexford and Dublin city.[27]

Wicklow, while the most consistently disturbed county in Ireland after the rebellion, was by no means the only source of instability in December 1798. The Limerick mails were robbed in the early part of the month at Monas-terevin (Kildare) and a gun battle was fought between rebel raiders and the military in Gracefield Wood. One of those arrested after the clash was implicated in the killing of five Clare militiamen. The activities of Wexford's 'babes in the woods' were also widely reported, a sizeable gang of former insurgents and deserters active in the Killan/ Newtownbarry/ Enniscorthy triangle.[28] Raiders also carried off weapons from the Knocktopher yeomanry in Kilkenny without resistance in the first week of December 1798, possibly the same group which disarmed members of the Iverk yeomanry near Waterford. Another Waterford based gang of raiders, meanwhile, lost three of its members during an attempted raid on an East Indiaman moored in Dungarvan.[29]

Mounting instability on a national level in the winter of 1798–9 was indicated by fresh disturbances in Antrim, Down, Armagh, Louth, Mayo, Cork, Limerick, Clare and Tipperary.[30] County Clare was in a state of rebellion for the first time from 4 to 14 January 1799 when thousands of local United Irishmen menaced Ennis, Corofin, Miltown Malbay and

27 Chambers, *Kildare*, p. 110; O'Donnell, *Aftermath*, pp 106–8. Munster rebel leader Daniel Cullinane of Cashel, aka General Marcus Cleark, sent a letter to Dwyer by courier in June 1801 which credited the Wicklowman's 'good name and republican virtues' with having 'given much hopes to your suffering countrymen.' Cullinane was thought to have visited Tipperary, Waterford, Limerick, Cork, Donegal and Down on seditious business. See Marcus Cleark [Daniel Cullinane] to Dwyer, c.15 Jun. 1801 quoted in Dickson, *Dwyer*, pp 355–6. 28 *Hib. Jn.*, 30 Nov. 1798; *FLJ*, 1 Dec. 1798. 29 *Hib. Jn.*, 7 Dec. 1798; *FLJ*, 19 Dec. 1798. 30 *Hib. Jn.*, 26 Dec. 1798.

Ennistymon after arms raiding the previous month. Paradoxically, United Irish strength and militancy in Clare had burgeoned rather than diminished after the heavy defeat of Franco-Irish forces in late September 1798.[31] Their rising was seemingly inspired by expectations of fresh, larger scale landings from France and reports that military reinforcements were on their way. Clare insurgents swore the United Irish oath, used the term 'Defender' freely and employed Whiteboy tactics such as cattle houghing and issuing threatening notices. A document posted on Kiltoraght church on 4 January 1799 illustrated the complex agenda of its authors: 'That no rent, tithe money, church rates or any county rates whatsoever should be paid until further orders from the Directory of the United Irishmen who meant to plant the tree of liberty in a very short time.'[32]

The first major victim of their houghing attacks was Captain Thomas Crowe of the Ennis Cavalry, a natural enemy of agrarian radicals owing to his status as a magistrate and land owner, who incurred the wrath of the Claremen for supervising the flogging of republicans. Cattle on Crowe's Ballyvaskin farm were houghed on 4 January by a rebel band which included yeomen defectors and operated in the district commanded by Francis Lysaght of Miltown Malbay.[33]

Whilst welcoming the prospect of a French invasion and advocating an interest in the United Irish agenda, the traditional grievances and tactics of the Claremen explains in part the long term problems of extending the authority of the republican leadership into Connaught. Unusual latitude was allowed to pursue regional objectives although this hybridisation was by no means confined to the west. Radical propaganda regarding land re-distribution had been circulated in Leinster during the recruiting phase of 1797 and resurfaced on many occasions down to 1803. An important gauge of United Irish control in Clare, however, was the deep involvement of educated, socially secure men such as Lysaght, a minor landowner, and Moy schoolmaster Hugh Kildea. Lysaght and Kildea, in fact, may well have channelled popular discontent into pro-French republican schemes in keeping with earlier United Irish practices of the co-option of proto-trade union and Defender radicalism in rural towns. The real if unrealised prospect of French assistance, moreover, revived dormant Jacobite traditions.[34]

31 Two men were committed to Clonmel goal in September 1798 for having 'distributed seditious papers, tending to intimidate persons employed in the collection of county taxes, for the eastern division of the barony of Iffa and Offa, and the inhabitants of Carrick and Newtown from paying them.' *FLJ*, 19 Sept. 1798.   32 Information of J. Chappell quoted in K. Sheedy, *The United Irishmen of County Clare* (Ennis, 1998), p. 38.   33 Sheedy, *Clare*, pp 38-40.   34 The pre-rebellion United

Confidence in the French had been in evidence on 14 January 1799, the last day of the rising, when George O'Donnell met rebels going to Seafield 'to get arms and ammunition from a vessel they expected from France, and if they had any arms they need not fear the king's troops'. This proved illusory as the Romney Fencibles and other British forces arrived to re-occupy Ennis and quell resistance by their presence.[35] The government regarded the Clare rising as political in character and in March 1799 court-martialled captives in Ennis and Limerick city on charges of 'aiding and assisting in the present rebellion existing in this kingdom'. Cornwallis alluded to Clare when justifying his reimposition of martial law in the west and also acknowledged that elements of the yeomanry were politically unreliable.[36]

The anomalies of the Clare rising were contained by coercion which failed in counties where geography and primitive communications enabled unreconciled veterans of 1798 to assemble. Anti-government violence was consequently more extensive, violent and insidious than at any time between the Militia crisis of 1793 and May 1798. Formidable rebel factions remained under arms in 1799 in Wicklow, Wexford, Carlow, Kildare, Antrim and, to a lesser extent, Meath; their assembly in defiance of conventional law enforcement suggested a worsening crisis. The mobility of such groups, necessitated by their need to avoid encirclement and combat on disadvantageous terms and to obtain sustenance, ensured that county Dublin, Kilkenny and Waterford were also affected, despite having no significant native resident groups.

The movements of unpardoned fugitives and men returning home from areas to which they had gravitated as mobilised rebel units during the rebellion had an appreciable effect on rural Ireland. These were the 'shoals that crowded the rebel ranks' and that had 'migrated through the country like flights of locusts, devouring everything in their way'.[37] The fighting in Wexford had drawn large contingents from Wicklow, Dublin and Kildare and, according to Micheal Óg Ó Longáin, from as far afield as Tipperary. Thomas Judkin Fitzgerald, Tipperary's notorious hard line ex-high sheriff,

Irish Directory issued handbills discouraging 'the circulation of bank notes' and 'cautioning against the purchasing of quit rents, pursuant to a scheme then in agitation, declaring that, as such a sale was an anticipation of the future resources of the country, it should not be allowed to stand good in the event of a revolution.' Memoir of the State Prisoners in *Castlereagh corr.*, i, p. 364. Cows were killed near Fermoy, Cork, in mid-March 1798 by 'Captain Lightfoot, Governor General of Ireland.' *Saunders News Letter*, 24 Mar. 1798.   **35** Information of James Taaffe, quoted in Sheedy, *Clare*, p. 53.   **36** Sheedy, *Clare*, p. 61; Cornwallis to Portland, 16 Jan. 1799, PRO HO 100/85/87.   **37** *Hib. Tel.*, 26 Oct. 1798.

claimed in mid-January 1799 to have apprehended 'some of Holt's [Wicklow] gang' within two days of their arrival in the county and thereby prevented 'an attack' in conjunction with 'adherents' in Kilkenny.[38] Tipperary did not require such stimulus and in January 1799 was regarded as a county where disturbances and expectations of a French invasion had been common 'for some time'.[39] The county's organisation was 'more general and systematic than ever', a view reinforced by the lethal reprisals taken against assize witnesses and attributable to the efforts of Morres to preserve strength.[40]

There were also nightly robberies on the Cork/Waterford borderlands in January 1799, particularly in the barony of Kinnataloon, where 'the most savage cruelty' of a large gang of offenders 'spread terror and dismay'. Led by ex-Clare militiaman Michael Bryan and headquartered in Connagh, the well armed faction allegedly increased in size and looked 'forward with confident hope to the arrival of a French force'.[41]

The west of Ireland came into focus once more the following month when a massive upsurge in cattle mutilation in Mayo and Galway attained levels that threatened the 'total destruction' of livestock. Major-General John Moore was ordered on 20 February to convene courts martial and, contrary to previous instructions, to execute sentence on the 'most atrocious' offenders without referral to Dublin Castle.[42] The resurgence of the 'old system' of houghing in Galway and Mayo was linked by the viceroy to the simultaneous resurfacing in Cork of the 'usual' violent 'resistance' to tithes. Cornwallis readily bracketed these classic agrarian offences with those perpetrated by rebel veterans, brigands and deserter gangs in other parts of Ireland. The root cause of the disturbances was the near anarchic disaffection which had been assiduously cultivated by the United Irishmen since the advent of the rebellion of 1798 as the essential precursor to successful revolution. As far as the viceroy was concerned, anti-government violence in any form constituted 'rebellion' which, 'if less openly persisted in ... does not fail to show itself in various acts of outrage and depredation, not less destructive and infinitely more embarrassing than open insurrection'.[43]

While it is unlikely that houghing attacks were conceived as furthering republican objectives, the sudden appearance, scale and geographic spread

38 T.J. Fitzgerald to Castlereagh, 18 Jan. 1799, NA, SOC, 1018/22.   39 Cornwallis to Portland, 16 Jan. 1799, PRO HO 100/85/87.   40 R. Johnson to Downshire, 14 Feb. 1799, PRONI, D607/G/67.   41 W. Kirby to Castlereagh, 12 Jan. 1799, PRO, HO 100/85/95.   42 Adjutant-General G. Hewitt to Major-General J. Moore, 20 Feb. 1799, PRO HO 100/85/261; R. Johnson to Downshire, 14 Feb. 1799, PRONI, D607/G/67.   43 Cornwallis to Portland, 14 Feb. 1799, PRO HO 100/85/235.

of the outbreak, possibly the worst to afflict Connaught since 1712, implied organisation and purpose. In Ennis in March 1799 Judge Robert Day determined that the 'savage crime of houghing' emanated 'from some diabolical principle far above the ordinary flight of human atrocity ... it is but one of the bitter fruits of the tree of French liberty'. Attacks on cattle, Day assumed, represented an agreed if not co-ordinated ploy to deprive royal navy victuallers of the vital supplies exported to the fleets from Cork. His suspicions of underlying political motives deepened on arrival in Tralee on St. Patrick's Day ahead of the assizes. Day was then shocked by the numerous printed and manuscript seditious notices 'some reprobating tithes, taxes & even rents, some reprobating Union – all under different forms & pretences ... to agitate & excite the "Men of Kerry".'[44]

IV

Little discussion of post-rebellion violence had taken place in parliament, even though seemingly endemic unrest and the destabilisation it engendered was arguably the key context for union debates. On 20 December 1798 Castle under-secretary Edward Cooke noted the 'returning turbulence' and argued for the retention of martial law to quell the trouble before it became uncontainable. Cooke's secret service duty made him an uniquely qualified judge of such matters; yet his views were unpopular given the desire of Cornwallis and the Pitt government to dispense with the discredited coercion policy he had promoted under Camden from 1796.[45]

Cornwallis was obliged to inform Portland in December 1798 that 'the seeds of rebellion are again spreading' and in Carlow, Wicklow, Kildare and Wexford there was 'every appearance ... of an intended insurrection'. Numerous reports of timber being felled to make pikes handles, attempts to suborn the militia and the seditious activities of the large numbers of pardoned rebels living in the capital informed his opinion. It is unclear whether the viceroy's reports affected discussion of union in Westminster

44 Diary of Judge Robert Day, 5 March 1799, RIA, Ms 12.W.11., p. 65. Buckingham believed that 'the mischief done to private property by the new system (as ordered by the Directory here) is out of all calculation; none of the roads to Dublin are passable at any hour of the day save to large parties or military escorts; and this system is openly talked of as being more certain, and more destructive, than that of open force till their friends arrive, who are most impatiently looked for in the counties of Antrim, Galway, and Cork.' Buckingham to Grenville, 11 Mar. 1798 in *Fortescue*, iv, p. 497.   45 Cooke to Castlereagh, 20 Dec. 1798 in *Castlereagh corr.*, ii, p. 49.

but those privy to his dispatches would have been strengthened in their desire to tighten control of Irish security policy. It was on 24 December 1798, mindful of Cornwallis' position, that Britain's parliament endorsed an agenda to seek legislative union with Ireland. This set the scene for the first major debate in the Irish house of commons on 22 January 1799.[46]

Pitt favoured repealing coercive legislation in Ireland and was keen to restore habeas corpus and abolish martial law. A priority was the recommencement of civil assizes which would dispense with courts martial to try civilians for politically motivated offences. December 1798 witnessed the restitution of most peacetime civil rights and the resurrection of the shelved assize circuits. Wicklow, Wexford, Mayo and certain other counties had to be exempted owing to the dangers faced by judges and jurors, a point of political sensitivity. Cornwallis had no choice but to make provision for summary justice in Ireland's worst affected counties and to retain the services of the erratic yeomanry organisation and militia.

The problem of martial law demonstrated to the French that Ireland remained highly disaffected. Eliminating this perennial security nightmare was consequently one of the major objects of union for Westminster. Binding the allegiance of Irishmen to the state would be desirable at the best of times but absolutely necessary in wartime, if the expense and logistics of maintaining huge garrisons was to be avoided. The rebellion had required the dispatch to Ireland of more British troops than were available to defend their home country from invasion. The serious defence liability of Ireland was further reflected in contingency regulations for invasion which were issued by the government in the early 1800s: Irish communities were ordered to move inland in case of invasion to keep themselves and their goods out of the French controlled zone whereas Britons, who were much less likely to collaborate, were instructed to stay put.

An important assessment of United Irish plans and capabilities was sent to Dublin on 28 February 1799 by William Wickham. Having noted the conflicting opinions regarding the intentions of a French naval expedition fitting out in Brest, Wickham apprised Castlereagh that Ireland (as the Dublin United Irish leadership was known to have informed its 'friends') was the 'real object' of the fleet in the spring. That this proved incorrect offered only short term relief to Wickham who believed that there were 'many concurrent circumstances independent of the present state of the

---

46 Cornwallis to Portland in *Cornwallis corr.*, iii, p. 19; *FJ*, 13, 23 and 27 Dec. 1798. Wicklow, Wexford, Kildare and Meath were reputedly in a 'wretched state.' Patrickson to Downshire, 14 Jan. 1799, PRONI, D 607/6/17.

country in Ireland which must naturally tempt the enemy to an invasion'. Surveillance of rebel emissaries travelling between Ireland, Britain and France confirmed that United Irish strategy had reverted to that which had existed between 1795 and May 1798: mounting a 'general rising ... as soon as the French shall appear on the coast'.[47] A typical memorial from a United Irish officer in Hamburg to the French Directory boasted that the rebels in Ireland 'have the most part of the arms left by General Humbert at Killala, and immense quantities of pikes; are better organised, and more eager in the glorious cause of freedom than they ever have been'.[48]

British-based informers and agent handlers discovered plans to support an Irish invasion with diversionary activity in London, Manchester and Bristol where new communities of republican fugitives of the 1798 rebellion would inhibit the transfer of troops to Ireland. John Binns and Valentine Lawless were two well-regarded United Irishmen in Britain with close relatives who commanded authority in Dublin after 1798. Wickham's generally effective intelligence network ascertained that the United Irish state prisoners interned in Kilmainham, who had formerly comprised the Executive Directory, had sanctioned a replacement Directory in Dublin.[49]

Numerous reports by low level informers and infiltrators in April/May 1799 gave specific details of French assisted risings that never came to pass and alleged seditious contact between the state prisoners and their successors. A plot to seize Cork on Easter Sunday attracted more credence than most and was thoroughly investigated by Major-Generals William Myers and Charles Ross.[50] There were, however, many other mooted dates and locations, which, when supported by the sworn depositions of intended participants describing plausible scenarios, served to confuse the authorities. This may well have been a deliberate strategy of those privy to genuine intentions. Separating mischievous and garbled rising plans from those deliberately disseminated by an informed Dublin leadership in league with the French offered little comfort to the Castle. The salient feature remained

47 Wickham to Castlereagh, 28 Feb. 1799, PRO HO 100/85/281. Lt.-Gen. Gerard Lake toured the south of Ireland in April/May 1799 and reported that 'the disposition of the people is not good. They are ready to rise should the French land ... they will not shew unless the enemy arrive and make a successful stand in arms in any part of the Kingdom.' Lake to Cornwallis, 3 June 1799, PRO HO 100/89/55. 48 Memorial of Dennis O'Neill, 30 Jan. 1799 in *Castlereagh corr.*, ii, p. 234. 49 Significant information came from James McGucken, attorney to the Ulster Provincial Directory, who became a double agent after his arrest on 2 August 1798. Conway, 'one of the Directory at Cork', also supplied insights into United Irish plans in April 1799. Castlereagh to Wickham, 2 Apr. 1799, PRO HO 100/86/242. 50 Information of Joseph Holt, 27 Feb. 1799 in *Castlereagh corr.*, ii, pp 186-7.

that the 'agitators' were 'exceedingly active and busy throughout the whole kingdom'.[51]

The much-dreaded French fleet commanded by Admiral Eustache Bruix left Brest on 26 April 1799. By various ruses Bruix convinced British and Irish authorities that his destination was the west or south coast of Ireland. The French enjoyed United Irish support in concealing their strategic objectives, presumably with assurances that Ireland would later feature in their plans. Enemy landings in Bantry Bay were deterred in the spring of 1799 by twenty-three warships under Lord Bridport's control. These included Sir Edward Pellew's *L'Impetueux* which, ominously, experienced a mutiny attempt off Berehaven on 30 May to prevent its putting to sea against the French. Three men were hanged in Port Mahon the following week and others flogged but more immediate problems were caused by the desertion of 176 men who had taken advantage of the confusion to escape to the Kerry shoreline.

Ulster commander Major-General Nugent, more experienced and decisive than most senior officers in Ireland, detected signs that Antrim republicans had been disheartened by their heavy defeats in 1798 and would not rise without a 'formidable' French invasion. Agitation, nonetheless, was comparable in scale and nature to that afflicting Leinster. Thomas Archer and General James 'Holt' Dickey (aka Dickson and Dixon) were two veteran rebel officers of the rebellion who had remained out in 1799 at the head of small bands of comrades.[52] In March 1799 Nugent joined the growing number of regional army commanders who attributed malcontent to United Irish agents assuring locals of 'the intention of a landing' from Brest in their locality. The French dimension and United Irish membership bracketed east Ulster disturbances with those in Connaught and Leinster, even if wholly different local circumstances had disposed the activists to create unrest.[53]

Dickey's men flogged their enemies, a practice reminiscent of the punishments meted out by the Hearts of Steel in the 1770s and possibly

51 Cornwallis to Portland, 4 Mar. 1799, PRO HO 100/86/19. See also 25 Mar. 1799, PRO HO 100/86/195; 25 Mar. 1799, PRO HO 100/86/228; 31 Mar. 1799, PRO HO 100/86/239 and 6 May 1799, PRO HO 100/88/286. For the widely known plan in militia garrisons of Cork and Kerry to revolt at noon on 5 May 1799, see information of Owen Madden, 7 May 1799, PRO HO 100/88/314. For Leonard McNally's warning of 15,000 French troops landing in Ireland 'by the latter end of May [1799]', see [McNally] to D[ownshire], 17 Apr. 1799, PRONI, D 607/G/159.   52 Report of Major-General Nugent, 10 May 1799, PRO HO 100/88/340. Nugent noted of Dickey when captured: 'this fellow will not inform & is very impudent.'   53 Buckingham to Grenville, 11 Mar. 1798 in *Fortescue*, iv, p. 497.

indicative of some continuity of personnel with that earlier body. United Irish captain Samuel Hume of Moneyduff, County Antrim, was also active in disarming Rasharkin yeomanry in January 1799. In custody Hume divulged details of Defender/ United Irish leaders in Antrim, Down, Derry and Tyrone, insights which attest to efforts to maintain the republican organisation in Ulster after 1798. According to Hume, Tyrone man Patrick Mitchel had 'for some time … been travelling this county for the purpose of encouraging Defenderism', presumably by promising French military aid.[54]

On visiting Randalstown on 3 February 1799, Revd Edward Hudson noted that 'an armed and numerous banditti plundered several houses of arms within a mile of Antrim', killing one man and severely injuring a second. Raiders struck near Ballymena a few days later, attacking nine houses to obtain firearms and leaving one soldier and a loyalist badly wounded. Ten of the perpetrators were seized after a long chase but their comrades remained stoic and continued their depredations. The upsurge was attributed to expectations of an imminent French invasion which the 'disaffected … say will be within a month'. Hudson, whose yeoman curate was robbed of arms near Portglenone on 8 March, ascertained that 'the name of United Irishmen is never heard, it is merged in that of Defender'.[55] This new 'system' evidently spread from Antrim to Armagh and revealed its political motivation in reports of raiders declining to steal cash from their victims. An expected rising on St Patrick's Day failed to occur but the 'considerable progress' of Defenderism convinced Hudson that a French invasion would elicit 'terrible scenes'.[56]

Operating in east Ulster's militarised and comparatively open terrain did not permit long term activity by groups which acted in expectation of receiving imminent help from France. Life on the run took a steady toll of the rebels and disposed several to seek terms. One Randalstown area leader, a catholic veteran of the rebellion in Ulster and Connaught, outlined a plan to rise on 10 April 1799. The day elapsed without incident, suggesting to Hudson that the United Irish Directory had set spurious dates merely to 'keep up their spirits'.[57]

In mid-April 1799 fifteen members of Dickey's faction were rounded up in response to information given by an artillery regiment deserter. This was a timely breakthrough as east-Ulster loyalists were reeling from the 'nightly barbarities' inflicted on their communities and intimidated from reporting

54 Examination of Samuel Hume, 26 Jan. 1800 in Fitzpatrick, *Sham squire*, p. 345. 55 Hudson to Charlemont 3 Feb. 1799 in *Charlemont*, ii, p. 345. 56 Hudson to Charlemont, 22 Mar. in *Charlemont*, ii, p. 347. 57 Hudson to Charlemont, 8 Apr. 1799 in *Charlemont*, ii, pp 348–9.

rebel attacks.[58] This setback apparently prompted Dickey's offer to surrender on terms of transportation, an overture negated by his betrayal and capture by the Toome yeomanry on 8 May 1799. Other arrests hastened the disintegration of the Dickey faction, the target of wide ranging arrests. Dickey was seized just as news filtered through that the French fleet had left Brest and he was consequently deprived of the chance to augment his numbers. The reaction to the fleet's sailing in Antrim and other parts of the North was negligible although the loss of experienced leaders clearly accelerated the collapse of rebel factions.[59] Archer, an ex-yeoman, held out until March 1800 when he was 'executed and hung in chains in Ballymena'.[60]

Mass arrests had also taken place in late March 1799 in the Blessington area of west Wicklow, neutralising the harbouring ring which supported the Hughes faction. As in Antrim, the arrests derived effectiveness by being directed by a well placed insider, in this case the desperate Hughes who had been captured with a capital conviction over his head. Government forces had also utilised an informer's tip-off to strike a heavy blow against the Dwyer group on 15 February 1799 when he and eleven followers were trapped in Derrynamuck townland, Imaal, by the Glengary Highlanders. Two soldiers and three rebels died in the shoot-out and a further eight rebels were executed following court-martial in Baltinglass. Only Dwyer managed to escape, to reform his faction around a cadre of hardened Imaal and Glenmalure rebels who defied the authorities until December 1803.[61]

Intimidating rebel harbourers by even temporary detention lessened the capacity of later gangs to take root in that area, a useful procedure given the difficulty of sustaining convictions against harbourers at the assizes. It was not illegal to harbour a fugitive who had not been formally outlawed by the grand jury and this impediment to prosecution greatly hindered efforts to contain the Dwyer/Mernagh faction. Bounties also proved largely ineffective: sums of £300 to £500 failed to elicit the betrayal of either Holt or Dwyer between 1798 and 1803.[62]

The Rebellion Act of March 1799 was parliament's primary response to the continuing unrest and its passage through both houses elicited commentary regarding security matters that might otherwise have been aired in the concurrent union discussions. The act presaged a flurry of courts martial while acting as the spur for the release of hundreds of compromised

58 Hudson to Charlemont, 1 May 1799 in *Charlemont*, ii, p. 351.   59 Nugent, 10 May 1799, PRO HO 100/88/340; Wickham to Castlereagh, 26 May 1799, PRO HO 100/86/434.   60 Fitzpatrick, *Sham squire*, p. 351.   61 O'Donnell, *Aftermath*, pp 34-9.   62 Forty-two of Hughes' supporters were arrested. John Patrickson to Downshire, 26 Mar. 1799, PRONI, D 607/G/133.

United Irishmen from the Dublin Bay hulks and prisons. Those whose crimes were no longer deemed serious in the light of the liberal terms of the Amnesty Act or whose alleged offences were not easily proved were generally freed in 1799-1800.[63] Many rebels were excused their sentences, bailed or simply sent home if they enjoyed gentry and military patronage. All but a handful of the ninety men sentenced to terms of transportation and military service in King's County in April/May 1798 were freed by the close of 1799, the unfortunate minority being conscripted into regiments bound for the West Indies, the Prussian military and the penal colonies of New South Wales (Australia).[64]

The prison releases infuriated ultra-loyalists who stepped up their unofficial campaign of 'white terror' against Catholic clergy and chapels in Wicklow, Wexford, Carlow, Kildare and King's County. Pardoned ex-rebels were illegally killed in south Leinster, deaths which inspired revenge attacks on loyalists and, as such, helped perpetuate unrest. The violence of 'orange' yeomen from Rathdrum, Newtownmountkennedy, Ballaghkeen and other Wicklow and north Wexford centres encouraged hundreds of rebel veterans to settle in Dublin's south city liberties. Tensions were also inflamed by the execution of high profile United Irishmen, such as Patrick Grant of Kirikee and William 'Billy' Byrne of Ballymanus. The loss of these popular rebel officers motivated Dwyer to kill several state witnesses and jeopardised the lives of magistrates and yeomanries involved in their prosecution.[65]

Attacks on cattle in Connaught had ceased by early June 1799, possibly due to a sense of futility engendered by the non-arrival of the Brest fleet. Even so, small numbers of rebels active since the rebellion remained at large. Major-General Eyre Power Trench claimed that the appearance of Bridport's British squadron off the Mayo coast on 3 June 1799 drew the outstanding rebels into the nearby mountains, presumably hoping to catch sight of their French allies. The influence of James Joseph MacDonnell was detected in leading and supplying the north Connacht bodies, specifically a 'regularly organised and well armed' group on the Mayo/Galway border. The direct involvement of MacDonnell, one of the highest ranking Connacht United Irishmen to survive the rebellion, is doubtful as he escaped to France after the battle of Ballinamuck and joined the Irish Legion.[66]

63 McDowell, *Ireland*, pp 667-8.   64 R. O'Donnell, '"Marked for Botany Bay:" The Wicklow United Irishmen and the development of political transportation from Ireland', Ph.D. thesis, Australian National University, 1996.   65 Sir J. Caldwell to Cornwallis, 21 Aug. 1799 in *The tryal of William Byrne* (Dublin, 1799) pp 78-9; O'Donnell, *Aftermath*, pp 42-6.   66 For MacDonnell, see S. Molloy, 'General James

The disappointing absence of the French apparently inhibited fresh outbreaks of violence during the summer months but Wicklow, Wexford, Carlow, Kildare and Limerick remained volatile. The next major upsurge outside Leinster came in September/October 1799 owing to inter-provincial agitation by Tipperary-based militants with links to Kerry, Limerick, Clare and Waterford. Alexander Marsden noted:

> new attempts at rebellion of which we have serious proofs, will not impede the union, but in other views they are very unpleasant ... many were engaged, and their schemes nearly ripe for execution ... As the hopes of the disaffected are kept up partly by what the agitation of the question of union may produce, and partly by promise of succour from France, it is of the utmost importance that our military force should not be too much reduced.[67]

One of the main Munster based organisers in 1799 was United Irish officer Phil Cunningham, a Kerryman suspected of rescuing prisoners from the Essex Fencibles en route to Clonmel where he kept an inn and worked as a mason. When courtmartialled in October 1799, Cunningham was charged with having gone to Dungarvan on 1 August 1799 and to 'other places in the county Waterford with intent to foment rebellion and excite divers[e] subjects ... to raise & take up arms against His Majesty'.[68] Cunningham, deemed to have previously pursued this objective at Carrick-on-Suir and Kilmacthomas, narrowly avoided execution by virtue of a favourable technicality introduced by the Rebellion Act. He was transported to New South Wales on the *Anne* where he led the last rising mounted by the United Irishmen at Castle Hill (Sydney) in March 1804.[69]

Cunningham's arrest undoubtedly damaged the network of contacts he had built up, particularly as other insurgent officers such as Thomas Langan of Glin, Bill Leonard of Ahanagran and Manus Sheehy of Duagh were also captured and transported during the same period. Limerick and Kerry,

Joseph MacDonnell (1763-1848)' in *Co. Roscommon Historical and Archaeological Society Journal* vi (1996), pp 73-6. Denis Browne advised Cornwallis in 1799 that MacDonnell should not be permitted to return to Ireland as 'it is not compatible with the peace or safety of Connaught to make any terms whatever with this person who was the prime mover and promoter of the misfortunes of Mayo.' Quoted in Hayes, *Last invasion*, pp 277-8.   **67** Marsden to Castlereagh, 28 Sept. 1798 in *Castlereagh corr.*, ii, p. 407.   **68** 11 Oct. 1799, NA, 620/6/19/13.   **69** *Sydney Gazette*, 11 Mar. 1804; R. O'Donnell, 'Philip Cunningham: Clonmel's insurgent leader of 1798' in *Tipp. Hist. Jn.* (1998), pp 150-7; J. Gallagher, 'The revolutionary Irish 1800-1804' in *The Push from the Bush*, xix (1985), pp 2-33.

however, retained the services of higher ranking United Irishmen who evaded prosecution into the early 1800s, not least Gerald Fitzgerald (brother of the Knight of Glin), Nicholas Sandes of Listowel and the astronomer James Baggott of Ballingarry.[70]

The loss of Cunningham did not lessen the serious insurgent threat which emerged in Tipperary in September 1799 when attacks were mounted on members of the Clonmel yeomen and on Carrick magistrate John Mansfield. Another magistrate, John Bagwell, became unnerved and feared that the large numbers involved in the upsurge indicated that 'an immediate intended rising of the rebels' was planned.[71] Fethard loyalists added to the impression of a widespread conspiracy by reporting menacing fires 'blazing on all the surrounding hills' on the night of 6 September and that the military anticipated a rising. The garrisons of Clonmel and Carrick consequently went on full alert and martial law regulations were re-applied to Tipperary and Waterford on the 13th, another testament to the failure of the Irish administration.[72]

The sense of crisis spread further south and to the east; the Marquis of Waterford claimed that 'the entire lower class are on the point to rise and murder'.[73] An informer divulged the unsettling news that 'Ireland was all new organised, and meant to proceed on a new principle; that union was the word for rising all over the kingdom.'[74] Cooke's sources did not highlight the union question but led him to state that 'the Defender system is spreading dangerously' throughout the country and was gaining strength in King's County and Kildare in October. Opposition to the union, tithe grievances, migrating labourers and the succession of poor potato crops after 1798 were all correctly identified as sources of unrest but it was the ability of politically motivated agitators such as Cunningham to exploit such factors that troubled the government.[75]

Rebellious behaviour attributed to United Irishmen abroad in 1799 included the defection to anti-British forces in Jamaica of Irish rebels who

70 T. F. Culhane, 'Traditions of Glin and its neighbourhood' in *Jn. Kerry Arch. Hist. Soc.* (1969), pp 74-101.   71 J. Bagwell to —, 7 Sept. 1799, PRO HO 100/89/ 187.   72 J. King to —, 7 Sept. 1799, PRO HO 100/89/185; 13 Sept. 1799, PRO HO 100/89/213; Lake to —, 14 Sept. 1799, PRO HO 100/89/214.   73 Waterford to Castlereagh, 9 Sept. 1799 in *Castlereagh corr.*, ii, p. 394.   74 'Information', n.d. [Sept. 1799] in *Castlereagh corr.*, ii, p. 395.   75 Cooke to Castlereagh, 18 Sept. 1799 in *Castlereagh corr.*, ii, p. 403; Elliott to Castlereagh, 19 Oct. 1799 in Ibid., ii, pp 431-2; Lane to Downshire, 12 Oct. 1799, PRONI, D 607/G/200. John Dooane of Dungarvan, cousin of Cunningham's co-defendant, was impressed by the prediction of the emissaries that 'they w[oul]d be ruined' when the anticipated Act of Union came into effect. 4 Oct. 1799, NA, 620/6/69/13, p. 10.

had been conscripted into the army. In September 1799 a 'conspiracy' involving Irish recruits in the Prince of Wales regiment was uncovered in Guernsey and many of the almost 400 rebels shipped to Emden that month for induction into the Prussian military were punished for insubordination. United Irishmen in the Royal Newfoundland regiment revolted in April 1800 and, when detained, temporarily avoided execution by seizing the vessel taking them for trial in Nova Scotia. Mutiny plots also affected the *Minerva* and *Friendship* which sailed from Cobh in August 1799 with rebel prisoners bound for New South Wales. A defiant *Minerva* rebel declared: 'it was much better to die ... than live in a state of bondage ... they had ventured their lives for their freedom before and would now again venture'. Such incidents demonstrated the resilience of rebel prisoners who continued to create ferment when the opportunity arose.[76]

The authorities learned in January 1800 that William Putnam McCabe had visited Belfast to inform the United Irishmen that a renewed French invasion attempt would be mounted from Brest. McCabe had been implicated in virtually every aspect of the United Irish conspiracy in the late 1790s and had escaped to France after the suppression of the rebellion of 1798. His message may have been widely disseminated in republican circles and there was certainly an appreciable upsurge in rebel and agrarian activity in the spring of 1800, the last to occur before the union bill received its belated royal assent in August.[77]

As before, escalating attacks in one county took on regional and national importance when they coincided with similar crises in other regions. In Tipperary two 'loyal' men who had been denounced at a seditious meeting in Cashel were put to death near Cahir in early March 1800 and several others severely flogged near Newcastle. Reports of quasi-political and agrarian violence continued to emanate that month from Limerick and

---

76 Price journal, 8 Oct. 1799, BL Ms 13,880, p. 45. United Irish immigrants were blamed, possibly incorrectly, for a 1799 riot in Philadelphia and came under suspicion in Bath, Bristol, London and Manchester. 'Irish plots' were also detected in Port Jackson (New South Wales) in February, September and October 1800 and in the secondary outposts of Toongabbie and Norfolk Island in December of that year. An unsuccessful, fatal mutiny attempt struck the *Anne* in July 1800 and eighteen rebels were killed or mortally wounded attempting to seize the *Hercules* on 29 December 1801. O'Donnell, "Marked for Botany Bay," Chapter 9; 8 October 1799, *Castlereagh corr.*, ii, pp 417-18; Byrne, *Memoirs*, ii, pp 279-80; iii, pp 162-3; Madden, *United Irishmen*, i, p. 330; Wickham to Cooke, 5 Sept. 1799, PRO HO 100/89/177; J. Mannion, 'Transatlantic disaffection: Wexford and Newfoundland 1798-1800' in *Jn. Wex. Hist. Soc.* (1998-9), p. 56.   77 Castlereagh to J. King, 8 Jan. 1800, PRO HO 100/93/3.

Clare, resulting in the dispatch of military reinforcements to Connagh, Emly, Bruff and Cappagh to stop the agitators becoming 'more daring.'[78] Killings were also reported at this time in Carlow and Wicklow and note taken that 'a formidable banditti of the association of Defenders' had taken 'deep root' in Antrim, notwithstanding pre-emptive efforts by Brigadier-General Drummond and the execution of several known ringleaders. That those implicated in the Antrim disturbances were deemed to be the 'better kind of farmers' did not augur well for government and tended to discredit the conciliatory attitude that General Nugent had adopted towards privileged United Irish prisoners. Reports in April also noted Defender meetings at Hillsborough in Down, another county with a proven record in militant disaffection.[79]

March 1800 was also a significant month in Wicklow and other parts of Leinster where the Castle gained an insight into what appeared to be a centrally directed build up. Contact was established in March between the Dwyer group and three United Irish emissaries who were perfecting province-wide seditious communications. The agents, reputedly wealthy farmers from Kildare, had been 'long expected' by the time they called to Eadestown where Dwyer's father lived and were possibly known to the Wicklowmen from previous meetings. The delegates spent several days with Dwyer in Imaal; one of them (seized by the military in Carlow on 4 April) claimed to have also travelled through Wexford administering a new oath which bound those who accepted it to 'assist the French whenever they effect a landing'. This was the formula used by Robert Emmet's agents in 1802-3 and its utilisation in early 1800 may reflect his input as a member of the Dublin Directory.[80]

In early 1800 Emmet visited his brother and other high-ranking United Irishmen who had been relocated from Kilmainham to Fort George, Scotland, for the duration of the French war. Their continued support for the new Dublin leadership was canvassed and received by Emmet and he may have outlined a specific strategic plan to them. A European tour undertaken by Emmet and Delaney followed the Scottish trip and included meetings with Napoleon, Talleyrand and General Augereau, indicating that top level channels established by United Irish agents were offered to the new delegates. This lengthy excursion laid the basis for the plot attempted in Dublin and elsewhere in Ireland in July 1803, a drastically scaled down

78 General Sir J. Duff to Lake, 14 Mar. 1800, PRO HO 100/93/206; information of Thomas P[...], 14 Mar. 1800, PRO HO 100/93/204.   79 Cornwallis to Portland, 17 Mar. 1800, PRO HO 100/93/188; PRO HO 100/98/215.   80 N. Steele to Marsden, 18 Sept. 1800, NA, 620/49/59; 28 Jan. 1801, NA, 620/10/113/2.

version of one which had been intended to support a French invasion in August of that year.[81]

Long before the shock of 1803, it was clear that amidst the chaos of plebeian violence attributable to brigands, agrarian protesters and quasi-political agitators in post-rebellion Ireland, a loose but determined United Irish command structure had been rebuilt. When the Act of Union was passed on 1 January 1801, it was greeted with deceptive calm by an apathetic Dublin which did not reflect the disturbed mood of the country. Notwithstanding widespread misinterpretation, Emmet's actions five years after the Great Rebellion confounded those who had promoted union as the answer to disaffection and instability in Ireland and destroyed a central plank of their lobby in 1798-9. The burden of responsibility was shifted from Irish ascendancy conservatives to British administrators and with it the axis of republican enmity.

81 O'Donnell, *Aftermath*, pp 110-13.

14

Britishness, Irishness and the Act of Union[1]

Thomas Bartlett

W hen the British prime minister, William Pitt, learned on 26 May 1798 of the outbreak of insurrection in Ireland, he immediately thought that this crisis offered the perfect opportunity to move for a union between Britain and Ireland. This notion of union was very much in vogue at that time. The revolutionary French republic had already embarked on a series of incorporating unions (i.e. military annexations) with various minor states overrun by it in Europe; the former British colonies in North America had recently forged a strengthened union by means of a newly drafted and ratified constitution; and even the United Irishmen – the proximate cause of the crisis that engulfed Ireland in 1798 – had proudly referred to their movement as 'the Union'.[2] This latter irony was relished: once a codeword for the United Irishmen, 'that odious, detestable thing called union,' noted one anti-union pamphleteer, 'is suddenly purged from all its unnatural foulness by the regenerating breath of an English statesman'.[3] Pitt's action in calling for a union with Ireland, however, was no different to that of previous British ministers faced with acute difficulties there. Union had been mentioned at various points in the previous fifty years: during the Money Bill dispute in the early 1750s; when 'Free Trade' had been agitated in the late 1770s; when the constitutional concessions of 1782 had been

---

1 A version of this essay was delivered as my inaugural lecture as professor of Modern Irish History at University College Dublin on 24 Feb. 2000. 2 The French and American examples are explicitly addressed in *Necessity of an incorporating union between Great Britain and Ireland proved from the situation of both kingdoms* (Dublin, 1798), pp 29, 33, and M. Weld, *No union, being an appeal to Irishmen* (Dublin, 1798), p. 13. For the United Irishmen's 'Union', see 'Memoir or detailed statement of the origin and progress of the Irish union' in W.J. MacNeven (ed.), *Pieces of Irish history* (New York, 1807), pp 174 ff. 3 D. Taaffe, *The probability, causes and consequences of an union between Great Britain and Ireland discussed* (Dublin, 1798), p. 30.

demanded; during the controversy over the commercial propositions of
1785; at the time of the Regency crisis of 1788-9; and, especially, during the
crisis provoked by the catholic question in the years 1792 to 1793. Even
before the 1750s, the question of union with England had been a live one.
Indeed, in the early years of the eighteenth century, Irish protestants could
only look on glumly, their pleas and protests ignored, while the favoured
Scots were bribed, bullied and badgered into a union with England in 1707.
Since then much had changed in Anglo-Irish relations: by the 1790s, if not
long before, the burgeoning self-confidence of protestant Ireland, the
enhanced importance of their potent symbol of identity, the Irish parliament, indeed, their growing identification with Ireland and Irishness, meant
that all talk of union with Britain had to be dismissed since there was little
possibility of the Irish parliament voting itself out of existence. To be sure,
the Catholic Relief Act of 1793 had advanced substantially the cause of
union in both countries. The inability of the Irish parliament to defend the
protestant ascendancy had been then mercilessly exposed, and certainly
from that date on there had been an elite pro-union lobby in both England
and Ireland: but the primary difficulty had endured – the consent of the
Irish.[4] At a stroke, the rebellion changed the prospects for union, and British
ministers and their Irish allies hastened to seize the opportunity. The unionist moment had finally come: but it might as quickly pass; and there could
be no question of leaving the matter until quieter times prevailed. It is vital
to act, wrote one unionist, 'while the terror of the late rebellion is fresh', and
George III signalled his agreement for 'using the present moment of terror
for frightening the supporters of the Castle into a union'.[5] Accordingly, the
new lord lieutenant, the Marquis Cornwallis (and his chief secretary, the
Irish-born Lord Castlereagh) were entrusted with a dual mandate: first, to
crush rebellion, but then to put through a legislative union.

As Pitt saw it, his proposed union was a key instrument of counter-
revolution, a vital strategic imperative which would draw England and
Ireland closer and closer together, frustrating those Irish jacobins and their
French allies who had sought to prise them apart. Indeed, in his main
speech advocating the union proposals in the British House of Commons,
Pitt stressed this imperial strategic argument. On a constitutional level,
union could also be seen as the final solution to those problems that had –
from an English perspective – bedevilled Anglo-Irish relations since 1782.
Pitt stressed the profoundly unsatisfactory nature of the 'constitution of

4 For the origins of the union, see Kelly, 'Origins'.   5 Carysfort to Grenville, 15 Aug.
1798, *Fortescue*, iv, p. 280.

1782', the culpable failure to reform it in the 1780s, and, hence, the ever-present danger of a clash between two 'independent' legislatures – a clash, he claimed, only narrowly averted at the time of the Regency crisis.

Pitt now looked to the future: only in a united parliament could the catholic question be resolved, gratifying the political ambitions of Irish catholics without endangering Irish protestants. Other benefits would stem from union: Ireland would gain commercial advantages; there would be an infusion of 'English capital, English manners [and] English industry' so that Ireland would prosper from union with England as much as Scotland had done since her union of 1707. The ghost of Scotland hovered over the Irish union debates: her union with England had ushered in a prosperity largely based on Scotland's unrestricted access to the imperial emporium: surely Ireland could do as well, even better? Lastly, Pitt held out an attractive picture of the new parliament sitting as an impartial imperial legislature, far removed from the prejudice of local Irish factions, calmly and dispassionately adjudicating in the interests of all, an assembly where contentious matters such as tithes or the provision of salaries for catholic priests could be coolly deliberated on.[6] Central to Pitt's understanding of Ireland was his conviction that the Irish parliament had failed, that Irish politicians had failed and that there could now be no alternative but union. 'There is no circumstance of apparent or probable difficulty,' he declared, 'no apprehension of unpopularity, no fear of toil or labour that shall prevent me from using every exertion which remains in my power to accomplish [union].' Pitt's resolute determination to spare no effort guaranteed ultimate victory.

II

By the autumn of 1800, Lord Castlereagh could finally relax: the union had passed and would come into force at midnight on the last day of the year. Two years during which the projected union had been 'written up, spoken up, intrigued up, drunk up, sung up and bribed up' had come to an end.[7] In the circumstances, Castlereagh's comment on his ostensible triumph was a curious one: 'I feel very proud of myself, of being less an Irishman and more an Englishman than hitherto.'[8] This striking statement of longing as much as loathing, of anxiety as much as aspiration, is worth examination on two

6 *Parl. Hist. of England*, xxxiv, Pitt's speech, 23 Jan. 1799, pp 242–9; see also Pitt's speech of 31 Jan. 1799 in *A review of a speech of the Rt. Hon. William Pitt ... January 31st. 1799* (Dublin, 1799), p. 43.   7 Cooke to Auckland, 27 Oct. 1798, PRONI T3229/2/37.   8 Castlereagh to John King, 2 Aug. 1800, PRO HO 100/94/128–9.

counts. First, it encapsulated the most problematic aspects of union – those involving nation, nationality and identity. Second, it highlighted the union's supreme irony: at the very moment of its passing, Ireland and England were in fact moving further and further apart – industrially, agriculturally, demographically and, not least, religiously. There was no further geographic separation, but the Irish Sea might prove to be more than a wet ha-ha between England and Ireland. The two countries would be united politically but the 'join' would remain painfully evident. Was genuine union in fact desired – or possible? We now know how the Irish could become protestant: and how the Irish became 'white': and we are now told that we have become European; but could the Irish have become British?

To this question, Linda Colley has in fact given a resounding no, and in her fine study of the development of Britishness over the long eighteenth century, she chose to omit Ireland altogether:

> The invention of Britishness was so closely bound up with protestantism, with war with France and with the acquisition of empire that Ireland was never able to or willing to play a satisfactory part in it. Its population was more catholic than protestant. It was the ideal jumping-off spot for a French invasion of Britain, and both its catholic and its protestant dissidents traditionally looked to France for aid. And although Irishmen were (and still are) an important component of Britain's armed forces, and individual Irishmen played leading roles as generals, diplomatists and pro-consuls, Ireland's relationship with the empire was always a deeply ambiguous one. How could it not be so when London treated it as a colony. ... Ireland was cut off from Great Britain by sea but it was cut off still more effectively by the prejudices of the English, Welsh, and Scots, and by the self-image of the bulk of the Irish themselves, both protestants and catholics.[9]

The Irish, in short, could never be British. There could be an act of union, but the fact of union could not bring about assimilation, and the Irish would remain resolutely unassimilable. Colley's verdict has fuelled contemporary pre-occupations concerning the essential elements of 'Britishness' and 'Irishness'.[10] It is worthy of extended consideration.

9 L. Colley, *Britons: forging the nation 1707-1837* (New Haven, 1992), p. 8.   **10** On the topic of identities, see B. Bradshaw & P. Roberts (ed.), *British consciousness and identity: the making of Britain 1533-1707* (Cambridge, 1998); T. Claydon & I. McBride (ed.), *Protestantism and national identity: Britain and Ireland c.1650-c1850* (Cambridge, 1998); C. Kidd, *British identities before nationalism: ethnicity and nationhood in the Atlantic world 1600-1800* (Cambridge, 1999).

In all the public argumentation and special pleading that had accompanied the union negotiations, little had touched directly on national identity. The implications for the protestant nation of the loss of their parliament had rarely been addressed. Protestant nationalism, seemingly so vibrant in 1782, seeking and welcoming novel accommodation with the catholics, had barely survived the shock of 1798. The discredited Henry Grattan's 'national' objections to union fell on deaf ears, a marked contrast to the enthusiasm which had drowned out the commercial propositions of 1785, which Grattan had played a leading role in orchestrating. Charlemont, Grattan's ally in the anti-union camp, exclaimed 'we are yet a nation' on receipt of the news of a setback to the union's progress in January 1799; in fact, national feeling had little to do with the opposition to union in the Irish parliament.[11] The speaker, John Foster, the main opponent of union, regarded an Irish parliament as an essential badge of protestant nationhood (for him, pro-testant nationalism meant little more than protestant ascendancy) and he urged his fellow Irish MPs not to vote for a move from 'an independent kingdom to an abject colony.'[12] Like Grattan's pan-national sentiments, Foster's, too, were given short shrift. Edward Cooke, under-secretary at Dublin Castle and closely involved in monitoring anti-unionist speeches, reported that Foster's arguments were easily rebutted 'except the obvious and irrefutable objection *per se* of removing parliament to a distance'.[13] 'Distance' was important to his case, as it would be to a later nationalist argument, but the key problem for Foster and for those loyalists upholding the protestant ascendancy had little to do with remoteness. For them the Irish parliament should be the vital bulwark of the protestant interest in Ireland; was it desirable for an indifferent Westminster parliament to discharge that duty from afar? Could it be trusted with that task?

Beyond the walls of the Irish parliament, the 'national' argument had more of an airing. Anxieties were expressed that Irish orators would not succeed in transplanting themselves to an English environment: an Irish gentleman 'smell[ing] of the turf of boggy Ireland ... would be ashamed to exhibit the Irish brogue in the British senate'. In this regard, the cautionary example of Henry Flood was often cited: an Irish Demosthenes when speaking in the Irish parliament, yet at Westminster he suffered the humiliation of concluding 'a very able and eloquent speech amidst the

11 Charlemont to Haliday, 25 Jan. 1799, *Charlemont*, ii, p. 344.   12 *Speech of the Rt Hon. John Foster ... 11 April 1799* (Dublin, 1799), p. 46.   13 Cooke to Wickham, 12 Apr. 1799, *Cornwallis corr.*, iii, p. 87.

yawns and coughs of an English senate'. In addition, Foster circulated resolutions in county Louth forecasting 'the total extinction of national pride, spirit and independence'[14] while others predicted that Ireland would become 'a degraded and divided province',[15] and that Dublin would 'dwindle into a fishing town'.[16] The former United Irishman William Drennan protested at the probable fate that lay in store for Ireland, 'to be known in future only as a sound in the title of the sovereign.'[17] A correspondent of the barrister, Denys Scully, expressed his sorrow at the likelihood that a union – a measure 'so contrary and opposite to the wishes of the Irish people' – would pass. 'Are we then 'to become in the true and literal sense 'West Britons?'[18]

Moreover, if putative 'West Britons' viewed the future anxiously, a few longstanding 'North Britons' had no reassuring words for them. Mrs Leslie, a Scot, who had accompanied her husband on military service to Ireland during the rebellion, opposed union because it was 'a measure that would lose all the consequence of Ireland and sink her as poor Scotland has been sunk into a paltry despised corner of Britain. I will not deny the advantages Scotland has got in point of riches, civilisation etc. but as a nation she is totally lost and insignificant.'[19] For Castlereagh, the Irish parliament had ever been a tiresome, or a dangerous irrelevance, a drain on Irish resources, and a first call on Irish talent (like himself!) that could best be displayed in an imperial forum. Union for him would 'consolidate the strength and glory of the empire.'[20] The problem, however, remained: could Castlereagh and the Irish find a second identity by becoming British? Initial indications were not encouraging.

It was accepted that English politicians, and the English public, knew little about Ireland, and cared less: the lovelessness of the Anglo-Irish relationship had long been evident; and the ignorance that had underpinned it seemed comprehensive at the time of the union.[21] Certainly, the union provided a stimulus to Irish writers to explain their country to the English, to undertake 'advocacy before the bar of English public opinion,'[22] but that

14 Resolutions in circulation in the County of Louth [early 1799], PRO HO 100/85/77.   15 *An address to the Roman Catholics of Ireland on the conduct they should pursue at the present crisis on the subject of an union* (Dublin, 1799), p. 8.   16 *Reasons against an union in which* Arguments for and against an Union ... *are particularly considered* (Dublin, 1798), p. 18.   17 W. Drennan, *Fugitive pieces in verse and prose* (Belfast, 1815) p. 211. 18 Rev. John Murphy to Denys Scully, 23 Jan. 1799 in MacDermot (ed.), *Scully papers*, p. 18.   19 Mrs Leslie to Mrs Stewart, 28 Dec. 1798, PRONI D3167/3/A/37.   20 *A report of the debate in the House of Commons of Ireland ... 22 and 23 Jan. 1799, on the subject of union* (Dublin, 1799), p. 44.   21 The average Englishman, wrote Sir Robert Peel, 'knows as much of the state of Ireland as he does of the state of Kamschatka': Peel to Whitworth, 29 Feb. 1816, in Parker (ed.), *Peel corr.*, i, p. 211.   22 T. Flanagan, quoted

was work for the future. The Irish novelist (a writer who chose to set his or her stories in Ireland) was at the time of union largely unknown.[23] Admittedly, in 1800, Maria Edgeworth had published *Castle Rackrent*, but its impact was surely not what she had intended. She had written it as an historical novel, set 'before the year 1782', with its characters, the 'Sir Kits and Sir Condys', belonging to Ireland's 'former existence': however, her novel was widely read as an accurate representation of Irish life at the time of the union. None other than George III himself valued its insights. Maria's father claimed that the king (after reading the novel) had then 'rubbed his hands and said, "What, what – 'I know something now of my Irish subjects."'[24] The novel's title soon became shorthand for all that was bizarre and burlesque amongst the Irish governing elite. A year after publication, a clearly shaken Charles Abbot, the first post-union chief secretary, confided to his lord lieutenant, Hardwicke, that his party had 'dined one day at a thorough Castle Rackrent, but pray never say so'.[25]

Moreover, while the period 1775-1850 has been described as the 'great age of Irish travel writing', major accounts were actually relatively scarce up to 1800.[26] Few English visited Ireland for pleasure, fewer published their impressions, and fewer still had anything worthwhile to say. The casual tourist followed carefully insulated itineraries, 'handed about from one country gentleman to another who are interested to conceal the true state of the country ... handed about from squire to squire each rivalling the other entertaining their foreign guest and pouring falsehoods into his ears as to the disturbed state of the country and the vicious habits of the people'.[27] 'No man can know Ireland by inspiration' had remarked a correspondent of Lord Downshire's in 1798; however such information as there was on Ireland and the Irish drew as much on inspiration as observation.[28]

There was, for example, the English audience's view of the Irish and their traits as revealed on the London stage in the plays of the Irish dramatists Farquhar, Macklin, O'Keefe and Sheridan.[29] Their representations of the wild Irish – duellists, fortune hunters, and choleric army officers who

in J. Cronin, *The Anglo-Irish novel, vol. i. The nineteenth century* (Belfast, 1980), p. 14. **23** W.J. McCormack, *From Burke to Beckett: ascendancy, tradition and betrayal in literary history* (Cork, 1994), pp 96-7.   **24** Quoted in Cronin, *Anglo-Irish novel*, p. 25.   **25** Abbott to Hardwicke, 21 Aug. 1801, BL Add. Mss 35,711/98.   **26** C.J. Woods, 'Irish travel writings as source materials' in *IHS*, xxviii (1992), pp 171-83. The most important of those that were written at the time were published much later.   **27** Judge Fletcher's charge delivered at the Wexford Assizes, July 1814, PRO HO 100/176/56-112.   **28** Quoted in A. Malcomson, *John Foster: the politics of the Anglo-Irish ascendancy* (Oxford, 1978), title page.   **29** D. Hayton, 'From barbarian to burlesque: English images of the Irish c.1660-1775' in *Ir. Econ. Soc. Hist*, xv (1988) pp 5-31.

exhibited braggadoccio and brogue, artlessness, charm and ruthlessness –
influenced English perceptions of 'the wild little island' and its inhabitants.[30]
By the time of union (and for some decades before then), the preferred stage
Irishman had been Macklin's soldierly soldier, Sir Callaghan O'Brallaghan
rather than Sheridan's comic psychopath, Sir Lucius O'Trigger.[31]

Less happily, however, and in stark contrast to the sentimental and
romantic portrayal of Irishmen (and Irishwomen) on the stage, the dark side
of Irishness had had much publicity during the 1790s. English newspapers
and magazines published detailed coverage of Irish disturbances throughout
the 1790s; the London *Times* carried long accounts of Defender trials in the
early part of the decade, and newspaper coverage of the 1798 rebellion had
been sensational. The English protestant folk memory of Irish popish
superstition and barbarism had been reinvigorated by scarifying accounts of
the cruelties of the rebels, and cartoonists such as James Gillray had left
little to the imagination. The Englishman, Edward Cooke, on the day union
came into effect, predicted that the catholic demand for political rights in
the Westminster parliament would fall victim to 'the prejudices of 200
years', and that there would be a demand to maintain intact 'a constitution
purchased by the blood of martyrs and patriots who perished at the stake in
Smithfield and [who] fell upon the banks of the Boyne and on the plains of
Aughrim'.[32] Representing the rebellion as a sectarian bloodbath – a task
taken up enthusiastically by Sir Richard Musgrave – reinforced the English
public's view of Ireland as an enemy country, popish and barbaric.[33] How
could there be a real union – and the sexual element in that concept is
implicit – with such savages?

A further source of British information was the letters of English and
Scottish officials, judges and ecclesiastics who served in Ireland. In addition
to their normal official correspondence, it was expected that a lord lieutenant, chief secretary or chief justice should compose a statement of his
Irish reflections, and frequently these were of such length that they can only

30 Edward Monckton to Lord Caledon, 1 Apr. 1800, PRONI D2433/c/2/9. 31 J.
Leersen, *Mere Irish and Fíor Ghael* (Cork, 1996), pp 118-30. Christopher Wheatley
dates the more favourable view of the Irish soldier on the stage to an earlier period in
the eighteenth century: C. Wheatley, 'I hear the Irish are naturally brave:' dramatic
portrayals of the Irish soldier in the seventeenth and eighteenth centuries' in *Irish Sword*,
xix (1995) pp 187-96. For Irish recruits to British forces, see T. Bartlett, 'A weapon of
war yet untried': Irish catholics and the armed forces of the crown 1760-1820' in T.
Fraser & K. Jeffery (eds), *Men, women and war* (Dublin, 1993), pp 66-85. (This audience
preference was presumably linked to an increasing appreciation of the role of Irish
recruits in defending the empire.) 32 Quoted Bartlett, *Fall and rise*, p. 272. 33 R.
Musgrave, *Memoirs of the different rebellions in Ireland* (Dublin, 1801).

have been meant for circulation. Leading officials in Dublin Castle in the 1780s and 1790s wrote freely to England, delivering their uniformly unfavourable verdicts on Irish politicians whose capacity for rapacity was legendary, voicing the dangers of Irish reform, revealing the ignorance of the catholic Irish, and stating their suspicions of Irish presbyterians. Chief Secretary Thomas Orde's letters in the 1780s, for example, are so hysterically anti-catholic as to raise grave doubts about his sanity.[34] Even cooler heads could get carried away after a spell in Ireland. In 1797, Thomas Pelham, for example, stated his opinion that 'nothing short of the establishment of the catholic religion will satisfy those of that persuasion, and as the property of the country is in the hands of the protestants such an event can never take place without a civil war ... As long as the poor and the rich are of different persuasions in religious matters, there will always be a jealousy between the democratic and aristocratic parts of the constitution.'[35] The role of these 'Irish experts', the ex-lords lieutenants (Portland, Buckingham, Westmorland, Camden) and the former chief secretaries (Grenville, Hobart, Pelham) did not cease on their return to London: their 'reflections' on the coming revolution in Ireland are frequently found among Pitt's papers, and elsewhere. Lord Hobart, chief secretary in Ireland in the early 1790s, told Pitt at the time of the union that 'The leaders of the catholics of Ireland are decidedly hostile to the British connection; those of any religion are bigoted papists, those who have none (I believe the larger part) are jacobins. Their hatred to England induced the former to acquiesce with the latter in a conspiracy with the protestant dissenting democrats.' His conclusion was that the catholics will always be disaffected: 'as you cannot extirpate them, it is an evil that must be borne': he looked forward to union as an opportunity to revive the penal laws, in his opinion most unwisely repealed.

Army officers also provided information: arriving in Ireland wielding a sword, a surprising number soon took up the pen to record their impressions of the country and its inhabitants. In general, English officers found the Irish gentry contemptible, by turns cowardly and oppressive, and always uncouth. Irish officers in the yeomanry and militia were uniformly derided as savage, sectarian and incompetent. At the highest levels, the private letters and public statements of the two most recent commanders-in-chief, Sir Ralph Abercromby and Marquis Cornwallis, forcibly expressed their wholly unfavourable opinion of the Irish governing elite, both political and military. Cornwallis, echoing Edmund Burke, claimed that his uncouth Irish advisers

34 See his letters to Pitt and others in PRO, Chatham papers, 30/8.   35 Pelham to Portland, 29 Sept. 1797, PRO HO 100/70/146-9.

sought to establish 'a more violent and intolerable tyranny than that of Robespierre'; and Abercromby too was outraged by the conduct of the military forces allegedly under his command.[36] Less elevated witnesses stressed the wretched conditions of the poor in Ireland, the malign influence of priests ('ignorant, illiterate, bigotted wretches'),[37] the republicanism of the presbyterians, and the neglect of duty by the clergy of the established church.

The causes of the troubles in Ireland also attracted the attention of some officers who usually stressed the malign state of social relations in that country. Colonel Robert Craufurd was scathing in his depiction of class relationships; Captain Welsford, on duty in Connacht, wrote to the Scottish peer, Lord Minto, who, in a speech on union, had posed a question as to the origins of the 1798 rebellion.[38] Minto would never have asked, wrote Welsford, why a rebellion had broken out if he had known Ireland as he [Welsford] did:

> Had you witnessed the extreme misery of the peasantry, your surprise [at rebellion] would cease: almost naked, living in huts without windows, chimneys or doors. I believe the hut of any savage ... better with respect to comfort than the cabin of an Irish peasant who never tastes animal food. Milk and potatoes, with a quantity of whiskey on holidays [Holy Days] constitute his food two thirds of the year; potatoes and water the other three months. The lord, middleman or farmer never think of providing a comfortable habitation for their labourers. ... Until the condition of the poor is meliorated rebellion may, by a military force be kept down, but not destroyed.[39]

This notion that military force alone could maintain order in Ireland was echoed by other commentators.Colonel Craufurd, destined for a glittering career in the Peninsular war, summed up the prevailing view among army officers: 'The people of Ireland are and will long continue to be ripe for general insurrection.'[40] Cornwallis was sufficiently impressed by such gloomy assessments that he had a moment of doubt: 'What then have we

---

36 Cornwallis to Ross, 16 Nov. 1799: *Cornwallis corr.*, iii, p.145; for Abercromby's strictures, see T. Bartlett, 'Indiscipline and disaffection in the armed forces of the crown' in P. Corish (ed.), *Rebels, radicals and establishments* (Belfast, 1985), pp 115-34.   37 Capt. Welsford to Lord Minto, 6 Nov. 1799, Nat. Lib. Scotland, Ms 11229/73-5.   38 'I do not know why there is a rebellion in Ireland at all. I have never heard any adequate reason assigned for it:' *The speech of Lord Minto in the House of Peers, 11 April 1799 ... respecting an union* (Dublin, 1799), p. 52.   39 As footnote 34.   40 Crawfurd to Wickham, 28 July 1798, PRO HO 100/66/198-203.

done?' he asked just weeks before union came into effect: 'We have united ourselves to a people whom we ought to have destroyed.'[41]

A further element strongly reinforcing these negative perceptions of Ireland and the Irish were the letters sent by resident Irishmen and Irishwomen to England: these writings often confirmed and elaborated on stereotypes. Some Irish politicians clearly felt obliged to pander to English perceptions of Ireland by crying up the violence of Irish life, behaving as the earl of Donoughmore put it, a few years after the union, 'as if it was the chief business of an Irish member of parliament when on his mission on the other side of the water to collect together all the terrific tales which his correspondents may be willing to furnish him with for the sake of disquieting the ministers'.[42] Cornwallis warned Portland against attaching too much credence to reports from Ireland about 'dangerous plots [which] are heightened by the warmth of imagination'.[43] Throughout the 1790s and earlier, the correspondence carried on by key members of the unofficial, but hugely influential, 'Irish cabinet' of advisors to the lord lieutenant, such as John Beresford, head of the revenue commissioners, Lord Clare, the Irish lord chancellor, and Charles Agar, archbishop of Cashel, with leading British politicians, notably Lord Auckland, provided a quasi-official running commentary on events and personalities in Ireland during that period. Whatever merits Irish politicians had, mused Cornwallis, were entirely outweighed by 'the strength of ancient ... hereditary prejudices'.[44] Clare's letters in particular revealed his deeply pessimistic view of human nature, and he depicted the Irish as variously unregenerate, savage, and barbaric (if catholic), naive, foolish, and giddy (if protestant), and puritan, republican and levelling (if presbyterian): above all, he expressed his conviction of the futility of all attempts at reform in an Irish context. These despatches in the guise of private letters impacted on English perceptions of Ireland for they were circulated within the governing elite in London.[45]

Unfavourable English perceptions of Ireland were shared by some of the Irish. There was undoubtedly a positive Irish self-image: but there was also an unflattering one, typically colonial in that it accorded so well with metropolitan prejudices. It was an Irish commentator who denounced the lack of polish among the Tipperary gentry who 'consider a steeplechase the noblest work of human ambition and listen to the yapping of a parcel of

41 Cornwallis to Hardwicke, 1 Dec. 1800, BL Add. Mss 35644/38-9. 42 Donoughmore to Marsden, 1 Apr. 1805, BL Add. Mss 31229/104-5. 43 Cornwallis to Portland, 9 May 1801, *Cornwallis corr.*, iii, pp 360-1. 44 Cornwallis to Hardwicke, 1 Dec. 1800, BL Add. Mss 35644/38-9. 45 See the letters in the Sneyd (Fitzgibbon) transcripts, PRONI T3287.

curs with more pleasure than to the music of Rossini.'[46] Consider the revealing thoughts that the fastidious Scully confided to his commonplace book. He anticipated greater contact between Ireland and England after the union but cringed at the unfavourable impression Irish women would make on their more cultured English cousins:

> I have often heard Irish ladies (who possessed rank or birth, or fortune or education, or some or all of those advantages together) express themselves in words which would shock an ear of common delicacy in England, such as the following, 'stinking', 'dirty', 'nasty', 'fat woman', 'the fellow's carcase', 'swim in blood', 'rotten', 'to spit' – with fifty other phrases (nauseous to recollect) which are in England confined to the drunkard, debaucher, or the butcher and scavenger. Yet it is a fact that they possess as much native innocence of mind, genuine modesty and rather more prudery than the English women – and I impute the use of those coarse phrases (which are inconceivably grating to the ear from a female voice) to the ignorance of mothers in a few instances but more generally to their shameful neglect of cultivating the style of conversation and many other useful attainments.

Scully concluded with the suggestion that Irish women should substitute 'fetid, rancid or offensive' for 'stinking', 'soiled' for 'dirty, nasty', 'large, or embonpoint' for 'fat', and 'putrid, carious or decayed' for 'rotten'.[47]

Such anxieties voiced by a Scully, or indeed by a Lord Donoughmore, would have elicited a hoot of derision from those Irish commentators for whom the much vaunted 'English refinement' was a true oxymoron. Denis Taaffe, for example, derided the effrontery of those who had the impertinence to claim that 'our barbarous, poor, unpolished people would be refined etc by our intimacy with the elegant, agreeable, social, highly polished English!!! What strange tales we are destined to hear! Learn good breeding and politeness from the churling, growling, and selfish race of Englishmen!' Taaffe was prepared to concede that 'in the polite accomplishments of boxing, swearing, gluttony, rudeness, unfeeling avarice etc, [the English] stand unrivalled': and he offered his readers 'a specimen of their elegant conversation and style' which abounded with such imprecations as 'Nay, damn my eyes! God damn my eyes, face and nose! I'll be damned if! God damn my bloody eyes etc etc. Such are the flowers which cocknified Irishmen may borrow to adorn our isle!'[48]

46 John Hely-Hutchinson to Donoghmore, 30 Jan. 1831, PRONI T344459/E/372. 47 Scully's commonplace book, 7 Nov. 1799, in MacDermot (ed.), *Scully papers*, pp 43-4. 48 Taaffe, *Probability*, pp 31-2.

These unflattering views of England and the English, and of Ireland, its peoples and its prospects, were seriously at odds with the buoyant message in unionist speeches and declarations. The glaring discrepancy between the negative English perception of what Ireland was (shared at both popular and elite levels), and the positive act of seeking to unite with such a regressive country (a country in almost every respect the perceived antithesis of England herself) appeared to rule out any prospect of a real union or any likelihood of the emergence of a shared British identity. Colley's decision to omit Ireland from her study of Britishness may then appear to be justified. There is however a counter-case which should be made.

IV

There were no *a priori* grounds for ruling the Irish out of the British nation. Colley herself admits that it is no longer sufficient to think of nations 'only as historic phenomena characterised by cultural and ethnic homogeneity ... Most nations have always been culturally and ethnically diverse, problematic, protean and artificial.'[49] Other scholars have spoken of nations as essentially 'imagined communities' in which the invention of a shared identity took precedence over the realisation of one. There was no fundamental reason why the Irish could not belong to Britishness. As Bradshaw and Roberts have remarked: 'the genius [of Britishness] is found in its capaciousness: its capacity to seem to buttress the self-esteem of each of the constituent nationalities of the British conglomerate ... while at the same time subsuming these identities under a more comprehensive category of nationality'.[50]

While protestantism was an important stabilising and unifying force in Britishness, it could also be a disruptive element. The state church of Scotland was presbyterian, that of England was anglican and there were furious rivalries between them. By the 1790s in England itself, it was dissent and non-conformity, not catholicism, that aroused the greater anxiety – the Priestley riots of 1791 were a recent memory[51] – and there were sharp divisions within the church of England. Everywhere, it is the disunity of protestantism, rather than its unity, that has impressed some researchers:

49 Colley, *Britons*, p. 5.   **50** Bradshaw & Roberts (eds), *British consciousness*, p. 3.   **51** In 1791, in Manchester and Birmingham and surrounding areas, the homes and work-premises of protestant dissenters (notably those of the Unitarian minister, Joseph Priestley) were attacked and burned by what was generally described as a 'church and king mob;' N. Rogers, *Crowds, culture and politics in Georgian Britain* (Oxford, 1998), pp 192-3.

'There was no unifying protestantism on which a strong feeling of Britishness could be based.'[52]

Nor should too much weight be placed on English antipathy towards the Irish: 'We are a savage, immoral, ill-mannered race ... I well know such are the sentiments,' wrote one pamphleteer, 'which the low and the vulgar of your country entertain of the people of Ireland.' 'I am well aware of the rooted prejudices,' wrote another, 'I had almost said hatred, that lodges in the breast of some Englishmen towards Ireland.' English indifference towards Ireland and her concerns was also well attested. Some twenty years after union, the novelist Gerald Griffin (then living in England) candidly admitted that Ireland was not much thought of there: 'It is a doubt to me if the "dear little island" were swallowed by a whale, or put in a bag and sent off to the moon, if the circumstance would occasion any farther observation than a "dear me" at one end of the town, and a "my eyes" at the other.'[53] Such negative sentiments towards Ireland and the Irish could be multiplied: and yet, were they any different to the similarly unflattering views entertained by the English of their fellow-British, the Scots? The venom reserved for Scottish politicians such as Lord Wedderburn or Henry Dundas or Lord Bute – the latter widely depicted as entering George III's mother, as his countrymen were similarly penetrating England – may even have outdone anti-Irishness in ferocity.[54] Certainly, in the theatre, the portrayal of the Scot as a snivelling toady endured long after the stage-Irishman had mellowed. If the hateful Scots could be accepted as British, why not the amusing Irish?

Furthermore, a willingness by historians to accept that the Irish could never be assimilated into a British identity has meant that the increasing 'Britishness' of Irish life around the time of the union has been ignored. In 1803, Leonard McNally reported that at a theatre in Dublin 'the audience [is] peaceable and zealously loyal in their plaudits on every occasion that offers, and indeed every sentiment in favour of the British constitution, the British navy, British bravery etc etc is received and marked with the most zealous approbation'.[55] The recent welcome attention paid to Jacobitism in Ireland emphasises that it was at heart a British ideology, and not necessarily a plea for Irish separatism.[56] The Stuarts were, after all, indigenous British monarchs, the Hanoverians were German blow-ins. However, while the

52 J. Black, 'Confessional state or elect nation? Religion and identity in eighteenth-century England' in Claydon & McBride (ed.), *Protestantism and national identity*, p. 61. 53 Quoted in Cronin, *Anglo-Irish novel*, i, p. 13. 54 Colley, *Britons*, p. 122. 55 [MacNally] to A. Marsden, 3 Dec. 1803, in M. MacDonagh, *The viceroy's post bag* (London, 1904), pp 441-3. 56 B. Ó Buachalla, *Aisling ghéar: na Stiobhartaigh agus an t-aos léinn 1603-1788* (Dublin, 1996).

Britishness of Jacobitism – the primary allegiance of catholic Ireland for most of the eighteenth century – has been recognised, the British dimension to the United Irish conspiracy has still to be accorded its proper weight. Frequently depicted as Irish separatists, the United Irishmen can also be viewed as international republicans who advocated a series of republics in these islands, and further afield. 'What were the Bonds' and the Sheares's of this country,' asked an Irish writer, 'but the disciples of the Hardy's and Thelwall's of London, of the Muir's and Margarot's of Edinburgh?'[57] Their wider ambitions frustrated, the United Irishmen were reluctantly forced to settle for republicanism in one country.

Similarly, the large recruitment of Irishmen into the armed forces of the crown from the 1790s on should also caution against any notion that a British identity was simply impossible for Irishmen. By the 1840s, forty per cent of the rank and file of the Victorian army were Irish, and Irishness was clearly no barrier to enlisting in a British force. Furthermore, throughout the nineteenth century, the British army was constantly deployed on imperial service, and some Irish derived great satisfaction from their post-union role in the British empire, as soldiers, missionaries or traders. The union had been cried up as a gateway for the Irish into the British empire: following union, claimed Henry Dundas, the voice of Irishmen 'would be heard not only in Europe but in Asia, Africa and America;' and this promise had been, by and large, fulfilled.[58] Britishness resided in the empire and in the armies of that empire; Irishmen were prominent in both of these spheres.

Finally, while literary historians have legitimately focussed their attention on those Irish authors who created Irish characters and wrote on Irish themes, the work of Irish writers whose work celebrated Englishness has been largely neglected. Consider the curious case of Leonard MacNally, widely known to Irish historians both as a United Irishman and as a government informer: less well known as a playwright and composer. In the 1780s he wrote the still-popular song, 'The Lass of Richmond Hill' – a ballad so quintessentially English that MacNally's Irish authorship was periodically disputed in the pages of *Notes and Queries* during the nineteenth century. MacNally's writing for the stage was likewise almost entirely bound up with

57 An Irishman, *Reasons against an union in which* Arguments for and against an union ... *are particularly considered* (Dublin, 1798), p. 26: E. McFarland, *Ireland and Scotland in the age of the revolution* (Edinburgh, 1994); A. Goodwin, *The Friends of Liberty: the English democratic movements in the age of the democratic revolution* (London, 1979). 58 *Substance of the speech of the Rt Hon. Henry Dundas ... Thursday , February 7, 1799* (London, 1799), p. 17.

English themes. Admittedly, an early piece, *Prelude for Covent Garden* written in 1782 had flopped disastrously because of his insensitive portrayal of national character. One review described the uproar which led to the performance being abandoned:

> The author with a partiality to his own countrymen which we know not how to censure had drawn the character of an Irishman as one possessed of qualities which he had rather imprudently denied to the other persons of the drama consisting of English, Scotch, Welsh and French. This circumstance gave offense and before the conclusion of the piece the clamour became too great for anything to be heard.

However, the *Prelude* had been an uncharacteristic foray by MacNally into Irishness: later plays such as *Richard, Coeur de Lion*, but especially his major 'hit' *Robin Hood or Sherwood Forest. A Comic Opera* dealt with classic English heroes. MacNally's Irish birth and upbringing were obviously no barriers to his immersing himself in Englishness, or contributing to its invention. *Robin Hood* has even been credited with reviving interest in the famous outlaw of Sherwood Forest.[59] In the 1790s MacNally acted as a lawyer for the United Irishmen: at the same time he was an important government informer. He wrote a play extolling union in 1800, but it was never performed and has subsequently disappeared. MacNally died in 1820: he had been a protestant all his life, and he had spent twenty-five years secretly denouncing sundry catholic committees, catholic bishops, and clerics: but on his deathbed he summoned a catholic priest. His life illustrates the point that identities are not always fixed but rather are frequently overlapping and contingent.[60]

For all the possibilities of assimilation into a greater Britishness, the Irish were never quite accepted as being truly British. Hitherto, this 'failure' has been explained in various ways: the attempt was never made or it was doomed to failure from the beginning. In fact, failure was far from certain: at the time of the union, the Irish were possibly no more alien than the Scots or the Welsh, the concept of Britishness could embrace contrarieties, and a common interest in the empire would remain a powerful bond. The union, it may be suggested, could have worked: that it did not was not inevitable; its failure is a matter for investigation rather than something pre-ordained.

59 S. Knight, *Robin Hood: A complete study of the outlaw* (Oxford, 1990), p. 150.   60 For MacNally, see W.J. Fitzpatrick, *Secret service under Pitt* (London, 1892), chap. 14; and my 'The life and opinions of Leonard MacNally, playwright, barrister, United Irishman and informer' in H. Morgan (ed.), *Information, media and power through the ages* (Dublin, 2001), pp 113-36.

Index